Emerging Business and Trade Opportunities Between Oceania and Asia

Angus Hooke
Australian Institute of Higher Education, Australia

Hardik Vachharajani
Crown Institute of Higher Education, Australia

Harpreet Kaur
Australian Institute of Higher Education, Australia

Kevin E. Dow
University of Auckland, New Zealand

IGI Global
PUBLISHER of TIMELY KNOWLEDGE

A volume in the Advances in Business Strategy and Competitive Advantage (ABSCA) Book Series

Published in the United States of America by
IGI Global
Business Science Reference (an imprint of IGI Global)
701 E. Chocolate Avenue
Hershey PA, USA 17033
Tel: 717-533-8845
Fax: 717-533-8661
E-mail: cust@igi-global.com
Web site: http://www.igi-global.com

Library of Congress Cataloging-in-Publication Data

Names: Hooke, Angus, editor.
Title: Emerging business and trade opportunities between Oceania and Asia / Angus Hooke [and three others], editor.
Description: Hershey, PA : Business Science Reference, [2021] | Includes bibliographical references and index. | Summary: “This book is for existing and new business entrepreneurs in Oceania and Asia in the fields of economics and business-oriented disciplines to gain a deeper understanding of investment opportunities in areas such as education, health and tourism”-- Provided by publisher.
Identifiers: LCCN 2020018644 (print) | LCCN 2020018645 (ebook) | ISBN 9781799841265 (hardcover) | ISBN 9781799857693 (paperback) | ISBN 9781799841272 (ebook)
Subjects: LCSH: Asia--Economic conditions--21st century. | Oceania--Economic conditions--21st century. | Business enterprises--Asia. | Business enterprises--Oceania. | Investments, Foreign--Asia. | Investments, Foreign--Oceania.
Classification: LCC HC412 .E5833 2021 (print) | LCC HC412 (ebook) | DDC 330.95--dc23
LC record available at https://lccn.loc.gov/2020018644
LC ebook record available at https://lccn.loc.gov/2020018645

This book is published in the IGI Global book series Advances in Business Strategy and Competitive Advantage (ABSCA) (ISSN: 2327-3429; eISSN: 2327-3437)

British Cataloguing in Publication Data
A Cataloguing in Publication record for this book is available from the British Library.

Advances in Business Strategy and Competitive Advantage (ABSCA) Book Series

ISSN:2327-3429
EISSN:2327-3437

Editor-in-Chief: Patricia Ordóñez de Pablos Universidad de Oviedo, Spain

MISSION

Business entities are constantly seeking new ways through which to gain advantage over their competitors and strengthen their position within the business environment. With competition at an all-time high due to technological advancements allowing for competition on a global scale, firms continue to seek new ways through which to improve and strengthen their business processes, procedures, and profitability.

The **Advances in Business Strategy and Competitive Advantage (ABSCA) Book Series** is a timely series responding to the high demand for state-of-the-art research on how business strategies are created, implemented and re-designed to meet the demands of globalized competitive markets. With a focus on local and global challenges, business opportunities and the needs of society, the **ABSCA** encourages scientific discourse on doing business and managing information technologies for the creation of sustainable competitive advantage.

COVERAGE

- Value Creation
- Business Models
- Cost Leadership Strategy
- Small and Medium Enterprises
- Economies of Scale
- Globalization
- Innovation Strategy
- Value Chain
- Entrepreneurship & Innovation
- Core Competencies

IGI Global is currently accepting manuscripts for publication within this series. To submit a proposal for a volume in this series, please contact our Acquisition Editors at Acquisitions@igi-global.com or visit: http://www.igi-global.com/publish/.

The Advances in Business Strategy and Competitive Advantage (ABSCA) Book Series (ISSN 2327-3429) is published by IGI Global, 701 E. Chocolate Avenue, Hershey, PA 17033-1240, USA, www.igi-global.com. This series is composed of titles available for purchase individually; each title is edited to be contextually exclusive from any other title within the series. For pricing and ordering information please visit http://www.igi-global.com/book-series/advances-business-strategy-competitive-advantage/73672. Postmaster: Send all address changes to above address.

Titles in this Series

For a list of additional titles in this series, please visit:
http://www.igi-global.com/book-series/advances-business-strategy-competitive-advantage/73672

Ethical Standards and Practice in Managerial and Financial Accounting
Ionica Oncioiu (Titu Maiorescu University, Romania)
Business Science Reference • © 2021 • 300pp • H/C (ISBN: 9781799840121) • US $195.00

Sustainability Reporting, Ethics, and Strategic Management Strategies for Modern Organizations
Ionica Oncioiu (Titu Maiorescu University, Romania) Sorinel Căpuşneanu (Titu Maiorescu University, Romania) Dan Ioan Topor (1 Decembrie 1918 University, Romania) and Dana Maria (Oprea) Constantin (University of Bucharest, Romania)
Business Science Reference • © 2021 • 320pp • H/C (ISBN: 9781799846376) • US $195.00

International Perspectives on the Youth Labor Market Emerging Research and Opportunities
Samir Amine (Université du Québec en Outaouais, Canada)
Business Science Reference • © 2020 • 217pp • H/C (ISBN: 9781799827795) • US $170.00

Open and Innovative Trade Opportunities for Latin America and the Caribbean
Pablo Alberto Baisotti (University of Costa Rica, Costa Rica)
Business Science Reference • © 2020 • 255pp • H/C (ISBN: 9781799835035) • US $215.00

Cases on Performance Improvement Innovation
Darlene M. Van Tiem (Capella University, USA & University of Michigan – Dearborn, USA) and Nancy Crain Burns (Crain Burns Associates LLC, USA)
Business Science Reference • © 2020 • 377pp • H/C (ISBN: 9781799836735) • US $195.00

Handbook of Research on Entrepreneurship Development and Opportunities in Circular Economy
Neeta Baporikar (Namibia University of Science and Technology, Namibia & University of Pune, India)
Business Science Reference • © 2020 • 696pp • H/C (ISBN: 9781799851165) • US $265.00

For an entire list of titles in this series, please visit:
http://www.igi-global.com/book-series/advances-business-strategy-competitive-advantage/73672

IGI Global
PUBLISHER of TIMELY KNOWLEDGE

701 East Chocolate Avenue, Hershey, PA 17033, USA
Tel: 717-533-8845 x100 • Fax: 717-533-8661
E-Mail: cust@igi-global.com • www.igi-global.com

Table of Contents

Detailed Table of Contents

This chapter provides an overview of the economic performance and current situation of the economies in the Oceanic region. Oceania comprises the economically developed countries of Australia and New Zealand plus the more than 20 island countries and protectorates of Melanesia, Micronesia, and Polynesia. In 2018, Australia dominated the region in terms of population (71% of the total for Oceania) and gross domestic product (86%). Melanesia, which includes Papua New Guinea, Fiji, and New Caledonia, contained 26% of the region's population and generated 4% of its gross regional product. According to the authors' forecasting model, Oceania's share of both world population and gross world product will rise strongly during the coming three decades, admittedly from a low base. Reflecting the high degree of complementarity of the Oceanic economies with those of Asia, this strong growth in the Oceanic region should support increasingly attractive opportunities for trade and investment with the economies of Asia.

In 2018, East Asia accounted for accounted for 31% of gross world product (GWP). A global forecasting model developed by Hooke and updated by Hooke, Alati, and Kaur for the first three chapters of this book suggests that the region's share will remain at about this level until 2050, with the effects of global labour productivity convergence more than offsetting East Asia's relatively slow work force growth. Thereafter, the share will decline to 18% by 2100 due mainly to more rapid productivity and work force growth in West Asia and Africa. China is expected to retain its position as the world's largest economy until about the middle of this century, at which time its GDP will be more than 2.5 times that of the United States. An important driver of growth in East Asia during the coming decades will be Indonesia, whose share of GWP is forecast to rise from 2.6% in 2018 to 3.8% by 2050.

While East Asia has been the dominant economic region in Asia for several centuries, the gross regional product (GRP) of West Asia (comprising Southern, Central, and Western Asia) is projected to surpass that of East Asia by 2050 and to be 40% larger by 2100. In 2018, West Asia accounted for accounted for 17% of gross world product (GWP) compared with 31% by East Asia. It is projected that West Asia's share of GWP will rise to 31% by 2050 and 35% in 2060 before falling back to 25% in 2100. The dominant economy will be India, whose GDP is expected to surpass that of China by 2050 and to be 50% larger by 2100.

India is Australia's fourth largest export market and investment destination, and fifth largest trading partner, with access to a large and youthful market of 1.4 billion population. In 2018, India was the second largest source of skilled professionals after the UK and third largest source of immigrants after the UK and New Zealand. Increasing number of Indian nationals and businesses are choosing Australia as a destination of choice for education, tourism and for doing business. The Independent India Economic Strategy – 2035 was launched on 22 November 2018 for promoting bilateral trade and export market for Australian goods, services, and investment opportunities for mutual economic benefit. This chapter examines the economic significance of bilateral trade relationship between Australia and India and opportunities and challenges faced by the two countries with focus on education, tourism, health, agri-business, alternative energy, and mining sectors to meet the demand and supply gap and the sustainable development goals.

China becomes an aging society in a pace much faster than other countries because of its one-child policy implemented since 1980. This chapter examines the current situation of population aging in China, the government policies and regulations surrounding elderly care, and the experiences of other Asian and Oceanian countries in dealing with population aging. The rapid population aging poses severe challenges for the elderly care in China, which has not established an adequate social security system, but it also provides abundant opportunities for enterprises and entrepreneurs in the aging industry from other Asian and Oceanian countries as well as China. China can learn from the experiences of industrialized Asian and Oceanian countries and regions in developing its elderly care industry.

India is the world's largest democracy and second most populous country with nearly 1.4 billion people. With reduced birth rates and increasing lifespans, it had nearly 104 million 'senior citizens' in 2011, expected to grow to 300 million by 2050. Providing care for the elderly in India is a growing public and private concern. Filial piety is embedded in culture and long-term care for parents and the elderly is expected from children. However, over the last five decades there have been rapid changes in socioeconomic patterns with increasing mobility for work and rise of nuclear households. Despite this, elder care is still largely underdeveloped, with lack of formal training in geriatric care and geriatric care curriculum in medical education. Australia has a highly evolved elderly care system with care services that includes retirement villages, home care, residential care, and flexible care. These are provided by subsidization from the government and private user pay system. Australia is well poised to provide aged care expertise and services and shape elderly care in India.

Foreword

The countries of Oceania and Asia are diverse in both business and culture. The Oceanic countries include Australia and New Zealand, which have highly developed and globally competitive economies, as well as countries that have few complex markets and some that are in the early stages of economic development. The mixture and complexity of these countries, as well as their physical location, provide extensive opportunities for Oceania and Asia to grow their business and trade relationships. This book discusses these opportunities.

The editors divide the book into three sections. The first section gives an overview of the economies of Oceania, East Asia, and West Asia. The discussion provides insights into the differences and similarities in the economies of the two regions. The second section describes the emerging business and trade opportunities between the countries in Oceania and Asia. Tourism has always been a major economic component of the Oceanic and Asian economies, and both the range and depth of opportunities in the sector are increasing rapidly. One such new opportunity is health and elder care. As the world's population ages there will be many worthwhile and profitable opportunities for innovative and entrepreneurial providers in the sector. The third section of the book discusses the information technology and funding opportunities between the two regions.

The economic opportunities and incentives for companies in Oceania and Asia to work together are endless. The book presents these opportunities for entrepreneurs, researchers, and academics who seek to partake in developing and exploiting the emerging business and trade opportunities between these two great regions.

Vincent J. Shea
St. John's University, USA

Preface

EVOLUTION OF THE WORLD ECONOMY

Since 1950, real gross world product (GWP) has increased at an average annual rate of about 3.75 percent. The driving force on the demand side has been exports, which have grown at an average annual rate of about 5 percent, compared with 2 percent for home goods and services. As a result, the share of goods and services produced for export markets has risen from less than 10 percent in 1950 to 30 percent today.

Since 2016, the contribution of exports to the growth of GWP has exceeded the contribution of sales in domestic markets, and the gap between the two will increase over the coming decades. Of course, the share of exports in GWP and their relative contribution to the growth of GWP cannot rise indefinitely, and both will stabilize when and if the world economy becomes a single market. That will not occur in the first half of the 21st century.

Exports not only dominate contributions to growth on the demand side, they also support a reallocation of global resources along the lines of international comparative advantage. They therefore increase global economic efficiency and the average standard of living. A country's export sector is normally its highest-productivity sector – the sector that competes and wins on the global stage, without subsidies, and often on a playing field tilted against it.

Competition in product and factor markets ensures that the benefits gained by the export sector do not remain wholly within that sector but quickly spread over all parts of the economy. A hairdresser relocating from Mumbai to Sydney increases their real income 7-fold, not because they are better hairdressers in Sydney but because Australia's large endowment of natural and man-made resources per capita have increased the purchasing power of their Sydney customers and the demand of other Sydney industries for their labour services. Countries normally grow rich on the back of their export sector.

In 1950, the world's population was 2.5 billion, GWP (in purchasing power parity terms at 2018 prices) was I$ 11 trillion and per capita GWP was I$ 4,300. (I$, an international dollar, is a dollar with the same real purchasing power in all countries, sometimes described as what a dollar will buy in New York in July of the specified year.) By 2018, global population had risen to 7.7 billion, GWP was I$ 135 trillion and per capita GDP was I$ 17,670. The United Nations (UN) projects that the world's population could reach 9.6 billion in 2050 and 10.7 billion by 2100. The economic forecasting model developed by Hooke and Alati and enhanced for this book by Hooke, Alati and Kaur suggests that, if the UN projections are realized, GWP and per capita GWP could be about I$ 515 trillion and I$ 54,000, respectively, in 2050 and I$ 1,730 trillion and I$ 161,000, respectively, in 2100.

This book focuses on export, import, and investment opportunities between Oceania and Asia. It is organized into three sections: the economies of Oceania and Asia, the core opportunities, and the supporting opportunities. A brief description of the chapters in each section follows.

SECTION 1: THE ECONOMIES OF OCEANIA AND ASIA

Chapter 1 provides an overview of the economic and business environment in the Western-oriented economies of Australia and New Zealand and the traditional Oceanic economies of Melanesia, Micronesia, and Polynesia. Australia and New Zealand are high-income countries with well-developed resource sectors that are important suppliers of commodities to Asian markets. Their services sectors include health, education, finance, and Information industries that use global, cutting-edge technologies. Many of the key personnel in these industries, including managers and researchers who are temporary or permanent immigrants from Asia, understand the needs of Asian firms and consumers, and have family and other contacts in Asian countries. The smaller countries and protectorates in Oceania have abundant potential as tourist destinations and suppliers of marine products. Most of the economies of Oceania are growing strongly and are attractive destinations for the exports of Asian countries. The authors argue that since Oceania is adjacent to Asia and has economies that in many ways are complementary to those of Asia business and trade between the two regions should continue to flourish in the coming decades.

The number of economies in each of the three regions covered is quite large (25 in Oceania, 16 in East Asia and 34 in West Asia) and the authors do not provide detailed analyses of the economic prospects of each. They do, however, select one economy in each chapter for more in-depth consideration.

For Oceania, the economy chosen is that of Australia. Using population projections made by the UN, the authors suggest that the GDP of Australia, which increased from I$ 98 billion in 1950 to I$ 1.3 trillion in 2018, should rise to at least I$ 2.7 trillion by 2050 and I$ 6.7 trillion in 2100. They argue that the key to Australia's economic success will be its ability to generate and/or import innovative ideas, a precondition of expanding investment opportunities and rising labour productivity. With Australia's compulsory superannuation scheme providing adequate private saving and governments at all levels generally being fiscally responsible, exploitation of these opportunities should generate strong growth of GDP, with the combination of competitive markets and effective government income transfer policies ensuring that the benefits continue to be spread across all income classes. The authors suggest that Australia's pro-immigration policy, which focuses on skilled workers and university graduates, should contribute to the continued strong growth of innovative ideas.

Chapter 2 focuses on East Asia. The contribution of the gross regional product (GRP) of East Asia to GWP rose from 7 percent in 1950 to 31 percent in 2018. The authors suggest that this share will increase only slightly in the next two decades and will then decline to 30 percent in 1950 and 18 percent in 2100. The major reasons for the slowdown and subsequent decline are the already high levels of labour productivity in countries such as Japan, South Korea and Taiwan and the levelling off and then fall in population and thus workforce of major countries in the region. The authors predict that the economies of Southeast Asia will grow more strongly than those of their Northeast neighbors and that Indonesia's share of GWP, which was 2.6 percent in 2018, will rise to 3.6 percent in 2050.

The economy in East Asia chosen for more in-depth discussion is that of China. The authors argue that China may have had the largest economy in the world for about two of the last four millennia, with its share of GWP possibly peaking in the early 15th century, during the period of the Ming dynasty. They predict that the Chinese economy, which regained its earlier ranking of largest in the world in 2014, will maintain this position until the late 2040s and will continue to be the second largest in the world throughout the latter half of the 21st century. They point out that the UN expects China's share of the global population to fall from 19 percent in 2018 to 14 percent in 2050 and 10 percent in 2100. This will be reflected in a corresponding fall in China's share of the world's work force and, with globalization favoring convergence of labour productivity across all participating countries, a fall in China's share of GWP.

Chapter 3 focuses on West Asia, which the authors disaggregate into Southern Asia (9 countries), Western Asia (19 countries) and Central Asia (5 countries). This region's share of GWP was only 7 percent in 1950 (the same as that of East Asia) but had risen to 11 percent by 2018. The authors project that it will increase to 25 percent in 2050 and peak at 30 percent in 2060. They expect it to be powerhouse of the world economy for much of the next four decades, and to still account for more than a quarter of GWP in 2100.

The authors predict that the gross domestic product (GDP) of India will move ahead of that of the United States during the 2030s and of the GDP of China in the late 2040s. They note that the UN expects India's population to pass that of China in 2024, to be 23 percent larger in 2050, and to be 50 percent larger in 2100. In the near term, India will shed its demographic burden (a relatively low share of the workforce in total population) while China will lose its demographic gift (a relatively high share of the workforce in total population). The authors also suggest that India's relatively capitalistic economy may be more conducive to labour productivity growth than the more regulated economy of China.

SECTION 2: THE CORE OPPORTUNITIES

Chapter 4 addresses the Australia–India bilateral economic relationship, which has grown rapidly in the last two decades. Australia can benefit hugely from access to India's youthful market of 1.4 billion people. India is currently Australia's fifth largest export market and investment destination, fifth largest trading partner and second largest source of skilled labour and international students. In 2018, it was the second largest source of skilled professionals coming to Australia (after the UK), and third largest source of immigrants (following the UK and New Zealand). It can become an even more important partner in all these areas.

Trade in goods and services between Australia and India grew from $A 13.6 billion in 2007 to $A 27.5 billion in 2017. Appreciating the growing potential of the bilateral relationship, the Australian government commissioned a study entitled 'An India Economic Strategy-2035' (IES-2035), aimed at identifying bilateral trade and investment opportunities, mutual economic benefits, creation of jobs, economic growth, and economic prosperity for both Australia and India. The report, which was launched on 22 November 2018, spelled out a plan to transform the economic partnership between the two countries in ten key sectors. It was a major step in enhancing the bilateral economic relationship.

The plan predicts that India will be most populous and the third largest world economy after USA and China. However, the author suggests, there appears to be a lack of political will, among numerous other challenges, to tap the full potential from bilateral trade and realize the benefits from exploiting these economic and business opportunities.

The author argues that the bilateral relationship can help balance Australia's relationships with China and India. This will present some challenges. There are border disputes between India and China, with China claiming the eastern part of Kashmir and Arunachal Pradesh since 1962. Moreover, China is gaining strategic maritime and military control of the Indian Ocean region by investing in and building strategic infrastructure there. Australia could play a key role with defense arrangements that promote peace and security in the Indian ocean region trade route, and that dampen China's military ambition to access and control the Indian

Ocean by building roads, sea ports, and leasing islands from Burma, Bangladesh, Sri Lanka, the Maldives, Pakistan, and Mauritius through predatory economic policies that often lead to a debt trap.

Australia also faces challenges in doing business with India, given that country's complex regulatory environment, fluctuating import demands and tariff regimes, and bureaucratic red tape. India itself faces numerous challenges such as water scarcity, high demand for energy and power, food security, traffic jams, shortage of affordable housing, air and water pollution, limited transport infrastructure, inadequate healthcare facilities for the aged and poor waste disposal systems.

The author suggests that, despite the many challenges, Australia and India can each benefit considerably from bilateral trade agreements in six key sectors of the economy, namely education, tourism, health, mining, alternative energy. and agribusiness

Chapter 5 examines the situation and outlook for population aging in China, business opportunities that are opening up in the sector especially for suppliers from other parts of Asia and from Oceania; and experiences of some of the countries in the two regions that have been relatively successful in addressing the economic and social problems caused by rapid aging.

The authors suggest that the elderly-care care sector could become the biggest sector in the Chinese economy. China has both the world's largest population and one of the most-rapidly aging populations. It will take only 20 years for the proportion of aged persons in the population to double, compared with more than 60 years in Germany and Sweden, which are commonly cited as aging countries. By 2050, the number of aged persons in China will exceed the population of the USA today.

Also, attitudes toward elderly care are changing. The one-child per family policy that was in place from the early 1980s to 2015 has led to a fall in the fertility rate to 1.2 (compared to the figure of slightly above 2.0 that is needed to prevent the total population from eventually falling) and the emergence of a 4:2:1 family structure (family units comprising 4 grandparents, 2 parents and 1 child). There is growing recognition that one person cannot look after two aged parents and four even-more elderly grandparents. Also, the emigration of several hundred million working-age people away from the rural areas to the cities has physically separated many elderly persons from their children. These developments are causing an increasing number of people to change their understanding of how the elderly should be cared for, with less emphasis resting on family care and more emphasis being placed on society/community care.

The authors note that the Chinese government has been lowering the thresholds for foreign investment in the elderly care industry. To identify business opportunities, they divide the elderly-care sector into three industries: core industry (such as housing, social services and medical care), related industry (providers of elderly-care products and services such as education and training of doctors and nurses specializing in elderly care), and extensional industry (including financing and insurance). They suggest that the most attractive opportunities will be in the high- and middle-end of the market (e.g. high-quality nursing homes) and that upper-income countries where aging commenced earlier than in China, such as Australia, Japan and Singapore, are well-placed to exploit these opportunities.

This chapter provides essential reading for policy makers in all countries experiencing population aging (which encompasses most middle- and upper-income countries). It describes the aging problem and the many government and community responses, not only in China, but also in other countries including Japan (which has been successful in attracting private capital into the industry), Australia (with its "Living Longer, Living Better" program, which supports a better-funded and more flexible elderly-care industry), South Korea (which has 65,000 elderly-care centers that receive favorable ratings from users), Singapore (which, the authors claim, has one of the best healthcare systems in the world), Hong Kong (which has a reverse mortgage program that provides funding for retirees while putting minimal pressure on the government's budget), and Taiwan (where elderly care is one the country's eight "key" industries).

Chapter 6 examines the demand for and supply of elderly care in India, recognizes that supply falls short of demand in many areas, and identifies opportunities for Australian aged care service providers to meet segments of the shortfall. It addresses specific questions such as: What is the profile (prevalence, demography, socioeconomic status, religious and cultural status) of the aged in India? How are the aged currently cared for? What are the factors driving the demand for elderly care services? What legislation, regulation and policy frameworks exist for elderly care? What is the current supply of aged care services? And, what are the major challenges and opportunities facing firms, especially foreign firms that seek to enter India's aged care industry?

Since rapid economic development is a recent phenomenon in India, only a small part of the elderly population can afford high-quality aged care services. However, a small proportion of a very-large number can still be a large number. There are currently more than 100 million elderly persons in India, and it is estimated that 5 percent of these are in the middle- or upper-income categories, implying that 5 million elderly persons can currently afford high-quality products and services. This number will grow rapidly, with the number of elderly persons forecast to rise to 300 million over the next three decades and the proportion with comfortable assets and incomes expected to rise sharply as India continues to reap the benefits of global economic convergence. As the authors note: "There is no better time than now for Australia to provide expertise and play a positive role in shaping the sector."

The chapter provides essential reading for any Australian aged-care provider considering entry into the Indian market. It notes that a one-stop shop is available, which provides valuable insights into local market conditions and approval processes, and assistance in establishing networks. It also describes the nine formats of the elderly care industry in India, policies related to foreign investment, and the pros and cons of different ownership structures (incorporation of a private limited company as a wholly owned subsidiary of a foreign company or joint venture is the least expensive, easiest, and fastest mode of entry to the Indian market by foreign companies).

Chapter 7 notes that the services sector has been growing in importance in most economies and focuses on business and trade opportunities in this sector, with reference mainly to the travel and tourism industries and the economies of India and Australia. In India, the travel and tourism industries account for about 10 percent of GDP and provides employment for 75 million workers. The author conducts a detailed analysis of the historical sources of tourists to India and their contributions to the foreign exchange earnings of the Indian economy. He notes that the shares of both India and Australia in global tourism receipts are small and suggests that more pro-active measures could increase these shares.

The chapter includes the kind of in-depth description of the range and depth of India's tourism offerings that can only be provided by someone who has spent most of his life connected to the industry at the highest levels in the Indian government. The author's descriptions of heritage tourism, wildlife tourism, adventure tourism, rural tourism and religious tourism (including the Buddhist circuits) contain unique insights and are rich in detail.

The author provides a thorough discussion of the many initiatives the Indian government has undertaken to promote the tourism and travel industry. These are addressed from the viewpoint of a person who has been deeply involved in the deliberations that lead to the identification, evaluation, and development of these initiatives. The initiatives include the Incredible India campaign, the Atithi Devi Bhava (social awareness) campaign, Hunar se Rozgar Tak (Skill Development program) Earn while you Learn program, and the statue of Sardar Vallabhbhai Patel (which, at a height of 183 meters, is the world's tallest statue). The author also identifies the many tourist attractions that Australia has to offer and proposes steps that Australia could take to make these better known to prospective Indian tourists.

Chapter 8 addresses opportunities in the travel and tourism sector. The authors note that this sector has become a major source of income and employment growth for emerging economies like India, which did not have well-developed tourism sectors in the pre-liberalization era. Travel and tourism are rapidly becoming mainstream growth industries in India. Currently, they generate around 8 percent of total employment opportunities in the country, a figure that is expected to rise over the next few decades. One of the largest contributors to the sector's growth has been medical tourism. India attracts patients from Asia, the Middle East, Africa, and Europe as well as from the large Indian diaspora in the developed world including Oceania. India offers quality, affordable care with world class facilities backed by a strong, indigenous pharma industry. Its medical tourism industry compares well with those of other Asian nations like Singapore, Thailand, and Malaysia.

SECTION 3: THE SUPPORTING OPPORTUNITIES

Chapters 9 and 10 discuss the contribution that well-designed and targeted coaching can make to the ability of foreign companies to thrive in China. Given the current and predicted high growth of the Chinese economy, it is likely that Sino-Foreign partnerships will become the 'new normal', with Western executives working in teams with Chinese executives, both in China and globally. Such partnerships are likely to struggle with a significant cultural gap, as they seek to both upskill executives and ensure that knowledge is effectively developed and shared across teams. It is highly likely that such teams will need to place greater emphasis on soft skills, such as coaching, and the effective use of people analytics.

Chapter 11 provides crucial information and guidance to foreign companies seeking to implement an enterprise resource planning (ERP) system in China. It notes that these systems constitute the informational backbone of intelligent manufacturing, a core objective of the Chinese government's "Made in China 2025" initiative, It also recognizes that there are major differences between Chinese and Western cultures and that failure to fully take these differences into account has been a barrier to the successful implementation of ERP systems in the past.

The author uses information gained from a research study that included a large survey and an in-depth analysis of the data gained from the survey. The study asked the following questions: (1) What are the major barriers to success in ERP development? And (2) How can these barriers be overcome? Among the barriers, it identified cultural differences, in particular the "one hand" tradition where all decisions need to be approved by top management, and the practice of using knowledge as a bargaining tool rather than an asset to be shared willingly across the organization.

The author suggests that there are several components to overcoming these barriers. First, it is essential to gain the strong support of senior management; this can lead to rapid acceptance of an ERP system throughout the organization. Second, it is often helpful re-engineer business processes to accommodate the preferred ERP system. The chapter notes instances where this has been done, resulting in dramatic reductions in cost and improvements in quality, service, and speed. Third, training and education on the business potential of ERP systems and the contribution knowledge sharing makes to realizing this potential can help develop a culture of acceptance and sharing. The author concludes that companies in the economically advanced countries of Oceania may be better placed than companies in other western countries to overcome these barriers and to succeed in implementing ERP in China.

Chapter 12 provides a wealth of practical advice from a practitioner with years of successful experience in raising funds, especially for start-ups and cross-border companies. The author notes that the rapidly changing scale and structure of the economies of Oceania and Asia are opening up opportunities for the establishment of new enterprises and the expansion of existing enterprises in traditional industries such as resource extraction and farming as well as industries in the smart-manufacturing, finance, health, training, and tourism sectors. New enterprises can play an especially important role in exploiting these opportunities.

However, the author observes, most start-ups including those in the hi-tech sector and with promising new products are poorly funded and struggle to survive. He describes the many sources of funds available to start-ups including bootstrapping, families and friends, angel investors, venture capitalists and private equity providers. Governments are also promising source of funds, and the author describes some of the types financial assistance afforded by governments in Australia, China, India, Malaysia, Indonesia, and South Korea.

The chapter's prime focus is on how to access funds from these sources. The author points out that it is not enough to have a marketable product that can generate an attractive profit. The new entrepreneur with limited finance must also know how to get the attention and then the confidence of those who allocate the funds. To do this, they must focus on what the investor wants. Emphasis is placed on the importance of a well-prepared business plan, a honed elevator pitch, an attractive pitch deck, and later, a convincing due diligence pack. The author also provides important advice on what does and what does not work with these tools. The ability to understand how the tools work and how they are presented to investors are vital to a start-up's success in raising the funds it needs to become established, to survive and to prosper.

Section 1

Chapter 1
The Economies of Oceania

Angus Hooke
Australian Institute of Higher Education, Australia

Lauren A. Alati
Argon & Co., Australia

ABSTRACT

This chapter provides an overview of the economic performance and current situation of the economies in the Oceanic region. Oceania comprises the economically developed countries of Australia and New Zealand plus the more than 20 island countries and protectorates of Melanesia, Micronesia, and Polynesia. In 2018, Australia dominated the region in terms of population (71% of the total for Oceania) and gross domestic product (86%). Melanesia, which includes Papua New Guinea, Fiji, and New Caledonia, contained 26% of the region's population and generated 4% of its gross regional product. According to the authors' forecasting model, Oceania's share of both world population and gross world product will rise strongly during the coming three decades, admittedly from a low base. Reflecting the high degree of complementarity of the Oceanic economies with those of Asia, this strong growth in the Oceanic region should support increasingly attractive opportunities for trade and investment with the economies of Asia.

OVERVIEW

The economies of Oceania, individually and in total, are small compared to those of Asia. In 2018, Oceania's population was 41 million, or 0.9 percent that of Asia. Oceania's per capita gross domestic product (GDP), of just over I$ 38,500, was 2.6 times that of Asia, and its gross regional product (GRP), of I$ 1.6 trillion, was

DOI: 10.4018/978-1-7998-4126-5.ch001

2.4 percent of the GRP of Asia.[1] The economies of Oceania, comprising about 25 countries and protectorates, had average population of about 1.6 million and GDP of I$ 63 billion while for the 49 countries of Asia average population was 86 million and average GDP of I$ 1.3 trillion. However, the difference in scale, there is a high degree of complementary between the economies of the two regions, with Oceania being an important source for Asia of raw materials and education, health and financial services, Asia being the leading supplier for Oceania of a wide range of manufactured products and each region providing a market for the other in tourism, investment products.

For the purposes of this chapter, Oceania is divided into four regions: Australia and New Zealand (Table 2), Melanesia (Table 5), Micronesia (Table 6) and Polynesia (Table 7). Table 1 shows the performance of these regions in 2018 with respect to labour force, labour productivity, gross regional product (GRP), population, and per capita GRP. The ANZ region dominated in all categories: it accounted for 74 percent of the labour force, 71 percent of the population and 95 percent of GRP. Its labour productivity and per capita GRP were 7.6 and 7.8 times the corresponding averages in the rest of the region. Among the three smaller regions, Melanesia had the largest GRP (I$ 62 billion) and Micronesia had the highest per capita GRP ($15,116).

Table 1. The Major regions in Oceania, 2018

	Labour force (m)	**Labour productivity (I$)**	**GRP (I$ bn)**	**Population (m)**	**Per capita GDP (I$)**
ANZ	15.7	96,745	1,520	29.6	51,424
Melanesia	4.6	13,473	62	10.7	5,811
Micronesia	0.2	34,684	7	0.5	15,116
Polynesia	0.6	13,912	8	0.7	12,013
Oceania	**21.1**	**75,636**	**1,598**	**41**	**38,579**
Asia	2,086.5	31,001	64,683	4,286	15,091
World	3,415.2	39,627	135,334	7,676	17,630

Sources. World Bank's World Economic Indicators, IMF's World Economic Outlook, UN Population Division, CIA's World Factbook

Notes. (1) GRP is measured in purchasing power parity (PPP) terms, at 2018 prices.

(2) ANZ refers to Australia and New Zealand

AUSTRALIA AND NEW ZEALAND

In 2019, the Australian Bureau of Statistics announced that the population of ***Australia*** had passed 25 million and was growing at an annual rate of about 1.5

percent (compared with a global average of 1.1 percent). In 2018, Australia's GDP of I$ 1.3 trillion was 19th highest in the world, and its per capita GDP of I$ 52,809 was second only to that of the United States among the world's larger economies (those with population above 20 million and GDP more that I$ 1 trillion). Australia has an open market economy with a small but highly productive agricultural sector (4 percent of GDP) and a large, cutting-edge services sector (71 percent of GDP). Its main trading partners are China (28 percent of exports plus imports). Japan (8 percent) and South Korea (6 percent). Australia is an important exporter of natural resources (coal, iron, copper, gold, natural gas, and uranium) and farm products (wheat, wool, meat, milk, and cheese), as well as education, financial services, and tourism. Its major import commodities include motor vehicles, petroleum products, telecommunications equipment, and computers. Australia's proximity to and increasingly close cultural ties with what might be three of the world's four largest economies by 2050 – India (largest), China (second largest) and Indonesia (fourth largest) – should make it an increasingly attractive source and destination for both international trade and foreign investment during the coming decades (Hooke, 2019).

Well into the second half of the 20th century, ***New Zealand*** had an agrarian economy that was heavily dependent on concessionary access to the British market (Hawke, 2015). Over the last four decades, the economy has become industrialised, innovative, and internationally competitive. Important goals of the government are to continue expanding its network of free trade agreements and to increase the development and use of non-fossil sources of energy. In 2018, New Zealand's population was 4.7 million, per capita GDP was I$ 44,128 and total GDP was I$ 208 billion. The country's main trading partners are China (21 percent of all trade), Australia (14 percent), the United States (10 percent) and Japan (7 percent). New Zealand's leading exports are dairy products, meat, logs, other wood products, fruit, crude oil, and wine. Its major imports include crude petroleum, mechanical and electrical machinery, motor vehicles, and textiles.

Table 2. The ANZ economies, 2018

	Labour force (m)	Labour productivity (I$)	GDP (I$ bn)	Population (m)	Per capita GDP (I$)
Australia	13.0	100,625	1,312	25	52,809
New Zealand	2.7	77,833	208	5	44,128
Total	**15.7**	96,745	**1,520**	**30**	**51,424**
Rest of Oceania	5.4	14,353	78	12	6,552
Oceania	21.1	75,636	1,598	41	38,579

Sources. World Bank's World Economic Indicators, IMF's World Economic Outlook, UN Population Division, CIA's World Factbook

Table 3 shows the performance of key macro variables of the Australian economy from 1950 to 2015 and projections for these variables in 2050 and 2100. The macroeconomic projections in this and the following two chapters are derived from a World Income Model (WIM) developed initially by Hooke (2019) and modified and updated by Hooke, Alati and Kaur to provide a framework for the first three chapters of this book. The model includes data and projections for 167 countries and protectorates. The projections are based partly on convergence theory and the strong empirical support for this theory across economic eras (Snooks, 1996), in East Asia since World War II (Hooke, 2019), and in many developing countries in the first two decades of this century.

Table 3. Economic Performance and Prospects of Australia, 1950-2100

Australia	1950	2000	2018	2050	2100
Work force (m)	4	10	13	17	19
Productivity (I$)	22,260	76,509	100,625	165,213	358,518
GDP (I$ bn)	96	763	1,312	2,747	6,653
Population (m)	8	19	25	32	41
Per capita GDP (I$)	11,682	40,153	52,809	85,911	161,333

Source. World Bank's World Economic Indicators, IMF's World Economic Outlook, UN Population Division, CIA's World Factbook; Hooke, Alati and Kaur's World Income Model

The key assumptions of the model are that:

§ Labour productivity in the United States will maintain its current average annual growth rate of just over 1 percent.

§ Labour productivities and labour force participation rates will converge across all regions apart from Africa by 2060.
§ Labour productivities and labour force participation rates in Africa will converge with those in the rest of the world by 2080.

Table 4. Illustrative Effects on Incomes of Investment in Australia of $100

	Primary Incomes	**Transfers**		**Public goods**	**Overall**
		Taxes (-)	**Benefits**		
Investors	10	-4		1	7
Workers	30	-12		5	23
Welfare recipients	0		6	4	10
Total	40	-16	6	10	40

Source. Angus Hooke, *Global Economic Development: Past, Present and Future*

Workshops and questionnaires have been used to produce refinements for individual economies on an as-need basis – i.e., when a request has been made for an in-depth analysis and/or a projection for a specific economy.

During 1950-2018, the average annual growth rates of Australia's work force and labour productivity were 1.6 percent and 2.2 percent, respectively, resulting in average annual growth of GDP of 3.9 percent. The growth of labour productivity was especially strong during the third quarter of the 20th century, reflecting the reaping of gains foregone during the Great Depression and (for peacetime goods and services) during World War II.

It is projected that Australia's work force will continue to grow strongly, due mainly to the Australian government's strong support of immigration and the country's appeal to skilled workers in neighbouring developing countries. It is forecast that labour productivity will grow at just over 1.5 percent a year, higher than the OECD average due mainly to the positive contribution that migration makes to innovation and the creation of investment opportunities. This does, however, depend on the government following through with its stated policy of freeing up labour markets and reducing red and green tape.

The forecast is also highly dependent on strong growth of productive investment. Analysis by the authors suggests that growth of productive investment may be the most important condition for realising this scenario, not only because of its direct contribution to growth of GDP but also because of it tends to raise the incomes of all major income classes and thus to gain broad political support. A numerical example, while only a broad generalisation, may clarify the effects of investment in Australia.

In Australia, the ratio of the productive capital stock to GDP is about 2.5. Assuming a capital depreciation rate of 10 percent, the ratio of productive capital to net domestic product (NDP) is about 2.0. Normally, an investment of $100 will increase NDP by $40, generating primary incomes for both workers and investors – the rise in the capital stock pushes outward the national demand curve for labour, causing wages to rise by $30 and leaving $10 for investors (Primary Incomes column in Table 4). Fortunately, investors seem reasonably content with receiving a return of 10 percent on their capital.

Australia has three levels of government and each has its own suite of taxes. In total, there are more than 120 different taxes. Of these, only the personal income tax can lay a plausible claim to being progressive and, overall, the system is best characterised as being proportional, with a rate equivalent to about 40 percent of NDP. So, investors pay about $4 of the increase in their primary income as taxes, and workers contribute about $12 (Taxes column in Table 4). A little more than a third of tax revenue, or about $6 in our example, is paid to welfare recipients (Benefits column), leaving two-thirds ($10) for the government to spend on infrastructure (such as roads, hospitals and schools) and current goods and services (such as wages of nurses, teachers and police). These expenditures are likely to favour welfare recipients and workers over investors, suggesting that after the government interventions have been completed, the beneficiaries of a productive investment, in order, are workers (58 percent), welfare recipients (20 percent) and investors (15 percent).

Investment does not occur in a vacuum. On the supply side, it depends on the availability of private savings. Australia generates most of its private savings through a compulsory superannuation scheme and so long as the work force is growing strongly the new contributions to the scheme by current workers vastly exceed the withdrawals by retired workers. Australia's policy of high immigration, together with a planned increase in the compulsory superannuation rate from 9 per cent to 12 percent, should ensure private savings sufficient to realise the above scenario.

Investment also needs a continuing stream of profitable opportunities. Specifically, it needs innovation. The Australian government places heavy emphasis on innovation and has a raft of policies to support those with new and promising business ideas. Innovation is also facilitated by the policy of attracting skilled migrants, who are generally more motivated than residents, have fewer opportunities for entering the established workforce and bring new ideas to the local business environment. There is reason for optimism that Australia has the conditions needed to generate new business ideas as well as the resources needed to place these ideas in investments that increase the level of NDP and raise incomes across all social classes.

MELANESIA

Fiji, which became an independent country in 1970 (Lal, 1992), has a population of almost 900,000 and GDP of I$ 9.7 billion. Increasing political stability is improving the environment for international trade and inward FDI. Fiji's main trading partners are Australia (17 percent of all trade), the United States (14 percent) and New Zealand (12 percent). The country's main exports are bottled mineral water to the United States, tourism (850,000 tourists visited the country in 2017), fuel, fish, sugar, and gems. Its main imports are machinery and transport equipment, manufactured goods, and petroleum products.

Table 5. The economies of Melanesia, 2018

	Labour force ('000)	**Labour productivity (I$)**	**GDP/GRP (I$ mn)**	**Population ('000)**	**Per capita GDP/GRP (I$)**
Fiji	355	27,399	9,726	885	10,989
Papua New Guinea	3,742	10,340	38,698	8,571	4,515
New Caledonia	120	92,583	11,110	283	39,258
Norfolk Island	1	3,575	3	2	2,000
Solomon Islands	249	6,428	1,598	652	2,451
Vanuatu	142	6,741	954	292	3,266
Total	**4,609**	**13,473**	**62,090**	**10,685**	**5,811**
Rest of Oceania	16,521	92,976	1,536,029	30,740	49,969
Oceania	21,129	75,636	1,598,118	41,425	38,579

Sources. World Bank's World Economic Indicators, IMF's World Economic Outlook, UN Population Division, CIA's World Factbook

Papua New Guinea (PNG) has been an independent country since 1975. Its economy has been reasonably well managed since then (Goodman and Lepani, 1987). PNG has a largely agrarian economy, with about 85 percent of the population dependent on farming. The formal economy is still quite small but is growing steadily. In 2018, the country's population amounted to 8.6 million (second highest in Oceania), per capita GDP was I$ 4,515 and total GDP was almost I$ 39 billion (third highest in Oceania). PNG's main trading partners are Australia (25 percent of all trade), Singapore (18 percent), and China (15 percent). Its main exports include minerals (copper, gold, and oil account for about two thirds of all exports), coffee, cocoa, crayfish, and prawns. The country's leading imports are machinery and transport equipment, manufactured goods, food, fuels, and chemicals. The PNG government is seeking to develop a more open economy and, in 2017, launched its first ever national trade policy, focusing on providing an environment favouring the expansion of exports and inward foreign direct investment (FDI).

New Caledonia has been a special collectivity of France since 1998. In a referendum held in 2018, residents voted against independence and in favour of retaining territorial status. In that year, its population was 283,000, per capita GDP was I$ 39,258 and total GDP was more than I$ 11 billion (the highest among the Oceanic protectorates). France provides financial assistance equal to about 15 percent of the protectorate's GDP. Other key foundations of the economy include the mining and processing of nickel (New Caledonia possesses 11 percent of the world's nickel reserves) and tourism (Kushnir, 2019). The protectorate's main trading partners are China (18 percent of all trade), France (16 percent) and South Korea (10 percent). Its main exports are ferronickel, nickel ore, tourism, and fish. New Caledonia's major imports are chemicals, machinery & equipment, and fuels.

In the late 18th and early 19th century, ***Norfolk Island*** was the site of two failed attempts by the British to establish a penal colony. In 1856, following the departure of the British, it was resettled by Pitcairn Islanders, who were descendants of the Bounty mutineers and their Tahitian companions. It now has the status of non-self-governing overseas territory of Australia. Since July 2016, the Norfolk Island Regional Council has been responsible for planning and managing a wide range of public services. In 2018, the island's population was 1,750, its per capita GDP was estimated to be about I$ 2,000 and its total GDP was I$ 3 million. Norfolk Island has a small agricultural sector and is self-sufficient in beef, poultry, and eggs. However, 80 percent of the workforce are employed in the services sector. Tourism is growing in importance. The territory's main commodity exports are postage stamps, seeds of the Norfolk Island pine and Kentia palm, and avocados.

The ***Solomon Islands*** achieved independence in 1978. Ethnic divisions and poor government led to instability and civil unrest over the following two decades. During 2003-17, a Regional Assistance Mission to the Solomon Islands (RAMSI) achieved considerable success in restoring law and order and rebuilding government institutions, leading to improved prospects for trade and inward FDI. In 2018, the country had a population of about 650,000, per capita GDP of a little under I$ 2,500 and total GDP of I$ 1.6 billion. The Solomon Island's main exports are timber, fish, copra, palm oil, cocoa, and coconut oil. Its leading imports are food, manufactured products, and equipment. The country's main trading partners are China (44 percent of all trade), Australia (12 percent) and Singapore (6 percent).

Vanuatu was administered by an Anglo-French Condominium for most of the early and middle 20th century but became an independent country in 1980. Since then, political and social divisions along linguistic lines appear to be weakening and political institutions are slowly becoming stronger. The government is undertaking ambitious projects to increase resort development and cruise ship facilities in order to support the tourism industry. In 2018, the country had a population of 292,000, per capita GDP of I$ 3,266 and total GDP of I$ 950 million. Vanuatu's leading exports comprise fish products, offshore financial services, tourism (about 330,000 arrived tourists in 2017), copra, beef, cocoa, coffee, and coconut products. Its main imports are machinery and equipment, food products, and fuels. The country's main trading partners are Russia (20 percent of the total), Australia (18 percent) and the Philippines (16 percent).

MICRONESIA

Guam is an unincorporated, organised territory of the United States. It provides an important defence base for the States, which has several thousand military personnel on the island. Defence expenditures by the United States generate about a third of the territory's GDP, with tourism providing another one fifth (Hiles and Webb, 1995). In 1918, Guam had a population of 168,000, per capita GDP of close to I$ 35,500 and total GDP of I$ 5.8 billion. The country's main commodity exports are construction materials, and fish. Its leading commodity imports are foodstuffs, manufactures, and fuels. The country's major trading partners are Singapore (25 percent of all trade), Japan (18 percent) and Palau (8 percent).

Kiribati (formerly the Gilbert Islands) became a completely independent nation in 1979. Geographically, it comprises 33 scattered atolls. In 2018. The country's population was 116,000, its per capita GDP was I$ 2,361 and its total GDP was I$ 273 million. Apart from foreign aid, Kiribati's main sources of foreign exchange are fishing licenses, and seafarer remittances. However, the country also exports fish and coconut products. Kiribati's leading imports are food, machinery & equipment, manufactured products, and fuels. Its major trading partners are the Philippines (27 percent of all trade), Australia (15 percent) and Malaysia (10 percent)

The ***Marshall Islands*** have been independent since 1986. The foundations of the economy are its hosting of both a US missile test site and one of the four dedicated ground antennas that support the Global Positioning System (GPS). The governments of the Marshall Islands and the United States are building a trust fund that will provide a continuing income stream for the country from 2024. In 2018, the Marshall Islands had a population of 58,000, per capita GDP of I$ 4,165 and total GDP of I$ 242 million. About 11 percent of the population work in the agricultural sector, with coconuts and breadfruit being the main commercial crops. In addition to the services it provides to the US government, the country exports copra cake, coconut oil, fish, and handicrafts. Its main imports are foodstuffs, machinery & equipment, and fuels.

Table 6. The economies of Micronesia, 2018

	Labour force ('000)	Labour productivity (I$)	GDP/GRP (I$ mn)	Population ('000)	Per capita GDP/GRP (I$)
Guam	73	79,452	5,800	168	34,524
Kiribati	42	6,433	273	116	2,361
Marshall Islands	11	21,707	242	58	4,165
FS of Micronesia	38	11,102	420	113	3,727
Nauru	4	41,271	160	10	16,508
N Mariana Islands	28	4,429	124	5	24,314
Palau	16	21,583	347	18	19,261
Total	**212**	**34,684**	**7,366**	**487**	**15,116**
Rest of Oceania	20,917	76,051	1,590,752	40,938	38,858
Oceania	21,129	75,636	1,598,118	41,425	38,579

Sources. World Bank's World Economic Indicators, IMF's World Economic Outlook, UN Population Division, CIA's World Factbook

The ***Federated States of Micronesia*** comprise four islands that, along with Palau, originally formed the Caroline Islands. Micronesia has been independent since 1986. Its economy has been heavily dependent on direct assistance from the United States under an Agreement that will expire in 2023; however, the Agreement makes provision for the establishment of a trust fund that is intended to provide a comparable income stream from 2024. A consequence of the Agreement is that about two-thirds of the work force are employed by government, with the private sector being small and not very innovative. In 2018, the country had a population of 113,000, per capita GDP of I$ 3,727 and total GDP of I$ 420 million. Its major export products are fish, kava, betel nut, and black pepper. Its main imports include food products, clothing, computers, and household electronic products.

Nauru has a land area of only 26 square kilometres. Little is known of the origins of the Nauruan people, and their language bears no similarity to any other language in the Pacific region. The country achieved independence in 1966 and joined the United Nations in 1999 as its smallest independent republic. In the 20th century, considerable revenue was generated by the mining and export of phosphates, but the coastal reserves were exhausted by 2006. However, mining has recommenced inland on a deeper layer of "secondary phosphate" and is expected to continue for several more decades. Growth was further stimulated in 2013 by the opening of the Australian Regional Processing Centre for asylum seekers. In 2018, the country's population was about 10,000, per capita GDP was I$ 16,508 and total GDP was I$ 160 million. Nauru's main export is phosphate. Its main imports are foodstuffs, manufactured products, and building materials. The country's major trading partners are Australia (40 percent of all trade), Nigeria (20 percent) and Japan (10 percent).

The ***Northern Mariana Islands*** is a commonwealth under US administration as part of the UN Treaty of the Pacific. In the 1970s, it voted against independence and in favour of close ties with the United States. The protectorate's relative prosperity depends importantly on contributions from the United States, which fund about a quarter of the government's budget. The protectorate has a small but efficient agricultural sector focused on cattle ranches and small farms growing coconuts, breadfruit, tomatoes, and melons. Tourism is growing strongly, with China and South Korea replacing Japan as the major source countries. In 2018, the Northern Mariana Islands had a population of a little over 5,000, per capita GDP of I$ 24,314 and total GDP of I$ 124 million. The country's main commodity exports are garments. Its major commodity imports are foodstuffs, construction materials & equipment, and petroleum products.

In 1978, ***Palau*** chose to be an independent nation rather than part of the Federated States of Micronesia. The country's economy is dominated by subsistence agriculture, tourism, and fishing. In 2018, population was 18,000, per capita GDP was I$ 19,261 and total GDP was I$ 347 million. Palau's major trading partners are Japan (35 percent of all trade), the United States (25 percent) and China (10 percent). The country's main exports are tourism (168,000 tourists in 2015) and fish including especially shellfish and tuna. Its major imports are machinery & equipment, fuels, and foodstuffs. Prospects for tourism are especially bright due to the rapid industrialisation of East Asia and the high quality of the country's tourism infrastructure (reflecting largely the attractiveness of its business climate to foreign investors).

POLYNESIA

American Samoa is an unincorporated, organised territory of the United States. It has a traditional Polynesian society, with more than 90 percent of the land being communally owned. In 1918, the island's population was 51,000, per capita GDP was I$ 12,902 and total GDP was I$ 658 million. The economy depends heavily on financial and other support provided by the United States. However, American Samoa does have a strong tuna fishing and processing industry – in 2018, the tuna processing industry accounted for 16 percent of total employment and processed tuna was the island's leading export product. Tourism is growing strongly, and the government is very supportive of efforts to promote this industry.

The ***Cook Islands*** are named after Captain James Cook, who landed there in 1773 during the second of his three voyages to the south Pacific. In 1975, its residents chose self-government in free association with New Zealand. The Cook

Table 7. The economies of Polynesia, 2018

	Labour force ('000)	Labour productivity (I$)	GDP/GRP (I$ mn)	Population ('000)	Per capita GDP/GRP (I$)
American Samoa	18	36,863	658	51	12,902
Cook Islands (NZ)	11	21,487	240	8.574	27,980
French Polynesia	126	43,468	5,490	290	18,931
Niue	1	15,083	10	1.6	6,250
Pitcairn Islands	0	7,200	0	0.054	2,000
Samoa	57	20,000	1,140	201	5,672
Tokelau	0	4,545	2	1	2,000
Tonga	338	1,775	600	106.1	5,655
Tuvalu	36	1,162	42	11	3,818
Wallis and Futuna	5	12,392	60	16	3,806
Total	592	13,912	8242	686	12,013
Rest of Oceania	20,537	77,417	1,589,876	40,739	39,026
Oceania	21,129	75,636	1,598,118	41,425	38,579

Sources. World Bank's World Economic Indicators, IMF's World Economic Outlook, UN Population Division, CIA's World Factbook

Islands government has responsibility for internal matters while the New Zealand government, in consultation with the Cook Islands government, looks after external affairs and defence. About a quarter of the workforce is engaged in agriculture, with manufacturing being limited to fruit processing, clothing, and handicrafts. In 2018, the Cook Islands had a population of about 9,000, per capita GDP was I$ 15,957 and total GDP was I$ 143 million. Its main exports are black pearls and pearl shells, but fish, copra, papayas, fresh and canned citrus fruit, coffee, and clothing are also important. The economy benefits considerably from foreign aid, which comes mainly from New Zealand, as well as remittances from emigrants working in neighbouring countries. The country's major imports are foodstuffs, textiles, fuels, timber, and capital goods.

French Polynesia, which is formally an overseas collectivity of France, is often referred to as an overseas country of France because of the high degree of autonomy it possesses (Blanchet, 1991). The economy has a developed farming sector and is self-sufficient in many farm products. However, services dominate economic activity, accounting for about 85 percent of GDP. Tourism is the largest single industry and employs more than 15 percent of the workforce. In 2018, French Polynesia had a population of 290,000, per capita GDP of I$ 18,931 and total GDP of just under

I$ 5.5 billion. The country's main commodity exports are cultured pearls, mother-of-pearl, coconut products, vanilla, and shark meat. Its main imports are processed food products, machinery & equipment, and fuels. French Polynesia's main trading partners are France (20 percent of all trade), the United States (14 percent), and Japan and Hong Kong (12 percent each).

Niue (formerly known as Savage Island) has been a self-governing territory in free association with New Zealand since 1974. During 1966-2018, its population declined from 5,200 to 1,600, reflecting strong emigration to New Zealand where employment and business prospects were much brighter. In 2018, per capita and total GDP were I$ 6,250 and I$ 10 million, respectively. Niue's agriculture sector is a mixture of subsistence gardening and commercial farming. The manufacturing sector comprises mainly very small businesses that process agricultural products for export. The main commodity exports are canned coconut cream, copra, honey, vanilla, passionfruit products, footballs, and postage stamps (which are sold to stamp collectors abroad). Most commercial consumption items are imported, with imports exceeding exports by a ratio of 40:1. The large trade deficit is funded by foreign aid and remittances from family members working mainly in New Zealand.

The ***Pitcairn Islands*** were settled in 1790 by the Bounty mutineers and their companions from Tahiti. It has been a British colony since 1838 and is the last vestige of the British Empire in the Pacific. In 2018, its population was 54 (down from 233 in 1937), with per capita GDP estimated at no more than I$ 2,000. The colony has a mainly subsistence economy and barter is still an important method of exchange. Its main export products are handicrafts sold to passing ships, postage stamps sold to foreign stamp collectors, and honey, fruits, and vegetables.

Samoa (the name may mean "People of the Deep Sea") has been a parliamentary republic since it gained independence from New Zealand-Administered UN Trusteeship in 1962. Its economy has traditionally been heavily dependent on foreign aid, remittances from family members working abroad, agriculture, fishing, and tourism. The largest industry is now tourism, which accounts for 25 percent of GDP. In 2012, Samoa joined the WTO and in 2014 graduated from developing country status. The government has a welcoming approach to business and is endeavouring to stimulate economic growth by deregulating the financial sector and encouraging private investment from foreign as well as domestic sources. Samoa's main trading partners are Australia, New Zealand, and American Samoa, each with shares of about 20 percent of the total. Its main commodity exports are fish, coconut oil and cream, nonu, copra, taro, auto parts, garments, and beer. The main commodity imports are machinery & equipment, industrial supplies, and foodstuffs.

Tokelau has been a territory of New Zealand since 1925. In 1918, its population was about 1,300, its per capita GDP was I$ 2,000 and its total GDP was I$ 2.6 million. Foreign aid from New Zealand amounted to I$ 11,000 per person. The small population is evenly distributed across three atolls. Tokelau's main commodity exports are postage stamps to foreign stamp collectors, copra, and handicrafts. Its main commodity imports are foodstuffs, building materials and fuels.

Tonga (historically known as "The Friendly Isles") is unique among the smaller Oceanic countries in both never having completely lost its independence and still being a constitutional monarchy (though most government powers were relinquished by the then-King George TUPOU V leading up to the parliamentary elections in 2010). Most Tongans speak English and the work force is highly educated. Government policies are growth oriented, with strong support for the education and health-care industries. In 2018, the country had a population of 106,000, per capita GDP of I$ 5,655 and total GDP of I$ 600 million. Tonga's main sources of foreign exchange are foreign aid and remittances from Tongans working abroad, followed by exports of agricultural products (squash, vanilla beans, and yams) and tourism (it receives about 60,000 tourists a year). Its main trading partners are New Zealand (23 percent of all trade), Hong Kong (13 percent) and Australia (10 percent).

Tuvalu (formerly the Elise Islands) became independent in 1970. The country comprises nine scattered coral atolls, covers an area of only 26 square kilometres and is home to 11,000 people. Its highest point is less than five metres above sea level. In 2018, Tuvalu's per capita GDP was I$ 3,818 and its total GDP was I$ 42 million. The country's major industry is fishing - in 2013, revenue from fishing licences amounted to 45 percent of GDP. Tuvalu's main exports are copra and fish. Its major imports include foodstuffs, manufactured goods, fuels, and machinery. The country's main trading partners are Singapore (20 percent of all trade), the United States (12 percent) and Bosnia and Herzegovina (10 percent).

In 1959, the inhabitants of the islands of ***Wallis and Futuna*** voted to become a French overseas territory. In 2003, the status of the islands was changed to overseas collectivity. The collectivity's economy consists largely of traditional agriculture (focusing on coconuts, vegetables, pigs, and fishing) and a large public sector funded mainly by contributions from France. A major problem is the scarcity of employment and business opportunities, resulting in high emigration of younger adults. In 2018, the population was 16,000, per capita GDP was I$ 3,806 and total GDP was I$ 60 million. The territory's main commodity exports are copra, chemicals, and construction materials. Its major commodity imports are chemicals, machinery, and consumer goods.

CONCLUSION

Oceania comprises the western-oriented countries of Australia and New Zealand plus the more-than 20 generally small, independent, and semi-independent island countries of Melanesia, Micronesia, and Polynesia. In 2018, Australia and New Zealand accounted for 71 percent of the region's population and 95 percent of its GRP. Melanesia, which is dominated by Papua New Guinea, Fiji, and New Caledonia, contained 26 percent of the region's population, and generated 4 percent of its GRP. According to the forecasting model developed by the authors, Oceania's share of both world population and GWP will rise strongly during the coming three decades, admittedly from a low base. Reflecting the high degree of complementarity of the Oceanic economies with those of Asia, this strong growth in the Oceanic region should support increasingly attractive opportunities for trade and investment with the economies of Asia.

REFERENCES

Blanchet, G. (1991). *A Survey of the Economy of French Polynesia, 1960 to 1990*. The Australian National University.

Goodman, R., & Lepani, C. (1997). *The Economy of Papua New Guinea*. The Australian National University.

Hawke, G. R. (1985). *The Making of New Zealand: An Economic History*. Cambridge University Press.

Hiles, G., & Webb, R. (1995). *The Economic Impact of Tourism in Guam*. Bureau of Labor Statistics, Guam Finance Commission.

Hooke, A. (2019). *Global Economic Development: Past, Present and Future*. Lakeland House.

Jinks, B., Biskup, P., & Nelson, H. (1973). *Readings in New Guinea History*. Angus & Robertson.

Kushnir, I. (2019). *Economy of New Caledonia*. Independently published.

Lal, B. V. (1992). *Broken Waves: A History of the Fiji Islands in the Twentieth Century*. University of Hawaii Press.

ADDITIONAL READING

AusTrade. (2019). *Australia's Tourist Arrivals Exceed 9 Million in 2018*. https://www.austrade.gov.au/news/economic-analysis/australias-tourist-arrivals-exceed-9-million-in-2018

CIA. (2020). *The World Factbook*. https://www.cia.gov/library/publications/the-world-factbook/

DFAT. (2019). *New Zealand Market Insights*. https://dfat.gov.au/geo/new-zealand/pages/new-zealand.aspx

DFAT. (2019). *Solomon Islands Insights*. https://dfat.gov.au/geo/solomon-islands/Pages/solomon-islands.aspx

Dixon, T., & O'Mahony, J. (2020). *Australia in the Global Economy*. Pearson.

Hirsch, E. (2019). *The Melanesian World*. Routledge Handbooks Online. doi:10.4324/9781315529691

Martin, K. (2019) *The Polynesian World*. Routledge Handbooks Online, Quanchi, M. (2019). *The Melanesian World*. Routledge Handbooks Online.

Siwatibau, S. (1993). Macroeconomic Management in the Small Open Economies of the Pacific in the Future of Asia-Pacific Economies: Pacific Islands at the Crossroads? National Centre for Development studies, Canberra.

Trading Economics. (2019). *Ease of Doing Business in Fiji*. https://tradingeconomics.com/fiji/ease-of-doing-business

Trading Economics. (2019). *Ease of Doing Business in Australia*. https://tradingeconomics.com/australia/ease-of-doing-business

ENDNOTE

1 I$ refers to an "international dollar", which has the same purchasing power across countries and over time. In this chapter, I$ refers to purchasing power in 2018.

Chapter 2
The Economies of East Asia

Angus Hooke
Australian Institute of Higher Education, Australia

Harpreet Kaur
Australian Institute of Higher Education, Australia

ABSTRACT

In 2018, East Asia accounted for accounted for 31% of gross world product (GWP). A global forecasting model developed by Hooke and updated by Hooke, Alati, and Kaur for the first three chapters of this book suggests that the region's share will remain at about this level until 2050, with the effects of global labour productivity convergence more than offsetting East Asia's relatively slow work force growth. Thereafter, the share will decline to 18% by 2100 due mainly to more rapid productivity and work force growth in West Asia and Africa. China is expected to retain its position as the world's largest economy until about the middle of this century, at which time its GDP will be more than 2.5 times that of the United States. An important driver of growth in East Asia during the coming decades will be Indonesia, whose share of GWP is forecast to rise from 2.6% in 2018 to 3.8% by 2050.

OVERVIEW

In 1950, East Asia accounted for 32 percent of the world's population but only 7 percent of gross world product (GWP). By 2018, the region's share of world population had fallen slightly, to 30 percent; however, reflecting very strong growth of labour productivity, especially in Northeast Asia, its share of GWP had increased more than fourfold to 31 percent. It is projected by the United Nation's Population Division that East Asia's population will rise modestly in the coming decades, to 2.4 billion

DOI: 10.4018/978-1-7998-4126-5.ch002

in 2050, but will then decline to less than 2 billion by 2100. The model developed by the authors, which is described briefly in the preceding chapter, suggests that East Asia's gross regional product (GRP) – the sum of the gross domestic products (GDPs) of all the countries in East Asia - will be 29 percent of GWP in 2050 but, reflecting its own declining population as well as strong growth of population, labour force participation rates and labour productivity in West Asia and Africa, will decline to 18 per cent by 2100 (Table 1).

THE MAJOR REGIONS OF EAST ASIA

In 2018, East Asia accounted for 36 percent of the world's work force. Labour productivity, at I$ 33,607, was 85 percent of the global average.[1] The GRP of East Asia was I$ 41.5 billion, accounting for 31 percent of GWP. With total population of 2,288 million, per capita GRP was I$ 18,150, or 4 percent above the world average. Within East Asia (comprising Northeast Asia and Southeast Asia). Northeast Asia had the larger GRP (79 percent of the East Asia total) and larger population (72 percent of the total).

Northeast Asia

In 2018, Northeast Asia's population accounted for 21 percent of world population and 72 percent of the population of East Asia. Its per capita GDP (I$ 20,178) was 16 percent above the global average (I$ 17,630) (Table 2). The region's share of gross world product (GWP), which was 24 percent in 2018, is projected to fall to 20 percent by 2050 and 11 percent by 2100, due mainly to relatively low work force growth.

China passed the United States as the world's largest economy in 2014. In that year, its labour productivity was only about one-fifth that of the United States, but its work force was five times larger. With productivity growth in the United States constrained by the slow outward movement of the global technology frontier, and productivity in China benefitting from both the outward movement of the frontier and inside movement toward the frontier, labour productivity has continued to grow more rapidly in China, and in 2018 its GDP was almost 20 percent larger than that of the United States.

Table 1. Major Economic Indicators, 1950-2100

	1950	2000	2010	2018	2050	2100
Population (mn)						
East Asia	818	2,004	2,156	2,288	2,375	1,952
West Asia	505	1,501	1,795	1,998	2,879	2,753
America	424	1,115	1,233	1,365	1,161	1,148
Europe	547	720	731	741	704	626
Africa	222	791	1,013	1,243	2,424	4,171
Oceania	14	32	37	41	57	76
World	2,530	6,164	6,966	7,676	9,599	10,727
Total GDP (I$ tn)						
East Asia	0.8	13.4	27.6	41.5	153	315
West Asia	0.8	9.3	15.6	23.2	159	444
America	3.6	23.2	28.0	33.0	84	185
Europe	5.3	23.6	24.7	29.2	55	101
Africa	0.3	3.6	5.3	6.8	60	673
Oceania	0.1	0.9	1.2	1.6	4	12
World	11	74	102	135	515	1,731
Per capita GDP (I$)						
East Asia	984	6,671	12,794	18,150	64,285	161,333
West Asia	1,530	6,214	8,689	11,591	55,258	161,333
America	8,386	20,832	22,705	24,197	72,675	161,333
Europe	9,721	32,702	33,726	39,390	78,220	161,333
Africa	1,366	4,611	5,232	5,504	24,680	161,333
Oceania	8,450	29,141	32,963	38,380	63,816	161,333
World	4,297	12,016	14,697	17,630	53,612	161,333

Sources. World Bank's World Economic Indicators, IMF's World Economic Outlook, UN Population Division, CIA's World Factbook, authors' forecasting model.

Note. GDP is measured in purchasing power parity (PPP) terms, at 2018 prices.

China's recent move to the top of the global GDP ladder was not a new occurrence (Hooke, 2019). For two of the last four millennia, China may have had the largest economy in the world. This was due to both its relatively large population – and thus work force – and its comparatively high level of technology and economic organisation throughout most of the period. Hooke (2019) suggests that China had the world's largest GDP during the latter half of the Chou period (1111-21 BC), during the Ch'in period (221-206 BC), probably during much of the Han period

(206 BC – AD 220) and for most of the millennia that commenced with the Sui ascendancy in AD 581. China's relative decline began in the 1420s, during the reign of the Ming dynasty, when concerns about the meagre returns from costly foreign trade excursions and external conflicts with relatively poor neighbours caused the central government to adopt progressively isolationist and conservative economic policies. China's share of GWP fell from above 40 percent in the early 15th century to less than 2 percent in the late 1970s, before the country under Deng Xiaoping's leadership re-joined the world economy (Naughton, 2007).

Table 2. Economies of the East Asia Regions, 2018

	Labour force (m)	Labour productivity (I$)	GRP (I$ b)	Population (m)	Per capita GRP (I$)
East Asia	1,235	33,607	41,520	2,288	18,150
Northeast Asia	918	35,909	32,952	1,633	20,178
Southeast Asia	318	26,959	8,568	655	13,088
Rest of world	2,180	43,040	93,814	5,389	17,410
World	3,415	39,627	135,334	7,676	17,630

Sources. World Bank's World Economic Indicators, IMF's World Economic Outlook, UN Population Division, CIA's World Factbook

Table 3. Economies of Northeast Asia, 2018

	Labour force (m)	Labour productivity (I$)	GDR/GWP (I$ bn)	Population (m)	Per capita GDP/GWP (I$)
China	810	30,867	24,993	1,426	17,525
Japan	65	88,112	5,714	127	44,961
South Korea	28	77,007	2,146	51	42,003
North Korea	14	4,000	56	26	2,191
Mongolia	1	34,400	43	3	13,537
Northeast Asia	**918**	**35,909**	**32,952**	**1,633**	**20,178**
Rest of world	2,498	40,994	102,382	6,043	16,942
World	3,415	39,627	135,334	7,676	17,630

Sources. World Bank's World Economic Indicators, IMF's World Economic Outlook, UN Population Division, CIA's World Factbook

China became the world's largest exporter of commodities in 2010 and, by 2018, was exporting 50 percent more than the second largest exporter, the United States. China's leading export destinations are the United States (19 percent), Hong Kong (12 percent) and Japan (9 percent). Its main export products are electrical and other machinery, apparel, furniture, and textiles.

In 2013, China became the world's largest trading nation; however, by 2018 its total imports were still only 70 percent of those of the United States. The main sources of China's commodity imports are South Korea (10 percent), Japan (9 percent), the United States (8 percent) and Germany and Australia (5 percent each). China's main commodity imports are machinery including integrated circuits and other computer parts, oil and mineral fuels, optical and medical equipment, metal ores, motor vehicles, and soybeans.

The forecasting model developed by the authors suggests that China will remain the world's largest economy until the late 2040s, at which time its GDP will be passed by that of India. According to forecasts made by the UN Population Division, India's population will be 23 percent larger than that of China by 2050 and the ratios of the working age population to total population, which currently is about 60 percent in China and only 40 percent in India, will be quite similar. In the latter half of the century, the ratio of China's GDP to that of India will fall to about 67 percent as per capita incomes converge globally and China's population declines to a little over 1 billion. China will, however, remain the world's second largest economy, with its GDP in 2100 being about double that of third-placed Nigeria and 2.5 times the GDP of fourth-placed United States.

Table 4. Economic Performance and Prospects of China, 1950-2100

	1950	2000	2018	2050	2100
Work force (m)	309	733	810	663	472
Productivity (I$)	555	3,946	30,867	136,936	358,519
GDP (I$)	171	2,892	24,993	90,773	169,207
Population (m)	544	1,291	1,426	1,387	1,049
Per capita GDP (I$)	315	2,240	17,525	65,460	161,333

Source. World Income Model developed by the authors

In the 17th and 18th centuries, under the Tokugawu shoganate, ***Japan*** had a closed but reasonably prosperous economy. However, as is common experience when an autarky opens its economy to those of wealthier neighbours, the GDP of Japan accelerated during the eight decades following the 1854 Treaty of Kanugawa between Japan and the United States. After being defeated in World War II, Japan was again required to adopt an open trading and investment system, leading to average annual GDP growth of about 10 percent in the 1950s and 1960s, 5 percent in the 1970s and 4 percent in the 1980s. However, reflecting partly a steady decline in competitiveness associated with the rigid Keiretsu supply chain system, the guarantee of lifetime employment for urban employees and strong political support for some traditional industries, the economy has stagnated since the turn of the 1990s (Flath, 2019). Nevertheless, while Japan now accounts for only 4 percent of GWP, it holds 15 percent of the world's financial assets, implying that the country's share of world income is much higher than its share of world production. In 2018, Japan was the world's fourth largest exporter of commodities, after China, the United States and Germany. Its main exports are motor vehicles, iron and steel, semiconductors, and power-generating equipment. Its main export partners are the United States (20 percent), China (19 percent) and South Korea (8 percent). Japan's leading imports are petroleum products, liquefied natural gas, coal and clothing. The main source countries for its imports are China (25 percent), the United States (11 percent) and Australia (6 percent).

The name ***Korea*** is derived from the Chinese name Goryeo, the dynasty that united the Korean peninsula in the 10th century AD. Korea was mostly an independent kingdom for the next nine centuries. However, following a war with Russia, Japan occupied the peninsula in 1905 and annexed it five years later. After World War II, Korea was split into the northern half, which was supported strongly by the Soviet Union and later China, and the southern half, which was closely aligned with the United States.

South Korea was among the world's poorest countries in the early 1960s. However, its economy developed rapidly in the following three decades (Lee, 1998) and, in 1997, South Korea was admitted to the ranks of the advanced economies by the OECD. In 2018, South Korea's per capita GDP was about I$ 42,000, second highest in Northeast Asia to that of Japan. The country's economic success has been due largely to its open approach to free trade – it now has free trade agreements that cover three-quarters of global trade – and inward FDI. Being a relatively high-income country and located close to the global technology frontier, South Korea's GDP growth rate has declined in recent years, to an average annual rate of about 3 percent in 2014-18. However, it does have scope for higher growth by further narrowing its labour productivity gap with the global majors, particularly the United States and Japan. Exploitation of this scope will require continuation of its open approach to international trade and investment. Currently, South Korea's main commodity exports are semiconductors, petrochemicals, automobiles and automobile parts, wireless communication equipment, plastics, TV sets, and computers. The main destinations for these exports are China (25 percent), the United States (12 percent) and Vietnam (8 percent). The country's main commodity imports are petroleum, natural gas, steel, coal, semiconductors, computers, automobiles, fine chemicals, and textiles. The main sources of its imports are China (20 percent), Japan (12 percent), and the United States (11 percent).

The local name for ***North Korea*** (Democratic People's Republic of Korea -DPRK) is "Choson", which translates to "Land of the) Morning Calm". With its larger endowment of minerals and stronger history of industrialisation, per capita GDP at the turn of the 1950s was higher in North Korea than in South Korea. Since the Korean War of 1950-53, and especially following the collapse of the Soviet Union in 1989, North Korea has followed a policy of strict economic independence and it has become one of the most centrally directed and closed economies in the world. The focus on political stability has hampered economic development, with the average standard of living falling to a fraction of that of South Korea. In 2018, North Korea's per capita GDP was estimated to be about I$ 2,200. The government has identified economic development as a priority and in 2016 used two mass mobilisations – one of about 70 days and the other of 200 days – to stimulate production and speed up the completion of important development projects. To date, there is little evidence that these efforts have gained traction. However, the North Korean president Kim Jong Un is increasing the country's political interactions with the rest of the world, meeting several times with the presidents of South Korea and the United States in 2019. If this approach leads to a more open economy, considerable trade and investment opportunities may emerge. Currently, North Korea's main export products are minerals, metal products, textiles, agricultural goods, and fish. Its leading imports are fuels such as petroleum and coking coal. More than four-fifths of the country's international trade is with China.

In the 13th century, ***Mongolia*** under Ghengis Khan may have been the most powerful and richest empire in the world. Following Khan's death, the empire broke up into several states and eventually fell under Chinese rule. Independence for the area that is now Mongolia was achieved in 1921. For the next seven decades, Mongolia was a communist state and a recipient of considerable aid from its western neighbour, the Soviet Union. In 1990, following the collapse of the Soviet Union, Mongolia experienced a relatively peaceful revolution that led to a democratic form of government. Aid from the former Soviet area dropped sharply but market reforms, privatisation of inefficient government enterprises and a more welcoming approach to inward FDI led to strong economic growth, albeit from a low base. Mongolia is well endowed with mineral resources such as copper, gold, tin, and uranium and is slowly creating an environment that encourages FDI to assist in their development. In 2018, the stock of FDI was US $18 billion, or more than US $5,000 per citizen. Mongolia's main export products include copper, apparel, livestock, cashmere, and coal. About 85 percent of all exports go to China. Mongolia's main commodity imports, of which a third come from China, are machinery & equipment, cars, and fuels.

Table 5. Economies of Southeast Asia, 2018

	Labour force (m)	Labour productivity (I$)	GDR/GWP (I$ bn)	Population (m)	Per capita GDP/GWP (I$)
Brunei	0.2	174,758	36	0.4	84,989
Cambodia	9.0	7,643	69	16.2	4,265
Indonesia	126.0	27,696	3,491	267.4	13,056
Laos	3.6	14,259	52	7.1	7,348
Malaysia	15.1	66,215	1,003	31.5	31,782
Myanmar	22.5	15,732	354	53.7	6,589
Philippines	43.4	21,689	942	106.5	8,849
Singapore	3.7	156,367	582	5.8	100,737
Thailand	38.5	34,615	1,332	69.4	19,205
Timor-Leste	0.3	33,727	10	1.3	7,866
Vietnam	55.3	12,603	697	95.4	7,302
SE Asia	**318**	**26,959**	**8,568**	**655**	**13,088**
Rest of world	3,097	40,927	126,767	7,022	18,054
World	3,415	39,627	135,334	7,676	17,630

Sources. World Bank's World Economic Indicators, IMF's World Economic Outlook, UN Population Division, CIA's World Factbook

Southeast Asia

In 2018, the population of Southeast Asia accounted for 9 percent of the world's population and 21 percent of the population of Asia. However, its per capita GDP (I$ 13,088) was only 74 percent of the global average. Reflecting mainly the effects of per capita income convergence, the region's share of GWP, which was 6 percent in 2018, is projected to rise to 9 percent in 2050 before falling back to 7 percent by 2100.

During the 15th to 17th centuries, ***Brunei*** controlled the coastal areas of both northwest Borneo and the southern Philippines. However, its influence declined during the 18th century, due to both internal disputes over royal succession and external expansion of major European powers, and in 1888 Brunei became a British protectorate. The country regained its independence and status as an absolute monarchy in 1984. It now boasts one of the world's most enduring monarchies, with one family occupying the throne for more than six centuries. Brunei has large reserves of petroleum and natural gas, well-developed infrastructure, a highly educated and largely English-speaking work force, and a stable government that encourages international trade and investment. It is one of the few countries in the world that does not levy an income tax. In 2018, Brunei's population was 430.000, per capita GDP was just under I$ 85,000 (about 5 times the world average) and total GDP was I$ 36 billion. Brunei's exports are dominated by crude oil and natural gas. Its main imports are machinery and motor vehicles. The country's major trading partners are Japan (24 percent of the total), Malaysia (16 percent) and Singapore (2 percent).

The history of ***Cambodia*** can be traced back to the Angkor Empire that ruled most of Southeast Asia during the 10th to 13th centuries AD. In 1863, following attacks from neighbouring entities, the king of Cambodia placed the country under French protection. It became part of French Indochina in 1887 but gained full independence from the French in 1953. It is officially a parliamentary constitutional monarchy. Cambodia experienced considerable internal conflict in the late 20th century, but the defeat of the Khmers and increased concentration of power within the Cambodian People's Party (CPP) has resulted in greater political stability. The average annual growth of GDP was about 8 percent during 2000-10 and 7 percent in 2011-17. Growth came mainly from the tourism sector (international arrivals rose from 2 million in 2007 to 5.6 million in 2017) and the garment and construction industries. As a result of this growth, the World Bank moved Cambodia from low-income to lower-middle income status in 2016. In 2018, population was 16 million, per capita GDP was I$ 4,265 (24 percent of the global average) and total GDP was I$ 69 billion. Exports are dominated by textiles (68 percent of the total in 2018), followed by timber, rubber, rice, and fish. The main imports are petroleum products, cigarettes, gold, and construction materials. Cambodia's major trading partners are China (20 percent of the total), the United States (12 percent) and the European Union (10 percent). The stock of inward FDI is still very low (US $ 30 billion in 2018) but there are signs of growing investor interest in developing the country's deposits of bauxite, gold, iron, and gems.

Indonesia was colonised by the Netherlands in the 17th century and occupied by Japan during 1942-45. It achieved independence in 1949, but then experienced several decades of authoritarian government before democracy was restored in 1999 (Palmer, 2018). Indonesia is the world's largest archipelago, third most populous democracy, and largest Muslim-majority nation. It has the 3rd largest economy in Asia and 7th largest globally. In 2018, its population was 267 million, per capita GDP was I$ 13,056 (three-quarters of the global average) and GDP was I$ 3.5 trillion (2.6 percent of GWP). In recent years the government has strengthened its fiscal situation (the ratio of public debt to GDP fell from more than 100 percent in 1999 to 34 percent in 2017), achieved strong economic growth (average of 5 percent a year during 2013-18) and had its sovereign credit risk upgraded by Standard & Poor to investment grade. Indonesia's main commodity exports comprise mineral fuels, palm oil, electrical machinery, rubber, and mechanical appliance parts. Its major imports are mineral fuels, boilers, and machinery. The country's main trading partners are the United States (18 percent of the total), Japan (10 percent) and Singapore (8 percent).

Laos also has a rich history. Commencing in the 13th century AD, the Lao Kingdom of Lan Xang had a flourishing economy and influence that extended to present-day Thailand and Cambodia. The kingdom's prosperity and power started to decline in the 16th century and the country came under the domination of first, Siam in the late 18th century, and then France in the late 19th century when it became part of French Indochina. It achieved independence from France in 1954. In 1975, the communist Pathet Lao took control of government and replaced the six-centuries-old monarchy with a one-party communist state. Following poor economic performance, the government introduced reforms from 1986 that included decentralisation of political control and encouragement of free enterprise. The reforms were followed by average annual GDP growth of 6 percent during 1990-2009 and 7 percent in 2010-17. As a result, per capita GDP reached I$ 7,348 in 2018, or 42 percent of the global average. Laos' main commodity exports are wood products, coffee, electricity, tin, coffee, and gold. Its major imports include machinery & equipment, fuel, motor vehicles, and consumer goods. The country's leading trading partners are Thailand (50 percent of the total), China (25 percent) and Vietnam (10 percent). The government encourages inward FDI and has established several special economic zones that provide generous tax and other incentives to foreign investors. In 2017, the stock of inward FDI was US $15.4 billion, or US $2,160 per capita.

In the 18th and 19th centuries, Great Britain established colonies and protectorates in the area that now includes ***Malaysia*** ("land of the Malays"). The independent federation of Malaysia was formed as a constitutional monarchy in 1963. The current boundaries were established when Singapore withdrew from the federation in 1965. At that time, the economy was resource-based, and per capita income was low. It has since developed into a multi-sector, upper middle-income economy. In 2018, population was 31.5 million, per capita GDP was I$ 31,782 and total GDP exceeded I$ 1 trillion (26th largest in the world). The government aims to make Malaysia a high-income country by 2020 and to move industry further up the high-value production chain by attracting FDI in latest-technology, knowledge-based manufacturing, and services. Malaysia's main commodity exports are semiconductors and electronic equipment, palm oil, petroleum and liquefied natural gas, wood and wood products, chemicals, and solar panels. Its leading imports include electronics, machinery, motor vehicles, and plastics. The country's main trading partners are China (17 percent of the total), the United States (13 percent) and Singapore (8 percent). In 2017, the stock of inward DFI reached US$140 billion or about US$ 4,500 per capita.

During 1824-86, Britain incorporated the many ethnic groups that occupy modern ***Myanmar*** into its Indian Empire. In 1937, Myanmar became a self-governing colony, and in 1948 attained complete independence from Britain. For the remainder of the 20th century and in the first decade of the 21st century Myanmar maintained a relatively closed economy. The transition to a civilian-led government, which commenced in 2011, has led to reforms aimed at opening the economy and encouraging investments from abroad. However, rivalries among different groups continue to constrain economic development. In 2018 per capita GDP was I$ 6,589 – roughly half the average for Southeast Asia and about one third of the global average. Myanmar's main exports include natural gas, wood products, pulses & beans, fish, rice, and jewellery including jade and gems. The country's main imports are petroleum, fertilisers, construction materials, and foodstuffs. Official figures greatly underestimate trade due to widespread smuggling of products through Thailand, China, Bangladesh, Malaysia, and India.

The islands that make up the ***Philippines*** became a Spanish colony in the 16th century. They were ceded to the United States in 1898 following the Spanish-American war. In 1935, the Philippines became a self-governing commonwealth and entered a 10-year transition period aimed at achieving full independence. This was interrupted by World War II, and the Philippines was occupied by the Japanese during 1942-45. However, it achieved complete independence in 1946. The country comprises more than 7,600 islands. The topography of the major islands is generally rugged with narrow coastal lowlands (Canlas and Fujisaki, 2001). In recent years, the economy has been reasonably strong: the current account has generally been in surplus, the tax-to-GDP ratio is low, the public debt-to-GDP ratio is about 40 percent (compared to a global average of 67 percent) and economic growth is averaging about 6 percent a year. The government has pledged to enhance the county's infrastructure and to make doing business easier. In 2018, population was 106 million, per capita GDP was I$ 8,849 and total GDP was I$ 942 billion (29th highest globally). Inward FDI, though still low by international standards, reached a record level in 2017. The Philippines' main commodity exports are electrical machinery & equipment (almost half of total exports) followed by computers & optical readers (14 percent). Its leading imports are also machinery & equipment (about 25 percent of the total) and mineral fuels including petroleum (12 percent). About 80 per cent of trade is with other Asian countries and 10 percent is with North America.

Legend has it that ***Singapore*** was founded a few millennia back when a Sumatran prince saw a lion on the island, interpreted this as a very good omen and founded a settlement there that he named Singapura (meaning "Lion City"). More credible evidence indicates that the island was supporting settlement in the 3rd century AD and was a Malay trading post (known as Temasek) in the 14th century. It changed hands several times during the next few centuries, and by the early 19th century was controlled by the Jahor Sultanate. In 1819, in return for support of the successful brother in a succession struggle and an annual payment, Sir Stamford Raffles negotiated a transfer of the island to the British East India Company. In 1867, it became a British colony, ruled directly by the British government. Singapore prospered under British rule, becoming a major producer of rubber and tin and a leading trading port, attracting many migrants from China. The colony was occupied by the Japanese during 1942-45 but reverted to British rule after World war II. In 1959, it achieved independence from the British. In 1963, Singapore joined with Malaya to form the Federation of Malaysia, but political differences between major parties of the new country led to Singapore's expulsion in 1965. Under its first prime minister, Lee Kuan Yew, and his successors, the country has maintained an effectively corruption-free government environment, has promoted free markets, and has produced one of the world's most prosperous economies. The government has not borrowed to finance expenditures since the 1980s, and it has no external debt. In 2018, Singapore's population was 5.8 million, the country's total GDP was almost I$ 600 billion and its per capita GDP exceeded I$ 100,000. Singapore's main commodity exports are electronic and communication equipment, pharmaceuticals and other chemicals, and refined petroleum products. The country's main commodity imports are machinery and equipment, foodstuffs, and consumer goods. Its major trading partners are China (15 percent of the total), Malaysia (12 percent) and Hong Kong (7 percent).

Thailand (known as Siam until 1939) is the only Asian country never to have been colonised by a European power. It was established in the 14th century and became a constitutional monarchy in 1932. Since 2005, the kingdom has experienced considerable political unrest; however, apart from a dip in the growth rate following a military coup in 2014, the economy appears to have been largely insulated from this development (Nidhiprabha, 2018). In 2018, per capita GDP was I$ 19,205 – about 10 percent above the world average. Thailand's robust economic performance is underpinned by well-developed infrastructure, supportive investment policies and free and open markets. The industry and services sectors contribute about 90 percent of GDP, and have attracted more than three million migrant workers, mainly from neighbouring Asian countries. Exports account for about two thirds of economic activity. The main export commodities are agricultural products such as rice, sugar, cassava, and poultry; and manufactured products including processed foods, electronic goods, and automobiles. Thailand imports a wide range of commodities including soybean, wheat, cotton, dairy products, machinery, computers, jewellery, and precious metals including silver bars and gold. Its main trading partners are China (16 percent of the total), Japan (12 percent) and the United States (9 percent). In 2017, the stock of inward FDI was US $228 billion, or about US $3,300 per capita.

During the last four centuries, the area covered by ***Timor-Leste*** has been colonised or occupied by Portugal, the Netherlands, Japan, and Indonesia. Since 2002, Timor-Leste has been internationally recognised as an independent, semi-presidential republic. Following an unsuccessful coup attempt in 2008, the country has enjoyed a high degree of political stability, allowing the government to place more emphasis on economic development. Timor-Leste has rich deposits of oil and natural gas, and revenue from oil constitutes about 90 percent of the government's budgetary receipts. The major economic challenge facing the government is how to use the country's natural wealth to develop the non-resource economy, both to continue growing GDP and to provide some insulation against unstable global oil and gas prices. Because infrastructure and production facilities are limited, oil is currently being piped to Australia for processing. In 1918, Timor-Leste's population was 1.3 million, per capita GDP was I$ $7,866 and total GDP was I$ 10 billion. In addition to oil and gas, the country exports coffee, sandalwood, and marble. It may also have the potential to develop vanilla as an export industry. Timor-Leste's main imports are machinery, processed fuels, and foodstuffs. Because political and economic stability are very recent phenomena in Timor-Leste, the stock of inward FDI is low, but can be expected to increase strongly as the relatively new economy matures.

Vietnam was colonized by France during 1858-84 and became part of French Indochina in 1887. It achieved independence in 1954 but was divided into two countries – North Vietnam, which was communist; and South Vietnam, which was market-oriented. In 1975, the country was reunited under communist rule. Economic growth was negligible during the following decade. However, since introduction of the government's "doi moi" ("renovation") policy in 1986, which focused on economic liberalisation and more competitive, export-oriented industries, Vietnam has become one of Asia's best-performing economies (Phan et al, 2006). It joined the WTO in 2007 and has entered into trade agreements with many major countries and regions. Since 2013, per capita GDP has been growing by 6 percent a year, reaching I$ 7,302 in 2018. Vietnam's major exports include clothes, shoes, electronic products, crude oil, seafood, rice, and coffee. Its leading imports are machinery & equipment, fuels, raw materials for its clothing & shoe industries, and electronic products. The country's main trading partner is China (20 percent of the total,) followed by South Korea (14 percent) and the United States (10 percent).

CONCLUSION

In 2018, East Asia accounted for 31 percent of GWP. Within the two regions of East Asia, namely Northeast and Southeast Asia, the larger share was produced by Northeast Asia (24 percent of GWP). The authors' forecasting model suggests that the GRP of East Asia will rise strongly throughout the 21st century. Nevertheless, the region's share in GWP will decline slightly in the coming decades to 29 percent in 2050, and then more rapidly to 18 percent in 2100. However, reflecting stronger effects of global per capita income convergence and more rapid work force growth, the share of Southeast Asia in GWP will rise from 6 percent in 2018 to 9 percent in 2050 before falling back to 7 percent in 2100. Among the leading economies, the share in GWP of China is forecast to remain at about 18 percent until 2050 and then to decline to 10 percent by 2100. An important mover in Southeast Asia will be Indonesia, whose share in GWP is forecast to rise from 2.6 percent in 2018 to 3.8 percent by 2050.

REFERENCES

Canlas, D., & Fujisaki, S. (2001). *The Philippine Economy: Alternatives for the 21st Century*. University of Philippines Press.

Flath, D. (2014). *The Japanese Economy*. Oxford University Press.

Hooke, A. (2019). *Global Economic Development: Past, Present and Future*. Lakeland House.

Lee, J. (1998). *Han Unbound: The Political Economy of South Korea*. Stanford University Press.

Naughton, B. (2018). *The Chinese Economy*. MIT Press Ltd.

Nidhiprabha, B. (2018). *Macroeconomic Policy for Emerging Markets: Lessons from Thailand*. Routledge. doi:10.4324/9781315627472

Palmer, I. (2018). *The Indonesian Economy Since 1965: A Case Study of Political Economy*. Routledge. doi:10.4324/9780429461491

Phan, T., Harvie, C., & Tran, V. (2006). *Vietnam's Economic Transition: Policies, Issues and Prospects*. ICFAI Books.

ADDITIONAL READING

Chun, S. (2018). *The Economic Development of South Korea: From Poverty to a Modern Industrial Estate*. Routledge. doi:10.4324/9781351215749

CIA. (2020). *The World Factbook*. https://www.cia.gov/library/publications/the-world-factbook/

Hill, H. (1996). *The Indonesian Economy Since 1966: Southeast Asia's Emerging Giant*. Cambridge University Press.

Jwa, S. (2017). *The Rise and Fall of Korea' Economic Development: Lessons for Developing and Developed Nations*. Palgrave Macmillan. doi:10.1007/978-3-319-58065-4

Piketty, T. (2014) *Harvard University Press.*

Shishido, S. (2019). *Growth Alternatives of the Japanese Economy*. World Scientific. doi:10.1142/11210

ENDNOTE

1 I$ refers to an "international dollar", which has the same purchasing power across countries and over time. In this chapter, I$ refers to purchasing power in 2018.

Chapter 3
The Economies of West Asia

Lauren A. Alati
Argon & Co, Australia

Harpreet Kaur
Australian Institute of Higher Education, Australia

ABSTRACT

While East Asia has been the dominant economic region in Asia for several centuries, the gross regional product (GRP) of West Asia (comprising Southern, Central, and Western Asia) is projected to surpass that of East Asia by 2050 and to be 40% larger by 2100. In 2018, West Asia accounted for accounted for 17% of gross world product (GWP) compared with 31% by East Asia. It is projected that West Asia's share of GWP will rise to 31% by 2050 and 35% in 2060 before falling back to 25% in 2100. The dominant economy will be India, whose GDP is expected to surpass that of China by 2050 and to be 50% larger by 2100.

WEST ASIA IN THE WORLD ECONOMY

In 1950, shortly after the end of World War II, West Asia accounted for 20 percent of the world's population, compared with 32 percent by East Asia. However, both regions had the same share (7 percent) in gross world product (GWP). indicating that per capita gross regional product (GRP) was significantly higher in West Asia. By 2018, West Asia's share of GWP had risen to 17 percent. It is projected by the United Nation's Population Division that West Asia's population will rise strongly in the coming decades, to 2.9 billion by 2050.and 3 billion in 2070, but will then decline to about 2.8 billion, or 26 percent of the global total, by 2100. The macroeconomic forecasting model developed by Hooke (2019) and the authors of

DOI: 10.4018/978-1-7998-4126-5.ch003

this chapter, which is described in Chapter 1, projects that West Asia's GRP will increase six-fold in the coming three decades, to I$ 159 trillion in 2050, and will more than double in the following half century. West Asia will account for a third of GWP in the 2050s and a still sizeable 25 percent in 2100 (the decline in share in the last half century reflecting mainly West Asia's declining population as well as strong growth of population, labour force participation rates and labour productivity in Africa) (Table 1).

THE MAJOR REGIONS OF WEST ASIA

In 2018, West Asia accounted for 25 percent of the world's work force. Labour productivity, at I$ 27,218, was 69 percent of the global average. The GRP of West Asia was I$ 23.2 trillion, accounting for 17 percent of GWP. With total population of almost 2 billion, per capita GRP was I$ 11,591, or two thirds the world average. Within West Asia, Southern Asia accounted for 62 percent of the region's output and 88 percent of its population.

Southern Asia

In 2018, the population of Southern Asia accounted for 22 percent of the world's population and 21 percent of its workforce. Its per capita GDP, of I$ 8,530, was 48 percent of the global average. It is projected that the region's share of GWP, which was 11 percent in 2018, will rise to 25 percent in 2050 and 29 percent in 2060 as a result of strong labour force and labour productivity growth, but will fall back to 21 percent, in 2100.

Afghanistan ("Land of the Pashtuns/Afghans") was formed in 1747 when Ahmad Shah Durrani unified the tribes of Pashtun. It later came under British control but gained independence from the British in 1919. Afghanistan is nominally a presidential Islamic republic, but large internal divisions have made effective government difficult. The strongest opposition comes from the Taliban, which claim that their political organisation is the legitimate government, have a strong presence in all provinces and are committed to the withdrawal of all foreign forces and the establishment of sharia law. In 2018, with only a quarter of the population in the work force and labour productivity low in all sectors, per capita GDP was I$ 1,896, the lowest in Southern Asia. Agriculture contributes a quarter of GDP, with opium, wheat, fruit, and nuts being the major crops. The services sector comprises about 60 percent of GDP, much of which is dependent on spending by foreign militia. Afghanistan's main commodity exports are opium, fruit & nuts, handwoven carpets, gems, and medicinal herbs. The major destinations for these exports are India (57 percent) and Pakistan (30 percent). Imports exceed exports by a ratio of 10:1. The leading imports are machinery & equipment, petroleum, textiles, and foodstuffs. The main sources of imports are China and India (20 percent each), Pakistan (12 percent) and Kazakhstan (10 percent).

Table 1. Major Economic Indicators, 1950-2100

	1950	2000	2010	2018	2050	2100
Population (m)						
West Asia	505	1,501	1,795	1,998	2,879	2,753
East Asia	818	2,004	2,156	2,288	2,375	1,952
America	424	1,115	1,233	1,365	1,161	1,148
Europe	547	720	731	741	704	626
Africa	222	791	1,013	1,243	2,424	4,171
Oceania	14	32	37	41	57	76
World	2,530	6,164	6,966	7,676	9,599	10,727
Total GRP (I$ tn)						
West Asia	0.8	9.3	15.6	23.2	159	444
East Asia	0.8	13.4	27.6	41.5	153	315
America	3.6	23.2	28.0	33.0	84	185
Europe	5.3	23.6	24.7	29.2	55	101
Africa	0.3	3.6	5.3	6.8	60	673
Oceania	0.1	0.9	1.2	1.6	4	12
World	10.9	74.1	102.4	135.3	515	1,731
Per capita GRP (I$)						
West Asia	1,530	6,214	8,689	11,591	55,258	161,333
East Asia	984	6,671	12,794	18,150	64,285	161,333
America	8,386	20,832	22,705	24,197	72,675	161,333
Europe	9,721	32,702	33,726	39,390	78,220	161,333
Africa	1,366	4,611	5,232	5,504	24,680	161,333
Oceania	8,450	29,141	32,963	38,380	63,816	161,333
World	4,297	12,016	14,697	17,630	53,612	161,333

Sources. World Bank's World Economic Indicators, UN Population Division, IMF's World Economic Outlook and CIA's World Factbook, authors' projections.

Note. GDP, GRP and GWP are measured in purchasing power parity (PPP) terms at 2018 prices.

Table 2. Economies of Major West Asia Regions, 2018

	Labour force (m)	Labour productivity (I$)	GDP/GRP (I$ bn)	Population (m)	Per capita GDP/GRP (I$)
West Asia	851	27,218	23,163	1,998	11,591
Southern Asia	726	19,907	14,455	1,695	8,530
Central Asia	98	79,334	7,796	271	28,742
Western Asia	27	34,257	912	32	28,103
Rest of world	2,564	43,746	112,171	5,678	19,756
World	3,415	39,627	135,334	7,676	17,630

Sources. World Bank's World Economic Indicators, IMF's World Economic Outlook, UN Population Division, CIA's World Factbook

Bangladesh incorporates the large delta formed at the confluence of the Ganges and Brahmaputra Rivers north of the Bay of Bengal. This area was the site of trading posts of different tribes in the first millennia AD. Muslim conversion of the region commenced in the 10th century. Along with India and Pakistan, Bangladesh became part of the British Empire in the 18th century, formed part of Pakistan in 1947 and was established as an independent parliamentary republic in 1971. Political unrest impeded economic development over the next few decades, but greater stability from the early 1990s has been followed by vastly improved economic performance, with the annual growth of GDP averaging about 6 per since 2000. In 2018, Bangladesh's population was 161 million and per capita GDP was I$ 4,251. Total GDP, of I$ 686 billion, accounted for 5 percent of the GRP of Southern Asia. Bangladesh's main export products are garments, knitwear, agricultural products, frozen fish, and jute. Its leading imports include cotton, machinery & equipment, chemicals, iron & steel, and foodstuffs. The country's major trading partners are China (17 percent of the total), India (9 percent) and the United States (7 percent).

Bhutan ("Land of the Thunder Dragon") was ceded to Britain following the Duar War in 1865. However, from 1910, Britain agreed not to interfere any more in Bhutan's internal affairs. In 1949, Bhutan entered into a roughly similar agreement with India, but the country remained subject to "guidance" by India with respect to foreign policy. By 2007, Bhutan had regained full policy independence. Following the drafting of its first constitution in 2005, Bhutan became a constitutional monarchy, with its current king being Jigme Khesar Namgyel Aangchuck. Bhutan's economy is based largely on hydropower, agriculture, and forestry. The government places high priority on protecting the natural environment and cultural traditions; for example, visits to tourist destinations are restricted to environmentally conscious tourists. Hydropower contributes about 25 percent of the government's revenue and

40 percent of export receipts. The export of hydropower to India and Bangladesh, which is currently being severely constrained by long delays in approved construction projects, will be increased many-fold once these projects are completed, In 2018, Bhutan's per capita GDP was I$ 10,743, reflecting the spread of revenue from its abundant hydropower resources over a relatively small population (800,000). The average annual growth of total GDP during 2014-18 was 7 percent. Bhutan's main commodity exports are electricity (currently only to India), ferrosilicon, cement, cardamom, and calcium carbide. Its major imports include fuel & lubricants, airplanes, machinery & equipment, and rice. India is the destination of 95 percent of the country's exports and the source of 90 percent of its imports.

Table 3. Economies of Southern Asia, 2018

	Labour force (m)	Labour productivity (I$)	GDP/GRP (I$ bn)	Population (m)	Per capita GDP/GRP (I$)
Afghanistan	8.7	8,066	70	37	1,896
Bangladesh	67.3	10,187	686	161	4,251
Bhutan	0.4	20,258	8	1	10,743
India	527.8	19,530	10,309	1,352	7,627
Iran	30.9	58,996	1,821	82	22,328
Maldives	0.2	35,254	8	1	15,643
Nepal	17.0	5,006	85	28	3,018
Pakistan	64.8	18,093	1,172	212	5,531
Sri Lanka	9.0	32,953	297	21	14,126
Southern Asia	**726**	**19,907**	**14,455**	**1,894**	**7,633**
Rest of world	2,689	44,952	120,879	5,783	20,904
World	3,415	39,627	135,334	7,676	17,630

Sources. World Bank's World Economic Indicators, IMF's World Economic Outlook, UN Population Division, CIA's World Factbook

India has a long and impressive economic history. Settled farming began to replace nomadic scavenging and hunting in north India about nine thousand years ago, with wheat and barley being the major crops grown and sheep and goats the main animals grazed. Globally, economies with small manufacturing and services sectors emerged about 6,000 years ago and, according to Hooke (2019) the geographical area roughly corresponding to a major part of current India may have housed the largest economy during at least three significant periods since then.

First was the Mauryan period. In 325 BC, Candra Gupta Maurya formed the first Indian empire. It was large, covering almost the entire subcontinent. Unlike many great conquerors its founder, Candra Gupta, was not wholly captivated by power. He abdicated in 297 BC, joined the Jaina religion and died in the traditional Jaina manner, committing suicide slowly by starvation. His son (Bindusara) continued to develop the economy. Since the government's main source of revenue was rural taxes, based on the amount of land used and its output, Bindusara's policies favoured the expansion and development of farming. The empire reached its zenith under Asoka who died in 238 BC. It collapsed in 185 BC when Brhadratha Maurya was assassinated by his Brahmin commander-in-chief.

Second was the period from AD 320 to 540, when the Gupta dynasty ruled the country. This was a time of comparative stability, and both the economy and classical Indian culture flourished.

Third was the Mughal period, which commenced in AD 1526. At its zenith, from the accession of Akbar the Great in 1556 until 1707, the Mughal Empire covered the whole subcontinent and commanded resources unprecedented in Indian history. Economic expansion was based on trade, which was supported by an efficient, centralised administration. The requirement that farmers pay their taxes in cash contributed to the development of a money economy as well as a network of grain markets, bazaars, and small towns. This was the period of the so-called "three great rulers" – Jahangir, Shah Jahan[15] and Aurangzeb. During their reign Lahore, Delhi and Ahmadabad were among the most prosperous cities in the world and Goa, under the control of the Portuguese, was referred to as the "golden city".

Following Vasco da Gama's voyage to India in 1498 the Portuguese, Dutch, British and French developed a strong commercial interest in the country. However, from the middle of the eighteenth century, power was increasingly appropriated by the British. In 1757 the British defeated a combined French-Mughal force and established a stronghold in Bengal. Thereafter, British control spread rapidly and by 1818 they had defeated the Hindu Marathas who, in turn, had conquered the Mughals in the late seventeenth century. The British victory over the Sikh kingdom in 1849 brought the whole of India under British rule.

India attained independence from Britain in 1947. Economic growth was slow during the following four decades, reflecting inward-looking policies and bureaucratic controls that hindered competition and discouraged initiative. The economy began to open up and adopt more market-friendly policies during the 1990s and these have led to a steady and sustained rise in the growth rate of GDP, which reached an annual average rate of 7 percent during 2014-18 (the highest rate among the major economies). In 2018, India's GDP of I$ 10.3 trillion was third highest in the world (after China and the United States).

Table 4. Economic Performance and Prospects for India, 1950-2100

India	1950	2000	2018	2050	2100
Work force (m)	147	413	528	743	709
Productivity (I$)	3,206	6,749	19,530	122,795	358,519
GDP (I$ bn)	471	2,786	10,309	91,218	254,200
Population (m)	376	1,057	1,352	1,704	1,576
Per capita GDP (I$)	1,252	2,636	7,627	53,520	161,333

Sources. World Bank's World Economic Indicators, IMF's World Economic Outlook, UN Population Division, CIA's World Factbook, authors' projections.

The forecasting model developed by Hooke and the authors of this chapter projects that India's GDP will rise above that of the United States in the early 2030s and will pass the GDP of China in the late 2040s. By 2100, when GWP will be about 13 times larger than in 2018, India's GDP will be 50 percent higher than that of China (which will still be the second-ranked economy). These developments reflect both demographic factors and the effects of per capita income convergence in the period to 2050, and manly demographic factors in the latter half of the century. The UN's Population Division predicts that India's population will surpass that of China in 2024, will be 23 percent higher in 2050 and will be 50 percent higher in 2100. China is currently enjoying what is often referred to as a "demographic gift", with the workforce comprising 60 percent of its population compared with 46 percent for the world. India, on the other hand, is shouldering a "demographic burden", with the workforce comprising only 40 percent of its population. Hence while, in 2018, India's per capita GDP was only 44 per cent that of China, its labour productivity was 65 percent of China's. The authors' forecasting model projects that China's demographic gift and India's demographic burden will largely disappear and that labour productivity convergence mechanisms, supplemented by differences in market orientation versus maintenance of the political landscape, will increase the ratio of per capita GDP in India to 82 percent of that of China by 2050 and will close the gap by 2060. If present political boundaries are unchanged the Indian economy will, during the latter half of this century, not only be the largest in the world but will be the largest by an increasing margin.

Iran ("Land of the Noble Ones") changed its name from Persia in 1935, but continued as a monarchy until 1979 when, following an internal revolution, it became a theocratic (Islamic) republic. Ultimate political authority is now vested in a learned religious scholar, generally referred to as the Supreme Leader, who is responsible to an Assembly of Experts (AOE), which is a popularly elected body of 88 clerics. In 2018, Iran's per capita GDP was I$ 22,328. It was the highest among the Southern

Asia economies and was 26 percent above the world average. With its relatively high per capita GPD and large population (82 million) and work force, Iran's total GDP, of I$ 1.8 trillion, was 19th largest in the world. However, the country has the potential to move much higher on the global GDP ladder. While the economy has maintained its historically well-developed agricultural, industrial and services sectors, it has many economic distortions as a result of public ownership of hundreds of enterprises, government intervention in the activities of many other enterprises, price controls and subsidies. The election of President Hasan Ruhani in 2017 has generated expectations that some economic reforms may be implemented and that the economy may become more attractive as a location for trade and a destination for FDI. Iran's leading commodity exports are petroleum (60 percent of all exports), chemical and petroleum products, carpets, fruit, and nuts. Its main imports include industrial supplies, machinery & equipment, foodstuffs, and consumer goods. Iran's major trading partners are China (22 percent of total exports and imports), UAE (mainly for imports), and India.

The ***Maldives*** was a sultanate from the 12th century until 1887, when it became a British protectorate. The islands achieved independence in 1965 and became a republic in 1968. For the next 30 years, the new country had single-party elections and the same person as president. Political parties became legal in 2005. In 2008 a new constitution was ratified, the first multiparty elections were held, and a new president was elected. Possible irregularities and associated changes in leadership led to an uncertain political climate, which appears to have been resolved by the election of Ibrahim Mohamad Solih from the Maldivian Democratic Party (MDP) as President in 2018. The Maldives is now a middle-income country, due mainly to strong growth of its fisheries and tourism sectors. In 2015, foreign ownership of land was legalised subject to the conditions that at least 70 percent of the land is reclaimed from the oceans and a minimum of US $1 billion is invested in government-approved projects. Global warming is a concern since 80 percent of the land area is 1 metre or less above sea level. During 2013-18, per capita GDP increased at an average annual rate of 4 percent, to I$ 15.643. The Maldives' main exports are tourism and fish. The major imports are petroleum, clothing, intermediate goods, and capital goods. The country's major trading partners are Thailand (25 percent of the total), UAE (10 percent) and India (8 percent).

Nepal (the "Newar" people of Kathmandu and surrounding valleys) was formed in the 18th and 19th centuries by unifying the principality of Gorka with the many other principalities and states of the Himalayan region. Following the Anglo-Nepal War of 1814-16, Nepal and Britain have maintained generally friendly relations. Nepal has experienced considerable political instability during the last six decades, and in 2008 the monarchy was formally abolished and replaced by a federal parliamentary republic. In May 2018, the two parties that had formed a coalition government – the

Nepal-Unified Marxist-Leninist party and the Communist Party of Nepal-United - merged to form the Nepal Communist Party (NCP), which is now the ruling party in parliament. Nepal is one of the world's poorest countries, with one quarter of its population living below the poverty line. In 2018, the country's per capita GDP was only I$ 3,018. Nepal's major economic problems are that it is landlocked, the transport and electricity infrastructure are poor, the political situation is unstable, and the business environment is difficult. On the positive side, Nepal is located between the largest (China) and third largest (India) markets in the world, has thousands of its citizens studying IT abroad who could provide the basis for a global information services industry and has geographical attractions that could make it a world leader in high-value-added tourism. It could become the Ireland of Asia with respect to the export of IT services and the Switzerland of Asia regarding the export of high value tourism. In 2017, the United States and Nepal entered a US $500 million Millennium Challenge Corporate Compact to develop the country's transport and electricity infrastructure. Nepal's main export products are clothing, pulses, carpets, and jute. Its major imports include petroleum, machinery & equipment, gold, and medicines. The country's main trading partners are India (60 percent of all trade), the United States (7 per cent) and China (5 percent).

For an even longer period than India, the area that is currently ***Pakistan*** may have been home to the world's largest economy (Hooke, 2019). Approximately 5,500 years ago, settlements that started in the Middle East began to spread throughout the Indus Valley of modern Pakistan. The next few millennia led to the emergence of a mature civilisation, the Indus Civilisation, in about the middle of the third millennium BC.

The Indus economy covered approximately 500,000 square miles, larger than the area of Pakistan today. The two largest cities were Harappa and Mohenjo-daro, each housing about 35 thousand people. Material culture was uniform throughout the region, suggesting an effective, centralised administration. Concomitants of civilisation included writing, standardised weights and measures and monumental architecture. The main domesticated animals were cattle, sheep, and goats; however, buffalos, pigs, camels, asses, and fowls were also important. Crops included wheat, barley, dates, melons, field peas, and cotton. The last was brought to the cities in bales where it served as raw material for a spinning, weaving and dyeing industry. There is evidence that mass production techniques based on the foot-wheel were used in the manufacture of pottery. Trade included the importation of raw materials (including gold and copper) and other goods from village communities and from forest tribes in adjoining regions. There was also considerable trade with the cities on the Sumer plain, with the Indus valley exporting timber, precious wood, ivory, and gold beads and importing silver, tin, woollen textiles, and grains. During the latter half of the third millennium BC the economy of the Indus Valley was probably the largest in the world.

The Indus civilisation collapsed during the first few centuries of the second millennium BC. Its demise has been attributed variously to climate change, tectonic events leading to the flooding of the Mohenjo-daro valley, invasion by tribespeople from the surrounding hills and an epidemic. Unlike in China, where historical gains have been preserved during less dynamic periods, the cities of the Indus Valley along with writing and many specialised crafts disappeared, nomadic pastoral groups became the dominant economic unit and living standards fell.

Pakistan was part of the British Empire from the 18th century until the middle of the 20th century. Independence was gained in 1947, and Pakistan's present boundaries were established in 1971. During the following decades, economic development was adversely affected by internal and external security issues. However, the growth of GDP has been rising from 2012, and averaged 5 percent a year during 2014-18. In 2018, per capita GDP was I$ 5,531 and total GDP was I$ 1.2 trillion, or 0.9 percent of GWP. Pakistan's commodity exports are dominated by textiles, apparel, and rugs, but rice and surgical instruments are also important. Its main imports include petroleum products, machinery, iron & steel, and tea. The country's leading trading partners are China (16 percent of the total), the United States (13 percent) and the United Kingdom (6 percent). Inward FDI has been increasing, albeit from a low base, due partly to an upgrading of Pakistan's credit rating following a moderately successful restructuring program with the IMF and commencement of the "China-Pakistan Economic Corridor" (CPEC), which focuses on developing the country's energy resources and public infrastructure.

Sri Lanka ("Resplendent Island") was inhabited first by the Sinhalese who arrived from north India in the 6th century BC. A south Indian dynasty established a Tamil Kingdom in the northern part of the island in the 14th century AD. The Portuguese, who controlled the coastal areas of the country in 16th century, were followed by the Dutch in the 17th century. Under its then-name of Ceylon, the island became a crown colony of the British in 1948. In 1972, it achieved independence, adopted a presidential republic form of government, and changed its name to Sri Lanka. Economic development has been sound, despite war between the Tamils and the Sinhalese during 1983-2009 and considerable political unrest since then. In 2018, Sri Lanka's per capita GDP was I$ 14,126. The country's main export products are textiles & apparel, tea and spices, rubbers, precious stones, and coconuts. Its leading imports are petroleum, textiles, machinery & equipment, and building materials. Sri Lanka's main trading partners are the United States (16 percent of the total), India (14 percent) and China (10 percent).

Western Asia

In 2018, Western Asia accounted for 14 percent of West Asia's population but contributed 35 percent of its GRP. This reflected mainly the region's abundant petroleum and its successful management of these reserves. The largest country in terms of population was Turkey with 82 million (30 percent of the total) followed by Iraq with 38 million and Saudi Arabia with 33 million. Turkey also had the largest GDP, of I$ 2.4 trillion, ahead of Saudi Arabia with I$ 1.9 trillion and UAE with I$ 748 billion. Per capita GDP for the whole region was I$ 28,742, more than 60 percent above the global average. It was highest in Qatar (I$ 131,377), followed by UAE (I$ 77,424), Kuwait (I$ 77,313) and Saudi Arabia (I$ 57,743).

Armenia (the name derives from Aram, who is believed to have been a descendant of Noah) claims to have been the first nation to have formally adopted Christianity as its state religion (in the early 4th century). The country has been occupied by many empires. More than one million Armenians were killed during a period of forced resettlement under the Ottoman Empire. Since 1988 (three years before gaining independence), Armenia has been providing support to the primarily Armenian-ethnic region of Nagorno-Karabakh, which was transferred by Russia to Azerbaijan in 1923. Reflecting this dispute, Armenia's trade border with Azerbaijan has been closed since 1991 and that with Turkey (which supports Azerbaijan in the dispute) since 1993. Under the central planning system in the Soviet era, Armenia imported raw materials and energy from other Soviet republics and transformed them into machine tools, textiles, and other manufactured products that it exported to these republics. While this model has largely been dismantled and more attention is being given to agriculture, large monopolies in important business sectors have been carried over from the Soviet era and these reduce Armenia's competitiveness on world markets. In 2018, per capita GDP was I$ 10,283, population was 3 million and total GDP was I$ 30 billion. Armenia's main exports are unwrought copper, pig iron, nonferrous metals, gold, diamonds, mineral products, foodstuffs, brandy, cigarettes, and energy. Its major imports are natural gas, petroleum, tobacco, foodstuffs, diamonds, pharmaceutical products, and cars. The country's main trading partners are Russia (26 percent of total trade), China (9 percent) and Bulgaria (7 percent).

Azerbaijan ("Land of Fire" - the country has recurring natural fires on ancient oil pools and discharges of natural gas) is a secular nation with a majority-Shia Muslim population. It gained independence following dissolution of the Soviet Union in 1991. Since 1988, there has been conflict with separatist groups, supported by Armenia, in the primarily ethnic-Armenian region of Nagorno-Karabakh, located in the western part of the country adjacent to Armenia. The parties involved are availing themselves of international assistance aimed at reaching a peaceful resolution of the dispute. The Azerbaijan economy is heavily dependent on oil and gas, and the growth of the country's GDP tends to move in tandem with the international prices of these commodities. The government has made some progress with both implementing market-based reforms and reducing corruption, which has been endemic in both the private and public sectors. In 2018, per capita GDP was I$ 18,744 or 6 percent above the global average. Azerbaijan's main exports are oil and gas (90 percent of all exports), machinery, foodstuffs, and cotton. The leading destinations for these exports are Italy (23 percent) and Turkey (14 percent). The country's major import products are machinery & equipment, foodstuffs, metals, and chemicals, sourced mainly from Russia (18 percent), Turkey (15 percent) and China (10 percent).

Table 5. Economies of Western Asia, 2017

	Labour force (m)	**Labour productivity (I$)**	**GDP/GRP (I$ bn)**	**Population (m)**	**Per capita GDP/GRP (I$)**
Armenia	1.5	20,245	30	3	10,283
Azerbaijan	5.2	35,947	186	10	18,744
Bahrain	0.9	89,965	76	2	48,628
Cyprus	0.4	77,196	33	1	27,818
Georgia	2.0	21,392	43	4	10,686
Iraq	9.1	77,008	703	38	18,346
Israel	4.1	89,143	364	10	37,008
Jordan	2.3	40,962	96	10	9,756
Kuwait	2.7	115,808	316	4	77,313
Lebanon	2.1	43,996	94	7	14,039
Oman	2.3	89,490	206	5	43,211
Qatar	2.0	183,172	365	3	131,377
Saudi Arabia	14.0	136,117	1,909	33	57,743
Palestine	1.3	19,399	24	5	5,048
Syria	3.9	24,718	96	17	5,514
Turkey	31.5	77,216	2,429	82	29,632
UAE	5.4	137,903	748	10	77,424
Yemen	7.6	10,426	79	28	2,782
Western Asia	**98**	**79,334**	**7796**	**271**	**28,742**
Rest of world	3,317	38,451	127,538	7,405	17,223
World	3,415	39,627	135,334	7,676	17,630

Sources. World Bank's World Economic Indicators, IMF's world Economic Outlook, UN Population Division, CIA's World Factbook

Bahrain (the name refers to the "two seas" that surround the archipelago) is an absolute monarchy that has been ruled by the family of Sunni Al Khalifa since 1783. In return for protection, it became a British protectorate in the 19th century, but regained its independence in 1971. The political situation is challenging since the Shia comprise a substantial majority of the population. In the face of declining oil reserves, the government has implemented a reasonably successful policy of economic diversification, and Bahrain now has strong petroleum processing & refining, aluminium, hospitality, retail and (Islamic) finance industries. Nevertheless, oil continues to provide about 85 percent of the government's revenue, and the weak international oil market and Bahrain's falling reserves caused three rating agencies to downgrade the country's sovereign debt rating in 2016. In August of that year, Bahrain entered into a free trade agreement with the United States, the first such arrangement between the United States and a Gulf country. In 2018, per capita GDP was I$ 48,628, population was 1.6 million and GDP was I$ 76 billion. Bahrain's main exports are petroleum and petroleum products, aluminium, and textiles. Its major imports are crude oil, machinery, and chemicals. The country's main trading partners are the UAE (14 percent), the United States (9 percent) and China (7 percent).

Cyprus (the name may refer to the copper that used to be mined on the island) was a British protectorate but, after years of resistance to British rule, gained independence in 1960. The island contains two main ethnic groups – Greek Cypriots and Turkish Cypriots. Following tensions and fighting between the two groups, Turkey intervened in favour of the Turkish Cypriots in 1974 and gained control over the northern one third of the island. In 1983, this area was declared the "Turkish Republic of Northern Cyprus" a title that is recognised only by Turkey. Negotiations to resolve the dispute between the two groups are ongoing. The area of the country under government control has a market-oriented economy with a services sector that generates about 80 percent of GDP. It performed well during the upswing that preceded the GFC, but the high exposure of Cypriot banks to the Greek economy led to a severe economic crisis when the Greek economy effectively collapsed during the GFC. In 2018, per capita GDP was I$ 27,818, population was 1.2 million and GDP totalled I$ 33 billion. The country's main exports are citrus fruits, potatoes, pharmaceuticals, cement, and clothing. Its major imports are consumer goods, petroleum & lubricants, machinery, and transport equipment, Cyprus' main trading partners are Greece (14 percent of total exports and imports), Germany (6 percent) and Libya (5 percent).

The region that is currently ***Georgia*** ("Land of the Wolves") once included the ancient kingdoms of Colchis and Kartli-Iberia. During the first millennia AD, it was dominated successively by the Romans, Persians, Arabs, and Turks. These periods of occupancy were followed by the Georgian Golden Age that witnessed military expansion by the state and the flourishing of Georgian architecture, paintings and poetry, which were expressed frequently in ecclesiastical art as well as in the first major works of secular literature. The period of great prosperity was ended by persistent Mongolian attacks and onset of the plague (Black Death), which was brought by the Mongolian warriors. Georgia became part of the Russian Empire in the 19th century and the Soviet Union in the 20th century. In 2003, growing resentment over rampant corruption and poor government led to the Rose Revolution, a subsequent change in government, and the introduction of some modest political and economic reforms. The latter, however, have been impeded by separatist movements (supported by Russia) in the regions of Abkhazia and South Ossetia. Recently, government policies have focussed on building up the country's infrastructure, supporting entrepreneurship and reducing regulations in order to attract foreign and domestic investment, especially in the areas of transportation, tourism, hydropower, and agriculture. In 2018, per capita GDP was I$ 10,686 and population was 4 million, resulting in total GDP of I$ 43 billion. Georgia's main export products are vehicles, ferro-alloys, fertilisers, nuts, scrap metal, gold, and copper ores. Its major imports are fuels, vehicles, machinery & parts, grains and other foods, and pharmaceuticals. The country's main trading partners are Turkey (13 percent of total trade), Russia (12 percent), and Azerbaijan and China (9 percent each).

Iraq was originally part of the Ottoman Empire. It was occupied by the British during World War 1 and, under a UN mandate, was managed by the British for a brief period after that war. The country achieved independence in 1932. The monarchy was abolished and nominally replaced by a democratic republic in 1958. However, government for the next three decades was autocratic. In 2005, the country adopted a parliamentary republic form of government, which has become increasingly democratic and technically strong. Iraq fought a war with Iran over territorial disputes during 1980-88 and was later twice invaded by US-led forces. In 2014-17, it was engaged in a war with the Islamic State of Iraq and ash-Shan (ISIS). The economy is largely state-run, and antiquated commercial laws, over-regulation, and corruption make it difficult for both foreign and domestic enterprises to do business. Per capita GDP grew at an average annual rate of 4 percent during 2013-18, to I$ 18,346, which was slightly above the world average. The economy of Iraq is heavily dependent on oil, which provides 85 percent of both the government's revenue and the country's export receipts. The major destination of these oil exports are India and China (20 percent each), the United States (15 percent) and South Korea (10 percent). Iraq's main imports are from Turkey (28 percent) and China (26 percent).

Israel (the name dates back to the Jewish patriarch Jacob who was given the title "Israel" or "He Who Wrestles with God" after he had wrestled a whole night with an angel of the Lord) was formed in 1948 and became a member of the United Nations in 1949. The country has direct access to both the Mediterranean Sea in the west and the Gulf of Aqaba in the southeast. Since 1948 Israel has fought several wars with its Arab neighbours. It occupied the West Bank and Gaza Strip in 1967, later granted Palestinian self-rule in both regions and in 2005 withdrew from Gaza. Israel has a free market economy led by several hi-tech, cutting edge sectors. In 2018, per capita GDP was I$ 37,008, or about twice the global average. The country's main exports are machinery & equipment, software, cut diamonds, agriculture products, chemicals, and textiles & apparels. Its major imports are raw materials, military equipment, capital goods, rough diamonds, fuels, grains, and consumer goods. Israels main trading partners are the United States (21 percent of both exports plus imports), the United Kingdom (7 percent) and China (6 percent).

Jordan (named after the Jordan River, which forms a segment of the country's northwest border) was part of the Ottoman Empire until the latter was dissolved after World War I. It then became part of the Middle East mandate that the league of Nations assigned to Britain. The region gained its independence from Britain in 1946 and became the Hashemite Kingdom of Jordan. King Hussein (1953-99) successfully managed most external (the United States and the Soviet Union) and internal pressures but was forced to cede the West Bank to Israel following the Six-Day War in 1967. Hussein's son and successor, King Abdallah II, has introduced some modest political reforms, aimed mainly at decentralising political and administrative decision-making and implementation. He also introduced economic reforms focused on increasing internal trade and investment and expanding the role of the private sector. These reforms contributed to average annual GDP growth of about 8 percent during the period leading up to the GFC. Since then, a period that has witnessed increased turmoil in West Asia, the growth of Jordan's GDP has averaged about 3 percent a year. The country's most challenging economic problems include providing employment opportunities and subsistence to the more than one million refugees who have entered the country following the outbreak of war in Syria and developing its own energy resources (energy imports comprise about a quarter of total imports). The government is encouraging domestic and foreign investment in projects aimed at exploiting natural gas, wind, sun, nuclear, and oil shale resources. In 2018, per capita GDP was I$ 9,756. The country's main exports are textiles, fertilisers, potash, phosphates, vegetables, and pharmaceuticals. Its major imports include crude oil & refined petroleum products, machinery & equipment, iron, and cereals. Jordan's main trading partners are the United States (18 percent), Saudi Arabia (14 percent) and China (8 percent).

Kuwait ("Fortress") has been a monarchy ruled by the Al-Sabah dynasty since the 18th century. To protect the kingdom from Ottoman invasion, the Amir ceded responsibility for foreign affairs and defence to Britain in 1899. Kuwait regained full control of these functions in 1961.The country was occupied by Iraq from August 1990 to February 1991 and has since experienced often violent internal protests by different minority groups (Sunni Islamists and tribal populists). Kuwait has more than 6 percent of the world's oil reserves, and the oil industry contributes about 50 percent of GDP and 90 percent of both export receipts and government revenue. Every year, the government places about 10 percent of its revenue into a Fund for Future Generations. The government's long-term development plan seeks to diversify the economy and provide a larger role for the private sector; however, implementation of the plan has been slowed by poor relations between the legislative and executive branches of government. In 2018, per capita GDP was I$ 77,313 or more than four time the global average. With population of 4 million, total GDP was I$ 316 billion. Kuwait's main export commodities are petroleum, oil-related products, and fertilisers. Its major import commodities are food, construction materials, vehicles & parts, and clothing. The country's main trading partners are China (15 percent), the United States (10 percent), and South Korea (9 percent).

Lebanon ("the wells/fountains", referring to the country's accessible water table) gained independence from France in 1923. Since then it has experienced short periods of prosperity built on its position as a regional centre for trade and finance but also longer periods of civil war (1975-90) and external wars with Israel and Syria (it was occupied by Syria during 1976-2005). Lebanon's boundary disputes with Syria in the north and west and with Israel in the south are still unresolved. The country has a strong laissez-faire tradition and there are few restrictions on foreign investment and trade. However, government interventions associated partly with the civil and international wars have led to institutional corruption and bureaucratic over-regulation that deter private-sector activity. Most government spending is allocated to debt servicing (the public debt to GDP ratio is 3rd highest in the world), wages of public servants and electricity subsidies, leaving little to restore and expand the infrastructure. Lebanon has received about 1.3 million refugees from Syria. In 2018, per capita GDP was I$ 14,039, about four-fifths of the global average. Lebanon's main commodity exports are jewellery, base metals, chemicals, consumer goods, fruits & vegetables, tobacco, and construction materials. Its major imports are petroleum products, cars, medicines, clothing, meat & live animals, and consumer goods. The country's main trading partners are China (12 percent of all trade), UAE (6 percent) and Turkey (5 percent).

Oman is bordered by the UAE, Saudi Arabia, and Yemen in the west and the Arabian Sea in the east. For many centuries, its long coastline enabled it to be a leader in trade across the Indian Ocean. In the 18th and 19th centuries Oman sought British assistance on several occasions but was always politically independent of Britain. It is an absolute monarchy and has been ruled since 1970 by Sultan Qaboos, who has modernised the economy and introduced decentralisation policies that allow greater public participation in local government. Oman has large deposits of oil and gas, and exploitation of these resources provides about three-quarters of the government's revenue. Economic policy is directed toward both enhancing recovery techniques to boost oil production and promoting industrialisation and privatisation to produce a more diversified pattern of production. The main target industries of the diversification strategy are tourism, shipping & logistics, manufacturing, mining, and aquaculture. In 2018, per capita GDP was I$ 43,211 or 2.4 times the global average. With population of 4.8 million, total GDP was I$ 206 billion. Oman's main exports are petroleum, re-exports, fish, metals, and textiles, which are sold mainly to China (44 percent), UAE (11 percent) and South Korea (8 percent). The country's major imports are machinery & equipment, manufactured products, foodstuffs, livestock, and lubricants, sourced mainly from UAE (36 percent), the United States (28 percent) and Brazil (4 percent).

Until the middle of the 20th century, ***Qatar*** was a small, poor British protectorate known mainly for its pearling activities. Since 2007, the country has boasted the highest per capita GDP in the world. Its success has been due to the discovery and successful exploitation of large oil and natural gas resources (Qatar possesses 13 percent of the world's natural gas reserves) as well as to development-focused policies adopted by Amir Hamad bin Khalifa Al Thani during 1995-2013 and by his son and current Amir, Tamin bin Hamad. Qatar's great wealth and proven ability to develop and manage infrastructure and other resources supported its successful bid to host the World (Football) Cup in 2022. Qatar's support of popular revolutions, including in Libya and Syria, have caused Saudi Arabia, the UAE, Bahrain, and Egypt to place some restrictions on trade with the country, and these have led the Qatar government to develop alternative trading arrangements. In 2018, Qatar's per capita GDP was I$ 131,377 (highest in the world), population was 2.8 million and total GDP was I$ 365 billion. The country's main exports are liquefied natural gas, petroleum products, fertilisers, and steel. Its major imports are machinery & transport equipment, food, and chemicals. Qatar's main trading partners are China and Japan (each with 11 percent of the total), India (9 percent) and South Korea (8 percent).

Saudi Arabia is the birthplace of Islam and home to two of the religion's holiest shrines located in the cities of Mecca and Medina (The king's official title is "Custodian of the Two Holy Mosques"). The modern state of Saudi Arabia was founded in 1932. Since 2015, it has moved along a path of steady political, social, and economic reform. The political reforms include allowing elections for municipal councillors from 2005; major social reforms include lifting the ban on women driving cars and allowing women to both vote and stand as candidates at municipal elections. Economic reforms include expanding the role of the private sector by privatising parts of the power generation, telecommunications, natural gas exploration and petrochemical sectors, increasing employment opportunities for local male and female nationals (there are 6 million foreign workers in Saudi Arabia), and providing a more safe and attractive environment for inward FDI. The country has 16 percent of the world's proven oil reserves (2015 estimate) and is the world's largest exporter of petroleum. The oil sector dominates the economy, accounting for more than 40 percent of GDP, 90 percent of export earnings, and about 85 percent of government revenue. Saudi Arabia's major import products are machinery & equipment, foodstuffs, chemicals, motor vehicles and textiles. The country's main trading partners are China (12 percent of the total), the United States (12 percent), and Japan and South Kores (8 percent each). The stock of inward FDI is very high (US $264 billion in 2017), most of which has been placed in the petroleum sector. The Saudi government has indicated that it welcomes private investment, both foreign and domestic, in the healthcare, education and tourism sectors.

The ***Palestine Authority*** was established in the late 1990s. Under the Oslo Accords, Israel transferred to the Authority security and civilian responsibility for both the West Bank (on the eastern boundary of Israel and to the west of the Jordan River and the Dead Sea) and the Gaza Strip (on the south-west boundary of Israel). However, hostilities among factions and against Israel have stalled progress toward agreement on a final status for the two areas. Currently, Israel occupies about 60 percent of the West Bank, the Palestine Authority manages the remaining part of the West Bank and the Islamic Resistance Movement (HAMAS) controls Gaza. Per capita GDP is estimated very roughly to be about I$ 5,000. For the West Bank, the main exports are stone, olives, fruits & vegetables, and limestone. The main imports are food, consumer goods, construction materials, and fuels. For Gaza, the major exports are strawberries, carnations, vegetables and fish, and the main imports are foodstuffs, consumer goods, and fuels.

Until the early 20th century, ***Syria*** was a province of the Ottoman Empire. It came under the mandate of France following World War I and attained independence after World War II. In 1958 Syria merged with Egypt to form the United Arab Republic, but unity was short-lived, and the arrangement was dissolved in 1961. Ethnic divisions, aggravated by corruption within government and perceived excessively tight controls led to intermittent unrest from 2011, which escalated into civil war. Prior to 2011, the government in Damascus began reforming the economy by allowing the opening of private banks (which led to reductions in interest rates), consolidating multiple exchange rates, reducing distorting subsidies to produce a more level business playing field and opening a stock exchange for secondary trade in financial securities. The reform was halted by the outbreak of hostilities. In addition, major countries imposed sanctions on aspects of trade with Syria. In 2018, per capita GDP was I$ 5,514, population was 17 million and total GDP was I$ 96 billion. Syria's main export commodities are crude oil, minerals, petroleum products, fruits and vegetables and cotton fibre. Its leading imports include machinery & equipment, food & livestock, and metal & metal products. The country's main trading partners are Russia (18 percent of the total), Lebanon (16 percent) and Turkey (12 percent).

Turkey ("Land of the Turks") was founded in 1923 out of the remnants of the once-powerful Ottoman Empire. The country experienced one-party rule for several decades but adopted a multiparty-political regime in 1950. The period since then has been marked by political instability and military coups (1960, 1971 and 1980). In 2018, the parliamentary system of government was replaced by a presidential system. In 1963, Turkey became an associate member of the EU and in 2005 began negotiations aimed at full membership. Following a severe financial crisis in 2001, Turkey privatised many government-owned enterprises and introduced more market-friendly policies. Thereafter, GDP growth averaged about 6 percent a year until the onset of the global financial crisis (GFC) in 2008. Due partly to the reforms made to its banking and financial markets system, Turkey recovered quickly form the crisis, and GDP growth increased to 9 percent in 2010-11. Since then, the pace of economic reform has slowed and the business outlook has become more challenging, with suspicions that the government has been using economic measures to target political opponents. In response to these developments, three credit rating agencies downgraded Turkey's sovereign credit ratings in 2016 and 2017. The overall economic performance has, nevertheless, been quite strong. During 2013-18, per capita GDP rose at an average annual rate of 5 percent, to I$ 29,632 or about two-thirds above the global average. Turkey's main export products are apparel, foodstuffs, textiles, metal manufactures, and transport equipment. Its major commodity imports are machinery, chemicals, semi-finished goods, fuels, and transport equipment. The country's main trading partners are Germany (10 percent of the total), the United States (6 percent) and Italy (5 percent).

UAE ("United Arab Princes/Lords/Commanders") is a federation of seven monarchies bounded by the Persian Gulf, Saudi Arabia, and Oman. In the 19th century, the small desert principalities occupying the area that comprises present-day UAE granted control over defence and foreign affairs to Britain. Following the discovery of oil and gas in the 1960s, the economies have been transformed. The governments of UAE have used the incomes generated from the country's rich oil and gas resources to build productive infrastructure and diversify economic activity. As a result, the non-oil / non-gas sectors now contribute about 70 percent of GDP. In 2018, per capita GDP was I$ 77,424 which was 20 percent higher than that of the United States and 40 percent higher than the average of all OECD countries. UAE.s main product exports are crude oil (45 percent), natural gas, re-exports, fried fish, and dates. Its major imports are machinery & equipment, chemicals, and foodstuffs. UAE's trading partners are quite diversified, with the leading countries being India (8 percent of exports plus imports), China (7 percent) and Iran (6 percent).

The Republic of ***Yemen*** ("Fertile/Happy Arabia") was formed in 1990 with the unification of the Yemen Arab Republic (North Yemen) and the communist-controlled People's Democratic Republic of Yemen (South Yemen). Several hundred thousand

Yemenis from the south then moved to the north, contributing to subsequent hostilities within the country. Intermittent fighting broke out between the government and the Huthis (a Zaydi Shia Muslim minority) during 2004-10, and then again from 2014. In 2016, the government and the Huthis participated in UN-sponsored peace talks. In 2019, the Yemen parliament convened for the first time since 2014. Prior to the conflict, the Yemen economy was heavily dependent on declining oil and gas resources for foreign exchange and government revenue. Some measures were introduced to diversify the economy, but the conflict has halted the small progress that had been made. Per capita GDP fell from I$ 3,500 in 2015 to I$ 2,782 in 2018. The economy is currently in disarray, with the Central Bank's foreign exchange reserves (which amounted to US $5.2 billion in 2014) now exhausted, about a third of the work force unemployed, more than 7 million people at risk of famine and 80 percent of the population in need of humanitarian assistance. When current hostilities cease, Yemen will need considerable foreign assistance, including from experienced social entrepreneurs, to restore economic stability and promote economic growth.

Central Asia

In 2018, Central Asia accounted for 2 percent of West Asia's population and contributed 4 percent of its GRP. The largest country in terms of population was Uzbekistan with 32 million followed by Kazakhstan with 18 million and Tajikistan with 9 million. Kazakhstan had the largest GDP, of I$ 513 billion, ahead of Uzbekistan with I$ 231 billion and Turkmenistan with I$ 112 billion. Per capita GDP for the whole region was I$ 12,659, or 72 percent of the global average. It was highest in Kazakhstan (I$ 28,032), followed by Turkmenistan (I$ 18,973), and Uzbekistan (I$ 7,127).

Kazakhstan ("Land of the Wanderers") was settled by nomadic tribes from Turkey and Mongolia commencing in the 13th century. It was conquered by Russia in the 18th century and was made a Soviet Republic in 1936. During the 1950s and 1960s, the Soviet's "Virgin Lands" program led to large-scale immigration, especially from Russia, and by the time the country regained its independence in 1991, the ethnic Kazakhs were in a minority. However, considerable reverse migration occurred from the mid-1990s and the Kazakhs now account for about 70 percent of the population. Kazakhstan was the second largest member (after Russia) of the Former Soviet Union. In 2018 it accounted for more than half the GRP of Central Asia. The country has large deposits of petroleum, uranium, copper, and zinc. The super-giant Kashagan oil field commenced production in 2015 and a US $37 billion expansion of the premiere Tengiz oil field should be completed by 2022. Kazakhstan's main exports are oil and oil products, natural gas, ferrous metals, and chemicals. Its major imports are machinery & equipment, metal products, and foodstuffs. The country's main trading partners are Russia (25 percent of the total), China 14 percent, and Italy (10 percent).

Table 6. Economy of Central Asia, 2018

	Labour force (m)	Labour productivity (I$)	GDP (I$ bn)	Population (m)	Per capita GDP (I$)
Kazakhstan	9	56,666	513	18	28,032
Kyrgyzstan	3	8,661	25	6	3,949
Tajikistan	3	10,069	31	9	3,377
Turkmenistan	2	46,349	112	6	18,973
Uzbekistan	18	12,643	231	32	7,127
Central Asia	**36**	**25,557**	**912**	**72**	**12,659**
Rest of world	3,380	39,776	134,423	7,604	17,677
World	3,415	39,627	135,334	7,676	17,630

Sources. World Bank's World Economic Indicators, IMF's world Economic Outlook, UN Population Division, CIA's World Factbook

Kyrgyzstan ("Land of the Forty Tribes") was annexed by Imperial Russia in 1876. In an unsuccessful revolt against the Tsarist regime in 1916, almost one sixth of the population was killed. Kyrgyzstan was a member of the Soviet Union from 1936 until 1991. It is now a parliamentary republic, with power distributed evenly between the president who is head of state and the prime minister who oversees the Kyrgyz government. Like several other Central Asian economies, Kyrgyzstan is landlocked, mountainous, and heavily dependent on mineral extraction and remittances from nationals working abroad. Per capita GDP in 2018 was I$3,949. Like several other countries in the region, economic development is hampered by endemic corruption, an opaque bureaucracy, a difficult business environment, and an inability to attract foreign investment. In 2018, Kyrgyzstan's main exports were gold, cotton, wool, garments, meat, mercury, uranium, and electricity. Its major imports were oil & gas, machinery & equipment, chemicals, and foodstuffs. The country's main trading partners are Switzerland (30 percent of the total), China (15 percent), and Russia (15 percent).

The residents of ***Tajikistan*** ("Land of the Tajik People") came under Russian rule in the 1860s and 1870s. The country was fully incorporated into the Soviet Union by 1925. The latter made changes to the status and boundaries of both Tajikistan and Uzbekistan in 1929. placing a large minority of ethnic Uzbeks in Tajikistan (and an even larger Tajik minority in Uzbekistan). Tajikistan obtained its independence in 1991 but was rent by civil war during 1992-97. The current president, Emomali

Rahmon, banned the last opposition party in 2015. He also declared himself "Founder of Peace and National Unity, Leader of the Nation" and gave himself a limitless term and lifelong immunity from prosecution. With per capita GDP of I$ 3,377 in 2018, Tajikistan is the poorest country among the members of the former Soviet Union. Only 7 percent of the land is suitable for farming (compared with 30 percent for the global economy). The production of and trade in narcotics account for more than a third of total GDP. Remittances from Tajiks working abroad (mainly in Russia) generate income equivalent to about a third of GDP. The country is mountainous, but does possess deposits of minerals such as silver, gold, uranium, antimony, tungsten, and coal. It also has vast hydropower potential and has contracted an Italian firm to build a major dam (the Roghun Dam) to allow further exploitation of this potential. Tajikistan's main exports are aluminium, electricity, cotton, fruits, vegetable oils, and textiles. Its major imports are petroleum products, aluminium oxide, machinery & equipment, and foodstuffs. The country's main trading partners are Russia (25 percent of the total), Turkey (15 percent) and China (13 percent).

Turkmenistan ("Land of the Turkmen People") differs from other countries in Central Asia in not being landlocked – the Caspian Sea marks its western boundary. Because of its location, it has been at the crossroads of western and eastern civilisations for more than two millennia. The city of Merv was once a famous Islamic city and an important trading and resting place on the Silk Road. Turkmenistan has been conquered, often after considerable resistance. by the Persians, Alexander the Great, Muslims, Mongols, Turkey and, in the 18th century, Russia. It achieved independence following the dissolution of the Soviet Union in 1991, and now has a presidential republic form of government. Turkmenistan's economy is based on the exploitation of large reserves of natural gas and petroleum, with hydrocarbon exports (mainly to China) contributing about a quarter of GDP. In 2018, per capita GDP was I$ 18,973 but it was very unevenly distributed. About half the population is engaged in farming, growing mainly cotton and wheat on irrigated oases; however, farming generates only 8 percent of GDP. Turkmenistan's main exports are gas, crude oil, petrochemicals, textiles, and cotton fibres. Its leading imports are machinery & equipment, chemicals, and foodstuffs. The country's major trading partners are China (50 percent), Turkey (15 percent) and Algeria (8 percent).

Uzbekistan ("Land of the Free") is the geographic and population centre of Central Asia. Its different territories were united by Russia in the late 19th century and, after considerable resistance, became part of the Soviet Union in 1924. Under Soviet rule, intensive production of cotton and grains, over-use of chemicals and depletion of the water supply led to degradation of much of the farmland and a drying up of rivers and the Caspian Sea. The country regained its independence following dissolution of the Soviet Union, and in 1994 adopted a presidential republic form of government. During the following decades, the government imposed a command-type economy, with tight controls over production, prices, and access to foreign currencies. Those policies, together with freezing of the local assets of some overseas companies, have discouraged foreign investment. Since the election of Shavkat Mirziyoyev as Prime Minister in 2016 there has been some loosening of controls and adoption of measures aimed at encouraging FDI. Uzbekistan is the world's 7th largest producer and 5th largest exporter of cotton. Its exports also include natural gas, mineral fertilisers, non-ferrous metals, and gold. The country's major imports are machinery & equipment, foodstuffs, and chemicals. Uzbekistan's main trading partners are Switzerland (22 percent of the total)., Russia (20 percent) and China (20 percent).

CONCLUSION

In 2018, West Asia accounted for 34 percent of the GRP of Asia and 17 percent of GWP. Within West Asia, GRP was highest in Southern Asia followed by Western Asia. The World Income Model developed by Hooke, Alati and Kaur suggests that the share of West Asia in GWP will rise to 31 percent by 2050, as convergence mechanisms narrow the gaps in average labour productivity among countries. It is projected that Southern Asia's share will more than double, to 25 percent. The Model also projects that, by 2050, the GDP of India will have passed that of China, and that India will continue to have the world's largest economy, and by a growing margin, through the remainder of the twenty-first century.

REFERENCES

Bayly, S. (1999). *Caste, Society and Politics in India from the Eighteenth Century to the Modern Age*. Cambridge University Press. doi:10.1017/CHOL9780521264341

CIA. (2020). *The World Factbook*. https://www.cia.gov/library/publications/the-world-factbook/

Damodaran, H., & Nilekani, N. (2011). *India's New Capitalists: Castes, Business, and Industry in a Modern Nation*. AIAA.

Hooke, A. (2019). *Global Economic Development: Past, Present and Future*. Lakeland House.

Khan, A. R. (2016). *The Economy of Bangladesh: A Quarter Century of Development*. Palgrave Macmillan.

Kushnir, I. (2019). *The Economy of Nepal*. Independently published.

Nilekani, N. (2010). *Imagining India: The Idea of a Renewed Nation*. Allen Lane.

Piketty, T. (2014) *Harvard University Press.*

Saeed, K. A. (2010). *The Economy of Pakistan*. Oxford University Press.

ENDNOTE

1 Shah Jahan had an unpromising start to his reign. Upon assuming power, he ordered the blinding and imprisonment of his brother. He then arranged for his father-in-law to slay all the other princes who were potential rivals for his throne. However, he became a candidate for the historical improvement prize by later commissioning the famous Peacock Throne and building the Taj Mahal, one of the Seven Wonders of the World, outside the city of Agra.

Section 2

Chapter 4
Australia-India:
Bilateral Trade Opportunities and Challenges

Anita Medhekar
https://orcid.org/0000-0002-6791-4056
Central Queensland University, Australia

ABSTRACT

India is Australia's fourth largest export market and investment destination, and fifth largest trading partner, with access to a large and youthful market of 1.4 billion population. In 2018, India was the second largest source of skilled professionals after the UK and third largest source of immigrants after the UK and New Zealand. Increasing number of Indian nationals and businesses are choosing Australia as a destination of choice for education, tourism and for doing business. The Independent India Economic Strategy – 2035 was launched on 22 November 2018 for promoting bilateral trade and export market for Australian goods, services, and investment opportunities for mutual economic benefit. This chapter examines the economic significance of bilateral trade relationship between Australia and India and opportunities and challenges faced by the two countries with focus on education, tourism, health, agri-business, alternative energy, and mining sectors to meet the demand and supply gap and the sustainable development goals.

DOI: 10.4018/978-1-7998-4126-5.ch004

INTRODUCTION

Since independence in 1947, the Indian economy followed a protectionist, inward-looking policy with the objective of achieving self-sufficiency and import substitution through a five-year planning strategy of green (agriculture), white (dairy), and industrial (technology and manufacturing) revolution. After the financial crisis of the early 1990s, the Rao government's 'New Economic Policy' reform package moved the country away from inward-looking restrictive trade policies to outward-looking policies and opened the Indian economy to international competition, deregulation, trade liberalisation, export promotion, privatisation and globalisation initiatives (Bhagwati, 1993; Chatterjee, Rae, & Ray, 2006; Medhekar, 2003).

The New Economic Policy reform package opened the economy to foreign direct investment (FDI), and public-private-partnerships (PPPs) for achieving Millennium Development Goals (MDGs) and economic growth (Ahluwalia & Little, 1998). India is a member of the World Trade Organisation (WTO), G-20 and General Agreement on Tariffs and Trade (GATT), like Australia. Further, the South Asian Association of Regional Cooperation (SAARC) is not functional due to the 1971 war that led to the creation of Bangladesh, cross-border skirmishes over Kashmir and distrust, and cancellation of SAARC meetings and bilateral economic, trade and cultural ties between the two countries. SAARC, which is the world's largest organisation with 22 percent of the world's population constituting eight countries, has not led to trade convergence, but more trade divergence between SAARC countries rather than to achieve positive economic outcomes for peace and prosperity of the region (Patra, 2016).

During 1947-80, it was difficult for Australia to establish any fruitful trade relationship with India, because India was not considered important for Australia, the international Kashmir issue, a tilt of Australia with Pakistan, and Australia-US strategic alliance and trade relationship with China (Gurry, 1993; Gurry, 2013). However, commencing in 2006 under then-Prime Minister John Howard, Australia–India bilateral strategic relationship improved significantly. In 2009. Prime Minister Rudd's government progressed beyond cricket diplomacy and took the relationship to the next level of strategic and bilateral trade relationship (Bergenwall, 2016; Bhagwati, 1993; Gurry, 2012; Mayer & Jain, 2010; Mishra, 2012; Ranjan, 2016; Thakur & Sharma, 2018). Prime Minister Abbot and Morrison's coalition government has also sought to strengthen bilateral trade relations with India- the sixth largest economy in the world and the single largest source of permanent migration to Australia (Asialink, 2019).

Australia and India have much in common given both were British colonies and are now part of the commonwealth group of nations. Besides, they share English as the official language of business, the rule of law and democratic leadership; however, with different cultural values (Gurry, 1993). Various bilateral trade initiatives such as mining and export of coal and particularly uranium, to harness nuclear energy required for India's development, could not take place, and is still a challenge. This was due to the risk factor of mining uranium at all stages and to producing nuclear weapons by India; as India has not signed the Nuclear Non-Proliferation Treaty (NPT) (Brewster, 2010; Smith, 2010). However, the two-way bilateral trade in goods and services increased to $A 18 billion in 2014-15 and grew to $27.5 (27 percent) billion in 2017 (Department of Foreign Affairs and Trade {DFAT}, 2018a). Further, since the Modi government came to power in 2014, it's foreign policy has been transformed from Look-East to Act-East towards South-East Asia, Japan and Australia to form bilateral trade, investment and defence security ties with the countries (Ganguly, 2017; Hall, 2015; Nguyen, 2017; ORF, 2019; Ranjan, 2016; Raghuramapatruni & Chary, 2017; Wojczewski, 2019).

Since 2015-2018, India has been Australia's fifth largest export market and FDI destination, and fifth largest two-way trading partner. India ranks 10th as the source of imports to Australia (CECA, 2019; Commonwealth of Australia, 2010). Bilateral trade between Australia and India has increased in the 21st century, with Australia having access to a large and youthful market of 1.4 billion people. However, there is lack of political will and numerous challenges to tap the full potential from bilateral trade and realise the benefits from economic and business opportunities. Following the national elections in May of 2019 in Australia and India, the Free Trade Agreement (FTA) between the two countries is still on the table for discussion (Chacko & Davis, 2018).

India has one of the fastest developing economies of Asia, with a huge market (Bergenwall, 2016). In 2018, India was the second largest source of skilled professionals to Australia following the UK, and third largest source of immigrants following UK and New Zealand (Bhosale, 2018). An increasing number of Indian nationals, students, and businesses are choosing Australia as a destination of choice for tourism, education, doing business, reflecting the shared history of colonisation by the UK, the Westminster style of democratic government and judicial governance, a love for cricket and the English language (Bhosale, 2018; Brewster, 2010).

Australia is seeking a balance in its relationship between India and China, as China is Australia's key trading partner, and India is Australia's future growth market for export of resources, tourism, and education. Further, there are also increasing tensions between the US and China over trade, and border disputes between India and China, where China claims to occupy the eastern part of Kashmir and Arunachal Pradesh since the 1962 war. Furthermore, China is gaining strategic maritime and military control of the Indian Ocean region by investing and building strategic infrastructure projects as the One-Belt-Road initiative, airports and seaports for South Asian countries bordering India (Brewster, 2010; Gurry, 2013; Phillips, 2013;

Singh, 2016). Moreover China, with its One-Belt-Road initiatives in the Pacific island countries, military ambitions, maritime power, and disputes over the South China Sea with South Korea, Vietnam, and Malacca in South-East Asia, is looked upon as a global threat, with fear and anxiety in Australia, the USA, India and ASEAN economies (Davis, 2020; Goodman, 2017; Nguyen, 2017).

In May 2011, the Comprehensive Economic Cooperation Agreement was launched by Australia-India, and since then they have had nine rounds of negotiations to enhance economic trade and investment relationships (CECA, 2019). These were followed by the Australian Government commissioning a report, that was launched on 22 November 2018, on An India Economic Strategy-2035 (IES-2035), which sought to identify bilateral trade and investment opportunities, mutual economic benefit, create jobs, growth and prosperity for Australia and India. It predicted that India will be the most populous and the third largest economy after the USA and China. It is an ambitious plan to transform Australia's economic partnership with India in ten key sectors and in other areas of the bilateral relationship (DFAT, 2018b).

In reply to this report, it is suggested that Australia should make India one of its top three export markets for Australian goods, services and people-to-people contacts and government diplomacy with a long-term strategy for bilateral trade and Australian investment in India. India can benefit from Australian expertise and investment in urban transport infrastructure, logistics, water management, resources, agri-business food processing and storage, and renewable solar energy (DFAT, 2018b). Moreover, with the global coronavirus COVID-19 situation, Australia cannot afford to depend just on China for its investments, import and export of resources, beef, grains, goods and services, tourism, and international students.

The purpose of this chapter is to: (i) critically examine the economic significance of bilateral trade in goods and services, and investment, between Australia and India; (ii) identify opportunities and challenges faced by the two countries in promoting trade and investment with a focus on the education, health, tourism, agri-business, alternative energy, and mining sectors; (ii) suggest a PPPs framework between Australia and India for inclusive economic growth for meeting Sustainable Development Goals (SDGs) via bilateral trade and investment such as (a) no poverty, (b) zero hunger (c) good health and well-being, (d) quality education, (e) gender equality, (f) clean drinking water and sanitation, and (g) affordable and clean energy (United Nations, 2019).

The chapter is structured as follows: The first section introduces the growing economic importance of bilateral trade between Australia and India. Section two provides background and an overview of the Australian and the Indian economies in the context of bilateral trade in goods and services. Section three discusses the challenges and opportunities for economic partnership in the six sectors of education, tourism, health, agri-business, alternative energy, and mining. The final section presents discussions and recommendations for management and policy, conclusions, and future research directions to advance knowledge in the field of bilateral trade and PPPs between Australia and India for mutual economic benefit and achieving 17-SDGs (United Nations, 2019) for inclusive economic development and growth.

BACKGROUND

India is Australia's fastest growing export market for goods and services. Investing in human capital has a direct bearing on the sustainability of a country's competitiveness and economic growth, besides improving Track-1 and Track-2 diplomatic relationship due to nearly a million diasporic Indians living in Australia, including Indian students, who are essential for future diplomatic ties and trade investment opportunities (Ranjan, 2016; Thakur & Sharma, 2018). Menon (2009) has identified general and specific motivating factors that drive countries to sign bilateral free trade agreements which could be mutually beneficial to both parties and could be in the interest of one party than other. The view is that World Trade Organisation and multilateral trade agreements have failed to deliver in case of various countries interest. Therefore, bilateral trade agreements are pursued by numerous countries. Other motivating factors are market-driven economic, political, and foreign policy, and defence strategy programs between countries.

OVERVIEW OF THE AUSTRALIAN AND THE INDIAN ECONOMIES

The Australian economy. Australia is an island continent in the southern hemisphere, with approximately 24.5 million population and a natural birth rate of 1.6 percent. Nearly 86 percent of the population are concentrated in urban cities. Australia was the only OECD country that did not experience a recession during the global financial crisis, and it experienced the highest GDP growth rate among the developed countries (Hubbard, Garrett, Lewis, & O'Brian, 2019). In 2018, Australia's GDP growth rate of 3.2 percent was driven by private business and the government sectors. The inflation rate in 2018 was around 2.2 percent and is expected to rise to 2.5 in 2020. There is also weaker capital investment from China, since the Australian government rejected the sale to China of an electric power plant in Victoria and the largest ranch constituting 2.5 percent of the entire country's farmland (NORDEA, 2019). There are various challenges faced by Australia such as impact of climate change, reduction of green-house gas emissions, drought, forest fires, water shortage, ageing population, and with COVID-19, there are nearly one million people unemployed, with increasing pressure on the health system, international trade, investment, decline in-bound tourists and students impacting on tourism and education sectors and overall slowing down of the economy.

Australia's top ten exports in 2018 were iron-ore, coal, education-related travel services, natural gas, gold, aluminium, beef, wheat, crude petroleum and personal travel services for tourism and business. Likewise, the top ten imports were machinery including computers; mineral fuels and oils; vehicles; electrical machinery and equipment; optical, technical and medical apparatus and pharmaceuticals; gems and precious metals; plastic and plastic articles; iron and steel articles, furniture bedding, lightening, signs, and prefabricated buildings (ABS, 2019; DFAT, 2018a).

The service sector is the largest contributor (67 percent) to the GDP of Australia, employing 78.3 percent of the working population in business, banking and finance, healthcare, education, travel and tourism sectors. The agriculture and mining sectors are the other two important export sectors. Australia exports, wheat, wool, cotton, pulses, lentils, fresh fruits and vegetables, besides coal, iron ore, uranium, gold, liquid natural gas and other minerals and precious stones like diamonds and emeralds (DFAT, 2018a; RBA, 2020; ABARES, 2019). In 2018, Australia's health and social sectors grew by 7.1 percent, followed by mining 6.3 percent and 4.8 percent for other services (RBA, 2020). The export of goods and commodity performance grew from 2017, due to rise in resources and energy prices (minerals including iron ore, coal and gold), and growth of the services such as education related travel services and tourism. Table 1 provides an overview of the key macroeconomic data for the Australian economy. It indicates that GDP growth rate slowed down from 2.6 percent in 2016 to 1.8 in 2018, unemployment was 5.2 percent and inflation at 1.7 percent was below the RBA's target inflation rate of 2-3 percent. As a result, the Reserve Bank of Australia (RBA) adopted an expansionary monetary policy, and cut the official interest rate three times in 2019 by quarter of a percent, and twice in March 2020 by another quarter, to what is now historically the lowest official cash rate (0.25 percent), to support employment growth, increase business and consumer confidence due to negative economic impact of COVID-19 pandemic (RBA, 2020).

Table-2 shows that in two-way trade with Australia, China, Japan and US have the top three positions and India has the 5th position.

Table-3 data shows that India ranks 5th in Australia's merchandise export market and ranked 13th in merchandise source country of import, with a total share of 2 percent and growth of 23.3 percent over 2016-18 period (DFAT, 2018a, pp.27-28).

Table-4 shows India is ranked 6th as Australia's two-way trading partner in services, with a growth rate of 18.7 percent over two years 2016-18 (DFAT, 2018a, p.37). Further, regarding Australia's source country of services imports, India is ranked 13th, with a total share of 2.6 percent and growth of 21.6 percent over 2016-18 (DFAT, 2018a, pp.37-38).

Table 1. Australia: Macroeconomic Indicators

Australia Macro-Economic Indicators	2016	2017	2018	2019
GDP (US$ b)	1,266	1,379	1,330	1,432
GDP per capita ($A b)	51,903	55,690	56228	56919
GDP ($A b) purchasing power parity	44493	44648	45000	45100
Annual GDP Growth (%)	2.6%	2.2%	2.3	1.8
Current account ($A b)	-17961	-10726	-11886	-2900
Current account balance (% of GDP)	-3.1	-2.5	-3.4	-1.5
Inflation (% change)	1.3	1.9	1.8	1.3
Unemployment (% of labour force)	5.7	5.6	5.2	5.19
Govt. Debt to GDP ratio (%)	40.5	40.7	40.7	40.7
Official interest rate (%)	1.5	1.5	1.5	1.0
Imports $A billion (BOP basis)	350,649	376,552	34730	35839
Exports $A billion (BOP basis)	336,89	336,67	36798	41585

Source: Trading Economics; DFAT (2017)

Table 2. Australia's top two-way trading partners ($A million)

Rank	Country	2015-16	2016-17	2017-18	Share of total (%)	Growth (%) in 2 years	5-year trend (%)
1	China	152,061	174,242	194,620	24.4	11.7	7.8
2	Japan	60,553	68,519	77,595	9.7	13.2	0.8
3	US	70,672	65,599	70,177	8.8	5.4	4.3
4	Rep of Korea	34,130	38,616	52,303	6.5	35.4	8.3
5	**India**	**19,963**	**25,733**	**29,116**	**3.6**	**13.1**	**12.9**
6	New Zealand	24,431	26,403	28,275	3.5	7.1	5.0
7	UK	28,363	27,585	27,793	3.5	0.8	5.3
8	Singapore	23,281	24,679	27,773	3.5	12.5	-2.6
9	Thailand	21,555	21,819	24,688	3.1	13.2	4.3
10	Germany	20,039	20,914	22,355	2.8	6.9	6.2
11	Malaysia	18,500	19,793	21,506	2.7	8.7	2.6
12	Hong Kong	15,706	19,704	18,820	2.4	-4.5	5.7
13	Indonesia	16,138	16,556	16,775	2.1	1.3	1.6
14	Taiwan	12,474	14,717	15,926	2.0	8.2	4.8
15	Vietnam	10,549	11,763	13,051	1.6	11.0	10.3

Source: DFAT (2018a, p.27)

Table 3. Australia's merchandise export and import source markets ($A million)

Rank	Export	2015-16	2016-17	2017-18	Share of total (%)	Growth (%) in 2 years	5-year trend (%)
1	China	87,829	110,012	123,274	30.6	12.1	7.5
2	Japan	37,975	44,455	51,328	12.7	15.5	-0.9
3	Rep of Korea	19,971	22,761	23,628	5.9	3.8	1.6
4	US	21,897	20,684	21,424	5.3	3.6	7.0
5	**India**	**13,338**	**19,268**	**21,145**	**5.2**	**9.7**	**12.3**
6	Hong Kong	11,560	15,861	14,506	3.6	-8.5	6.5
7	New Zealand	13,162	13,671	14,370	3.6	5.1	5.2
8	Singapore	10,070	11,349	13,164	3.3	16.0	3.3
9	UK	12,647	12,753	11,757	2.9	-7.8	6.8
10	Taiwan	7,670	9,987	10,952	2.7	9.7	5.5
11	Malaysia	7,651	8,436	8,944	2.2	6.0	4.1
12	Indonesia	7,029	8,347	8,391	2.1	0.5	5.9
13	Thailand	4,709	5,155	6,610	1.6	28.2	0.1
14	Vietnam	5,017	5,747	6,106	1.5	6.2	15.3
15	UA Emirates	3,780	3,847	4,344	1.1	12.9	7.4
Rank	**Import source**	**2015-16**	**2016-17**	**2017-18**	**Share of total (%)**	**Growth (%) in 2 years**	**5-year trend (%)**
1	China	64,222	64,230	71,346	18.0	11.1	8.4
2	US	48,775	45,915	48,754	12.3	6.2	3.2
3	Rep of Korea	14,159	15,854	28,674	7.3	80.9	17.9
4	Japan	22,577	24,064	26,267	6.6	9.2	4.6
5	Germany	16,290	16,567	18,185	4.6	9.8	5.9
6	Thailand	16,846	16,663	18,078	4.6	8.5	5.9
7	UK	15,716	14,832	16,036	4.1	8.1	4.2
8	Singapore	13,211	13,330	14,610	3.7	9.6	-6.6
9	New Zealand	12,269	12,732	13,905	3.5	9.2	4.8
10	Malaysia	10,849	11,357	12,562	3.2	10.6	1.6
11	Italy	7,802	7,989	9,131	2.3	14.3	4.4
12	Indonesia	9,110	8,210	8,348	2.1	2.1	-1.9
13	**India**	**6,625**	**6,465**	**7,971**	**2.0**	**23.3**	**15.0**
14	France	6,985	6,645	7,416	1.9	11.6	3.3
15	Vietnam	5,532	6,016	6,945	1.8	15.4	6.6

Source: DFAT (2018a, pp.27-28)

Table 4. Australia's services two-way trading partners ($A million)

Rank	Country	2015-16	2016-17	2017-18	Share of total (%)	Growth (%) in 2 years	5-year trend (%)
1	US	24,439	23,900	26,159	14.4	9.5	5.6
2	China	15,255	17,188	20,169	11.1	17.3	17.4
3	UK	13,619	13,609	14,021	7.7	3.0	4.5
4	NZ	9,080	9,921	10,993	6.1	10.8	8.3
5	Singapore	10,112	10,531	10,465	5.8	-0.6	5.1
6	**India**	**5,499**	**6,107**	**7,248**	**4.0**	**18.7**	**15.3**
7	Hong Kong	5,782	5,919	6,354	3.5	7.3	7.9
8	Japan	5,453	5,605	6,247	3.4	11.5	6.6
9	Indonesia	4,9444	5,404	5,544	3.1	2.6	5.8
10	Germany	4,599	4,695	5,125	2.8	9.2	7.6
11	Thailand	3,429	3,792	4,333	2.4	14.3	2.4
12	Malaysia	3,282	3,519	3,668	2.0	4.2	0.9
13	UA Emirates	3,064	2,980	3,552	2.0	19.2	5.2
14	France	3,291	3,057	3,257	1.8	6.5	7.5
15	Vietnam	2,539	2,693	3,159	1.7	17.3	7.9

Source: DFAT (2018a, p.37)

As seen from Table 5, total merchandise exports to India were $A 9,708,059, in 2015-2016 increasing to $A 15,158,186 (2016-17), and $A 16,325,643 in 2017-18, with a 2-year percentage growth of 7.7 percent. Further, total merchandise imports from India were $A 4,756,123 in 2015-16 increasing to $44,67,670 (2016-17) and $55,542,235 in 2017-18, with a 2-year growth of 24.1 percent.

The Indian Economy: India is the world largest democracy with a population of approximately 1.4 billion, a growing middle class, and nearly 300 million living below the poverty line with 20 percent of the world's working population (DFAT, 2018a). It is one of the world's fastest growing economies underpinned by a structural shift from agriculture to the manufacturing and service sectors, increase in employment, business friendly opportunities, 45 percent of population below 25 years, with increased consumption and urbanisation. Table 6 provides India's key macroeconomic indicators during 2016-18. The economy grew by 7.3 percent in 2018 while the unemployment rate has been stable at 3.5 percent.

Table 5. Australia's merchandise trade with India ($A '000)

Rank	Top Exports to India	2015-16	2016-17	2017-18	2016-18 Growth (%)	5-year Trend (%)
1	coal	5,010,019	8,730,850	9,907,331	13.5	16.3
2	copper ores & concentrate	511,071	682,071	852,330	25.0	-7.5
3	gold	685,504	409,597	731,927	78.7	-15.0
4	vegetables	744,370	1,428,741	727,539	-49.1	32.2
5	Iron ores & concentrate	6,315	5,250	299,273	....	0.6
6	wool & animal hair	215,275	222,831	246,357	10.6	9.0
7	non-ferrous waste & scrap	127,846	122,514	185,772	51.6	26.5
8	fruit & nuts	122,410	145,676	153,795	5.6	13.5
9	ferrous waste	96,493	86,902	145,868	67.9	-0.2
10	lead	110,800	116,907	127,646	9.2	7.0
11	cotton	62,813	394,002	122,942	-68.8	53.3
12	paint & varnish	62,810	83,958	117,530	40.0	18.5
13	crude petroleum	41,607	23,752	108,770	357.9	....
14	aluminium	48,296	79,730	60,643	-23.9	20.3
15	silver & platinum	78,978	....	50,012	....	....
16	paper & paperboard	19,546	74,485	46,769	-37.2	9.2
17	zinc	20,211	20,354	36,275	78.2	18.5
18	other ores & concentrate	123,521	44,001	29,837	-32.2	-33.5
19	pulp & wastepaper	22,107	44,001	24,901	68.4	28.6
20	Confidential trade item	1,051,985	1,340,600	1,883,757	....	....
Rank	**Top Imports from India**	**2015-16**	**2016-17**	**2017-18**	**2016-18 Growth %**	**5-year Trend %**
1	refined petroleum	1,573,010	1,081,048	1,642,595	51.9	97.5
2	medicine & veterinary	320,971	343,270	353,633	3.0	16.0
3	railway vehicle, hovertrains	33,330	123,560	338,912	174.3	138.1
4	pearls & gems	271,661	268,054	280,080	4.5	9.2
5	jewellery	175,455	172,273	179,620	4.3	4.8
6	made-up textile articles	165,543	176,356	176,169	-0.1	10.1
7	passenger motor vehicles	85,134	63,979	104,708	63.7	-18.8
8	women's clothing exl. knit	88,484	95,077	97,472	2.5	21.0
9	floor covering	91,001	88,560	89,062	0.6	13.9
10	textile clothing	73,362	79,929	85,604	7.1	20.6
11	manufactured base metals	52,442	56,041	81,945	46.2	12.0
12	travel goods, bags, containers	60,485	63,169	70,485	11.6	19.0
13	inorganic compounds	79,509	120,282	69,471	-42.2	0.6
14	rice	54,004	51,262	60,553	18.1	11.5
15	electrical distributing equip.	16,269	18,983	60,220	217.2	34.9
16	furniture, mattress, cushion	58,871	58,039	54,448	-6.2	15.8
17	electrical equipt.	45,902	46,908	53,296	13.6	4.6
18	rubber tyres & tubes	33,380	35,871	45,043	25.6	4.9
19	electric machinery parts	15,249	20,135	44,291	120.0	25.7
20	crude vegetable matter	40,190	39,073	43,540	11.4	-0.4
21	Confidential items of trade	27,215	33,830	34,483	....	....

Source: DFAT (2018a, p.90)

Table 6. India-Macroeconomic Indicators

India Macro-Economic Indicators	2016	2017	2018
GDP current price (US$ b)	2,273.6	2,602.3	2,690.0
GDP per capita (US$ b)	1,749.2	1,976.1	2,016.2
GDP (US$ b) purchasing power parity	8,714.8	9,473.8	10,401.4
Real GDP Growth (%)	7.1	6.7	7.3
Current account balance	- 14.4	-48.7	-80.4
Current account balance (% of GDP)	-0.7	-1.9	-3.0
Inflation (% change)	4.5	3.6	4.7
Unemployment (% of labour force)	3.5	3.5	3.5
Debt to GDP ratio (%)	69.5	71.18	69.55
Official Interest rate	6.75	6.50	6.0

Source: Compiled from: RBI: Trading Economics; DFAT, 2018a

Bilateral Trade in Goods and Services. Former Australian Prime Minister, Malcolm Turnbull, visited India in April 2017 with the aim of strengthening the two-way strategic partnership for economic growth, and knowledge sharing (Thakur & Sharma, 2018). The trade in goods and services was $A 13.6 billion in 2017. The major Australian exports are coal ($A 5.5 billion), education related travel services ($A 2.1 billion), gold ($A 903 million), agriculture goods such as chickpeas and lentils (DFAT, 2018a). Australia has nearly $US 2.7 billion trade surplus in agriculture sector with India (Indian Express, 2018). Major Australian imports from India in 2014-15 were refined petroleum ($A 910 million), personal travel/tourism services ($A 561 million) and business services ($A 481 million). The bilateral trade in goods between the two countries was valued at $A 27.4 billion in 2017, with key imports from Australia being coal, pulses, and wheat worth $A 5.7 billion; and exports to Australia were refined petroleum, medication and jewellery worth $A 5.1 billion. Two-way service trade between the countries was valued at $A 6.6 billion, with 300,000 Indian visitors to Australia in 2017 (education and tourism) and FDI of Australia in India was worth $A 1.827 billion (DFAT, 2018a).

Table 7. Australian exports and imports to India 2017-18

Australian exports to India 2017-18	**$A m**
Coal	9,907
Copper ores & Concentrates	852
Gold	732
Vegetables & Fruits	728
Australian imports from India	
Refined Petroleum	1,643
Medicaments (Incl. veterinary)	354
Railway Vehicles (incl. hovertrains	339
Pearls & Gems	280
Australian service exports	
Education-related travel	3,793
Personal travel excluding education	581
Australian service exports	
Personal travel excluding education	1827
Professional, technical & other business	609
Australia's Investment Aus $m Total	**FDI**
Australia's Investment in India= 13,957	1,827
India's investment in Australia =15,494	880

Source: Compiled from DFAT, 2018a; ABS, 2019

Table-7 provides information regarding Australian exports and imports of goods and services and investment in the financial year 2017-2018. India's principal export destination is USA (15.6 percent), UAE second (9.7 percent), Hong Kong third (5.1 percent), and Australia (1.3 percent) is in 22nd position. In the case of India's source of importing countries, China is first (16.2 percent), USA second (5.4 percent), UAE third (5.2 percent), and Australia (3.2 percent) is in 9th position. Its about time, that India and Australia establish sustainable bilateral trade and strategic relationships in the coming decade.

OPPORTUNITIES FROM BILATERAL TRADE BETWEEN AUSTRALIA AND INDIA

Australia and India can benefit from bilateral trade agreements in various sectors such as science and innovation, defence security, financial services, transport infrastructure, sports, besides the key six sectors of the economy discussed below.

(i) ***Education:*** Australia is the second largest destination for international students from India. Australia is a safe, multicultural destination with a large Indian diaspora, and is also an attractive destination for skilled emigrants. Education is the third most important Australian export product after coal and iron-ore due to its high quality, comparable to coals from the UK and the USA. It is projected that if Australia maintains its share of Indian international student numbers from the peak of 2010, Australia's education exports by 2035 to India would be worth $A 12 billion (DFAT, 2018b). Australia needs to diversify its education market to various developing countries to source international students and establish institutional research collaboration. Indian private and public sector educational institutions alone cannot meet the growing population's demand for secondary, vocational and university education. Large numbers of Indian students travel to the UK, the USA, Australia, and Canada, and are willing to pay the fees for quality education in healthcare, medicine, tourism, agri-business, management, engineering, and information technology.

Australia is well placed to provide affordable, quality education to meet the growing Indian demand, where the youth population between 18-25 years is expected to peak at 126 million in 2026 and still be 118 million by 2035 (DFAT, 2018b). According to the Indian Economic Strategy 2035 report, the Indian education sector has limited international collaboration with top overseas universities, outdated curricula and lack of focus on research and job ready skills as well as shortage of secondary schools, vocational training institutions, and universities. Australia can establish PPPs with top universities in India or with the Indian government regulatory approval to allow Australian universities to open offshore campuses in India for offering on campus, distance and online quality education to Indians to fill the gap between demand and supply, and meet the skilled labour market demand for the growing economy. Australian educated Indian students, when they return home, are ambassadors for Australia, as well as future leaders to build a fruitful bilateral relationship between the two countries in terms of diplomacy, exchange of research scholars for innovation, start-up investment and trade programs.

(ii) ***Tourism:*** Australia is a popular destination not just for education but also for tourism amongst the growing affluent Indian upper middle class. According to Tourism Research Australia (2019) March report, India is the third ranked market after China and New Zealand, showing the strongest growth for inbound Indian visitor numbers, which increased by 21.1 percent from 278,000 in 2016-17 to 337,000 in 2018-19 resulting in 21 percent increase in night stays worth $A 20.9 million, and 12 percent increase in spending worth $A 1.7 billion. Nearly 53 percent of Indian tourists visit friends and relatives, besides education and business-related travel. Indians spend an average of $A 4,933, compared to $A 5,195, due to staying with relatives (TRA, 2019). Australia needs to invest in tourism infrastructure, speed up visa processing, provide motel style self-contained accommodation facilities for families, allow franchise of retail Indian fast food chain in Australia such as Barista Lavazza, Bikanervala, HaldiRam's, Indian Coffee House, and Darshini, and provide country specific Indian cultural literacy to tourism staff with multi-lingual skills. There is an opportunity for leveraging on Indian diaspora and international students to be trained and employed in mining, engineering, tourism and hospitality customer service sectors of the Australian economy. However, the future of international tourism, travel and education does not look that optimistic due to the global COVID-19 pandemic.

(iii) ***Health:*** There is an increasing gap between the supply and demand for primary, secondary and tertiary level healthcare in India, due to growing population. On one hand, India is the second most popular inbound medical travel destination to treat foreign patients, and on the other hand millions of people do not have access, availability and cannot afford primary healthcare (Medhekar, Wong, & Hall, 2019). Further, nucleus families with children settled overseas have seen older parents left alone, giving rise to a demand for privately managed aged-care centres. Investing in health not only creates employment opportunities, joint medical research opportunities and entrepreneurship and innovation in health-related sectors such as medical devices, pharmaceuticals and diagnostic machinery; but also, a healthy population, which is essential to increase productivity and gross domestic product of the nation. India is the largest source of allied-healthcare workers, nurses and doctors to Australia, (Walton-Roberts & Rajan, 2020). Further, Australia imports from India pharmaceuticals and veterinary worth $A 335 million in 2017; and exports to India pharmaceuticals, and medical technology. Given the ageing population problem in Australia and its expertise in aged-care facilities and management, it can train Indian private aged-care service providers in managing and establishing aged-care facilities and training aged-care nursing assistants and staff through University collaboration.

(v) ***Mining:*** Australia's major resource exports to India will continue to grow in metallurgical coal, copper, gold and iron ore along with mining equipment and technology services, given India's increasing demand for goods and services with economic development, growth of industries, manufacturing and urbanisation of population (AIC, 2019). Bilateral collaboration with Australian geological sciences, university researchers and mining expertise will assist India to explore its natural resources and training skills in the use of modern mining equipment, technology, health and safety.

(v) ***Alternative Energy:*** The wheels of an economy turn because of energy sources. Energy shortage is a bottleneck for economic development. Demand for domestic and industrial energy usage in India is driven by economic development, rising population and consumption. India is already harnessing various renewable energy technologies (RETs), through hydropower, wind farms, biogas and solar, but it is still to reach its full potential to meet the growing demand by the industrial, manufacturing, agricultural and household sectors (Bhattacharya & Jana, 2009). Solar and hydro power are considered the cleanest source of energy production and consumption (Sharma, Tiwari, & Sood, 2013). Australia has many opportunities to collaborate with India, given its strong research base in renewable innovations, regulatory and legal framework, financing solar technology, besides having a competitive advantage to provide expertise in harnessing solar power and export liquid natural gas, coal, and uranium to meet India's growing demand.

(vi) ***Agribusiness:*** India can ensure its supply from Australia to meet the demand for staple food such as rice, wheat, chickpea, oil, and lentils in all times for its growing population; and not just in the drought period, and achieve the goals of food self-sufficiency, future food security, but also provide income support for farmers. Australian farmers can form partnerships and work with Indian farmers and scientists to supply and export staple crops, value-added processed food, and expertise to improve farmer's output, irrigation methods, income and maintain sustainable supply of grains, pulses, fruits, and vegetables. Australia exports 80 percent of chickpeas and 40 percent of Australian vegetables to India (ABARES, 2019). The Australian export of chickpeas, lentils and dried peas to India is worth $A 300 million per annum (ABS, 2019; DFAT, 2018; AIC, 2018).

According to the Indian Economic Strategy-2035 report, India was the sixth largest market in 2016-17 for bilateral Australian agricultural exports, which are dependent on Indian domestic production based on fluctuating monsoonal rains. Australia can provide expertise in agricultural research, innovative methods to increase productive efficiency, land and water management, reduce food wastage at farm level with integrated transport related value supply chains for export, strategies to adapt to climate change, develop high safety standards in clean and green food production. According to Singh (2016), *Australian Defence White Paper* released in 2016, demonstrates "a growing convergence in strategic approaches…as Australia looks towards the West and India begins to Act East" (Singh, 2016, p. 600) in the Indo-Pacific region with common maritime security interests. Further, due to Australia's location in the southern hemisphere, it can supply off-seasonal crops to northern hemisphere countries, as well as help India to meet the SDG goal of zero hunger, no poverty, food security, good health and wellbeing, clean drinking water, quality education and affordable and clean energy.

CHALLENGES FOR AUSTRALIA AND INDIA

India faces numerous challenges such as high density of population, congested cities, water scarcity, high demand for energy and power, food security, traffic jams, inadequate housing, air and water pollution, transport, infrastructure bottlenecks, insufficient healthcare facilities for the aged, and poor waste disposal systems. As Smith (2010) points out, India and Australia, "need to solve pressing regional and global problems which reach beyond the global financial crisis: the prospect of energy and food crises made worse by disruptive climate change; the ongoing search for international security in a world of nuclear weapons, rising powers and conflict between states; and the challenge of groups engaged in terrorism against civil populations" (p. 567). Similarly, Australia faces challenges of doing business with India, given India's regulatory environment, fluctuating import demands, complicated tariff regimes, and bureaucratic red tape.

The key challenges for both countries are discussed for the following six sectors:

(i) ***Education:*** Against the background of economic globalisation, the development of human capital very much depends on the internationalisation of educational services. International education is Australia's third largest export sector after mining and tourism. Australian universities and research institutions need to increase their collaboration with India on science and research into agriculture, bio-medical devices, food and water security, nanotechnology, and stem cell vaccines (DIIS, 2019). After China, India constitutes the second largest foreign

> student enrolment in Australia. With an increasing middle class and 45 percent of the population below 25 years, there is an increased demand for school and university education and highly skilled labour demanded by different sectors in India now and in the future. India is the second largest source of foreign students studying in Australia. The Australian government's policy of granting to foreign students who have graduated from an Australian university, working, and living rights for two years is a welcome move. In 2008-09, Australia's key export to India was education-related travel services, which amounted to US$ 2.1 billion. Australia can deepen its education engagement with India, by 'giving-back' like Central Queensland University does by donating and sponsoring Salaam-Balak orphan's scholarship for university education and increase its share of the Indian student market (Salaam Balak Trust, 2019).

Australian universities need to establish partnerships and collaboration with accredited universities for student and research-staff exchange and by offering vocational education and training and TAFE opportunities in India. Australian universities can open campuses in India and collaborate with locally- recognised institutions to offer TAFE qualification in India to supply a skilled labour force and help create job opportunities in trades, electricians, nursing attendants and hospitality sector. However, the challenge is for India to allow Australian foreign investment in the education sector, open off-shore university campuses and offices in India, accredit Australian and Indian degrees, provide mutual recognition of qualifications and credit transfer program from accredited universities to encourage student and staff mobility and exchange, regulation, including a small percentage of repatriation of profit share to Australia, by Australian educational investors in India.

Challenges in the case of education travel relate to an expensive and bureaucratic process of visa application for Indian students and academics and for Australians travelling to India for education and conferences. The governments of both countries should simplify the visa application process and make it online for international students and academics to encourage students to choose Australia as a study destination. Similarly, Australian universities need to provide on-campus and affordable purpose-built housing for international students with all facilities for example as Deakin University's excellent on campus student accommodation at Melbourne Burwood and Geelong with all essential facilities and services available for international students. In the current global COVID-19 scenario and travel-ban across countries, Australian universities can capitalise on their online distance education expertise and be a leader in the future in attracting distance enrolments from India and the Southeast Asian countries.

(ii) ***Tourism:*** An increasing number of Indians and Australians are travelling between the two countries for studies, health and medical treatment, and business-related travel combining these with tourism. Likewise, in the last decade the affluent and the upper middle-class Indians are travelling to Australia for business travel, sightseeing, honeymoon, and a destination for filming Bollywood movies. The perception of Australia as a safe location, inclusive of all races and multicultural society must be promoted in India. Direct flights from major cities in India and Australia can be introduced with ease of visa application for visitor-tourists, student-medical tourists and business travellers. However, due to COVID-19 travel-ban the future of trade, travel and tourism is very uncertain given the grounding of airlines, cruises and domestic and international travel restrictions across the world.

(iii) ***Health:*** With its rapidly growing population, India's supply of healthcare does not match its demand. There is a shortage of medical professionals and hospital infrastructure, with only 1 bed per 1000 of population. Public health expenditure is 1.4 percent of GDP (Golechha, 2015) and the Modi government aims to increase it to 2.5 percent of GDP by 2025 (The Economic Times, 2018). Healthcare in India is provided by both the public and the private sectors. Private hospitals, which have state-of-the-art medical equipment and technology, and employ overseas-educated medical staff, are engaged in the business of medical tourism and treating foreign patients who visit India for complex surgeries such as hip and knee replacements, cardiac, cancer, organ transplants and reproductive and cosmetic. This has resulted in a dual healthcare system: private-sector care for the affluent locals and foreign patients and under-resourced public sector for the local population (Medhekar, 2012; Medhekar, 2019). Further, in the future, high density of population per/square kilometre, homelessness and poverty, will give rise to public health concerns related to infections and lifestyle-related diseases such as obesity, cancer, diabetes, heart, infections, and respiratory diseases due to pollution emission and COVID-19 virus.

(iv) ***Mining:*** Japan, China and India are the key markets for Australian export of mining resources. Recently, there has been an increasing demand from India for Australian mineral resources such as coal, iron ore, copper and gold. Likewise, India also needs Australian mining expertise and services to extract its own natural endowments and mineral resources. There are many bureaucratic delays, legal and licencing disputes, issues in interpreting contractual agreements, corruption, regulatory and environmental challenges faced by Australian mining and engineering companies doing business in India, which need to be simplified and streamlined to facilitate trade and investment. Further, the Reserve Bank of India imposes a 20 percent withholding tax on foreign businesses which is a deterrent for Australian businesses to invest in partnership or solely without a Permanent Account Number (PAN) in Indian and unpredictably of the business conditions and Indian market (Indian Budget, 2019).

(v) ***Alternative Energy:*** There is an ever-increasing demand for energy in India. It is essential to ensure energy security for all and meet climate change goals (Chandel, Shrivastava, Sharma, & Ramasamy, 2016). Further, traffic pollution and the impact of coal-fired power stations are linked with climate change and accompanying public-health issues. India's supply of energy cannot meet its growing demand from the agriculture, industry, household and transport sectors, with increasing power shedding. With plenty of sunshine, Australia can help India, to harness solar energy to meet the energy needs of urban and rural household, and electrification of roads, small businesses and industries. However, there are political, institutional, regulatory, technological, fiscal and financial barriers to the development of renewable energy in India (Khare, Nema, & Baredar, 2013). Australia faces many challenges in trying to export coal and uranium to India, which are surrounded by political debate and protest not supported by the environmental lobby, against Adani coal mining in Abbot point Mackay (ABC News, 2019).

(vi) ***Agri-Business:*** Australian agribusiness exports to Southeast Asia and China are on the rise. There will be an increasing future demand for agriculture produce in India, which is driven by an increasing youth population below 25, a growing middle class, diet change, and a growing demand for high-value processed food and protein (Chatterjee, 2006). In India fluctuating monsoonal rainfall, crop failure, small subsistence holdings, bank loan debt and bankruptcy, result in a high incidence of farmer suicide (The Indian Express, 2019). Further, crop failure, lack of rainfall, drought and bad weather conditions, highly inefficient farm practices and logistical supply chains result in food waste at the farm level and shortage of staple crops such as rice, wheat, pulses, canola oil seeds, onions, fruits, and vegetables.

In the future, there will be numerous constraints and challenges for Australian exporters to India, such as: the unpredictable tariff and protectionist trade regime, irregular supply contracts based on food output, and cold-food storage supply chain logistics bottlenecks, lack of transparency and global pandemic, which can have a significant impact on Australian exports. For example, in December 2017, India increased the tariff on chickpeas from 0 to 30 percent and up to 66 percent in Feb 2018 (AIC, 2019; DFAT, 2018a; The Indian Express, 2018). Therefore, in the future, there is a need for certainty in regulation and tax regime transparency related to bilateral trade to take place without any trade barriers, for the mutual benefit of the two countries.

RECOMMENDATIONS AND DISCUSSION

Since the Modi government's Act-East policy, the trade relationship with Australia has somewhat improved (ORF, 2019; Ranjan, 2016), that "favours economic development, enhanced regionalism, improved security and greater soft power" (Hall, 2015, p. 250). Further, Modi cabinet recently approved the New National Education Policy 2020 reforms on 31 July, which has opened opportunities for 200 top foreign universities to set up operations in India. The following recommendations are made in order to build business-to-business and people-to-people links to build business contacts and hold art, culture, sporting events, teaching of Indian language (e.g. Hindi and Urdu) and film festivals between the two countries so as to tap into mutually beneficial trade, travel, health, agri-business, education, joint start-up innovative projects, and investment opportunities.

- ***Education:*** Sister university memoranda of understanding and alumni contacts can be established for research collaboration, which have significant impact to meet 17-SDGs, holding joint conferences, and exchange of students and academic scholars with mutual recognition of qualifications and credit transfers. Encourage establishment of Australian off-shore campuses, academic research collaboration between Indian and Australian universities, Indian companies and research institutes with an aim of solving numerous Indian economic problems related to poverty, pollution, infant and maternal mortality, quality education, gender equality, clean drinking water, waste management, and sanitation issues, affordable and clean energy, food security, pollution, sustainable cities and housing, and climate change impact. The future of online education is very promising due to COVID-19, and Australia has expertise in internet broadband-based working from home online education to train Indian universities to provide innovative affordable access to education in remote villages.
- ***Regional Security:*** The challenge of security concerns in the Indian and the Pacific Ocean region where Australia could play a key role in providing regional defence ties with India and the ASEAN countries to ensure peace, global stability and security in the Indian ocean trade route. Here the Indian, Australian and ASEAN role becomes more strategic to dampen China's military and maritime ambitions, to access and control the Pacific Island and Indian Ocean economies by building roads, sea ports, and leasing islands from Burma, Bangladesh, Sri Lanka, the Maldives, Pakistan, and Mauritius through predatory economic policies of debt trap, and surrounding India with its military "String of Pearls strategy" (Brewster, 2010).

- ***Connectivity and Communication:*** More direct flights between Australia and India should be established once the pandemic is over to the major cities of Cairns, Brisbane, Sydney, Melbourne, and Perth to encourage ease of in/out bound travel between the two countries. Australia can be the chosen destination for the increasing Indian demand for education and tourism. Further, Australia can help India in improving internet and telecommunication connectivity in the remote and rural villages, given their expertise in broadband -implementation across the country, in telemedicine, tele-health and online distance education.
- ***Public Work Projects:*** With increasing urbanisation in India, Australia can provide its expertise and FDI in the smart-city programs of the Indian government such as environmental management, public transport, highways, public utilities and services such as water, electricity, public washroom facilities, waste management, and road safety.
- ***Agriculture:*** The Indian agriculture sector needs greater predictability of the tariff regimes for cash crops, export of value-added processed food, sustainable import demand, and smart supply chain and cold storage logistics to avoid food waste. Australia is known for its expertise in efficient agriculture production, and management pre- and post-harvest at the farm level and in terms of crop-disease, supply-chain logistics of harvesting, storage and transportation of grains and fresh produce can ensure future food security for millions in India.
- ***Energy:*** There is a shortage of natural gas, electricity and water, resulting in queuing and rationing managed through load shedding. India depends on coal, gas and water for power, with increased demand from its domestic and industrial sectors. In the future, Australia can provide alternative green solar and wind energy solutions and harness of rainwater capture and storage as regulatory building requirement.
- ***Mining Resources*:** Indian's future demand, for Australian mineral resources such as coal, iron ore, uranium and gold, will continue to rise, with increase in per-capita income, economic development and growth. Australia can also provide its expertise in mining technology, geology, and equipment required to modernise the Indian mining sector, health, and safety workplace training.
- ***Health:*** Australia can provide expertise and partner with hospitals and medical research teams in India and assist in developing and solving health-related problems. Further, it can assist with establishing public and private aged-care facilities, special schools for physically and mentally challenged and solving the lifestyle related health problems of obesity, diabetes and communicable diseases and early detection of cancer.

- ***Cultural Sensitivity:*** Australia needs to have greater collaboration and partnership to train the Australian workforce to be culturally sensitive to provide tailor-made tours for Indian visitors, language interpreters, educational programs, local Asian retail food court chains such as (Miss India) to meet the demand for inbound Indian tourists, international students and business travelers to build better social, economic and bilateral relationships.
- ***Business Friendly Environment:*** India needs to still eliminate current bureaucratic red tape, corruption, delays in processing licenses and visas so that the business-friendly environment is created which is more trustworthy and transparent in doing business with democratic western countries as Australia in the future. Similarly, to attract Australian tourists, businesses, scholars and students, India needs to organise travel, tourism and international trade fairs and provide safety and security, a clean environment, safe transport, food, and safe tourists facilities along with ease of doing business in India.
- ***Marketing Australia for doing Business***: Australia has a business-friendly environment and marketing Australia to India, as an attractive destination for making Bollywood films is very promising. Tourism Australia can produce a documentary by using known Indian Bollywood celebrities such as Sharukh Khan and Aishwarya Rai taking a holiday with their children; and showing off the natural beauty Australia has to offer from city, country to coast, and outback to ocean geographical diversity, besides museums and Gold Coast theme parks to attract visitors from India, having a multiplier impact on the economy.
- ***Public-Private-Partnerships:*** The framework for PPPs performance model proposed by Campos, Morini, de Moraes and Inacio (2018) between the two countries for bilateral trade facilitation and international supply chain operation can be implemented. This involves PPPs between the government, business and consumers to mutually benefit from trade in goods and services, food security due to structural shifts in high protein food consumption, strengthening existing economic collaboration and in meeting SDG 17-goals such as (i) no poverty, (ii) zero hunger, (iii) good health and well-being, (iv) quality education, (v) gender equality, (vi) clean drinking water and sanitation, (vii) affordable and clean energy, (viii) decent employment, (ix) industry innovation and infrastructure development, (x) reduce inequality, (xi) sustainable cities and communities, (xii) responsible production and consumption, (xiii) climate change action, (xiv) life below water, (xv) life on land, (xvi) peace justice and strong institutions, and (xvii) global partnerships to achieve SDGs for inclusive economic development and growth (United Nations, 2019).

FUTURE RESEARCH DIRECTIONS

India is the second largest populated country after China. Over the last century Australia has neglected India, when it comes to forming bi-lateral trade relations, and has focussed more on China, USA, and Japan. The Australian-Indian diaspora has continued to play a significant role in the Australian economy from academia, running successful businesses to medical and other service sectors. International education and travel services being the largest exports of Australia to India, future research could look at the affordable housing problems faced by the Indian students and the contribution of these students to the Australian economy. Further, Australia's attractions of sun, sea, wildlife, and natural forests can be promoted in India as an affordable location for making Indian Bollywood films. Australia has many Indian doctors and nurses working in its public and private hospitals. Study can be conducted to see how shortage of medical professional in the remote regional areas can be filled by sending the new migrant medical professionals to these regional areas to service the remote communities of Australia, and meet United Nations SDGs related to poverty, access to good health and wellbeing. Studies can be conducted to see how Australia can help Indian rural and farming communities to solve problems related to their health, wellbeing, poverty, and hunger and to harness solar energy, water and recycling, reduce food waste at farm and supply-chain cold storage level, and provide better farm practices in drought prone areas to build situatable farming communities and reduce rural-urban migration of workers. In the area of agribusiness and mining, there is great potential for research into trade, investment opportunities and research between the two countries.

CONCLUSION

It is important for the democratic countries of Australia and India, where English is widely spoken and is the language of business, to establish social, political, economic, and Indian Ocean region strategic defence security relationship; given that India has no military ambitions to expand its control over other's lands and oceans, except for security of Indian coast and its borders with neighbouring countries. As Gurry (1993) in her paper 25 years ago, rightly asserted, "India should rank as one of Australia's most important neighbours" (p.5.10) for trade and economic relationships. However, now with the global COVID-19 pandemic, trade and travel between countries is at standstill with focus being on global efforts to promote hygiene, stop the spread of virus by closing borders, and to discover a vaccine for cure. The world will be a different place once the pandemic is over and countries will depend more on innovative online internet communication technologies to do business.

A Free Trade Agreement between Australia and India could offer significant opportunities for collaboration and cooperation in the areas of Australian expertise in education, tourism, healthcare, mining, alternative energy and agri-business industry for a peaceful and progressive bilateral trade relationship which is also mutually profitable. India will continue to be a key driver in the future growth of the Australian economy and source of export market in education, tourism, and mining resources and services, military expertise, internet and communication technologies, tele-medicine, alternative energy, agri-business, banking and insurance, healthcare, and information and communication technology services. Public-private partnerships are essential to have peace across borders and maritime trade route to have bilateral trade between any two countries to meet SDG's for inclusive development and growth.

The key is to capitalise on and harness Australia's Indian diaspora community from business, academics of Indian origin, alumni students, public and private sector skilled Indian migrants expertise in specific areas, their language skills and Indian links as part of Australia's future strategy for doing business with India and increase Australia's engagement with the Indian market, in order to grow trade in goods and services, travel, tourism, start-up innovation projects, and investment opportunities with India and vice versa. It is important to recruit highly skilled Indian migrant diaspora from different professions such as academics, medical, engineering and business entrepreneurs in Australian trade commissions to help in overcoming local challenges that Australians businesses face in India and to build a fruitful bilateral relationship at all levels people-to-people, education and research institutions, business and governments, with the aim of promoting the welfare of the population in both countries. Australian-Indian bilateral trade and diplomatic relationship will become more important, to develop a post- COVID-19 economic recovery, bi-lateral trade, investment maritime security and development strategy.

REFERENCES

ABARES. (2019). *Australian Agriculture Import--export*. Retrieved from http://www.agriculture.gov.au/abares

ABC News. (2019). *Adani protesters pick peak hour in Brisbane to 'stop the city'*. Retrieved from https://www.abc.net.au/news/2019-07-05/adani-protest-brisbane-cbd-promp-train-delay-warnings/11282030

ABS. (2019). *Statistics*. Retrieved from https://www.abs.gov.au/

Ahluwalia, M. S., & Little, I. M. D. (1998). *India's Economic Reforms and Development: Essays for Manmohan Singh*. Oxford University Press.

Asialink. (2019). *Where we Live. Address to Asialink PM Scott Morrison*. Retrieved from https://asialink.unimelb.edu.au/stories/australia-and-the-indo-pacific-an-address-by-prime-minister-scott-morrison

Australia-India Council (AIC). (2019). *Australia-India Council*. Available from dfat.gov.au/people-to-people/foundations-councils-institutes/australia-india-council/governance/Pages/australia-india-council-strategic-plan-2017-2020.aspx

Bergenwall, S. (2016). Assessing India's Rise and the Road Ahead. *Strategic Analysis*, *40*(5), 386–404. doi:10.1080/09700161.2016.1209905

Bhagwati, J. (1993). *India in Transition: Freeing the Economy*. Clarendon Press. doi:10.1093/acprof:oso/9780198288473.001.0001

Bhattacharya, S. C., & Jana, C. (2009). Renewable Energy in India: Historical Developments and Prospects. *Energy*, *38*(8), 981–991. doi:10.1016/j.energy.2008.10.017

Bhosale, S. (2018). Why India is Emerging as Australia's Natural Ally. *The Sydney Moring Herald*. Retrieved from https://www.smh.com.au/world/asia/why-india-is-emerging-as-australia-s-natural-ally-20180905-p501yp.html

Brewster, D. (2010). Australia and India: The Indian Ocean and the limits of strategic convergence. *Australian Journal of International Affairs*, *64*(5), 549–565. doi:10.1080/10357718.2010.513369

Campos, M. L., Morini, C., De Moraes, G. H., & Inacio, E. (2018). A Performance Model for Public–Private Partnerships: The authorized economic operator as an example. *RAUSP Management Journal*, *53*(2), 288–279. doi:10.1016/j.rausp.2017.07.002

CECA. (2019). *Comprehensive Economic Cooperation Agreement*. Retrieved from https://dfat.gov.au/trade/agreements/negotiations/aifta/Pages/australia-india-comprehensive-economic-cooperation-agreement.aspx

Chacko, P., & Davis, A. E. (2017). The natural/neglected relationship: Liberalism, identity and India-Australia relations. *The Pacific Review*, *30*(1), 26–50. doi:10.1080/09512748.2015.1100665

Chandel, S. S., Shrivastava, R., Sharma, V., & Ramasamy, P. (2016). Overview of the initiatives in renewable energy sector under the national action plan on climate change in India. *Renewable & Sustainable Energy Reviews*, *54*, 686–873. doi:10.1016/j.rser.2015.10.057

Chatterjee, S., Rae, A., & Ray, R. (2006). *Food Consumption, Trade Reforms and Trade Patterns in Contemporary India: How Do Australia and NZ Fit in?* Centre for Applied Economics and Policy Studies, Working Paper 2/06. Massey University, Palmerston North, New Zealand.

Commonwealth of Australia. (2010). *Australia-India: Joint Free Trade Agreement Feasibility Study*. Australian-Indian Government, DFAT.

Davis, M. J. (2020). Australia and China: Framing an Ambivalent Relationship. *Asian Studies Review*, *44*(2), 278–296. Advance online publication. doi:10.1080/10357823.2019.1698006

Department of Innovation Industry & Science (DIIS). (2019). *Collaborating with India on Science and Research*. Retrieved from www.industry.gov.au/funding-and-incentives/science-and-research/collaborating-with-india-on-science-and-research

DFAT. (2017). https://dfat.gov.au/about-us/publications/Documents/cot-cy-2017.pdf

DFAT. (2018a). https://dfat.gov.au/about-us/publications/Documents/cot-2017-18.pdf

DFAT. (2018b). *Indian Economic Strategy 2035*. Department of Foreign Affairs and Trade. Retrieved from https://dfat.gov.au/geo/india/ies/index.html

Ganguly, S. (2017). Had Modi truly changed India's foreign Policy? *The Washington Quarterly*, *40*(2), 131–143. doi:10.1080/0163660X.2017.1328929

Golechha, M. (2015). Healthcare agenda for the Indian government. *The Indian Journal of Medical Research*, *141*(2), 151–153. doi:10.4103/0971-5916.155541 PMID:25900948

Goodman, D. S. (2017). Australia and the China threat: Managing ambiguity. *The Pacific Review*, *30*(5), 769–782. doi:10.1080/09512748.2017.1339118

Gurry, M. (1993). Leadership and Bilateral Relations: Menzies and Nehru, Australia and India, 1949-1964. *Pacific Affairs*, *65*(4), 510–526. doi:10.2307/2760317

Gurry, M. (2012). India, the new centre of gravity: Australia-India relations under the Howards Government. *Journal of Southeast Asian Studies*, *35*(2), 282–305.

Gurry, M. (2013). A delicate balance: Australia's tilt to Pakistan and its impact on Australia-India relations. *Australian Journal of International Affairs*, *67*(2), 141–156. doi:10.1080/10357718.2012.750641

Hall, I. (2015). Is a 'Modi doctrine' emerging in India's foreign policy? *Australian Journal of International Affairs*, *69*(3), 247–252. doi:10.1080/10357718.2014.1000263

Hubbard, R. G., Garrett, A., Lewis, P., & O'Brian, A. (2019). Essentials of Economics, 4th (edn), Sydney: Pearson.

Indian Budget. (2019). *Indian Budget 2019*. Retrieved from https://www.indiabudget.gov.in/

Khare, V., Nema, S., & Baredar, P. (2013). Status of solar wind renewable energy in India. *Renewable & Sustainable Energy Reviews*, *27*, 1–10. doi:10.1016/j.rser.2013.06.018

Mayer, P., & Jain, P. (2010). Beyond Cricket: Australia–India Evolving Relations. *Australian Journal of Political Science*, *45*(1), 133–148. doi:10.1080/10361140903517759

Medhekar, A. (2003). Environmental, degradation, population and poverty in India. In R. Ghosh, M. Siddique, & R. Gabbay (Eds.), *Essays on development Issues: India and the Indian Ocean Region* (pp. 67–92). Atlantic Publishers and Distributors.

Medhekar, A. (2012). Managing the Growth of Medical Tourism by Public-Private Partnership in India. In K. Roy & S. Kar (Eds.), *Development Management in the Twenty First Century: Readings in World Development* (pp. 73–90). Nova Science.

Medhekar, A. (2019). Emerging Trends of Wellness and Medical Tourism in India. In S. Paul & S.K. Kulshreshtha, (Eds.), Global Developments in Healthcare and Medical Tourism. IGI Global. doi:091218-104208

Medhekar, A., Wong, H. Y., & Hall, J. E. (2019). Factors influencing inbound medical travel to India. *Journal of Health Organization and Management*, *33*(2), 155–172. doi:10.1108/JHOM-08-2018-0234 PMID:30950309

Menon, J. (2009). Dealing with the Proliferation of Bilateral Free Trade Agreements. *World Economy*, *32*(10), 1381–1407. doi:10.1111/j.1467-9701.2009.01187.x

Ministry of Education. (2020). National. *Educational Policy*, *2020*, •••. Retrieved from www.mhrd.gov.in/higher_education

Mishra, R. (2012). India-Australia Strategic Relations: Moving to the next level. *Strategic Analysis*, *36*(4), 657–662. doi:10.1080/09700161.2012.689537

Nguyen, T. H. (2017). Prospects of ASEAN-India Relations: An Analysis. *European Journal of Social and Human Sciences*, *4*(2), 1–8.

NORDEA. (2019). *Australia: Economic and Political Overview*. Retrieved from www.nordeatrade.com/en/explore-new-market/australia/economical-context

Observer Research Foundation (ORF). (2019). *Australia's Opportunity with the return ofNarendra Modi*. Retrieved from www.orfonline.org/expert-speak/australias-opportunity-with-the-return-of-narendra-modi-51897/

Patra, S. (2016). Role of SAARC in Convergence of South Asian economies. In Handbook of Research on Global Indicators of Economic and Political Convergence (pp. 144-169). IGI Global. doi:10.4018/978-1-5225-0215-9.ch007

Phillips, A. (2013). Australia and the challenges of order- building in the Indian Ocean region. *Australian Journal of International Affairs*, *67*(2), 25–140. doi:10.1080/10357718.2012.751965

Raghuramapatruni, R., & Chary, D. S. (2017). Trends and prospects of bilateral trading relations between India and Australia. *International Journal of Economic Research*, *14*(1), 599–616.

Ranjan, V. (2016). Australia and India *in Asia:* When 'Look West' Meets Act East. *Strategic Analysis*, *40*(5), 425–439. doi:10.1080/09700161.2016.1209906

Reserve Bank of Australia (RBA). (2020). *Monetary Policy*. Retrieved from https://www.rba.gov.au/

Salaam Balak Trust. (2019). *Industry Partnership Salaam Balak Trust*. Retrieved from www.cqu.edu.au/industry-and-partnerships/partnerships/community/salaam-baalak-trust

Sharma, N. K., Tiwari, P. K., & Sood, Y. R. (2013). A comprehensive analysis of strategies, policies and development of hydropower in India: Special emphasis on small hydro power. *Renewable & Sustainable Energy Reviews*, *18*, 460–470. doi:10.1016/j.rser.2012.10.017

Singh, U. B. (2016). Australia's 2016 Defence White paper: An Indian perspective. *Journal of Defence Studies*, *10*(2), 111–120.

Smith, G. (2010). Australia and the rise of India. *Australian Journal of International Affairs*, *64*(5), 566–582. doi:10.1080/10357710903544114

Thakur, R., & Sharma, A. (2018). India in Australia's strategic framing in the Indo-Pacific. *Strategic Analysis*, *42*(2), 69–83. doi:10.1080/09700161.2018.1439328

The Economic Times. (2018). *India to increase public health spending*. Retrieved from economictimes.indiatimes.com/news/economy/policy/india-to-increase-public-health-spending-to-2-5-of-gdp-pm-modi/articleshow/67055735.cms?from=mdr

The Indian Express. (2018). *Australian agriculture minister to visit India soon to resolve pulse trade issue*. Retrieved from www.newindianexpress.com/business/2018/jan/11/australian-agriculture-minister-to-visit-india-soon-to-resolve-pulses-trade-issue-1750925.html

The Indian Express. (2019). *80 percent framer suicide due to debt, loans from banks, not money lenders*. Retrieved from https://indianexpress.com/article/india/in-80-farmer-suicides-due-to-debt-loans-from-banks-not-moneylenders-4462930/

Tourism Research Australia (TRA). (2019). *International Tourism Results*. Retrieved from https://www.tra.gov.au/International/international-tourism-results

United Nations. (2019). *Sustainable Development Goals*. Retrieved from https://www.un.org/sustainabledevelopment/sustainable-development-goals/

Walton-Robert, M., & Rajan, S. I. (2020). Global demand for medical professionals drives Indians abroad despite acute domestic health-care workers shortages. *Online Journal of the Migration Policy Institute*. Retrieved from https://www.migrationpolicy.org/article/global-demand-medical-professionals-drives-indians-abroad

Wojczewski, T. (2019). Identity and world order in India's post-Cold War foreign policy discourse. *Third World Quarterly*, *40*(1), 180–198. doi:10.1080/01436597.2018.1552079

ADDITIONAL READING

Arora, S., Bahmani-Oskooee, M., & Goswamin, G. (2003). Lateral J-curve between India and her trading partners. *Applied Economics*, *35*(9), 1037–1041. doi:10.1080/0003684032000102172

Basrur, R. M. (2010). Scholarship on India's International Relations. *International Studies*. Advance online publication. doi:10.1177/002088171004600207

Panda, J. P. (2014). Factoring the RECP and the TPP: China, India and the Politics of Regional Integration. *Strategic Analysis*, *38*(1), 49–67. doi:10.1080/09700161.2014.863462

Rahman, M. M., & Mamun, S. A. K. (2016). Energy use, international trade and economic growth nexus in Australia: New evidence from an extended growth model. *Renewable & Sustainable Energy Reviews*, *64*, 806–816. doi:10.1016/j.rser.2016.06.039

Tandon, A. (2016). India's Foreign Policy priorities and the Emergence of a Modi Doctrine. *Strategic Analysis*, *40*(5), 349–356. doi:10.1080/09700161.2016.1209909

Wagner, C. (2016). The Role of India and China in South Asia. *Strategic Analysis*, *40*(4), 307–320. doi:10.1080/09700161.2016.1184790

Wilson, J. D. (2014). Mega-regional trade deals in the Asia-Pacific: Choosing between the TPP and RCEP. *Journal of Contemporary Asia*, *45*(2), 345–353. doi:10.1080/00472336.2014.956138

KEY TERMS AND DEFINITIONS

Bilateral Trade: Is an agreement of trade in goods and services, including tariff rates between two countries, such as Australia and India, which will mutually benefit both the countries in achieving sustainable development goals and inclusive economic development and growth.

Exports: When a country exports its good and services to another country. For example, Australia's major exports to India are coal, iron ore, education, and gold.

Free Trade Agreements (FTA): Where two or more countries have an FTA for certain good and services between them. FTA could be bilateral or multilateral.

Imports: When a country imports goods and services from another country. For example, Australia's main imports from India are refined oil, pearls and gems, and railway vehicles.

Inclusive Growth: Inclusive growth for developing country like India, means pro-poor growth, where there are equal opportunities for all, and the benefits from growth are allocated equally to all sections or members of the society, irrespective of class, creed, gender, religion, race or ethnicity.

Sustainable Development: Sustainable development aims to meet the human development goals along with sustainable use of natural resources, to meet the needs of the current and future generations.

Chapter 5
Population Aging and Prospect of China's Elderly Care and Its Related Industries

Mei Liu
https://orcid.org/0000-0002-3408-4914
Business School, Nottingham University, China

Qing-Ping Ma
https://orcid.org/0000-0002-4379-0378
Business School, Nottingham University, China

ABSTRACT

China becomes an aging society in a pace much faster than other countries because of its one-child policy implemented since 1980. This chapter examines the current situation of population aging in China, the government policies and regulations surrounding elderly care, and the experiences of other Asian and Oceanian countries in dealing with population aging. The rapid population aging poses severe challenges for the elderly care in China, which has not established an adequate social security system, but it also provides abundant opportunities for enterprises and entrepreneurs in the aging industry from other Asian and Oceanian countries as well as China. China can learn from the experiences of industrialized Asian and Oceanian countries and regions in developing its elderly care industry.

DOI: 10.4018/978-1-7998-4126-5.ch005

INTRODUCTION

Population ageing is poised to become one of the most significant social transformations of the twenty-first century, with implications for nearly all sectors of society, including labour and financial markets, the demand for goods and services, such as housing, transportation and social protection, as well as family structures and intergenerational ties (United Nations, 2019).

China is undergoing a population-aging process much faster than other countries. One key cause of the aging process is the one-child policy implemented very strictly by the Chinese government since 1980, which has dramatically reduced China's total fertility rate and changed the outlook of Chinese people on childbearing and family. Although the one-child policy was abolished in 2015 and now two children are allowed for all families, the most recent data on the birth rate suggest that the policy change has not increased the birth rate and that China's population is likely to decrease. Other East Asian countries such as Japan and Korea, which do not have any restriction on childbearing, also have a low birth rate, indicating that Chinese people may not change from having one child to having two or three, even though the Chinese government now encourages them to do so. The increased life expectancy and decreased birth rate will accelerate China's population-aging process and pose a serious challenge to China's social security system as well as to elderly care (Ma, 2014). As of 2018, people aged over 60 make up 17.3 percent of China's population, and the proportion of those aged 65 or above is 11.4 percent. If the new two-child policy fails to change people's outlook on childbearing and family size, the feared 4-2-1 pattern, i.e. one child is responsible for two parents and four grandparents, might become reality. In other parts of Asia and in Oceania, 27 percent of the population in Japan are aged 65 or above, and 16 percent are in Australia. China may benefit by drawing on their experiences of elderly care.

The challenge for China in social security and elderly care provides opportunities for the pension industry and elderly care and their related industries. The traditional elderly care system in China relies on adult children and parents living with their children when they need personal care. However, due to the 4-2-1 family pattern, a young adult or couple is certainly unable to care for six elderly people. The most efficient elderly care should be elderly residential care homes, with professional staff members providing services. The decrease in the total fertility rate may lead to a labor shortage and not enough workers being available for work in elderly care homes. Staff members in the elderly care homes will need many different tools to increase their productivity in terms of caring the elderly. Therefore, the production of equipment for elderly care may also become a promising manufacturing sector. Besides elderly care homes and equipment, pension and elderly-related other service sectors will also grow with the aging population. As the working population decreases, the demand for smart machines to help elderly people and their caregivers will increase.

The objectives of this chapter are to examine: 1) the current situation and future trend of China's population-aging process; 2) the prospects for China's elderly care industry and its related sectors; and 3) the potential for cooperation and business development for Asian and Oceanian countries in elderly care provision, technologies and related products and services. The rest of this chapter is structured as follows: the next section examines China's population-aging process; this is followed by a section investigating current issues and the Chinese government's policies and regulations regarding the elderly care industry; a section on other Asian and Oceanian countries' experience; and a section on the booming business opportunities in the Chinese elderly care market. The last section concludes the chapter.

POPULATION AGING IN CHINA

Population ageing refers to the increasing proportion of the elderly in the total population. Internationally, a country or region enters population aging when 10 percent of the total population is comprised of people who are 60 years or above, or when 7 percent of the population are aged above 65 years (Yang, 2014). According to the latest national population census in 2010,[1] 178 million people in China are aged 60 or above, which represents 13.3 percent of the total population, and is a 2.9 percentage points increase compared with the previous census in 2000. Around 120 million are aged 65 years or above, which accounts for 8.9 percent of the whole population, and is an increase of 1.9 percentage points from the previous census (S. Liu, 2011). It seems that since 1999, there is an acceleration of population aging in China. For example, there are over three million elderly people in Beijing, and the number is increasing rapidly. More than 500 people enter the ranks of the aged every day, and more than 120 people enter the 80-year-old and above category every day. In the next two or three decades, the elderly population will account for one-third of the total population (B. Li, Tai, & Xia, 2018).

As elsewhere in the world, population aging can be explained by a low fertility rate, rising life expectancy, and the cumulative effects of past changes in birth and mortality rates (Banister, Bloom, & Rosenberg, 2012). When the number of newborns is not sufficient to maintain a stable population, the proportion of elderly will increase (Ma, 2017). However, China is aging more rapidly than almost any other country in recent history because of the one-child policy that had been implemented for over 30 years. It led to a long period during which the birth rate was lower than the mortality rate. According to the United Nations (UN), China will take only 20 years for the proportion of the elderly population to double. By comparison, it took 61 years in Germany and 64 years in Sweden.

The total fertility rate is the average number of children a woman would bear over the course of her lifetime if current age-specific fertility rates remain constant throughout her childbearing years (Ma, 2014). When women on average give birth to fewer than two children each, the population will have fewer and fewer young people to work and contribute to the state pension systems (Ma, 2017). There has been large decline in China's fertility rate since the 1970s, as shown in Figure 1. From 5.8 in 1972, the total fertility rate of China declined in most of the years and reached a historical low of 1.0 in 2011. Since then it has remained at a stable level around 1.2.

Figure 1. Total fertility rate in China since 1970
Source: United Nations Population Division (2017a)

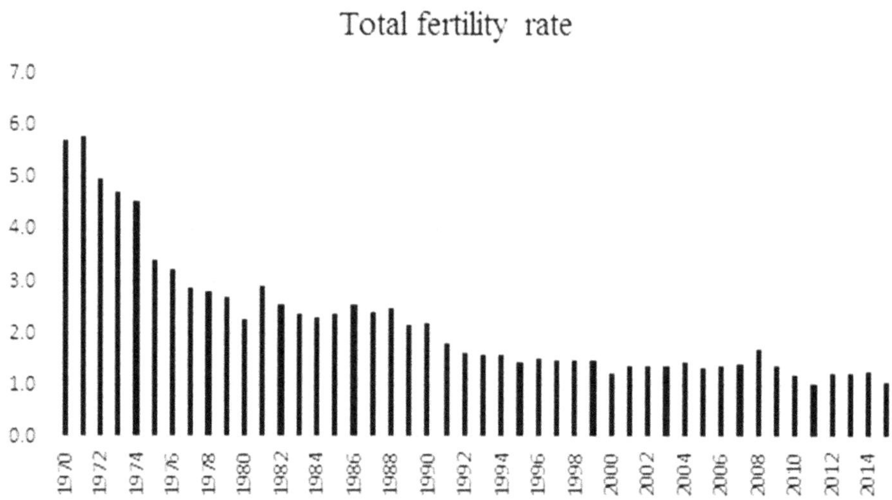

Unlike the declining total fertility rate, China's life expectancy has been rising rapidly. As shown in Figure 2, life expectancy at birth was 69.1 years in 1990. It rose to 76.7 in 2018 and is expected to rise further. Although some scholars argue that human longevity is approaching its limit (Sonnega, 2006), China's life expectancy is still below the lifespan limits that are proposed by researchers (Carnes, Olshansky, & Grahn, 2003; Fries, 1980; Olshansky, Carnes, & Cassel, 1990; Olshansky, Carnes, & Désesquelles, 2001) and may continue to increase further (Ma, 2012b).

Figure 2. Life expectancy at birth (years)
Source: United Nations Development Programme (2019)

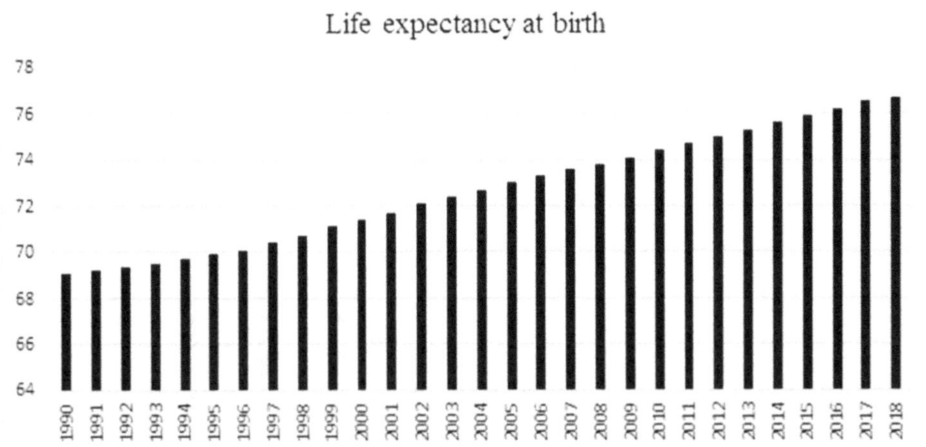

Due to the trends in fertility and life expectancy, the population aged 65 years and over have a rapidly growing share of the whole population in China. The dependency ratio is a widely used yardstick to measure the pressure of the young and elderly population on taxable income that is required to support entitlement programs. A high dependency ratio means that the working age population faces a greater burden in supporting the young and the aging populations. As shown in Figure 3, China's old-age dependency ratio (the ratio of the population aged 65 years or above per 100 population aged 20-64) was 14.5 percent in 2015. The UN estimates that this could rise as high as 47.9 percent by 2050 with the number of those over 65 rising from approximately 100 million in 2005 to approximately 330 million in 2050, roughly the population of the United States and twice the current population of Russia (United Nations Population Division, 2017b). It also shows from Figure 3 that from 2015 onwards, the dependency ratio rises more sharply than before. This implies that China's population aging will be more severe in the coming years.

Figure 3. Dependency ratio of China
Source: United Nations Population Division (2017b)

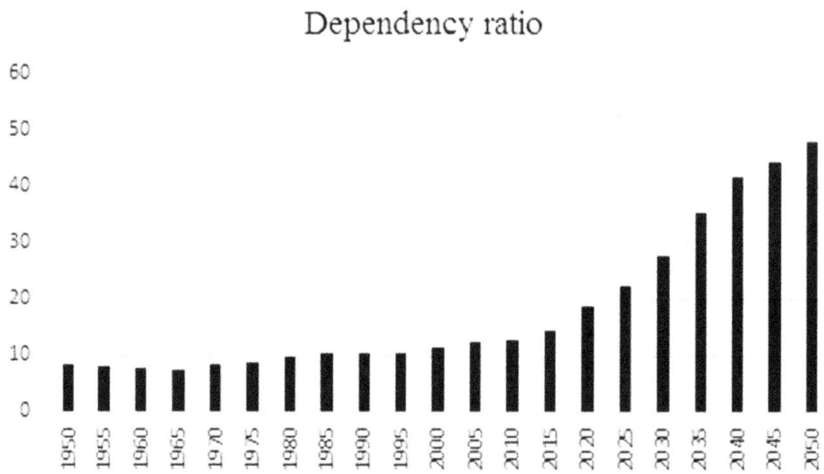

CURRENT ISSUES AND GOVERNMENT POLICIES

China's rapid aging process is reshaping society's view on elderly care, and the role of elderly care industry is gradually being appreciated. The Chinese government has long foreseen the challenges that may arise from an aging population. Besides the abolishment of the one-child policy in 2015, there has been a series of other policies and regulations to support the development of the elderly care industry (Jiangping Xu & Zhang, 2016).

Views on Elderly Care and Current Practices

People's views on the elderly have evolved over time. In primitive societies, there was "elderly killing" worldwide before "elderly care"; the elderly and sick were killed in many fishing and hunting tribes. Some scholars investigated 39 wild tribes in 1945 and found that half of them ill-treated their elderly (Y. Liu, 2018). Why does society change from "elderly killing" to "elderly care"? This has a close relationship with economic development. The higher productivity at more developed stages provides nearly enough food for everyone including the elderly. Moreover, people then began to realize the benefits and advantages for society of caring for their elderly.

In China, elderly care started from clan-elderly care and went through big-family elderly care and small-family elderly care before finally arriving at modern-elderly care. Each stage has been closely related to the economy and culture at the time

(Y. Liu, 2018). Family taking care of the elderly has long been a tradition and the dominant mode in Chinese society. Since the Chinese government began to implement the one-child policy in 1980 (Ma, 2017), the family size has been greatly reduced. With the increasing life expectancy, one child may have to care for two parents and four grandparents (the 4-2-1 pattern). The traditional family-elderly care is gradually transformed into modern-elderly care. Now elderly care is not only the responsibility of individuals, but also of the whole society. Although family elderly care is still the mainstream in China, the passive, dependent elderly care system will be transformed into an active and positive elderly care system in the future (Y. Liu, 2018).

According to Jiangping Xu and Zhang (2016), 90 percent of the elderly in China are cared for at home by family members. There are several reasons for this. Firstly, loyalty and filialness lie at the heart of traditional Chinese culture. People would like to take care of the elderly at home because they do not want to be regarded as being impious. Secondly, some old people have a bias against the nursing home. Thirdly, there are more freedom and privacy at home. Fourthly, the cost of family-elderly care is lower than that of nursing homes. However, there are disadvantages associated with family-elderly care as well. The children of the elderly may not have enough money or time for them, and emergency treatments may be delayed if there are few provisions for elderly care nearby.

Seven percent of the elderly population are taken care by the community. The community-elderly care mainly serves disabled and childless elderly people. It has several advantages. Firstly, the elderly people have more freedom and privacy. Secondly, the community provides help with food, transportation and living, thus it is very convenient for the old people. Thirdly and more importantly, the cost is low because the government provides allowances and support for community facilities. In addition, the community hospital can provide medical care for the elderly on a regular and timely basis.

Three percent of the old population are taken care at nursing homes. The nursing homes have three basic functions: 1) meeting the daily living requirements of the elderly with barrier-free facilities and necessary auxiliary function rooms; 2) providing rehabilitation care with facilities and equipment that can help the elderly to regain physiological functions to a certain extent or to slow down the decline of some physiological functions; and 3) providing emergency treatment and emergency services for the elderly experiencing sudden illness or other emergencies, so that the elderly can receive timely and effective help.

The main advantage of the nursing home is that the basic facilities are relatively complete, and safety is high. In addition, there are more people of similar age, which is a natural attraction for singles who like to be socially busy, and this can help them avoid a lonely life. However, freedom and privacy of the elderly are hard to achieve in most of the nursing homes. It is also more expensive to stay in the nursing home. The more comfortable a nursing home, the higher the fees it charges.

Challenges Faced by the Chinese Elderly Care Industry

The rapid aging of the population in China demands a rapid development of the Chines elderly care industry. However, unlike developed countries, China is aging at a time when its market economy is not mature, but the extent of aging is similar to that of the developed countries (Luo, 2015). It is estimated that China will become a developed country in the middle of the 21st century, but China's aging population will reach its peak before that (Johnston, 2019). The coming financial strains on the government due to aging of the population will force policymakers to re-evaluate spending and may slow down the pace at which pension cover is extended to everyone, an especially serious problem for low-income laborers with inadequate personal saving and no retirement coverage. The underdevelopment of the pension system will hinder the development of the elderly care industry.

Income inequality in China may also undermine the development of the elderly care industry. In 2012, the richest one percent owned more than one-third of the total national household wealth, while the poorest 25 percent owned less than two percent (Xie & Jin, 2015). In the elderly care industry, there is a big disparity as well. Although China has established a pension and medical insurance system for the whole society, the benefits depend on a person's employer (government, public utility, enterprise or self-employed), level of position, and residential registration (urban or rural). While many elderly people cannot enjoy many of the benefits provided by the system due to various reasons such as being farmers with rural residential registration in the west inland areas, some elderly people enjoy high-end pensions and medical care benefits. This exacerbates inequality within the society.

The development of the elder care industry is still on a low level, but it is unbalanced as well. The eastern region and coast cities entered the elderly care industry early and developed very fast, whereas the middle and western region of China entered the industry late and developed more slowly. The rural and urban areas are different in both residential income and infrastructure development. Most of the elderly people live in the rural area, where pensions are low and medical conditions are poor. The market for low-end elderly health care products has expanded in recent years, whereas there are few high- quality products in the market. While there is growing demand for elderly care services due to the huge amount of aging population, some facilities for the elderly are idle and some houses for the elderly are vacant. There are mismatches between supply and demand in different regions and in different segments of the market.

The rapid population aging in the rural areas also exacerbates the undersupply of elderly care. The one-child policy was more strictly implemented in urban than in rural areas. The birth rate in urban areas is lower than in rural areas (Wang, Zhao, & Zhao, 2017). Theoretically, the aging process should be faster in the urban areas. However, according to "Compilation of Statistics on Aging in China" published by the National Aging Committee, the aging process in rural areas surpassed that in urban areas in 2000. This appears to be caused by migration of rural young population to towns and cities, where there are more job opportunities with better incomes. The elderly population are left in the rural areas, which makes the population aging problem more severe in rural areas.

Government Regulations and Policies on Elderly Care

To promote and regulate the development of the elderly care industry, the State Council (the central government) issued its 35th Document on 6 September 2013, "Several Opinions of the State Council on Accelerating the Development of the Elderly Care Service Industry" (hereinafter referred to as the 35th document). The document provides an overall guideline for establishing a nationwide elderly care system for both urban and rural areas and developing the elderly care service industry. The Ministry of Civil Affairs, the Ministry of Finance, the National Development and Reform Commission, the Ministry of Education, and the National Bureau of Aging have also issued a number of policies and regulations in areas for which they are responsible to support the development of the elderly care industry. Although China's financial investment in the elderly care industry is still insufficient at present, fiscal policy can cover the basic needs in the elderly care service industry with increased input to weak areas (Jiangping Xu & Zhang, 2016).

The 35th document and related policies provide tax incentives to the elderly care institutions. These incentives include exemption from sales tax, property tax and urban land use tax, and corporate income tax for non-profit elderly care institutions. They also include exemption from half of the administration fees for establishing a profitable elderly care institution, and exemption from some administrative fees for elderly care services. There is a deduction from corporate income taxes for the donor to the amount of the donation to the non-profit elderly care institutions (Jiangping Xu & Zhang, 2016). A series of initiatives by the central and local governments provide preferential conditions for land use by elderly care facilities and elderly care institutions.

The 35th document also requires the development of courses for the training of elderly care professionals, better pay and subsidies to the elderly nursing staff and professionals, and encouragement of graduates from colleges and universities to engage in elderly care service. Local governments have also introduced policies that emphasize the importance of talent in the elderly care industry. They try to attract more working-age people into the elderly care industry by increasing the wages of elderly care staff.

Current policies and regulations encourage private capital to participate in the development of the elderly care service system. There are two main reasons for the lack of private capital in the elderly care industry. Firstly, the preferential policies on land use, taxes and fees lack operability because there is no detailed definition of "for-profit" and "non-profit" institutions. Secondly, some preferential policies are insufficiently rigid and are not effectively implemented (Guo & Zhang, 2014). The willingness of private capital to enter this field is not high. However, the government is now further increasing its support and encouraging private capital to participate in home care services, community care services, and the construction and renovation of elderly care service facilities. It also actively expanding the field of elderly care services in which private capital can participate and trying to create a welcoming policy environment for private capital to enter the industry.

The government also issued five national policies and guidelines to improve the infrastructure for elderly care facilities and equipment. They require that residential developers plan, construct, and inspect the residential buildings and the elderly care facilities at the same pace. They also require appropriate distribution of home and community care services for large-scale residential developments and appropriately centralized location in the vicinity for small-scale residential developments. The construction or renovation of cultural and sports facilities for the elderly should comply with the standards for the construction of old projects and the standards for the construction of barrier-free facilities. The Community Home Care Service Construction project was one of five major pension projects supported by the National Development Bank. The focus of support is the information platform for the aged care service and the facilitative community care service facilities that are conducive to the living conditions and living environment of the elderly.

The government also supports the development of the elderly care industry through the purchasing of public services. By purchasing public services, the government transfers public services originally undertaken by itself to social organizations, enterprises and institutions through public bidding, targeted entrustment, and invitation to bid, so as to improve the quality of public service supply and the efficiency of use of financial resources (Jialiang Xu & Zhao, 2013). The government uses four main modes to purchase elderly care services: delegation, indirect subsidy, service contract, and direct subsidy. In the delegation mode, the government hands over the management of the government-owned elderly care service institutions to the private firms and asks them to provide the corresponding elderly care services for the society. In the subsidy mode, the government subsidizes the clients according to certain standards to get elderly care services from private providers (Zhu, 2008).

In the service contract mode, the government signs service agreements or contracts with the elderly care service agencies, which provide specific elderly care services for the elderly. In the direct subsidy mode, the government provides direct funding to private elderly care institutions, which then provide basic elderly care services to low-income seniors, solitary, disabled and other elderly people in difficulties. The government purchase of elderly care services not only protects the benefits of the aged population, it also optimizes the use of limited resources. As a purchaser of elderly care services, the government should focus on the question of "what to buy" and "who to buy from", correctly handle the relationship between the purchaser and provider of the elderly care service, and realize the openness and transparency of the government's purchase of services (China Radio Network, 2014).

In sum, the Chinese elderly care industry is still in its infancy. As the aging problem has become more severe, central and local governments have been introducing policies and regulations to support the industry's development. The overall target is to lower the market access threshold for all nursing home ownerships, improve community facilities for at-home nursing for the elderly, train more professionals for the sector to expand services, and provide more employment opportunities. According to the "Smart Health and Pension Industry Development Action Plan (2017-2020)" issued by the Ministry of Industry and Information Technology recently, China will basically form a smart and healthy elderly industry system covering the whole life cycle, and create a group of smart health care services brand by 2020.

ELDERLY CARE IN INDUSTRIALIZED ASIAN AND PACIFIC COUNTRIES AND REGIONS

Several Asian and Oceanic countries and regions have established comprehensive social security systems. Their experiences could provide insights for China's policymakers and business practitioners. China may learn from these countries and regions as it develops its own elderly care and aging industry.

Japan's Aging Industry

As an Asian country deeply influenced by the Confucian culture, Japan regards elderly care as a virtue. Therefore, family elderly care has always been a tradition and core mode in Japanese society. Japan's aging population is large, and its aging process is the fastest among the developed countries. The increasing aged population and the declining proportion of children are serious problems faced by the Japanese society. Japan became an aging society in 1970 (Enomoto, 2008). Its life expectancy was highest in the world (Roser, Ortiz-Ospina, & Ritchie, 2013). Compared with other developed countries, its dependence ratio issue appeared to be especially severe (Ma, 2014). Its elderly care service system had obvious state-led welfare characteristics by that time. National and local governments have borne the main responsibility for elderly care services for a long time. Whether through annuity payments or community care, the government has led the design and operation of relevant systems. The government has also been the main source of funds.

In the 1970s and 1980s, the aging process of Japanese society accelerated. It became more difficult for the government to continue to bear the burden of providing elderly care services. The Japanese government began to attract private capital to the aging market. To regulate the behavior of private capital in the industry and protect the legitimate rights and interests of the elderly, the government set guidelines for industry operations. Subsequently, in response to the many problems in the elderly care industry, relevant associations and institutions in Japan proposed the "Aging Business Ethics Program" to regulate activities. The aging industry established a service quality standard certification committee to conduct quality certification and certification for the aged care service agencies and product suppliers. The certification results were made public, so that customers can make informed choices.

Japan officially implemented the "care insurance law" in 2000. A shared obligation between the individual and the government in the elderly care system was clearly stated. The law clarified the freedom of the elderly to choose the service provider based on their own needs. This free choice mechanism led to the formation of a competitive mechanism in the elderly care industry, which has alleviated supply shortages, improved efficiency, and improved service quality. At the same time, the care insurance system subsidized the demand side, which drove the demand for aged care, stimulated the enthusiasm of the supplier, and promoted the development of the Japanese elderly care market.

Japan's aging industry is characterized by a wide variety of health products and services. There are many health care products in Japan, from functional health drinks to health care tools, which are essential for Japanese life. The health industry is an important part of Abe's economic growth strategy that encourages private investment. In the "Healthy Longevity Industry Revitalization of Japan" event held in Tokyo in 2014, the head of the Japanese Ministry of Economy, Trade and Industry said that Japan's current health market is as high as 16 trillion yen, and he believed that the market would reach 26 trillion yen by 2020 (J. Liu, 2016).

Elderly care services in Japan are divided into two categories, namely, institutional pensions and window-time services. The institutional pension means that the elderly are accommodated in elderly care service institutions according to their economic situation, spiritual and cultural needs, and are personalized by a professional elderly care institution. The window-type service refers to service personnel entering the community. Door-to-door service provides services for the elderly at home. The serviced elderly can negotiate specific service plans with the service provider (Y. Liu, 2018).

The government has established cooperative relations with the private enterprises and with society (families and non-government organizations) and is committed to the improvement of the elderly service system. Japan's elderly care industry has moved on from the limitations of relying on state investment to develop the industry. The government can get the biggest social benefits at a small cost. The entry of a large number of private investors not only helps meet the needs of the elderly in Japan, it also contributes to a vibrant pension industry (Jiangping Xu & Zhang, 2016).

Australia's Aging Industry

Pension legislation has a history of over 60 years in Australia. In 1988, Australia became the first country in the world to establish a Minister for pensions. In 2015, the market value of the Australian aged-care industry totaled $A 18.3 billion, with a net income of $A 1.2 billion (Zhuang, 2017). The operating income of the industry comes mainly from government funds, which account for two thirds of the total revenue of the industry. For the residents, the expenses to be paid are mainly the basic daily expenses, which fully reflects Australia's "high welfare" characteristics. The market of Australian elderly care industry is relatively fragmented. Private enterprises have a market share of 37 percent, non-profit organizations account for 58 percent, and a 5 percent share is held by the government. The industry's largest company has a market share of only 4 percent. There are over 2,800 elderly care institutions in the market, of which about two-thirds have only care centers (Zhuang, 2017). Most of the small institutions do not have a sound operating system and lack skilled employees. The dispersed industry structure provides opportunities for large institutions to annex small competitors. Among private companies, Bupa is currently the oldest institution with the most beds, followed by Opal, Regis, Estia, Ality and Japara. Regis, Estia and Japara are listed on the Australian Securities Exchange (ASX).

The life expectancy of Australians has continued to increase. Currently, men have a life expectancy of 80 years old and women of 84 years. Australia's aging population is expected to increase gradually, and will exceed eight million by 2061 (Australian Bureau of Statistics, 2019). The growth rate of the population over 80 is significant, reflecting the improvement of the daily life and medical care quality and indicating that the demand for high-quality elderly care services will continue to rise. As early as 2011, the Australian government announced that, from July 2017, it would increase the retirement age by 0.5 years every two years. The retirement age in 2017 was 65.5 years old and will increase to 67 years from 2023.

At the same time, the government has been directly subsidizing individuals, and reducing its direct financial support for nursing homes. As early as April 2012, the government introduced the Living longer, living better (LLLB) reform plan, which aimed to gradually convert the entire nursing home subsidy system into a system based on "user pays". Such changes benefit the industry as a whole and deepen the level of competition in the industry. Operators with complete supporting services, reasonable price, and adequate beds can stand out, while relatively small and non-profit operators are negatively affected.

The LLLB reform program means that since July 1, 2015, the new payment standard allows nursing homes to charge their guests with either or both Daily Accommodation Payments (DAPs) or Refundable Accommodation Deposits (RADs). Prior to the new standard, most residents were only able to make DAPs. The government's relaxation of the payment standard has widened the sources of income for elderly care institutions. The conditions for receiving RADs are flexible. Institutions can now decide on the fees by themselves based on the standards, quality and location of the services, provided that the highest fees are disclosed on the government website to ensure transparency.

In addition to subsidies, additional policy support also contributes to the development of the elderly care industry. The most important change in the LLLB reform plan allows residents to make zero-interest loans to operators, providing them with more funds to increase their number of beds. The Australian Bureau of Statistics predicts that the population over the age of 85 years will double by 2031 and will then double again by 2045. There is a high probability that the elderly-care industry will be under-supplied. In order to cope with the rapid growth in the number of elderly people, Australia will need 70,000 extra beds by 2020. The government has gradually relaxed restrictions on the number of beds in nursing homes. In addition to competition within the industry, the boundaries between nursing homes, retirement homes and hospitals are becoming less and less obvious. Therefore, nursing homes seek diversification, especially diversification of services (such as nursing homes for Alzheimer's) and diversity of housing to meet the needs of different income groups and different health care demands.

From a broad perspective, the risks of the real estate market may impact the elderly care industry in Australia (Zhuang, 2017). The decline since 2017 in housing prices may reduce the ability of new residents to pay RADs, causing them to switch to paying DAPs. A risk also lies in the government's ability to continue to support the industry. The government's annual spending in the elderly care industry amounts to \$A 15.8 billion, and consumers themselves need to pay about \$A 4.4 billion (Grove, 2016). Considering the annual influx of people into Australia and the expansion of private wealth, the government may expect those who have the financial resources to bear the cost of elderly care by themselves. The ratio between payments from the government and consumers may shrink to 50:50 in the future.

Newly Industrialized Countries and Regions

Other industrialized Asian and Oceanic countries and regions also have successful experience in managing population aging. Elderly community centers are a unique feature in South Korea, with their diverse functions and dense concentration (Ahn Kwan-ok, 2016). There are 64,568 elderly community centers operating around South Korea, which provide places and services for elderly Korean citizens to pursue friendship, exchange information, and work on projects. The centers are primarily used by people aged between 75 and 84 years, the age when people begin to adopt a different lifestyle. People in the early stage of old age (65 -74) are reluctant to visit the centers since they remain in good health. People in the final stage of old age (85 or above) gradually drift away from the centers (Ahn Kwan-ok, 2016). The Korean Ministry of Health and Welfare conducted a survey of the elderly in 2015 and found that 85.5 percent of Koreans visit the center to socialize. Around three quarters of users were satisfied with the center. The main reasons given for being dissatisfied were that the centers do not meet users' needs (66.4 percent), poor quality of facilities (14.3 percent), shortage of programs (7.8 percent), and financial burden (5.6 percent). Central and local Korean governments provide large subsidies to the elderly community centers. South Korea's Ministry of Health and Welfare announced on 20 November, 2018 that it will be laying the foundation for comprehensive community care to provide the elderly with residential, medical, nursing, and care services in their homes and neighborhoods by 2025, shortly before Korea becomes a super-aged society (Hwang & Park, 2018).

Singapore has one of the best healthcare systems in the world. It spends less than 4 percent of GDP on healthcare, but has established the world's fourth best healthcare infrastructure (Institute for Management Development, 2010). The government's creative use of the Central Provident Fund (CPF), a mandatory savings plan for workers primarily to fund their retirement, has been a key factor in controlling healthcare costs (Coronado, 2015). Medisave, the CPF's medical savings component, enables Singaporeans to pay for much of their own medical care. The country's other two systems are a low-cost medical insurance program (MediShield) and a social safety net (Medifund). The 3Ms (Medisave, MediShield, and Medifund) play an integral role in the success of the system (Coronado, 2015). With the 3M system, most Singaporeans pay little or nothing for hospitalization. The affordable and sustainable healthcare financing model contributes a lot to elderly care in Singapore. Besides having a superior health care system, the Ministry of Health and the Ministry of National Development plan to launch a new assisted living scheme, which combines public housing with care services such as health screenings, exercise programs, housekeeping services, 24/7 emergency support, care coordination and personal care (Kit, 2019).

The Hong Kong Mortgage Corporation Limited (HKMC) launched the Reverse Mortgage Program on 11 July 2011. The Program aims to provide elderly people in Hong Kong with an alternative means of raising cash by using their dwelling place as collateral. Reverse mortgage is a loan arrangement. The elderly use their residential property as collateral to borrow from a lender. The elderly remain the owner of the property and can continue to stay in the property for the rest of their life. They will receive monthly payouts either over a fixed period of 10, 15 or 20 years or throughout their entire life, and they may borrow lump-sum amounts for specific purposes when needed. When the reverse mortgage loan terminates, the elderly (or the elderly's personal representatives) have the preferential right to redeem the property by repaying to the lender in full the outstanding loan amount owed under the reverse mortgage. If the elderly (or the elderly's personal representatives) do not exercise such right, the lender will sell the property to recover the outstanding loan amount. If the sale proceeds from the property exceed the loan amount owed, the lender will pass the surplus to the elderly. If there is any shortfall, the elderly (or their inheritors) need not worry as the shortfall will be borne by HKMC under an insurance arrangement between the lender and HKMC (HKMC, 2019). By 2014, the program had received only 624 applications. Likely causes for the low participation rate include lack of awareness and knowledge about the scheme, and an expectation that property prices would go up. The scheme is not a retirement welfare plan or an investment arrangement, and no government subsidies except for insurance by HKMC or investment gains or losses are involved (V. J. Li, 2016).

The elderly and long-term care service is one of the eight key industries in Taiwan. To promote the long-term care services, the government launched the "Long Term Care Act 1.0" plan in 2008. After eight years of implementation, they launched the "Long Term Care Act 2.0", which plans to ramp up spending on its elderly population. The new legislation greatly expands the type of services provided by the government to care for the elderly, as well as the scope of people capable of receiving the services (Ferry, 2017). The initial act covers low-income seniors or seniors suffering from severe disabilities. It offers services like home nursing, home and community-centered rehabilitation, subsidies for rent and other living costs, and transportation services. The services are provided through non-profit organizations under contract from local health and welfare departments using funding from the central government. The new act has increased the number of eligible seniors, as well as service items from eight to 17. Among the new categories are dementia care, family-care support, community-based preventive care, integrated services for aboriginal groups in remote areas, and hospital discharge plans and transition care (Lin & Huang, 2016).

BUSINESS OPPORTUNITIES IN THE ELDERLY CARE PROVISIONS

Broadly speaking, the aging industry includes three sub-industries: the core industry, related industry and extensional industry. The core industry includes providers of housing, social services and medical care that are directly related to elderly people's life. The related industry includes providers of elderly care products and other services besides the core services. For example, the supplier of the elderly care institutions, the training and labor market for elderly care services, the consultancies and suppliers that are related to the medical care services, as well as the entertainment for the elderly. The extensional industry includes the financing, insurance, and security markets (Y. Liu, 2018).

China has the largest number of aged persons in the world and it will also have the largest market for elderly care. Dang (2016) thinks that the aging industry will become the biggest industry in China. According to Y. Liu (2018), the total annual income of elderly is around ¥400 billion and will reach ¥5,000 billion in 2050. Since the elderly tend to have lower consumption expenditure proportionally, most of their income could go into the elderly care industries. Currently, the market value of goods and services in the aging industry is less than ¥200 billion. The difference implies a great gap between supply and demand in the aging industry. China has an urgent need to develop the elderly care industry, which will provide abundant business opportunities for enterprises and entrepreneurs from Asian and Oceanian countries.

Elderly Care Services

Elderly care services are the core of the aging industry. According to the sixth national census in 2010, 123 million households in China have at least one member that is 60-years old or above. Forty-three million households are empty nest families, and account for 35 percent of all households. Empty nest families are more common among the urban population. The number of households with a member 60 years old or above is 31 million, of which empty-nest families are 12 million, accounting for 37 percent. According to the National Population Development Strategy Research Report's estimate, the number of households with 60-year-olds or above people will reach 133 million by 2020. If the empty-nest family ratio is 35 percent, the number of empty-nest families is about 47 million (Lu, 2018). If there are no adult children taking care of the elderly at home, more elderly, especially elderly from the empty-nest families, can be expected to move into residential care homes.

According to the Ministry of Civil Affairs, China had 155,000 elderly nursing institutions and facilities in 2018, up by 10.6 percent year-on-year. The number of beds climbed to 7.44 million, an increase of 2 percent year-on-year (Hu, 2018). The nursing home projects are constructed by real estate developers and can be divided into three categories: high-end, middle-end, and low-end. The high-end nursing homes charge more than ¥1.5 million membership fee per resident, or have a selling price above ¥20,000 per square meter. The middle-end nursing homes charges a membership fee of ¥0.5 to 1 million, or a selling price of ¥10,000 to 20,000 per square meter. Low-end projects, mostly state-owned nursing homes under the welfare system, charge a few hundred or thousand yuan per month, and provide very limited services (Zhuang, 2017). In other words, only the high and middle-end nursing homes provide high-quality services for the elderly. The number of elderly people with an annual household income (including children's income) of more than ¥1.5 million in China is 10.2 million. That is, only 10.2 million people have the economic capacity to enjoy the true meaning of elderly services (Zhuang, 2017). More nursing homes are needed, especially in the rural areas of China where the income of the elderly is low and the working-age population is migrating to the cities.

The Chinese government has been lowering the threshold for private and foreign capital to invest in the elderly-care industry. In 2015, the Ministry of Civil Affairs and the National Development and Reform Commission jointly released a set of guidelines aimed at encouraging private capital to invest in the elderly nursing market, including at-home nursing, in-community nursing and professional institutions (Hu, 2018). Foreign investments have a lower market access threshold, which provides increasing opportunities to tap the potential of the Chinese market. So far, there are no leading Chinese brands in the field, and foreign companies can work with local partners (Hu, 2018). Elderly care homes owned and operated by non-government entities have proliferated across major urban centers in China, but little is known about the characteristics of these institutions (Feng et al., 2011). There is a great opportunity for Asian and Oceanic companies. Countries such as Japan, Australia, and Singapore all experienced population aging earlier than China and have aging markets that are mature. Companies in those countries could consider investing in the Chinese market. There have been some pioneering companies. On 16 November 2015 the Australian Trade Commission held the first "Australia China International Ageing Industry Summit" in Beijing. This was the first Australian aging industry delegation to visit China after the signing of the China-Australia Free Trade Agreement in June 2015. It is also the largest China-Australia pension and health industry high-level event held in China so far (Zhang, 2015). The Chinese government encourages overseas and private capital to invest in the elderly care service industry.

The elderly will have more choice on the market and will benefit from the diverse elderly care services provided by different institutions. The local and foreign firms have opportunities to cooperate and jointly exploit the market.

Elderly Care Equipment and Products

The providers of elderly care products and equipment form a key component of the elderly care related industry. The number of aging persons is increasing in China, but the products and equipment for the elderly are comparatively simple-functioned and of poor quality. The equipment and products for the elderly may be classified into four categories. The first category is equipment and products for personal use, which is to meet elderly's daily needs, such as eating, clothing, bedding, showering, and transportation. The second is equipment and products to make elderly's life more convenient and comfortable, such as wheelchairs and in future probably smart machines that could carry and lift heavy objects for the elderly and smart wheelchairs that carry the elderly to where they want to go. The third is tools for caregivers, who help both professional staff and family members in taking care of the elderly. The fourth is smart machines and robots that can replace caregivers partially or entirely in future. Traditionally, elderly care has been mainly to meet the basic requirements of the elderly. With new technologies, most of the efforts should be made to develop products and equipment that ultimately improve elderly's quality of life and dignity in old age.

For the first category, there is still great potential to develop food, clothes, and personal hygiene and cosmetic products for the elderly, compared with the market for young children. Delicious, soft, and easy to chew foods with nutrients for the health of the elderly could potentially have a large market. For the second category, products like walking sticks, wheelchairs, and trollies will provide convenience when the elderly go out. Furniture designed to be elderly-friendly will help them to live independently. Health-monitoring equipment, such as electrocardiography recorders, blood pressure monitors, blood glucose meters, blood oxygen monitors, body temperature detectors, weight detectors, and body fat detectors can help the elderly learn their health status without going to a hospital. Community caregivers can also use these tools to monitor the health of the elderly and help the elderly to live independently before they have to live in nursing homes. This will make these products belong to the third category of helping the caregiver's work. The positioning system, one-click calling device, and voice-calling equipment may provide convenience in case of emergency. Many trendy gadgets targeting young people can also be tailor-designed for the elderly, such as smart bracelets, smart watches, and smart phones that can monitor the vital signs of the elderly and alert relevant people in an emergency.

For the third category, tools to improve the efficiency and quality of the caregivers' work will have a huge market as the proportion of the aged population keeps growing. Tools for cleaning and lifting can greatly reduce the caregivers' physical workload. Portable health machines, rehabilitation training equipment and smart, integrated bed chairs can facilitate caregivers' daily work and improve efficiency. Detectors can be installed in toilets, living rooms and bedrooms. If an elderly person remains in the toilet over a certain period of time, an alarm can inform the caregiver, so that the caregiver does not need to accompany the elderly all the time. Furthermore, an information management and communication system can be built on a unified cloud platform. The information from the detectors can be synchronized to the community service center and the adult children. The life track and the living conditions of the elderly can be learned and notified in real time. Moreover, the accumulated data can help the caregiver and elderly care institutions to improve their service quality.

In January 2018, Chongqing Pomelo Robots cooperated with Longshan Nursing Home to pilot a smart retirement project. During the two months' trial, except for some elderly people who are particularly old and unable to experience, most of the elderly became deeply fond of the grapefruit robot. Every day, the robot chats with the elderly. It also plays their favorite drama, Peking operas, and news of interest to the aged population. Every night, the elderly have a video chat with their family members through the robot. The elderly can control the operations of the robot by simply speaking (speech), which is simple and easy to do (Lu, 2018).

Artificial intelligence technology is developing rapidly. In the future, elderly care robots as a device integrating most of the existing functions will gradually replace the simple smart product and become the product with the largest market share in the smart elderly care equipment industry. At the same time, it will replace some human caregivers and perform many of the tasks that are currently being undertaken by caregivers. Specifically, the aging population and the increase in the number of empty-nest families brought about by the one-child policy will make the demand for smart elderly care robots grow strongly, especially for smart-age robots with escort, daily care, medical care, and other versatile functions.

Financial Market for Elderly Care

Financial services play a key role in the extensional aging industry. To finance their retirement, most people save a part of their income when they are young and middle-aged and spend the accumulated capital to support their elderly life. The capital accumulation contributes to the growth of a country's whole financial system. The current financial market in China is underdeveloped in terms of supporting elderly care. Retired urban residents mainly live on their state pensions, while elderly citizens in rural areas depend largely on their personal savings and their working children. The state pensions for the rural elderly are much smaller than those for the urban retired workers. Although the government encourages enterprises to set up occupational pensions for their employees, most employees do not have occupational pensions. With the gradual opening up of China's financial market, there will be many opportunities for financial institutions from other Asian and Oceanic countries as well as from China.

Since China's state pension system will face increasing pressure from population aging, occupational or enterprise pensions (called enterprise annuities in China) and private pensions will experience strong growth in the future. The development of China's pension system is extremely uneven. International organizations such as the World Bank advocate three pillars for pension provision: the first pillar is basic state pensions; the second is occupational or enterprise pensions; and the third is private savings and private pension plans. The first pillar accounts for the largest proportion in China's pension insurance system, while the second and third pillars have very small proportions. Therefore, the second and third pillars need to grow tremendously to catch up with developed countries and there are business opportunities during this process. Financial institutions in Australia, Hong Kong, Japan, and Singapore with expertise in managing occupational pensions and private pensions and designing financial products according to customer needs could play an important role.

Financial institutions could develop different types of financial products that are tailored to different groups of elderly people. A key risk in pension provision which has not been adequately covered until recently is the longevity risk, i.e. the uncertainty of how long a person will live. Financial tools are being developed for trading, hedging and insuring longevity risk (Ma, 2014), so that enterprises, financial institutions and governments can insure longevity risk in their pension programs. The life market, where assets and liabilities linked to longevity (or mortality) are traded, is the world's newest capital market (Blake, Cairns, & Dowd, 2011). Mortality and longevity related derivatives have been developed. In the mortality and longevity (or survivor) swap, counterparties swap fixed series of payments in return for series of payments linked to the numbers of a given cohort who die in a given year (mortality swap) or who survive in a given year (longevity or survivor swap) (Dawson, Blake, Cairns, & Dowd, 2010). Longevity bonds can also be developed.

Reverse mortgage (discussed earlier) and other innovations using real estate for elderly finance have also been developed in China. Many regions have tried to support the elderly through the real estate owned by the elderly. Beijing, Shanghai, Guangzhou, and Wuhan are the pilot cities in China to finance the elderly through real estate (Jiangping Xu & Zhang, 2016). There are both successful and unsuccessful models. Under the renting model, the elderly nursing home and the real estate brokerage company collaborate, with the brokerage company responsible for letting out the houses of the elderly and using the rent obtained to pay the expenses for the elderly in the nursing home. Under the housing replacement model, the elderly mortgage their property and move into the nursing home after notarization. All the expenses in the nursing home are exempted for life, and the property rights of the house belong to the nursing home after the death of the elderly. Under the housing self-help model, the elderly sell their own property rights to the provident fund management center, and collect a one-off payment. The provident fund management center leases the house to the elderly according to the market price. The proceeds from the sale of the house can be freely used by the elderly after deducting the rent, deposit and related transaction costs.

CONCLUSION

As the currently most populous country with a population aging faster than in most major countries, China's future demand for elderly care will be enormous and its speed of population aging may make it less well prepared for this development than developed countries such as Japan and Australia. This will provide business opportunities not only for entrepreneurs in China, but also for enterprises in other Asian and Oceanic countries with expertise and technologies in elderly care and related equipment and products. China's elderly care industry is in its early growing stage and far from meeting the real demand of the society. Now the family structure makes it impossible for one child to look after several elderly people including parents and grandparents, which forces people to change their understanding of how elderly people should be looked after. There is an increasing number of people who accept the idea of receiving residential care in a care home when they can no longer live independently. The change of outlook on this issue will increase the demand for residential elderly care homes. The residential care homes should improve their operational and management ability, and diversify their services. Even for the elderly who can take care of themselves, equipment and products to facilitate their daily life will still be needed in large quantities as the population ages. Research and development in equipment and products for elderly care will grow in importance. More financial products targeting the elderly are also needed in the financial market. China's experience will also be helpful for other Asian and Oceanic countries seeking to provide quality care for their elderly population.

REFERENCES

Ahn Kwan-ok, G. (2016). *Elderly community centers a unique feature of aged life in South Korea.* Retrieved from http://english.hani.co.kr/arti/english_edition/e_national/776262.html

Australian Bureau of Statistics. (2019). *Population clock.* Retrieved from https://www.abs.gov.au/AUSSTATS/abs@.nsf/Web+Pages/Population+Clock?opendocument&ref=HPKI

Banister, J., Bloom, D. E., & Rosenberg, L. (2012). Population aging and economic growth in China. In M. Aoki & J. Wu (Eds.), *The Chinese economy, International economic association series* (pp. 114–149). Palgrave Macmillan. doi:10.1057/9781137034298_7

Blake, D., Cairns, A., & Dowd, K. (2011). The new life market: from survivor bonds to life settlements securitization. In Q.-P. Ma (Ed.), *Private capital and road to developed economy* (pp. 111–151). Economic Science Press.

Carnes, B. A., Olshansky, S. J., & Grahn, D. (2003). Biological evidence for limits to the duration of life. *Biogerontology, 4*(1), 31–45. doi:10.1023/A:1022425317536 PMID:12652187

China Radio Network. (2014). *A relatively complete government procurement service system will be established in 2020.* Retrieved from http://www.chinanews.com/gn/2014/10-06/6651510.shtml

Coronado, D. (2015). Singapore: Focus on eldercare. *Health Management, 15*(2).

Dang, J. (2016). *Aging industry is the largest new economy in the future.* Retrieved from http://www.cncaprc.gov.cn/contents/20/177814.html

Dawson, P., Blake, D., Cairns, A., & Dowd, K. (2010). Survor derivatives: A consistent pricing framework. *The Journal of Risk and Insurance, 77*(3), 579–596. doi:10.1111/j.1539-6975.2010.01356.x

Enomoto, N. (2008). *Changing Consumer Values and Behavior in Japan: Adaptation of Keio Department Store Shinjuku. In The Silver Market Phenomenon.* Springer.

Feng, Z., Zhan, H. J., Feng, X., Liu, C., Sun, M., & Mor, V. (2011). An industry in the making: The emergence of institutional elder care in urban China. *Journal of the American Geriatrics Society, 59*(4), 738–744. doi:10.1111/j.1532-5415.2011.03330.x PMID:21410445

Ferry, T. (2017). *Long-Term care for Taiwan's elderly*. Retrieved from https://topics.amcham.com.tw/2017/03/caring-taiwans-elderly/

Fries, J. F. (1980). Aging, natural death and the compression of morbidity. *The New England Journal of Medicine, 303*(3), 130–135. doi:10.1056/NEJM198007173030304 PMID:7383070

Grove, A. (2016). *Aged care: a quick guide*. Research paper series, 2016-17. Parliament of Australia, Department of Parliament Services, Social Policy Section.

Guo, L., & Zhang, Y. (2014). The changes and evaluation of China's private capital participating in the construction of elderly care service system. *Academic Forum,* (4), 90-94.

HKMC. (2019). *Reverse Mortgage Programme*. Retrieved from http://www.hkmc.com.hk/eng/our_business/reverse_mortgage_programme.html

Hu, Y. (2018). *Measures to boost care for the elderly*. Retrieved from http://www.chinadaily.com.cn/a/201812/04/WS5c05d3a6a310eff30328ed7f.html

Hwang, Y. R., & Park, H. J. (2018). *Comprehensive community care system to allow elderly Koreans to live in their homes by 2025*. Retrieved from http://english.hani.co.kr/arti/english_edition/e_national/871188.html

Institute for Management Development. (2010). *World Competitiveness Yearbook*. Author.

Johnston, L. A. (2019). The Economic Demography Transition: Is China's 'Not Rich, First Old'Circumstance a Barrier to Growth? *The Australian Economic Review, 52*(4), 406–426. doi:10.1111/1467-8462.12325

Kit, T. S. (2019). *New assisted living model for seniors in the works, public consultations to start soon*. Retrieved from https://www.channelnewsasia.com/news/singapore/new-assisted-living-model-for-seniors-in-the-works-public-11317046

Li, B., Tai, S., & Xia, K. (2018). *Coping with aging, see how the capital Beijing "toughs up"*. Retrieved from http://www.xinhuanet.com/2018-06/22/c_1123018685_2.htm

Li, V. J. (2016). *Housing Policies in Hong Kong, China and the People's Republic of China*. ADBI Working Paper. Tokyo: Asian Development Bank Institute (ADBI).

Lin, Y.-Y., & Huang, C.-S. (2016). Aging in Taiwan: Building a society for active aging and aging in place. *The Gerontologist, 56*(2), 176–183. doi:10.1093/geront/gnv107 PMID:26589450

Liu, J. (2016). The gap between social health and longevity industry and national health in Japan. *Chinese and Foreign Entrepreneurs,* (13), 114.

Liu, S. (2011). China's aging population status and countermeasures analysis. *Chinese Urban Economy,* (29), 298-298.

Liu, Y. (2018). The marketization development of China's aging industry. Beijing: Social Sciences Academic Press (China).

Lu, L. (2018). *Analysis of smart old-age equipment industry in 2018*. Retrieved from https://www.qianzhan.com/analyst/detail/220/180201-5ff84cbc.html

Luo, B. (2015). China Will Get Rich Before It Grows Old. *Foreign Affairs*, *94*, 19.

Ma, Q.-P. (2012b). Government and individual strategy for dealing with the increasing post-retirement life expectancy. In A. Tavidze (Ed.), *Progress in Economics Research* (Vol. 26, pp. 1–29). Nova Science Publisher.

Ma, Q.-P. (2014). Financing a fair and efficient pension system: issues and solutions. In T. Reilly (Ed.), *Pensions: policies, new reforms and current challenges* (pp. 1–25). Nova Science Publisher.

Ma, Q.-P. (2017). Pension provision in the robotic age. In A. Webb (Ed.), *Pensions: Global issues, perspectives and challenges* (pp. 1–38). Nova Science Publisher.

Olshansky, S. J., Carnes, B. A., & Cassel, C. (1990). In search of Methuselah: Estimating the upper limits to human longevity. *Science*, *250*(4981), 634–640. doi:10.1126cience.2237414 PMID:2237414

Olshansky, S. J., Carnes, B. A., & Désesquelles, A. (2001). Prospects for human longevity. *Science*, *291*(5508), 1491–1492. doi:10.1126cience.291.5508.1491 PMID:11234076

Roser, M., Ortiz-Ospina, E., & Ritchie, H. (2013). *Life expectancy*. Our World in Data.

Sonnega, A. (2006). The future of human life expectancy: have we reached the ceiling or is the sky the limit. *Research Highlights in the Demography and Economics of Aging, 8*, 1-4.

United Nations. (2019). *Ageing*. Retrieved from https://www.un.org/en/sections/issues-depth/ageing/

United Nations Development Programme. (2019). *Human Development Reports Data (1990-2018).* Retrieved from http://hdr.undp.org/en/data#

United Nations Population Division. (2017a). *World Fertility Data 2017*. Retrieved 2020/4/26 https://www.un.org/en/development/desa/population/publications/dataset/fertility/wfd2017.asp

United Nations Population Division. (2017b). *World population prospects 2017.* Retrieved from https://population.un.org/wpp/DataQuery/

Wang, F., Zhao, L., & Zhao, Z. (2017). China's family planning policies and their labor market consequences. *Journal of Population Economics*, *30*(1), 31–68. doi:10.100700148-016-0613-0

Xie, Y., & Jin, Y. (2015). Household wealth in China. *Chinese Sociological Review*, *47*(3), 203–229. doi:10.1080/21620555.2015.1032158 PMID:26435882

Xu, J., & Zhang, D. (2016). *Research on investment potential and policy of China's aging industry*. Beijing: Economic Daily Press.

Xu, J., & Zhao, T. (2013). The Realistic Dilemma and Path Innovation of Government Purchasing Public Service: Practice in Shanghai. *China Administration*, *8*, 26–30.

Yang, Y. (2014). *Report on the Development of Aging Society and Pension Security in China (2013)*. Tsinghua University Press.

Zhang, H. (2015). Australia wants to enter the Chinese pension market. *Youth Reference*. Retrieved from http://qnck.cyol.com/html/2015-11/25/nw.D110000qnck_20151125_1-11.htm

Zhu, Y. (2008). Public Policy Analysis of Government's Purchase of Elderly Care Services. *Journal of Tianshui College of Administration, 2008*(4), 72-76.

Zhuang, Z. (2017). *Focus on "Red Sunset", analyze the Australian aged care industry*. Retrieved from https://zhuanlan.zhihu.com/p/30365815

KEY TERMS AND DEFINITIONS

4-2-1 Pattern: One child is responsible for two parents and four grandparents.

Aging Industries: Industries that provide elderly care as well as elderly care associated products and services.

Empty Nest Family: Households without prime-age adults which include four types, family comprised of single elderly, family comprised of one elderly and juveniles, family comprised of an old couple, and family comprised of an old couple and juveniles.

Life Expectancy: The number of years a newborn infant could expect to live if prevailing patterns of age-specific mortality rates at the time of birth stay the same throughout the infant's life.

Old Age Dependency Ratio: The ratio between the population aged 65 or above and that aged 15-64 or 20-64.

Population Aging: The increasing proportion of the elderly in the total population. Internationally, a country or region goes into population aging when 10 percent of the total population is comprised of people who's 60 years above, or when 7 percent of population are aged above 65.

Total Fertility Rate: The average number of children a woman would bear over the course of her lifetime if current age-specific fertility rates remain constant throughout her childbearing years.

ENDNOTE

1 This refers to the sixth population census in China. The seventh population census will be undertaken in November 2020.

Chapter 6
Aged Care Services in India:
Challenges and Opportunities for Australian Aged Care Service Providers

Wadad Kathy Tannous
Western Sydney University, Australia

Divya Ramachandran
University of Sydney, Australia

ABSTRACT

India is the world's largest democracy and second most populous country with nearly 1.4 billion people. With reduced birth rates and increasing lifespans, it had nearly 104 million 'senior citizens' in 2011, expected to grow to 300 million by 2050. Providing care for the elderly in India is a growing public and private concern. Filial piety is embedded in culture and long-term care for parents and the elderly is expected from children. However, over the last five decades there have been rapid changes in socioeconomic patterns with increasing mobility for work and rise of nuclear households. Despite this, elder care is still largely underdeveloped, with lack of formal training in geriatric care and geriatric care curriculum in medical education. Australia has a highly evolved elderly care system with care services that includes retirement villages, home care, residential care, and flexible care. These are provided by subsidization from the government and private user pay system. Australia is well poised to provide aged care expertise and services and shape elderly care in India.

DOI: 10.4018/978-1-7998-4126-5.ch006

INTRODUCTION

Aims and Objectives

The aim of this chapter is to examine demand and supply of elderly care in India and opportunities for Australian aged care services in India. It begins by detailing the aged care sector in India including insights into Indian culture and possible impacts on services' provisions. This will be followed by description of this sector in Australia and its potential contribution to India's market.

Specific research questions are:

- What is the profile (prevalence, demography, socioeconomic status, religious and cultural status) of aged populations in India?
- How are elderly currently cared for in India?
- What factors are driving the demand for elderly care services in India?
- What legislation, regulation and policy frameworks exist for elderly care in India?
- What is the supply of aged care services in India?
- What are unique challenges and opportunities for aged care services in India?
- What are the supply and service provision of aged care in Australia?
- What opportunities are there for providers of Australian aged care service in supporting this sector in India?

BACKGROUND

Ageing is a global phenomenon, with an unprecedented growth in the number of persons aged over 65 years of age, attributed to increasing lifespans and reduced birth-rates. World over in 2019, 9% of people or 703 million were over 65 years of age, and projections indicate that this number will jump to 1.5 billion by 2050 (United Nations, 2019). India is no exception, with 87 million 'senior citizens' (over 60 years of age) in 2011, and an expected growth to 300 million by 2050 (United Nations Population Fund, 2017).

Providing care for the elderly in India is a growing public and private concern. Filial piety is embedded in Indian culture and long-term care for parents and the elderly is expected from children – particularly from sons alone, or sons and their spouses (Kadoya & Khan, 2017). However, over the last five decades, there have been rapid changes in socio-economic patterns in India. In particular, increasing mobility for work, and the rise of more nuclear households (Sathyanarayana, Kumar, & James, 2014), have affected the traditional social and cultural norms of elder care in the family, posing risks to emotional, physical and financial security (United Nations Population Fund, 2017). Despite the dire need, elder care in India is still largely underdeveloped, with lack of formal training in geriatric care and lack of specialised geriatric care curriculum in medical education (United Nations Population Fund, 2017).

India and Australia have a strong bilateral partnership. India is Australia's fifth largest export market and eighth largest trading partner overall (Department of Foreign Affairs and Trade, 2019). With its extraordinary scale, India is a market that offers significant growth opportunities for Australian business (Varghese, 2018). Australia has a highly evolved elderly care system, with a diversity of formal care services of home care, residential care and flexible care subsidised and regulated by the government (Australian Institute of Health and Welfare, 2019). In addition, this is complemented with private sector's provision of aged care, including retirement villages and community supports (Australian Institute of Health and Welfare, 2018). Further, the country has well developed education and training programs, from vocational to specialist levels, in aged and geriatric care (Ryan et al., 2018). Australia is well poised to provide aged care expertise and services and shape elderly care in India.

Methods

A literature search was carried out using AGELINE via EBSCO and Google Scholar with search terms "age*", "elderly", "geriatric", "senior", "aged care", and "India". Grey literature search was carried out on the Indian government websites, specific agencies and service providers' sites, news media, blogs and articles. Social and cultural aspects that are unique to elder care in India were examined, and an inductive process was used in the enquiry, adding further topics of interest to the research.

PROFILE OF THE AGED IN INDIA

Number of Aged People in India

India is the second most populous country in the world with a population of more than 1.3 billion. Per India's last census in 2011, 8.6% or nearly 104 million were 'senior citizens', aged 60 years of age and older. The official retirement age in India is 60 years and this age will be used for the term senior citizen or aged or older persons. The number is expected to grow to 300 million aged by 2050 (United Nations Population Fund, 2017). Two-thirds of this population were located in rural India with the remaining 30.6 million senior citizens live in urban areas (United

Nations Population Fund, 2017). Like many countries, including Australia, the gender ratio of the female senior citizens was slightly higher than males in both rural (9.2% females: 8.4% males) and urban areas (8.5% females: 7.7% males). The majority of senior citizens are in the age group of 60-69 years, with little over 1% of senior citizens, or 13.2 million, aged 80 years and above (known as the 'oldest old') (HelpAge India, 2015). The life expectancy is 72.5 and 73.3 years for men and females respectively. The Southern state of Kerala has the highest number of senior citizens, followed by Himachal Pradesh, Tamil Nadu and Punjab.

Marital Status of the elderly in India is shown in Figure 1. While the proportion of widowhood shows increase across both genders, the extents of widows are much higher than widowers, and grows from 35% among 60-64-year-olds to 69% among the oldest old.

Figure 1. Per cent distribution of elderly persons of various age-groups by marital status

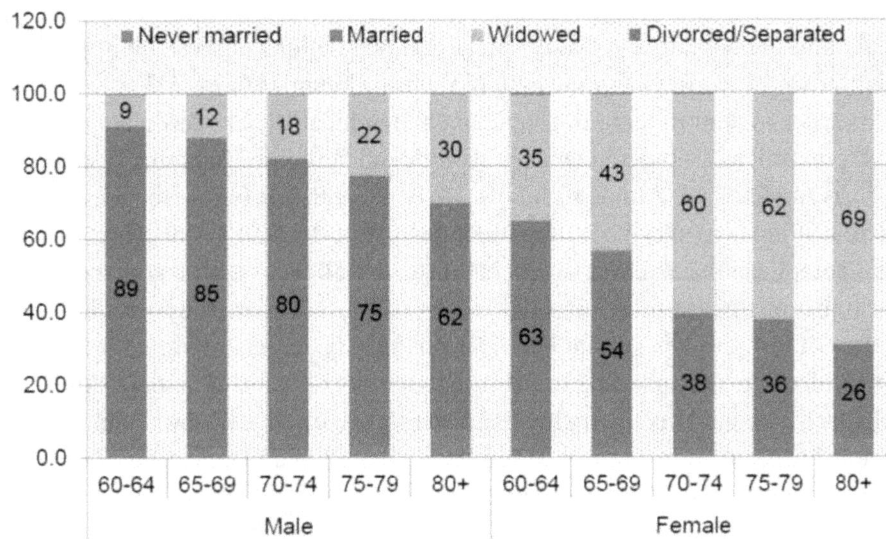

More than half of elderly persons in India live with their spouse followed by a third that live with their children. At 5%, or estimated 113,377 seniors were living alone and another 4% live with other relations or non-relations. (Ministry of Statistics and Program Implementation, 2016).

In India, a person who can read and write in any language, regardless of formal education, is considered literate. The literacy rates (number of literates in 100 persons) in urban areas are much higher at 66% compared to 34% in the rural areas. Amongst the states and union territories, the highest rates are in Mizoram (84%), followed by Kerala (79%) and Chandigarh (75%), and lowest in Arunachal Pradesh (20%). There are large gender disparities in literacy rates as well, with 71.5% of females being illiterate compared with 40.9% of males. In urban areas, 29.9% of senior citizens have completed an education qualification of year 10 equivalent (referred to as matric/secondary in India), compared to 7.1% in rural areas (United Nations Population Fund, 2017).

Religious and Cultural Beliefs

India's culture is among the world's oldest; civilisation in India began about 4,500 years ago. It is the birthplace of Hinduism, Buddhism, Sikh and Jain religions, and is characterised by a huge diversity of religious beliefs and practices, even within each religious grouping. Per the 2011 census, almost 80% of the population are Hindus and 14.2% are Muslims. The remaining 6% are composed of Christians, Sikhs, Buddhists, Jains and several indigenous faiths. While Zoroastrianism and Bahai faiths are not native to India, the largest populations of these faiths reside in India (Office of the Registrar General & Census Commissioner, 2020).

The caste system in India is a rigid and hierarchical social stratification system which groups Hindus based on nature of work and faith into Brahmins, Kshatriyas, Vaishyas and Shudras. Although believed to be more than 3,000 years old, the caste system continues to survive in large sections of society and is the cause of many social complications, such as untouchability, as well as systemic and entrenched discrimination against those considered lower castes, or 'outcastes' (Bayly, 1999). In terms of law, India is secular and does not have an official religion. Religion is an individual choice, and some social evils, such as exclusion of untouchables from public facilities and Hindu temples, are a punishable offence by law (Majid, 2012).

India boasts of a great language diversity, with 22 main languages, 13 different scripts and over 720 different dialects. While Indian states do not have a specific religion, languages are generally concentrated in different states. Hindi is the official language of the Central Government but is only spoken by about 40% of the population, mainly concentrated in Northern India. It is common to find Indians who cannot speak or understand Hindi throughout the majority of the country. English, a legacy of British colonialism, is currently the common language of the government, educational systems, national media and social elite (Ministry of Human Resource Development, 2016).

The culture, world views, ideas, customs, social behaviour, life style habits, and food preferences of Indians are shaped by their religions, languages and legacies of the caste system.

Vegetarianism

Recent surveys show 71% of Indians aged over 15 years eat non-vegetarian food. Telangana has the highest number of non-vegetarians (98.7%), followed by West Bengal (98.55%), Andhra Pradesh (98.25%), Odisha (97.35%) and Kerala (97%). Rajasthan has the least number of non-vegetarians (25.1%) (Bose, 2016).

However, India tops the list of countries practicing vegetarianism, with nearly 38% of the population being vegetarian (International Institute for Population Sciences, 2017). Vegetarianism spread through India after the fourth century BC and is deeply-rooted in through the Hindu religion and Ayurveda, an ancient system of medicine originating in India (Vecchio et al., 2014). While religious Hindu texts do not explicitly prohibit meat eating, the concept of ahimsa, or non-violence, and the belief that all lives are sacred and interconnected are at the root of vegetarianism. Many animals are considered as vehicles of god, and many gods take the form of animals. These gods occupy a position of respect and are worshipped by Hindus. Further, as per Ayurvedic teachings, food has the ability to affect the mind, body and emotions. For example, meat and fish are considered Rajasic food that promote Rajasic qualities such as aggression, greed, jealousy, lust, anger, egotism and irreligious feelings. On the other hand, Sattvic foods such as fresh fruits, vegetables and whole grains promote qualities of goodness, positivity, truth, serenity, balance, peacefulness, and virtuousness. With these beliefs, eating rules vary by caste. Brahmins are prohibited from meat, poultry and fish because it is said to undermine their spiritual quest. Vaishyas are prohibited from eating meat because qualities of anger are not good for trades people and business men (Sawe, 2019). Only Kshatriyas, or the warriors, are permitted meats as it allows power and passion to fight in a battlefield (Figure 2).

Figure 2. How India Eats

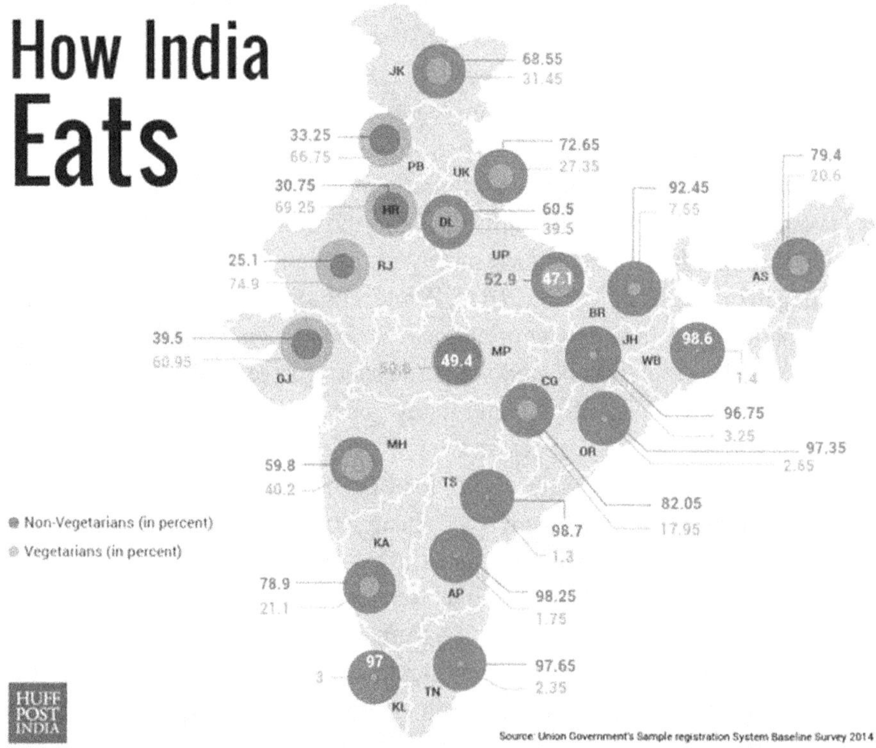

Because of these ingrained belief systems, it is not surprising vegetarianism has a huge prevalence in India. Even those who consume non-vegetarian foods will avoid meat consumption during religious ceremonies and events.

Socio-economic Status

The World Bank classifies India as 'lower-middle income country/South Asia'. However, there is a wide wealth disparity in the country, with India's richest 10 per cent holding 370 times the share of wealth that its poorest hold (Figure 3) (Rukmini, 2017).

Figure 3. Share of wealth by class

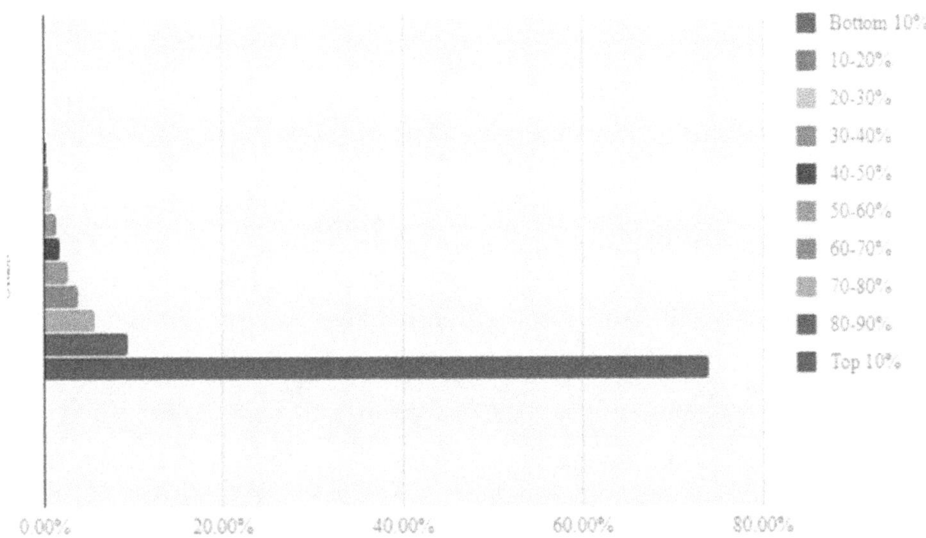

National sample survey data indicate that about 33.5% of the elderly are economically independent, 13.3% are partially dependent, and 51.8% are fully dependent on their children (Deloitte, 2014). India has limited mechanisms of social security, with benefits such as provident fund, pension schemes and gratuity available to those who were formally employed. The vast majority of the elderly are not eligible and cannot access these benefits.

There is an upward trend in old-age dependency ratio, number of people in the age group 60 or more per 100 persons in the age group 15-59 years, rising from 10.9% in 1961 to 14.2% in 2011 (Figure 4) (Ministry of Statistics and Program Implementation, 2016).

Figure 4. Old-age dependency ratio in India, 1961-2011

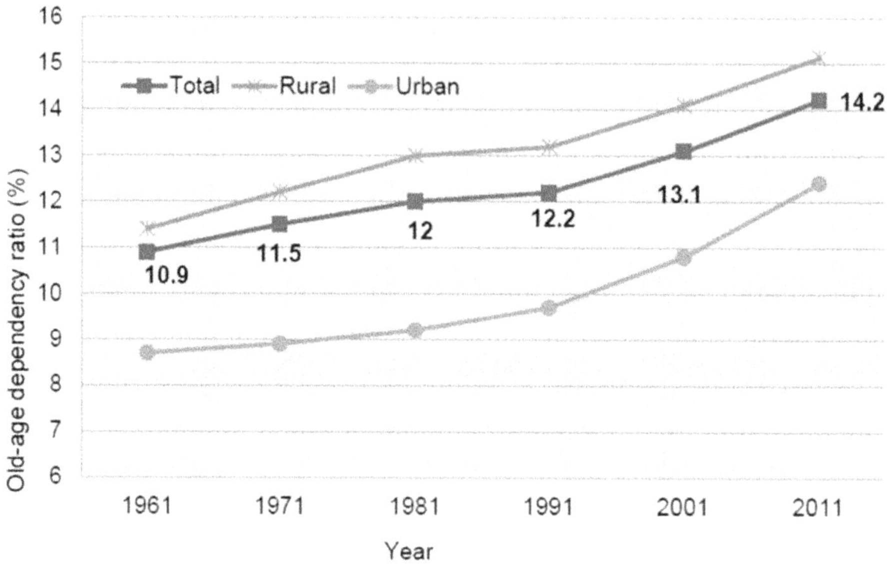

Urban populations indicate a lower dependency due to higher concentration of working age population in urban areas, with the old-age dependency ratio at 15.1 for rural and 12.4 for urban areas, respectively. Among the major states, the overall old-age dependency ratio varied from 10.4% in Delhi to 19.6% in Kerala. The ratio has increased over time for all these states but relatively higher rates of increase are seen in Kerala, Andhra Pradesh and Karnataka since 2001 (Ministry of Statistics and Program Implementation, 2016).

Health Status and Access to Healthcare

The Indian elderly are more likely to suffer from chronic than acute illness. There is a rise in chronic diseases, particularly cardiovascular, metabolic, and degenerative disorders. Hypertension, cataract, osteoarthritis, chronic obstructive pulmonary disease (COPD), ischemic heart disease, diabetes mellitus, benign prostatic hypertrophy, upper and lower gastrointestinal dysmotility (dyspepsia and constipation), and depression are common diseases among older patients that account for nearly 85% of all the diagnoses among the elderly. Diabetes, in particular, was described as an 'emerging epidemic' among the elderly (Dey, Nambiar, Lakshmi, Sheikh, & Reddy, 2012; Paul & Asirvatham, 2016).

India does not have a universal social security system, but a number of schemes are spread through a variety of legislation usually aimed at the disadvantaged. Benefits such as provident fund, pension schemes, and gratuity are available for those who worked in formal employment, and is lacking for majority of the elderly. There is no universal medical insurance and private health insurance penetration remains low. Even the elderly who are insured face significant out of pocket expenses and financial burdens as there is no coverage for outpatient care or pharmaceutical needs (Deloitte, 2014). When compared to other households, families with elderly persons spend a disproportionate amount of their total monthly consumption on healthcare needs.

Regulation and Legislation for Care of the Aged in India

From 1992, the Ministry of Social Justice and Empowerment (MOSJE) implemented the Integrated Programme for Older Persons (IPOP) that provides basic amenities of shelter, foods, medical care and entertainment opportunities and encouraging active aging. It provides financial assistance to local bodies, nongovernment organisations, educational institutions, charitable hospitals, nursing homes to implement a facilities including old age homes, mobile medical units for older persons living in the rural areas, day care centres and other supports for the aged (United Nations Population Fund, 2017).

The MOSJE enacted the *Maintenance and Welfare of Parents and Senior Citizens Act, 2007* (Maintenance Act) for the support of the elderly. Parents and grandparents, if unable to maintain themselves from their own income, can demand maintenance from their children, inclusive of food, clothing, residence, medical attendance and treatment. The tribunal can take action for any complaints. If the children themselves do not have sufficient means to maintain their aged parents or grandparents, the state governments are to provide old-age homes in each district to accommodate a minimum of 150 elderly (Jindal, 2012; United Nations Population Fund, 2017).

The implementation of IPOP and the Maintenance Act are left to the states with uneven implementation. As example, the Government of Tamil Nadu, issued a Gazette notification in February 2016 fixing minimum standards in old-age homes. This may encourage others to follow (United Nations Population Fund, 2017).

There is no formal aged care system in India and therefore there are no government (Central or State) supports to build retirement homes. There is no definition or any regulation for minimum standards of care. The issues surrounding contractual relations between elderly residents and several existing retirement homes and grievances with services have exposed exploitation of vulnerable senior citizens within aged care facilities. The Ministry of Housing and Urban Affairs have just very recently released model guidelines for aged care facilities (Ministry of Housing and Urban Affairs, 2019). Dalal and Basu (2019) describe these guidelines has missing specific provisions to safeguard the rights of vulnerable citizens living on their savings (Dalal & Basu, 2019).

Care for the Elderly

The elderly population access care through the general healthcare system. Health services consist of both allopathic treatments and medicine as well as alternative systems such as Homeopathy and Ayurveda.

The principal source of care for the frail elderly, including those with dementia (Kumar & Roy, 2016; Narayan et al., 2015) are still the family, and care is left to families' individual coping mechanisms. With the rise in chronic disease among the elderly, there is an urgent need for palliative care (Khosla, Patel, & Sharma, 2012). Several specialised geriatric hospitals are emerging as start-ups or not-for-profit organisations, however these still have very limited coverage.

Supply of Aged Care Services in India

The 2018 Confederation of Indian Industry (CII) report on the Senior Care Industry in India (Confederation of Indian Industry, 2018) provides a recent picture of supply of aged care services in India. The two categories of aged care services can be broken down into two broad categories: senior care and senior living services and home care services.

Home Care (HC)

Services provided to seniors within the senior's home address clinical and non-clinical support needs, including engagement activities, ADL assistance support, housekeeping, home engineering support, and nutrition support. Home services are provided through memberships or fee-per-service models and allow the elderly to utilise services in the comfort of their own home as required. The majority (63%) of home care companies provide clinical care, although there is an emergence of non-clinical home care services such as home engineering, housekeeping, nutrition services, and so on.

Senior Care and Senior Living

The formats of senior care and living services identified in the 2018 CII report are detailed below.

Independent Living Community (IL)

Apartment complexes, condominiums, cooperatives and other such retirement communities offering private residences designed for the independent senior. These types of communities do not provide medical services but instead provide seniors with hassle-free living, with some recreational facilities. A seniors-only housing community could be a standalone facility or a part of a larger housing project such as an area, tower or cluster of apartments/homes.

Assisted Living (AL) Community

Assisted living offers help with non-medical aspects of daily activities in an atmosphere of separate, private living units. It can be likened to congregate living for residents less able to function independently in all aspects of their daily lives.

Skilled Nursing Facility (SNF)

Skilled nursing facilities offer the most intensive level of care on the residential care continuum. Skilled nursing facilities are equipped to handle individuals with 24-hour nursing needs, post-operative recuperation or complex medical care demands, as well as chronically ill individuals who can no longer live independently. Such facilities may be freestanding or part of a senior community. SNFs may specialize in short-term or acute nursing care, intermediate or long-term skilled nursing care.

Continuing Care Retirement Community (CC)

A Continuing Care Retirement Community (CCRC) offers seniors a facility that combines housing, services and health care, allowing seniors to enjoy a private residential lifestyle with the opportunity of independence and the assurances of long-term health care. Within the CCRC, there are three types of care available, providing a phased approach to elderly living accommodations: Independent living, in which the person lives on their own in an apartment or cottage-style housing; Assisted living, offering some level of assistance for residents; and Skilled nursing care, for residents whose health is deteriorating.

Memory Care Facility (MC)

Memory care facilities provide increased levels of care and safety for individuals with Alzheimer's and dementia.

Figure 5. Formats of Senior Living

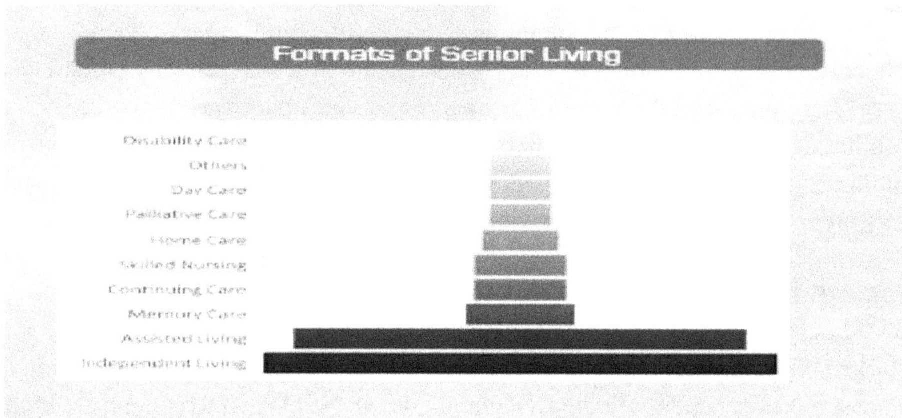

Senior Day Care Facility (SD)

Day care centres provide stimulation and rehabilitation to elders providing medical care and related procedures.

People With Disabilities Care (PWD)

These are for senior citizens who have children with special needs such as Autism, Cerebral Palsy, Down's Syndrome or Spastics. The model takes care of senior citizens with special needs children living in the Senior Care Centre and, after the demise of the parents, cares for the children until their death.

Figure 6. Number of Senior Living Communities (2018)

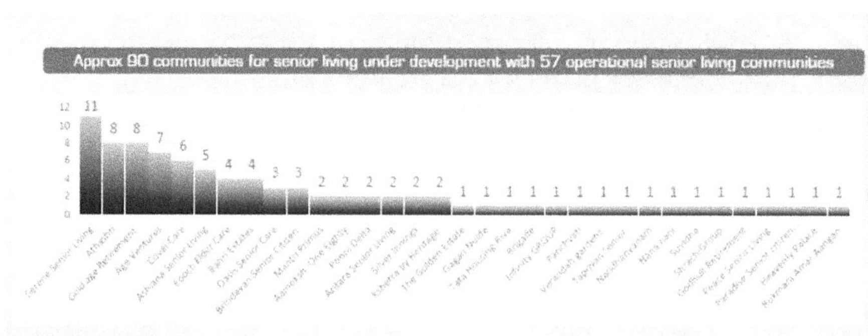

Palliative Care (PC)

Palliative care is a multi-disciplinary approach to specialized medical and nursing care for people with life-limiting illnesses. It focuses on providing people with relief from symptoms, pain, physical strain and mental stress relating to the terminal diagnosis.

As of 2018, there were 34 providers in India providing different senior care living formats (Figure 5). The majority of the facilities were spread across independent living and assisted living centres. There is a paucity of all other types of senior living services which require specialised health services, such as memory care, skilled nursing, palliative care, disability care and continuing care. Day care and home care formats are sparse as well.

Six operators have over 50% of the stock of 90 communities in formal senior living in the country.

Currently, the average communities per operator is 2.67, and most community growth has been witnessed over the last 8-10 years (Figure 6).

Senior living facilities in India have different price points in different regions across the country. While the median price of a senior living unit is at INR 45 lakhs (AUD 93,757), there are local peaks, as can be seen in North India with a few luxury projects. 41% of units have a price point between INR 20-50 lakhs (AUD 41,670-AUD 104,174) and only 6% of communities have a ticket price above 75 lakhs (AUD 156,262) (Figure 7). While the average price point for senior living communities has seen a steady increase, there are few players and projects at the higher end of the market.

Figure 7. Price Point of Senior Living Communities (2018)

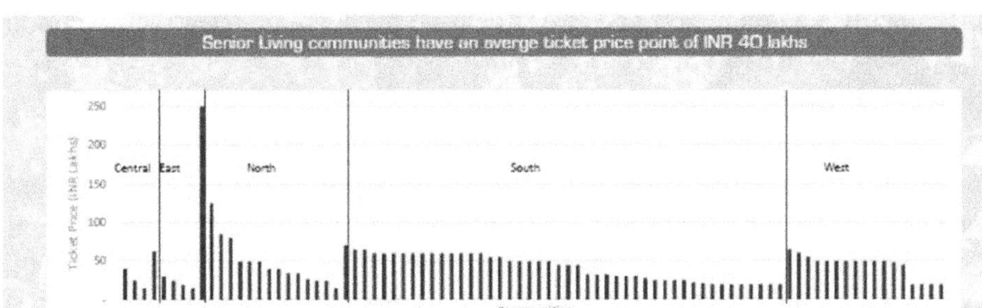

Old Age Homes

Old age homes are run by the government, not-for-profits or religious institutions to provide shelter mainly for the destitute, sick and elderly abandoned by family (HelpAge India, 2017). According to an estimate by HelpAge India, there were approximately 700 old age homes in India in 2017.

Factors Driving the Demand for Elder Care in India

The need for elderly services are immense and no longer relegated to the socially and economically disadvantaged, and there is a strong need among the middle and higher socioeconomic populations as well.

Indian society is collectivistic, fostering social cohesion and interdependence. Traditionally, multigenerational joint families are the most common family structure. The Hindu joint family is largely prevalent, where parents live with their sons and their spouses and children, as well as their unmarried daughters. Caring of the elderly by family members, especially by children and grand-children, had been the practice. Elderly parents expect and rely on their children for long-term care. Most families consider parental care the responsibility of the son and daughter-in-law (Kadoya & Khan, 2017). Filial piety is very strongly embedded in Indian culture, and with elderly parents having a respected position in the family, that is observed regardless of religious and economic background. The joint family structure and filial piety together have been beneficial for the elderly in India as they co-reside with their children, as well as enjoy special status and power within the living arrangement (HelpAge India, 2015).

A number of socio-cultural changes sweeping through India over the last few decades have affected family structures, placing physical, emotional and financial security of the elderly in a vulnerable position. These factors, together with the growth of the elderly population in India, drive the need for the senior care sector in India.

Rise of Nuclear Families

The last two decades have seen a rise of the nuclear family and extended family systems. While the latest data is not available, observations from the National Family Health Survey (2016) suggests that families are still taking care of the elderly in a big way. On average, the Indian elderly are residing in a household where at least seven members live, possibly indicating multigenerational households (International Institute for Population Sciences, 2017).

Gender inequalities abound in India as with the rest of the world. With feminism and social reform movements beginning in the mid-19th century, more women in India today participate equally in education and go on to join the workforce. While this change has seen improvements in female empowerment, it has presented challenges for women's traditional roles as the care giver for both children and seniors, driving the need for external help in care giving (Confederation of Indian Industry, 2018).

Decline in Fertility Rates

India has seen a steady decline in fertility rates, or the average number of children per the average number of women of child bearing age. Against a backdrop of anxieties of a population explosion, India began its Family Planning (Ministry of Health and Family Welfare, 2017) programs in 1948, immediately after acquiring independence, that included targeted approaches, contraceptive-specific incentives and family planning camp approach (Pachauri, 2014). The programme has been widely detailed to have had the single most important impact on changes in total fertility (Matthews, Padmadas, Hutter, McEachran, & Brown, 2009). The current fertility rate in India is 2.33 births per woman (The World Bank, 2020), halved since the 1980s (Figure 8).

Figure 8. Total Fertility Rate: India

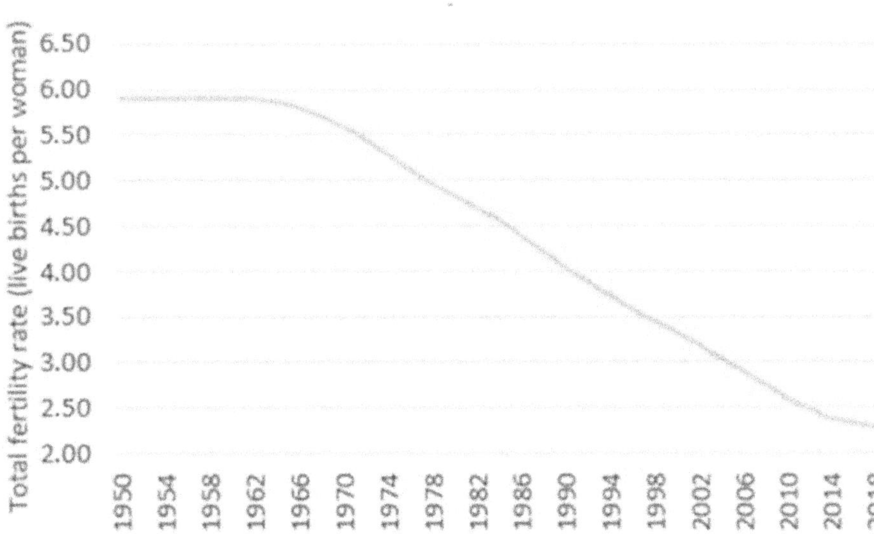

Migration

Urbanization and employment-related migrations have led younger families to move out of parental homes to bigger cities within India as well as overseas. One of the consequences of this increased mobility is the diminishing role of family in elderly care (Miltiades, 2002). The 2011 census pegs the number of internal migrants within India at 139 million, which includes both inter- and intra-state movement. The largest sources were Uttar Pradesh and Bihar, followed closely by Madhya Pradesh, Punjab, Rajasthan, Uttarakhand, Jammu and Kashmir and West Bengal. Major destination states were Delhi, Maharashtra, Tamil Nadu, Gujarat, Andhra Pradesh and Kerala (Sharma, 2017).

High-skilled migration from India is seen essentially as a middle-class phenomenon, and the aspiration to work and build a family overseas has become a norm among middle-class Indians. A Sridharan, chief of Covai Senior Care Constructions, explains:

A lot of young middle-class Indians left the country during the (1990s technology) boom. Their children don't want to be known as people who have their parents living in old age homes. So a need for such exclusive homes was felt and the rising middle-class is securing its retirement years by buying exclusive homes (Yadav, 2013).

As of 2017, 16.6 million persons from India were living in another country, and India has been among the world's top origin countries of migrants since the United Nations started tracking migrant origins in 1990. The number of international Indian migrants has more than doubled over the past 25 years, growing about twice as fast as the world's total migrant population (Knowledge Partnership on Migration and Development, 2018). In these transnational families, it is often the older adults who are left behind or choose to stay back. Economic remittances from those overseas are an important source of income for families where the elderly, and in some cases the spouse and very young children, stay back in India. India was identified to be the top recipient of economic remittances, with $69 billion USD remitted in 2017 (Knowledge Partnership on Migration and Development, 2018). While economically beneficial, the physical absence of children creates problems, from an emotional standpoint as well as with multitudes of tasks that comprise daily care giving, as well as more intensive care in times of ill health or emergency (Miltiades, 2002; Yadav, 2013).

Families where both members of the couple are working, or those living away from their family home or settled overseas, also constantly face the dilemma and guilt of not fulfilling their core responsibilities of parental care. Private operators have started addressing these needs and have begun offering a variety of services.

CHALLENGES UNIQUE TO AGED CARE SERVICES IN INDIA

Stigma Associated with Elderly Care

We are conditioned to feel guilty if we hire a professional to give our 85-year old mom a bath and not do it ourselves (Sinha, 2018).

Deep rooted beliefs and attitudes, in both Indian culture and ethos, as well as longstanding social conditioning place the responsibility of elderly care squarely on the young in the family. Indicators point to acute need for elderly care, there continues to be tremendous stigma associated with individuals and families that may seek professional help for looking after their old parents. They risk being judged by the society and often viewed as "abandoning their parents" or "shirking responsibilities". This frequently leads to avoidance of using professional elder care services, even at the cost of inadequacies in care.

You're just describing one of those new-fangled old age homes. That's not for me (Bhargava, 2015).

The country's popular media reinforce social and cultural stigmas around abandoning the elderly at a time when they need their children most. *Baghbhan* is a critically acclaimed Hindi film in 2003, depicted an elderly middle-class couple who devoted their lives to raising their four sons with the expectation that upon retirement, they would live with one of them, as is the social norm in India. The story goes on to depict callous and selfish sons and daughters-in-law preoccupied with their own lives, subjecting the couple to emotional and mental abuse. In the end, a foster son comes to the rescue (Elley, 2003). While it was one of the first films to highlight issues faced by the elderly, the film is a reflection that themes regarding care for parents and elders is not keeping pace with the socio-cultural and economic realities overtaking modern India (Elley, 2003).

Residential services for the elderly is not a new concept in India. Old age homes have been available as a welfare service in the country for many years through government, religious and not-for profit bodies. One qualitative study exploring why Indians do not prefer institutional care for the elderly describes not only inadequate infrastructure but poor treatment of residents by the staff, breaching basic standards of respect and dignity "even in upmarket exclusive homes"(Brijnath, 2012). These factors reinforce how elderly services are viewed (Ashiana Housing Ltd, 2019) and impact families' decision making processes for seeking retirement communities, day care centres or assisted living homes whose services can be paid for (Sinha, 2018).

However, India is beginning to see some shifts in thinking. There are those in their 60s and 70s who are comfortable financially and would prefer to live life on their own terms rather than at whims of children. In addition, for individuals that currently live in Western countries and have elderly parents and grandparents in India are more accepting of formal aged care services. These families are familiar with the vast array of specialised aged care services and are aware of both the beneficial effects and the down sides that elderly care services may bring.

Price Sensitivity and the Frugal Indian

Indian consumers, particularly the elderly, value frugality. This is not surprising in the absence of any social security. Seniors who are economically independent are primarily living off their savings, and others are partially or fully supported by children and family. Again, India does not have a universal health insurance coverage. Although more senior citizen health insurance products are becoming available, their market penetration is low. Further, most products typically do not cover pre-existing ailments or have long waiting periods for coverage. These conditions do not serve the needs of the elderly in wake of rising chronic disease.

In the case of seniors living in residential homes, after paying for the dwelling (or deposit for a lease arrangement), they would still need to have a regular source of income or savings to cover the monthly fees, health related costs and other out-of-pocket expenses. A recent study of seniors living in retirement homes indicated that that nearly 40% have paid over INR 20 lakhs (about AUD 40,500) for their retirement home investment. While almost the majority had a monthly outflow of INR 20,000 (about AUD 400), about half paid about INR 10,000 (about AUD 200) as monthly maintenance fees. Even at these modest rates, about 60% of respondents were concerned about affordability, and nearly half wanted better maintenance of facilities (Dalal & Basu, 2019). A Sridharan outlines,

India today has 100 million elderly people. If you take 5% of them as the middle class, it comes to five million people. It is a huge number and there is hardly any availability of old-age homes. (Yadav, 2015)

Thus, while the scale and the need is enormous, providers need to keep prices in check and consider the ability of people to pay higher charges in the long run.

Lack of Trained Personnel

India lacks trained and experienced human personnel across all streams – management, technical and clinical services – in elderly care. Current service providers hire professionals from hospitality, healthcare, and real estate backgrounds, and provide minimal on-the-job training to meet their requirements. While there is a dearth of skills across the spectrum of elder care workforce, there are acute shortages in roles that provide direct care, and often, these tasks are provided by untrained domestic help rather than professional personal care assistants, community support workers, nurses, and allied health professionals. Reports indicate that 12,000 care workers are employed just by the senior home-care sector as of date. In this sector alone, the demand for care workers is expected to go up to 40,000 to 50,000 by 2025 (Confederation of Indian Industry, 2018).

Working in the aged care sector is physically, emotionally and mentally demanding. Vital service-oriented staff with empathy for the elderly work unrecognized in a difficult environment. However, lack of training results in hiring staff that are ill-equipped to meet these challenges, leading to poor outcomes for the aged, the staff and the service providers. Only a small number of not-for-profits and universities offer geriatric training as shown in the table below. The National Institute of Social Defence (NISD) and the MOSJE also train eligible persons through its Regional Resources Training Centres (RRTCs) located at Delhi, Kolkata, Mumbai, Imphal, Bangalore, Hyderabad and Coimbatore (National Insititute of Social Defence, 2016; United Nations Population Fund, 2017).

Australia's Aged Care Sector

Australia spends on average 1.2% of its gross domestic product on support for the aged in 2019(Dyer et al., 2019). When compared to other like countries, it ranks highly for access and support for its population. It has one of the highest life expectancy. Australia has a rapidly ageing population with the proportion of people aged 65 years or over is 15% of the population in June 2017. This proportion is expected to increase to over 20% of the population over the next thirty years. The aged care service provides support for people aged 65 years or over and Aboriginal and Torres Strait Islander Australians aged 50 to 64 years (Productivity Commission, 2020).

Aged Care Service

The Australian aged care system delivers services through a range of provider and care types within residential and community-based settings. The Commonwealth Home Support Programme (CHSP) provides a basic level of aged care services to support continued independence for people aged 65 and over living at home and their carers. The Home Care Packages Programme (Home Care) assists frail older people to remain at home for longer. Usage rates of community aged care have increased consistently over time, and across sex and age groups.

Residential aged care provides permanent accommodation and care for people who can no longer live at home due to increased care needs (permanent residential aged care) and short-term accommodation and care for people who (or whose carers) need a break from their normal living arrangements (respite residential aged care).

Services that are approved to provide aged care receive Australian government funding to provide these services. They are required to meet minimum standards as well as demonstrate commitment to continuous improvement in quality of care (Productivity Commission, 2020). The *Aged Care Act 1997* and the accompanying Age Care Principles are the framework for aged care services. The Act covers service planning, user rights, eligibility for care, funding, quality assurance and other matters. In addition, there are statutory bodies that have responsibilities for this sector including the Aged Care Quality and Safety Commission, the Aged Care Pricing Commissioner and the National Aged Care Advocacy Program. Most of the residential aged care, home care and home support are delivered by non-government organisations. For Australian residential aged care, 41%, 23% and 18% are operated by private-for-profit, religious and charitable respectively in June 2019. The remained are operated by community based and state or territory governments (Productivity Commission, 2020). A significant portion of the cost of providing aged care is subsidised by the national government.

The ACATs consists of geriatrician, specialised nurse, physiotherapist, occupational therapist, social worker and or nutritionist that undertake comprehensive geriatric assessment and care focusing on mental and physical health, medication review, functional ability of the individuals. They provide recommendations for the services that the individuals are eligible for (Kim, Subramaniam, & Flicker, 2018).

Retirement Villages

Retirement villages refers to a purpose-built housing complex of multiple dwellings on a single site, designed for people in later life (typically aged 55 and over), who are provided with communal facilities and services but who are independent in the sense that they do not need the level of support provided by residential aged-care facilities. In the context of an ageing population, there has also been a growth in the number of facilities offering 'ageing-in-place' services, combining retirement-village independent living units, serviced apartment or hostel places and nursing homes in the one facility. The reasons for persons moving into retirement villages include lifestyle changes, home maintenance, social isolation, health and mobility. For one third of villages, co-locate with residential aged care facilities to provide health care services to residents on the concept of continuum of care. Each state and territory in Australia has its own legislation that covers diverse aspects of village development and operation, information disclosure and resolution of disputes. The number of retirement villages in Australia is almost 3000, with for profit organisations providing almost two-thirds of the villages followed by not-for-profit organisations (Hu, Xia, Skitmore, Buys, & Zuo, 2017).

Doing Business in India

A recent report by Australia's Department of Foreign Affairs (2018) recommended practical measures to cement India as a top economic partner for Australia (Department of Foreign Affairs and Trade, 2018). In response to the report, the Australian Government is taking a number of actions to help Australian businesses tap into India's economic potential. A Memorandum of Understanding between Austrade and Invest India agrees to create a one stop shop for businesses considering investing in respective markets, including insights on local market conditions, approvals processes and assistance to establish networks (Department of Foreign Affairs and Trade, 2018).

India's policy on Foreign Direct Investment (FDI) is regulated by the Department of Industrial Policy and Promotions (DIPP) (*Foreign Direct Investment*, 2019). As per regulations, FDI means any investment by non-resident entity/person resident outside India and encompasses all types of foreign investment in India, including investment by FIIs, investment by NRI, and investment by foreigners or foreign entities. FDI is prohibited in some sectors including real estate business, whereas in other sectors approval is required prior to investment. In general, if the investment is made in sectors not prohibited or requiring approval, FDI can be made through the automatic route.

Incorporation of a private limited company is the simplest and quickest type of India entry strategy for foreign nationals and foreign companies (VERVE Financial Services Private Limited, 2020). Foreign direct investment of up to 100% into a private limited company or limited company is under the automatic route, and Central Government permission is not required. Hence, incorporation of a private limited company as a wholly owned subsidiary of a foreign company or joint venture is the easiest, fastest and least expensive mode of entry to the Indian market by foreign companies.

Max India Limited, a multi-business corporate, is part of the USD $3 billion Max Group and is the holding company for Max Healthcare (Max@Home), Antara Senior Living and Max Bupa Health Insurance. Max Healthcare is a joint venture between Max India and Life Healthcare, South Africa (Max India Limited, 2016).

Incorporation of a Limited Liability Partnership by foreign nationals requires Government approval. Proprietorship Firms or Partnership Firms require prior approval from the Reserve Bank of India (RBI). Registration of Branch Office, Liaison Office or Project Office require approval by RBI as well the Government.

A private limited company must have a minimum of two shareholders and two Directors. A shareholder can be a person or a corporate entity, however, a Director must be a person. Foreign nationals are allowed to become Directors of an Indian Private Limited Company (Figure 9).

Figure 9. Popular Indian Company Structure

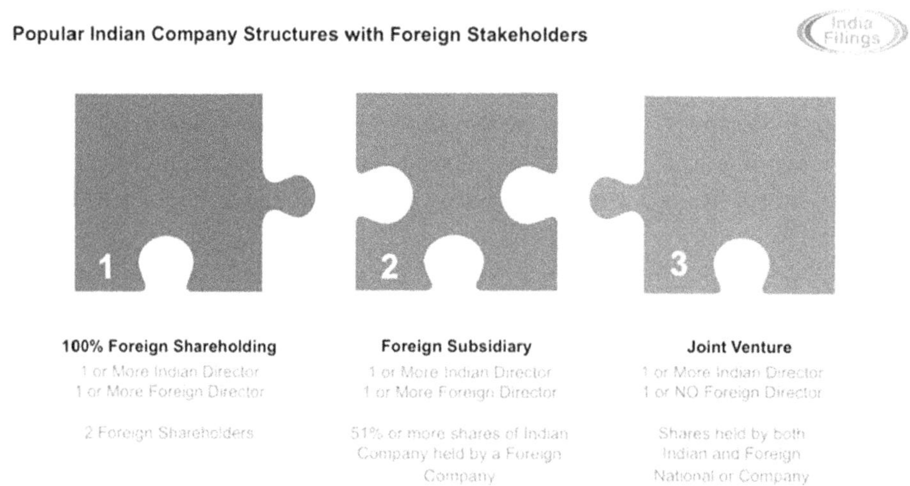

The Board of Directors of the Indian Private Limited Company must have one Director who is both an Indian Citizen and Indian Resident. However, there is no requirement for the Indian Director to be a shareholder in the company. Hence, most foreign companies or foreign nationals prefer to incorporate a company in India with three Directors – two Foreign National Directors and one Indian National Director.

The 100% shares of the Indian Company can be held by a combination of Foreign Companies and/or Foreign Nationals. Indian private limited companies require a minimum of two shareholders mandatorily. Hence, one corporate entity or person cannot hold all the shares of an Indian Private Limited Company.

Opportunities for Australian Entrepreneurs

Australia's aged care service market, retirement villages, home care and residential aged care, has developed and matured. It has strong presences of private for profit operates that have successfully operated in a highly regulated and structured system. In addition, the provision of care has evolved to be highly resident or consumer focused. They are well positioned to take their learnings for application and adoption into India and assist its' aged care sector it is development. Given the strong bilateral trade arrangements that exists between the two countries, coupled with highly multi-cultured exposure in providing care and workforce base, Australian businesses are well placed.

The staggering numbers of elderly people in India have made aged care a growing public and private concern. Despite more services making an entry, the sector is largely underdeveloped; India's supply cannot meet the demands. Australia has a highly evolved aged care system and is poised to provide expertise and services in the age care sector, shaping elderly care in India.

Key customer groups that would be inclined to consider senior living services include the recently retired elderly who are financially secure or non-resident Indians who are looking for care options for parents in India. They would find appealing a safe, secure and comfortable place to retire, living on their own terms with friendly social opportunities and without the hassles of day-to-day living.

With the growing proportions of an elder population and the associated increasing prevalence of chronic illnesses and dementia, there is a clear opportunity for Australian expertise in specialised residential care facilities with 24-hour health monitoring and nursing care services as well as services for people living with dementia or disabilities.

Australian entrepreneurs making a foray in the sector must be aware of and address the existing stigma and associations with "old age homes". This will require significant efforts on branding and promotion of senior citizen care. In addition, services need to keep the cultural context in mind and address the very diverse linguistic, spiritual and culinary requirements.

Even as India is awakening to the need for regulation in the elderly care sector, Australian entrepreneurs can provide expertise on best practice, processes and systems. They can shape the setting of standards in consumer centred care, quality of services and transparency in the sector. This may facilitate improving trust, eliminating stigma and bringing a change in perception of elderly care in India.

Training is a clear opportunity in India. Indian service providers in both the not-for-profit and private sectors are keen on building relations with Australia and are looking for knowledge partners, investment and joint venture opportunities. As Australia's vocational system is highly regarded in India, an abundance of training opportunities exist across the spectrum of geriatric services, specialised geriatric curriculum in medical education, dementia care and palliative care.

The outlook for Australian aged care providers considering setting up in India have been described as 'high volume, low margin'. This may pose challenges as Australia is typically a 'high-value, low-volume supplier'. Some segments of the Indian market are seeing an increased willingness to pay for better services, but in most instances, cost remains a primary driver. Australian providers will benefit if they are able to adjust their business models to reflect India's low-cost, high-volume environment.

CONCLUSION

With over 100 million senior citizens and an ageing population, as well as social and cultural changes sweeping its economy, India has a high demand for information, knowledge and expertise in the aged care services sector. Stigma persists, but some sections of society are seeing the value of specialised services. Despite challenges, India is beginning to see more innovative aged care services and senior living options. There is no better time than now for Australia to provide expertise and shape the sector.

Suggested areas for further research:

a) Market research and needs assessment of Australians of Indian origin with elderly parents in India, and learnings from Indian aged care services in Australia.
b) Requirements analysis for Australian trainings, accreditation, and expert consultancy services in India.

REFERENCES

Ashiana Housing Ltd. (2019). *Senior Living VS Old Age Homes VS Retirement Homes in India*. Retrieved from https://www.ashianahousing.com/real-estate-blog/old-age-homes-vs-retirement-village-vs-retirement-homes-in-india-and-senior-living

Australian Institute of Health and Welfare. (2018). *Older Australia at a glance*. Canberra: AIHW. Retrieved from https://www.aihw.gov.au/reports/older-people/older-australia-at-a-glance

Australian Institute of Health and Welfare. (2019). *Australia's welfare 2019 data insights*. Canberra: AIHW.

Bayly, S. (1999). *Caste, Society and Politics in India from the Eighteenth Century to the Modern Age*. Cambridge University Press.

Bhargava, A. (2015). Elderly care: Why India is one of the worst countries to grow old? *Daily News Analysis India*. Retrieved from https://www.dnaindia.com/analysis/standpoint-elderly-care-why-india-is-one-of-the-worst-countries-to-grow-old-in-2138686

Bose, A. (2016). Vegetarian India A Myth? Survey Shows Over 70% Indians Eat Non-Veg, Telangana Tops List. *Huffpost*. Retrieved from https://www.huffingtonpost.in/2016/06/14/how-india-eats_n_10434374.html

Brijnath, B. (2012). Why does institutionalised care not appeal to Indian families? Legislative and social answers from urban India. *Ageing and Society*, *32*(4), 697–717. doi:10.1017/S0144686X11000584

Confederation of Indian Industry. (2018). *CII - Senior Care Industry Report India 2018: Igniting potential in senior care services*. Retrieved from https://www.slideshare.net/saileshmishra1/cii-senior-care-industry-report-india-2018?from_action=save

Dalal, S., & Basu, D. (2019). *Retirement Homes in India*. Retrieved from Mumbai, Mharashtra, India: https://foundation.moneylife.in/memorandum/report-on-retirement-homes-in-india-by-moneylife-foundation-for-hdfc-ltd/48.html

Deloitte. (2014). *Ensuring care for the golden years - Way forward for India*. Paper presented at the FICCI 7th Annual Health Conference, New Delhi. https://www2.deloitte.com/content/dam/Deloitte/in/Documents/life-sciences-health-care/in-lshc-ficci-elderly-care-noexp.pdf

Department of Foreign Affairs and Trade. (2018). *Government response to An India Economic Strategy to 2035*. Retrieved from https://dfat.gov.au/about-us/publications/Pages/government-response-india-economic-strategy.aspx

Department of Foreign Affairs and Trade. (2019). *India Country Brief*. Canberra, Australia: Australian Government Retrieved from https://www.dfat.gov.au/geo/india/Pages/india-country-brief

Dey, S., Nambiar, D., Lakshmi, J., Sheikh, K., & Reddy, K. S. (2012). Health of the elderly in India: challenges of access and affordability. In *Aging in Asia: findings from new and emerging data initiatives*. National Academies Press.

Dyer, S. M., Valeri, M., Arora, N., Ross, T., Winsall, M., Tilden, D., & Crotty, M. (2019). *Review of International Systems for Long-Term Care of Older People*. Retrieved from Adelaide, Australia: https://agedcare.royalcommission.gov.au/publications/Documents/research-paper-2-review-international-systems-long-term-care.pdf

Elley, D. (2003, Nov. 24). Baghban. *Variety*.

Foreign Direct Investment. (2019). Retrieved from https://dipp.gov.in/foreign-direct-investment/foreign-direct-investment-policy

HelpAge India. (2015). *State of Elderly in India 2014*. Retrieved from New Delhi, India: https://www.helpageindia.org/wp-content/themes/helpageindia/pdf/state-elderly-india-2014.pdf

HelpAge India. (2017). *Old Age Homes*. Retrieved from https://www.helpageindia.org/our-work/welfare-development/old-age-homes/

Hu, X., Xia, B., Skitmore, M., Buys, L., & Zuo, J. (2017). Retirement villages in Australia: A literature review. *Pacific Rim Property Research Journal*, *23*(1), 101–122. doi:10.1080/14445921.2017.1298949

International Institute for Population Sciences. (2017). *National Family Health Survey (NFHS-4), 2015-16: India*. Mumbai: IIPS Retrieved from http://rchiips.org/nfhs/NFHS-4Reports/India.pdf

Jindal, B. (2012). *Maintenance and welfare of Parents and Senior Citizens*. Academic Press.

Kadoya, Y., & Khan, M. S. R. (2017). Can concern for the long-term care of older parents explain son preference at birth in India? *Journal of Women & Aging*, *29*(3), 254–266. doi:10.1080/08952841.2015.1138048 PMID:27029287

Khosla, D., Patel, F. D., & Sharma, S. C. (2012). Palliative care in India: Current progress and future needs. *Indian Journal of Palliative Care*, *18*(3), 149. doi:10.4103/0973-1075.105683 PMID:23439559

Kim, M.-Y., Subramaniam, P., & Flicker, L. (2018). The Australian Aged Care and its Implications for the Korean Aging Crisis. *Annals of Geriatric Medicine and Research*, *22*(1), 9–19. doi:10.4235/agmr.2018.22.1.9

Knowledge Partnership on Migration and Development. (2018). *Migration and Remittances: Recent Developments and Outlook*. Retrieved from https://www.knomad.org/sites/default/files/2018-04/Migration%20and%20Development%20Brief%2029.pdf

Kumar, C. T. S., & Roy, K. J. (2016). Bianca Brijnath, Unforgotten: Love and the Culture of Dementia Care in India, Berghahn Books, Oxford, 2014, 240 pp., hbk£ 60, ISBN 13: 9781782383543. *Ageing and Society*, *36*(5), 1111–1113. doi:10.1017/S0144686X1600012X

Majid, A. (2012). Future of untouchables in India: A case study of Dalit. *South Asian Studies*, *27*(1), 263.

Matthews, Z., Padmadas, S. S., Hutter, I., McEachran, J., & Brown, J. (2009). Does early childbearing and a sterilization-focused family planning programme in India fuel population growth? *Demographic Research*, *20*, 693–720. doi:10.4054/DemRes.2009.20.28

Max India Limited. (2016). *About Max India Limited*. Retrieved from https://www.maxindia.com/wp-content/uploads/2016/01/About-Max-India-Limited1.pdf

Miltiades, H. B. (2002). The social and psychological effect of an adult child's emigration on non-immigrant Asian Indian elderly parents. *Journal of Cross-Cultural Gerontology*, *17*(1), 33–55. doi:10.1023/A:1014868118739 PMID:14617974

Ministry of Health and Family Welfare. (2017). *National Family Planning Programme*. New Delhi: Government of India Retrieved from https://humdo.nhp.gov.in/about/national-fp-programme/

Ministry of Housing and Urban Affairs. (2019). *Model Guidelines for Development and Regulation of Retirement Homes*. New Delhi, India Retrieved from http://mohua.gov.in/upload/uploadfiles/files/Retirement%20Model%20Guidelines%20Book.pdf

Ministry of Human Resource Development. (2016). *Language Education*. Delhi, India: Government of India Retrieved from https://mhrd.gov.in/sites/upload_files/mhrd/files/upload_document/languagebr.pdf

Ministry of Statistics and Program Implementation. (2016). *Elderly in India - Profiles and Programes*. Retrieved from New Delhi, India: http://mospi.nic.in/sites/default/files/publication_reports/ElderlyinIndia_2016.pdf

Narayan, S. M., Varghese, M., Hepburn, K., Lewis, M., Paul, I., & Bhimani, R. (2015). Caregiving experiences of family members of persons with dementia in south India. *American Journal of Alzheimer's Disease and Other Dementias*, *30*(5), 508–516. doi:10.1177/1533317514567125 PMID:25735742

National Insititute of Social Defence. (2016). *Old Age Care*. Delhi, India: Government of India Retrieved from http://www.nisd.gov.in/content/128_1_OldAgeCare.aspx

Office of the Registrar General & Census Commissioner. (2020). *Census and You - Religion*. New Delhi: Government of India. Retrieved from http://censusindia.gov.in/Census_And_You/religion.aspx

Pachauri, S. (2014). Priority strategies for India's family planning programme. *The Indian Journal of Medical Research*, *140*(Suppl 1), S137. PMID:25673535

Paul, N. S. S., & Asirvatham, M. (2016). Geriatric health policy in India: The need for scaling-up implementation. *Journal of Family Medicine and Primary Care*, *5*(2), 242. doi:10.4103/2249-4863.192333 PMID:27843821

Productivity Commission. (2020). *Report on Government Services*. Retrieved from https://www.gen-agedcaredata.gov.au/Resources/Reports-and-publications/2020/February/Report-on-Government-Services-2020-part-f,-chapter

Rukmini, S. (2017). India's staggering wealth gap in five charts. *The Hindu*. Retrieved from https://www.thehindu.com/data/indias-staggering-wealth-gap-in-five-charts/article10935670.ece

Ryan, C., Ellem, P., Heaton, L., Mulvogue, J., Cousins, M., & De George–Walker, L. J. N. e. i. p. (2018). *Australian final year nursing students' and registered nurse supervisors' perceptions of a gerontology clinical learning experience: A preliminary appraisal*. Academic Press.

Sathyanarayana, K., Kumar, S., & James, K. (2014). Living arrangements of elderly in India: Policy and programmatic implications. *Population Ageing in India, 74*.

Sawe, B. E. (2019). *Countries with the highest rates of vegetarianism*. WorldAtlas.

Sharma, K. (2017). *India has 139 million internal migrants. They must not be forgotten*. World Economic Forum. Retrieved from https://www.weforum.org/agenda/2017/10/india-has-139-million-internal-migrants-we-must-not-forget-them/

Sinha, N. (2018, April 19). Why Elder Care Services is Unexplored in India? *Entrepreneur India*.

The World Bank. (2020). Fertility rate, total (births per woman) - India. Author.

United Nations. (2017). *Caring for Our Elders: Early Responses-India Ageing Report*. New Delhi, India: Author.

United Nations. (2019). *World Population Ageing 2019: Highlights*. New York: United Nations Population Fund.

Varghese, P. N. (2018). *An India Economic Strategy to 2035*. Retrieved from https://www.dfat.gov.au/geo/india/ies/pdf/dfat-an-india-economic-strategy-to-2035.pdf

Vecchio, M. G., Paramesh, E. C., Paramesh, H., Loganes, C., Ballali, S., Gafare, C. E., Verduci, E., & Gulati, A. (2014). Types of Food and Nutrient Intake in India: A Literature Review. *Indian Journal of Pediatrics*, *81*(1), 17–22. doi:10.100712098-014-1465-9 PMID:24928105

VERVE Financial Services Private Limited. (2020). *Guide to Indian Private Limited Company for Foreigners*. Retrieved from https://www.indiafilings.com/learn/guide-to-indian-private-limited-company-for-foreigners/

Yadav, S. (2013). Why India's Elderly are Moving to Retirement Homes. *BBC News India*. Retrieved from https://www.bbc.com/news/world-asia-india-23176206

Chapter 7
Emerging Business and Trade Opportunities Between India and Australia:
Tourism, Including Medical Tourism

Munish Kumar Duggal
https://orcid.org/0000-0003-3588-6940
Indian Economic Service, India

ABSTRACT

The travel and tourism sector is an important economic sector that contributes to the national income through job creation and export promotion. The sector accounted for 10.4percent of global GDP, 319 million jobs, and 9.9percent of total employment in 2017 In the same year, India was the seventh largest country after USA, China, Germany, Japan, UK, and Italy in terms of the contribution of T&T sector to its overall GDP growth. In absolute terms, the contribution of T&T sector to overall GDP was US $ 234 billion at real 2017 prices. As percent of overall GDP, the contribution of T&T growth in 2017 for India was 9.4percent and Australia 11percent against a global average of 10.4percent. Thus, T&T sector is important to both India and Australia and can be studied further for unlocking business and trade opportunities which could be of mutual interest to these countries.

DOI: 10.4018/978-1-7998-4126-5.ch007

BACKGROUND

Contribution of the Services Sector to Economic Growth

With economic growth, the relative shares of the primary, secondary and tertiary (broadly services) sectors in the overall growth of any economy undergo structural changes which, *inter alia*, are reflected in the rising share of the services sector and declining shares of the primary and secondary sectors. Thus, the services sector constitutes an increasing proportion of GDP in nearly all developing economies. Globally, services now make up 60-65 per cent of the total economy. The services sector in India has also grown on expected lines and in 2018-19, the sector contributed about 60 per cent of GDP including construction-related activities and 54 per cent without construction-related activities[1]. The share of the services sector in the Australian economy was close to 73 per cent at the end of 2017[2].

The services sector consists of subsectors relating to technology especially IT, healthcare, accounting & audit services, architecture and engineering, education, media & entertainment, space, legal, language, skills and travel & tourism. In India, the share of travel and tourism in total services exports rose from 12 per cent in 2012-13 to 15 per cent in 2017-18[3]. In what follows, an attempt is made to focus on the travel & tourism sector with special reference to India and Australia.

The Travel & Tourism (T&T) sector is an important component of the services sector, which contributes to the national income through job creation as well as export promotion. The sector accounted for over 10 percent of global GDP, 319 million jobs and 9.9 percent of total employment in 2017[4]. In that year, India was the seventh largest country after USA, China, Germany, Japan, UK and Italy in terms of the contribution of T&T to overall GDP growth. In absolute terms, the contribution of T&T to overall GDP was US $ 234 billion at real 2017 prices. As a percentage of overall GDP, the contribution of T&T growth in 2017 for India was 9.4 per cent compared with the global average of 10.4 percent. According to the World Travel and Tourism Council (2015), by 2025 the contribution of the sector to India's GDP may be close to 10.1 per cent and the sector may provide employment to 74.6 million persons including 29 million direct jobs (Prasad & Singh, 2016). The sector comprises travel, tourist attractions, travel agents and tour operators. T&T is important to both India and Australia and can be studied further for unlocking business and trade opportunities which could be of mutual interest to these countries.

Contribution of T&T to Overall Growth in INDIA

Table 1 provide details of the contribution of the T&T sector to India's GDP and employment from 2009-10 to 2017-18

Table 1. Tourism sector in India: Economic contribution

Year	Contribution of Tourism to GDP (percent)			Contribution of Tourism in Employment (percent)		
	Direct	Indirect	Total	Direct	Indirect	Total
2009-10	3.68	3.09	6.77	4.37	5.80	10.17
2010-11	3.67	3.09	6.76	4.63	6.15	10.78
2011-12	3.67	3.09	6.76	4.94	6.55	11.49
2012-13	3.74	3.14	6.88	5.31	7.05	12.36
2014-15*	2.2	6.7	8.9	NA	NA	12.1
2016-17	NA	NA	5.06	NA	NA	9.3
2017-18	NA	NA	9.4	NA	NA	12.38

Source: Ministry of Tourism, Government of India, 2017-18 & www.IBEF.org.
*Based on Travel and Tourism Economic Impact 2015 India, World Travel & Tourism Council, 2015

India has faced difficulties in credible data collection on employment in all sectors including travel and tourism due to an array of methodological issues and the presence of a very large unorganized sector, and detailed investigation of this aspect of data on employment is beyond the scope of this chapter.

Inbound Tourism in India: Aggregate

Table 2 provides details about the growth of Foreign Tourist Arrivals (FTA's) in India from 1981 till 2019 - the latest period for which firm figures are available.

The table clearly indicates a lack of any significant trend in tourist arrivals in India during the 1980s and 1990s. However, during the years 2003-07, 2010, and 2014 a double digit growth in foreign tourist arrivals is clearly visible. Negative growth in tourist arrivals in 1991, 2001, 2002 and 2009 is also indicated (Bureau of Immigration, 2017).

Inbound Tourism India: Region Specific

To understand the holistic picture about the inward tourist traffic into India in the immediate past, region-wise FTA's during 2014-16 are presented in table 3. Three major regions namely South Asia, North America and Western Europe have contributed close to 66 per cent of total tourists. During 2014-16, Australasia (Australia & New Zealand) has never accounted for more than 4 per cent of total tourists in India.

Table 2. Tourism Growth In India: 1981 to 2019

Year	Foreign Tourist Arrivals (Million)	Percent Change over Previous Year
1981	1.28	2.0
1991	1.68	-1.7
2001	2.54	-4.2
2002	2.38	-6.3
2003	2.73	14.7
2004	3.46	26.7
2005	3.92	13.3
2006	4.45	13.5
2007	5.08	14.2
2008	5.28	3.9
2009	5.17	-2.1
2010	5.78	11.8
2011	6.31	9.2
2012	6.58	4.3
2013	6.97	5.9
2014	7.68	10.2
2015	8.03	4.5
2016	8.80	9.6
2017	10.02	13.9
2018	10.55	5.3
2019 Jan-Apr	3.93	1.9

Source: Compiled, Bureau of Immigration, Government of India, 2017, India Tourism Statistics, Government of India, 2017. The data exclude arrivals of non-resident Indians.

Inbound Tourism India: Country Specific

Table 4 provides details of major countries contributing to inbound tourism in India during 1981-2003. Australia is one of the top 15 countries contributing to tourist arrivals in India during this period (Brewster, 2010). The tourist traffic from Australia to India during 1981 was 20,940 which increased to 58,730 in 2003 showing an average annual growth rate of 4.8 per cent. During 2003, Australia occupied the ninth position among top fifteen tourist-generating markets for India.

Table 3. Regional grouping wise FTAs in India- 2014-16

Region	Number of arrivals			Percentage Share			Percent Change	
	2014	2015	2016	2014	2015	2016	2015 over 2014	2016 over 2015
Australasia of which Australia	286294 (239762)*	312101 (263101)	348908 (293625)	3.73 (3.12)	3.89 (3.28)	3.96 (3.33)	9.01 (9.7)	11.8 (11.6)
North America	1387468	1494930	1614178	18.07	18.62	18.33	7.7	8.0
Central & S America	69926	70831	78730	0.91	0.88	0.89	1.3	11.2
Western Europe	1860580	1880203	2029412	24.23	23.42	23.05	1.1	7.9
Eastern Europe	422278	331051	406002	5.50	4.12	4.61	-21,6	22.6
Africa	280754	293569	302164	3.66	3.66	3.43	4.6	2.9
West Asia	413678	417616	451842	5.39	5.2	5.13	1.0	8.2
South Asia	1694857	1946207	2194555	22.07	24.25	24.93	14.8	12.8
South East Asia	685805	700298	746069	8.93	8.72	8.47	2.1	6.5
East Asia	546792	555770	617563	7.12	6.92	7.01	1.6	11.1
Unclassified	30667	24557	14988	0.40	0.31	0.17	-20	-39
Total	7679099	8027133	8804411	100	100	100	4.5	9.7

Source: Ministry of Tourism, Government of India
*Figures in parentheses reflect figures for Australia

Since 2003, the data can be obtained for top 10 rather than top 15 countries contributing to inbound tourist traffic to India. During this period, the top 10 countries contributing to inbound tourism traffic include Bangladesh, the USA, the UK, Canada, Malaysia, Sri Lanka, Australia, Germany, China and France. During 2003-16, the relative shares of tourists from the UK, USA, France and Canada declined in varying proportion. Table 6 illustrates that in 2003 a total of 58,730 Australian tourists contributed 2.1 percent to the total tourist traffic to India. There was a more than five- fold increase in the total number of tourists from Australia by 2016 to 293,625 tourists, with the total share of Australian tourists increasing to 3.3 percent.

Table 7 provides data on monthly variations in tourist traffic in India during 2001-15 clearly indicating the peak months of tourists during October to December and the lean months during April-June.

Having looked at several structural aspects of the total number of tourists visiting India in a historical perspective and in the recent years, we now give insights into the total earnings from such a tourist traffic.

Table 4. Tourist arrivals to India from 15 major countries: 1981 to 2003

Year	UK	USA	S Lanka	Canada	France	Japan	Germany	Malyasia	Australia
1981	116684	82052	75842	25358	57272	29032	55471	26458	20940
1982	120772	86806	76143	25991	59267	29103	50885	26552	23395
1983	136823	95847	81716	29857	50158	26662	52120	25796	23436
1984	124205	95651	75449	25135	47148	29566	48930	22993	24546
1985	119544	95920	69063	29022	44091	30573	45738	23265	22047
1986	160685	125364	75631	39837	65948	36402	64811	26209	33264
1987	166590	134876	74351	37677	64432	46240	72300	28480	32883
1988	200509	122888	70640	37498	69799	49244	77543	29635	31462
1989	229496	134314	67680	40306	78001	58707	78812	33120	30443
1990	235151	125303	68400	41046	79496	59122	71374	34278	30076
1991	212052	117332	70088	36142	69346	46655	72019	30617	22700
1992	244263	152288	71935	43386	74304	60137	84422	35201	26646
1993	274168	158159	76898	47800	70694	49616	83340	35334	28795
1994	300696	176482	89009	56441	73088	63398	85352	40762	33142
1995	334827	203343	114157	63821	82349	76042	89040	50039	36150
1996	360686	228829	107351	74031	93325	99018	99853	53370	48755
1997	370567	244239	122080	78570	91423	99729	105979	60401	50647
1998	376513	244687	118292	80111	97898	89565	93993	47496	57807
1999	345085	251926	120072	82892	85891	73373	85033	52613	73041
2000	432644	348292	129193	84013	100022	98159	83881	60513	53995
2001	405472	329147	112813	88600	102434	80634	80011	57869	52691
2002	387846	348182	108008	93598	78194	59709	64891	63748	50743
2003	430917	410803	109098	107671	97654	77996	76868	70750	58730

Table 8 provides information on foreign exchange earnings from tourism in India[5] from 1991 to 2003.

Total travel receipts in 2010-18 are given in table 9. The annual growth rates in tourism receipts in India show significant volatility irrespective of whether they are analyzed in local currency or US dollar terms indicating that tourism receipts appear to be dependent upon certain exogenous variables such as exchange rates over which the policy makers need to provide further insights through intensive research and data analytics[6].

In order to understand the significance of the tourism receipts or foreign exchange earnings in the Indian economy given in table 8 and 9 we need to understand their comparative significance in the economies of top 10 countries.

Table 5. **Tourist arrivals to India from 15 major countries: 1981 to 2003 continued**

Year	Singapore	Italy	Nepal	The Netherlands	South Korea	Israel
1981	17950	28503	11851	10780	2665	2569
1982	19026	29791	12115	10724	4110	3169
1983	21252	27947	12001	11358	3139	2548
1984	19204	23570	13401	12101	3078	1928
1985	18485	23187	15883	13158	3939	1448
1986	24189	38548	13957	15297	1767	1707
1987	26380	41151	16965	18819	2990	2473
1988	27565	47612	19715	21327	3572	2620
1989	29377	50751	19116	22716	3895	4634
1990	32570	49194	20614	24353	3986	5855
1991	28363	41129	21834	19845	3967	6882
1992	35039	51138	25244	30145	5171	9468
1993	40223	40315	28048	30856	4791	9646
1994	44157	43510	34732	35094	7227	12098
1995	48632	53015	34562	40147	9831	14806
1996	47136	49910	43426	40246	16173	18387
1997	52004	53854	43155	44843	15392	20162
1998	54328	54058	38199	54227	16321	21103
1999	53310	50677	25859	48820	19188	23417
2000	46612	50419	38801	46370	23411	25631
2001	42824	41351	41135	42368	27150	28774
2002	44306	37136	37136	31669	29374	25503
2003	48368	46908	42771	40565	35584	32157

Source: Bureau of Immigration, Government of India, various years

Table 10 lists top 10 countries in terms of international tourism receipts in 2016. International tourism receipts for USA were the highest at $US 205.9 billion. Spain, France, Germany, Italy, and the UK also find a place in the top 10 countries. Australia accounted for 2.6 per cent of total receipts and India was behind Australia with a share of around 1.8 percent. This clearly indicates that in the global context and for cross-section data for the year 2016, neither Australia nor India have significant shares in International tourism receipts. Revival of the growth in the global economies and pro-active measures by both India and Australia could increase their shares in international tourism receipts.

Table 6. Top 10 source countries for Foreign Tourist arrivals in India: 2016

S. No	Source Country	FTAs 2003	Percentage Share 2003	FTAs 2016	Percentage Share 2016
1	Bangladesh			1380409	15.68
2	United States	410803	15.1	1296939	14.73
3	United Kingdom	430917	15.8	941883	10.70
4	Canada	107671	3.9	317239	3.60
5	Malaysia	70750	2.6	301961	3.43
6	Sri Lanka	109098	4.0	297418	3.38
7	Australia	58730	2.1	293625	3.33
8	Germany	76868	2.8	265928	3.02
9	China	-	-	251313	2.85
10	France	97654	3.6	238707	2.71
	Total top 10 countries			5585422	63.43
	Others			3218989	36.57
	Grand Total			8804411	100

Source: Bureau of Immigration, Government of India, 2017.

Table 7. Month-wise Tourist arrivals in India: 2001 to 2015

	2001	2002	2003	2004	2005	2006	2007	2008	2009	2010	2011	2012	2013	2014	2015
Jan	1501	1229	1505	2055	3272	3970	4698	4599	4530	5593	5777	8623	10785	11664	12100
Feb	1405	1294	1442	2050	3136	3793	4401	5496	4610	6646	7653	8502	10255	11510	11642
March	1258	1177	1199	1812	2985	3378	4144	4312	4160	5507	5522	7843	9545	10479	11133
April	1289	1102	1153	1368	2156	2850	3218	3740	3873	4518	5724	6745	7226	9179	10091
May	957	947	1014	1134	1957	2350	2543	3153	3410	4358	5047	5562	6627	7936	9505
June	1119	906	1263	1364	2144	2566	2849	3538	3926	4751	5440	6485	7149	8366	9564
July	1242	1254	1489	1779	2556	2990	3436	4553	5042	5444	7116	8389	8620	10284	11982
Aug	1090	1127	1354	1552	2273	2698	3080	4041	4306	4620	5734	7260	8351	10385	11411
Sept	878	1108	1264	1476	2135	2640	2594	3602	3852	4678	5748	6652	7811	9057	10415
Oct	958	1111	1421	1906	2921	3355	3785	4234	4543	5219	7019	8154	8645	10041	10549
Nov	1172	1351	1585	2389	3560	3793	4533	5003	5361	6516	7941	9723	10663	11431	12649
Dec	1474	1588	1741	2589	4028	4642	5079	5023	6096	7039	8870	10549	11994	12988	14152
Total	14344	14195	16429	21472	33123	39025	44360	51294	53709	64889	77591	94487	107671	123320	135193

Source: data.gov.in, Ministry of Tourism, Government of India, various years

Table 8. Foreign Exchange earnings from Tourism: India

Year	Foreign Exchange earnings (INR Million)	Percent change	Foreign Exchange earnings (US $ Million)	Percent change
1991	43180	-	1861	-
1992	59510	37.8	2126	14.2
1993	66110	11.1	2124	-0.1
1994	71290	7.8	2272	7.0
1995	84300	18.2	2583	13.7
1996	100460	19.2	2832	9.6
1997	105110	4.6	2889	2.0
1998	121500	15.6	2948	2.0
1999	129510	6.6	3009	2.1
2000	142380	9.9	3168	5.3
2001	143440	0.7	3042	-4.0
2002	141950	-1.0	2923	-3.9
2003	164290	15.7	3533	20.9

Source: Reserve Bank of India and Ministry of Tourism, Government of India 2003

Table 9. Foreign Exchange Earnings in India: 2010-11 to 2018-19

Year	Foreign Exchange Earnings in India (US $ Billion)	Per cent Growth
2010 - 11	14.49	-
2011 – 12	17.71	22.2
2012 – 13	17.97	1.4
2013 – 14	18.39	2.3
2014 -15	20.4	10.9
2015 -16	21.4	4.9
2016 – 17	23.8	11.2
2017 – 18	28.7	20.6
2018 – 19 (P)	27.7	-3.5

Source: data.gov.in. Government of India for 2010-11 to 2013-14
Economic Survey 2018-19, Ministry of Finance, Government of India, 2018-19
P: Provisional data Foreign Exchange Earnings in India: 2010-11 to 2013-14

Table 10. Share of Top 10 countries of the World and India in International Tourism Receipts 2016

Rank	Country	International Tourism Receipts (US $Billion)	Percentage Share
1	United States of America	205.9	16.9
2	Spain	60.3	4.9
3	Thailand	49.9	4.1
4	China	44.4	3.6
5	France	42.5	3.5
6	Italy	40.2	3.3
7	United Kingdom	39.6	3.2
8	Germany	37.4	3.1
9	Hong Kong	32.9	2.7
10	Australia	32.4	2.6
	Total of top 10 countries	585.5	48.0
	India (P)[7]	22.2	1.8
	Others	612.3	50.2
	Total	1220.0	100

Source: Bureau of Immigration, Government of India, 2017.

During 1991-2003, the share of India in the world tourism receipts fluctuated between 0.62 percent to 0.69 percent and therefore, the share of about 1.8 per cent in 2016 was not exceptionally low by historical standards. The figures in Tables 10 and 11 clearly show the low foreign exchange earnings from tourism by India and the need to grow tourism at an exponential rate for it to make a meaningful contribution to GDP and employment.

Table 11. Share of India in the World Tourism Receipts

Year	World travel receipts (US $ Billion)	Total Travel receipts in India (US $ Million)	Per cent share of India
1991	276.9	1861	0.67
1992	315.4	2126	0.67
1993	321.9	2124	0.66
1994	354.9	2272	0.64
1995	405.3	2583	0.64
1996	436.5	2832	0.65
1997	439.7	2889	0.66
1998	442.5	2948	0.67
1999	457.2	3009	0.66
2000	477.0	3168	0.66
2001	463.6	3042	0.66
2002	474.0	2923	0.62
2003	514.4	3533	0.69

Source: India Tourism Statistics, Government of India 2003 and World Travel Receipts–World Tourism Organization

India Offerings[8]:

Tourism offerings of India - a country with continental dimensions, can be understood in terms of:

- **Heritage Tourism** arising out of deep rooted heritage and history dating back a few thousand years. Innumerable ancient heritage monuments, forts and palaces including the *Taj Mahal*, one of the seven wonders of the World, have a great tourism potential. Amongst centrally protected ticketed monuments, *Taj Mahal, Agra* (5.66 million) was the most visited monument in 2017-18 for domestic visitors followed by *Sun Temple, Konark* (3.22 million) and *Red Fort, Delhi* (3.04 million).
- **Wildlife Tourism** arising out of the fact that India hosts many wildlife sanctuaries and reserves including *Ranthambore, Bandhavgarh* and *Kanha National Parks, Bharatpur, Ranganathittu* and *Vembanad* bird sanctuaries.
- **Adventure Tourism** arising out of many regions having immense potential for adventure-intensive activities such as sports, skiing and trekking in the *Himalayas*, water rafting on the river *Ganges* and *Beas*, camels and Jeep

safaris in *Rajasthan*, water sports in *Goa*, Para Gliding in Hilly States and Scuba diving in *Lakshadweep* and *Andaman & Nicobar islands*.

- **Rural tourism** arising out of recent interest of the community and other stakeholders to showcase the roots of the fast moving urban life in India. In this category of rural tourism, the Ministry of Tourism is actively involved with many non-Government partners to organize fairs, village markets or *haats*, craft *bazaars* which provides a bird's eye view of Indian folks, arts, craft and local cuisines. The interests of tourists in 31 villages developed for this purpose is showing great potential.
- **Buddhist Circuits** are very popular among tourists of India as well as selected South Asian and South East Asian countries. The places like *Bodh Gaya, Rajgir, Nalanda, Patna, Vaishali, Kushinagar* are widely visited by Buddhists. In order to popularize these circuits, the Ministry of tourism undertakes various promotional activities on an ongoing basis in the international markets. These activities showcase and promote the Buddhist Heritage in India and provide a boost to tourism. Besides, the Ministry of tourism organizes an International Buddhist Conclave biennially. Participants in the conclave include eminent Buddhist scholars, opinion makers, tour operators and media personalities from overseas. The Indian Government successfully organized road shows in Yangon (Myanmar), Ho Chi Minh City (Vietnam), Phnom Penh (Cambodia) and Bangkok (Thailand) in May 2018 for promotion of India's Buddhist Heritage. The Ministry produced a short film on Buddhist sites which has been promoted through the digital and electronic media. The Government also launched a dedicated website on important Buddhist sites in India (*www..indiathelandofbuddha.in*) to promote and showcase the rich Buddhist Heritage in India.
- Due to India being a plural, multilingual, multi religious society, the extent of **religious tourism** arising out of innumerable historical/religious places of interest spread over length and breadth of the country is also significant. Religious places like *Vaishnodevi* and *Amaranth* in Jammu & Kashmir, *Tirupathi* in the State of Telangana, Rameshwaram and *Meenakshi* temple in the State of Tamil Nadu, *Padmnabhaswaminatahn* and *Guruvayoor* temples in the State of Kerala, *Haji ali* in the State of Maharashtra, *Ajmer Sherief* in the State of Rajasthan are just a few of many places of religious interest in India.

Most of the tourist circuits and religious sites mentioned above are being promoted under the *Swadesh Darshan Scheme*, under which the Ministry of tourism has identified 15 thematic circuits for development namely: Himalayan Circuit, North East Circuit, Krishna Circuit, Buddhist Circuit, Coastal Circuit, Desert Circuit, Tribal

Circuit, Eco Circuit, Wildlife Circuit, Rural Circuit, Spiritual Circuit, Ramayana Circuit, Heritage Circuit, *Tirthankar*[9] Circuit and *Sufi*[10] Circuit. These circuits cover religious, spiritual, cultural, natural, tribal sites in the country. These thematic circuits are being developed on the principles of high tourist value, competitiveness and sustainability in an integrated manner with an objective of enriching the tourist experience and enhancing employment opportunities in the sector.

In 2015, the Ministry of tourism launched the *'National Mission on Pilgrimage Rejuvenation and Spiritual, Heritage Augmentation Drive' (PRASHAD)* with the objective of creating pilgrimage infrastructure at important pilgrimage destinations. The total number of sites identified for development under the scheme at present is 41 in 25 States. By end 2018, 28 projects in 17 states have been approved under this scheme.

The above mentioned tourism offerings would not realize their full potential if connectivity issues are not integrated with the overall planning process. To achieve this objective of improving accessibility, the Indian Government announced a regional connectivity scheme called *Udan* - which literally means flight - covering 46 tourism routes. These routes include important Buddhist destinations such as Kushinagar, Varanasi (Sarnath) and Gaya (Bodhgaya). Some of the important destinations such as Gaya and Varanasi are already connected with important Buddhist source markets abroad such as Thailand, Sri Lanka and Bhutan. Besides, many places in Leh, Andaman & Nicobar Islands have the potential to develop as places of Eco-tourism which can attract tourists in large numbers. Eco-tourism is being promoted through development of Eco-circuit in the country.

Eco- circuit is one of the fifteen thematic circuits identified for development under the scheme and because of its significance needs further elaboration. The Government has identified eco-tourism as a *niche* tourism area for development. For promotion of various tourism destinations and products in the country including eco-tourism, the Government produces publicity material and collaterals in English and foreign languages and releases print, electronic and online media campaigns in important domestic and international markets under the '*Incredible India*' brand-line. Promotions are also undertaken through the website and various social media platforms.

The details of projects sanctioned by the Ministry under the eco-circuit theme of *Swadesh Darshan* scheme are given in Table 12.

Table 12. Eco-Tourism Projects in India

Serial Number	Name of the State	Project Name	Name of the circuit	Amount Sanctioned (INR Million)
1	Uttarakhand	Eco Circuit (2015-16)	Integrated Development of Eco-Tourism, Adventure Sports, Associated Tourism related Infrastructure for Development of *Tehri* Lake & Surroundings as New Destination-District *Tehri*, Uttarakhand.	709.2
2	Telangana	Eco Circuit (2015-16)	Integrated Development of Eco Tourism Circuit in *Mahaboobnagar* district, Telangana.	916.2
3	Kerala	Eco Circuit (2015-16)	Development of *Pathanamthitta – Gavi – Vagamon – Thekkady* as Eco Tourism Circuit in *Idduki* and *Pathanamthitta* Districts in Kerala.	765.5
4	Mizoram	Eco Circuit (2016-17)	Development of EcoAdventure Circuit *Aizawl -Rawpuichhip – Khawhphawp – Lengpui – Durtlang – ChatlangSakawrhmuituaitlang - Muthee – Beratlawng - Tuirial Airfield – Hmuifang"* in Mizoram under Eco circuit theme of *Swadesh Darshan* scheme	990.7
5	Madhya Pradesh	Eco Circuit (2017-18)	Development of *Gandhisagar DamMandleshwar DamOmkareshwar DamIndira Sagar Dam- Tawa Dam- Bargi Dam- Bheda Ghat- Bansagar DamKen* River under Eco circuit theme of *Swadesh Darshan* Scheme	996.2
6	Jharkhand	Eco Circuit (2018-19)	Development of Eco Circuit: Dalma- ChandilGetalsud- Betla national park- MirchaiyaNetarhat in Jharkhand under Swadesh Darshan Scheme	527.2
			Total	4905

Source: Ministry of Tourism, Government of India, 2018

Digital India Program

The Government of India launched electronic-visas or e-visas for tourists from 43 countries in November 2014 and widened eligibility to 150 countries in February

2015. Although the number of visitors using e-visas surged 11-fold to 445,300, they still accounted for only 5.5percent of total arrivals.

Table 13. Major countries availing e-Tourist visas in 2016 and first half of 2017

S. No	Source Country	2016	Percentage Share	2017 Jan -June	Percentage Share
1	United Kingdom	239005	22.1	151476	21.1
2	United States of America	157061	14.5	90378	12.6
3	France	65188	6.0	41755	5.8
4	Russia	63608	5.9	49365	6.9
5	China	62396	5.8	44577	6.2
6	Germany	49484	4.6	32224	4.5
7	Australia	47634	4.4	28789	4.0
8	Canada	40482	3.7	25744	3.6
9	Spain	23644	2.2	12138	1.7
10	Republic of Korea	21125	2.0	20055	2.8
11	The Netherlands	19077	1.8	11778	1.6
12	UAE	18599	1.7	7819	1.1
13	Malaysia	16822	1.6	11897	1.7
14	Singapore	16639	1.5	13804	1.9
15	Ukraine	15498	1.4	9364	1.3
	Others	223434	20.8	165913	23.1
	Total	1079696	100.0	717076	100.0

Source: Bureau of Immigration, Government of India, 2017

The e-visa eco system received a major boost under the Digital India initiative launched in 2015 under which the e-visa facility was extended to citizens of 166 countries. E-visa is allowed under three sub-categories: e-tourist visa, e-business visa, and e-medical visa. The window for application under e-visa has been increased from 30 days to 120 days and the duration of stay in India has been increased from 30 days to 60 days. As a result of the user-friendliness of the e-visa platform and appropriate media outreach by the Government, more than a million e-visas were issued during 2016. (Table 13). During January-September 2017 a total of 1.24million e-visa holders visited India registering a growth of 59.2 per cent over the same period of 2016[11]. Special immigration counters have been set up for seamless interface at major airports in India.

Box 1. Tourism Policies in India

The Government of India released a **National Tourism Policy** in 2002, under which tourism became a joint central-state government responsibility. The policy recognized tourism as an engine of growth in the Indian economy and laid a policy framework for increasing the number of international and domestic tourists. The government proposed to diversify the Indian tourism product and substantially improve the tourism infrastructure, undertake vigorous marketing and outreach, facilitate visa arrangements and improve connectivity through all modes of transport including air-travel. With the advent of online travel portals and low-cost carrier airlines, the sector experienced an increased movement in traffic, both international and domestic. After the announcement of this policy, many other initiatives aimed at promotion of tourism were undertaken. Prominent among these were:

Incredible India: This campaign was conceptualized in 2002 as a branding exercise for creating a distinctive identity for India for international tourists. The campaign included extensive advertising in print, electronic and visual media, with the sole aim of building the tourism brand.

Atithi Devi Bhava[12]: This social awareness campaign was initiated by the Ministry of Tourism in 2003 for promoting domestic tourism in the country which was assumed to have great unharnessed potential. It was aimed at providing the inbound tourists a greater sense of being welcomed in different states.

Hunar se Rozgar Tak- Skill Development Program: The program has been managed by the Ministry of Tourism to reduce the skills gap in the tourism sector, along with a focus on creation of employable skills among the youth from the economically weaker sections. Under this study-cum-training based program important courses such as (i) food and beverage service, (ii) food production, (iii) housekeeping, (iv) bakery and patisserie are included in the curriculum. The requirements of the tourism industry are suitably incorporated in this program.

Earn while you Learn Program: This program, a collaboration between the Ministry of Tourism and the Indian Institute of Tourism & Travel Management (IITTM), is targeted at college students/ graduates in the age group 18–25 years. It aims at inculcating tourism traits and knowledge among the trainees, enabling them to act/ work as student volunteers. Entirely funded by the Ministry of Tourism through the Scheme of Capacity Building for Service Providers, the 21-day program includes modules on Indian society and culture and an overview of the tourism travel and hospitality industry, as well as managerial and behavioural skills.

In October 2018, the Statue of *Sardar Vallabhbhai Patel*[13], also known as the *'Statue of Unity'*, was inaugurated as a tourist attraction. It is the tallest statue in the world, with a height of 182 metres. It is expected to attract tourists from India as well from abroad. The facility is equipped with e-bike tours. Foreign tourists show an immense interest in e-bike tours.

The Government has also been making serious efforts to boost investment in the tourism sector. In the hotel and tourism sector, 100 per cent FDI is allowed through the automatic route. A five-year tax holiday has been offered for 2, 3 and 4 star category hotels located around UNESCO World Heritage sites (except Delhi and Mumbai). Total FDI received by the Indian hotel and tourism sector was US$ 12.35 billion between April 2000 and March 2019.

Monument Friends (Mitra) is a novel Government initiative that has been received well by the corporate sector. In all, eleven memorandums of understanding have been signed under the *'Apni Dharohar, Apni Pehchaan'* – aimed at promoting different types of tourism mentioned above, the Indian Government is also alive to the prospective contributions of the corporate houses and public sector undertakings in the form of adoption of monuments having a world heritage tag and maintaining them under their Corporate Social Responsibility (CSR) programs. The prospective Monument

Mitras (meaning friends) who sign MOU's are free to select a monument/heritage/ tourist site of their interest under the *'Apni Dharohar, Apni Pehchaan* - Adopt a Heritage' project. The conservation of heritage/ancient buildings/monuments does not come under the *'Apni Dharohar, Apni Pehchaan* - Adopt a Heritage' project of the Ministry of Tourism. Hence, there is no pre-requisite Adopt a Heritage Project. Table 14 gives details of these projects.

Table 14. Heritage Projects adopted by Corporates in India

S. No	Monument *Mitra* (Corporate adopting the monument)	Name of Monument/ Heritage Site/Tourist Site or Technological Intervention
1	M/s Dalmia Bharat Ltd.	Red Fort, Delhi
2	M/s Dalmia Bharat Ltd.	Gandikota Fort, Andhra Pradesh
3	Adventure Tour Operators Association of India (ATOAI)	Area surrounding Gangotri Temple and Trail to Gaumukh, Uttarakhand
4	Adventure Tour Operators Association of India (ATOAI)	Mt. Stok Kangri Trek, Ladakh, Jammu and Kashmir
5	Yatra Online	Qutub Minar, Delhi
6	Yatra Online	Leh Palace, Jammu & Kashmir
7	Yatra Online	Ajanta Caves, Maharashtra
8	Yatra Online	Hampi (Hazara Rama Temple), Karnataka
9	M/s Bliss India Pvt. Ltd. (V-Resorts)	Surajkund, Haryana
10	M/s Apeejay Surrendra Park Pvt. Ltd.	Jantar Mantar, Delhi
11	M/s Resbird Technologies Pvt. Ltd.	Development of Multi-lingual Audio Guide Application for five Iconic Tourists Sites: • Colva Beach, Goa • Amer Fort, Rajasthan • Kaziranga, Assam • Kumarakom, Kerala • Mahabodhi Temple, Bihar

Source: Ministry of Tourism, Government of India, 2018

Despite the efforts of the Indian government and the private sector in addressing the issues faced by the growth of travel and tourism sector, as detailed in Box 1, India remains on such a low base of tourist numbers that it needs to grow exponentially (Sengupta & Nundy, 2005). For such exponential growth one has to understand the issues and challenges faced by the sector. They include:

- Problems arising out of co-ordination failures between various stakeholders from the government as well as private sector. These coordination failures need to be minimized through robust, productive and sustainable coordination mechanisms based on consultation and forging of viable partnerships among stakeholders.
- Issues arising out of huge interstate disparities in tourism infrastructure, which prevent the harnessing of the full tourism potential and providing less than optimal value of money to the tourists. All state governments, therefore, need to treat tourism as a major driver of employment and poverty alleviation so that the tourism system becomes dynamic and caters to the ever-evolving needs of the industry.
- Inadequate budgetary allocation to the various government schemes and programs leads to a thin spread of available resources. The Government should ensure adequate funding for the various schemes and abstain from announcing new schemes if it cannot ensure matching financial resources.
- Slow and inefficient government clearances at the level of federal/central as well as state governments for various projects such as building new hotels or adding rooms to the existing hotels. Time bound, technology based and fast paced clearances of such projects should be ensured. Wherever possible, human interface with the government departments providing clearances should be avoided.
- Land related issues are posing a big challenge to the tourism growth in the metropolitan cities. Availability of varying sized land parcels should be ensured for tourism and hospitality sector. The sectoral requirements should be integrated with land planning and Urban planning initiatives.
- Lack of globally competitive taxation regime on hospitality industry is often cited as a big constraint which prevents substantial tourism growth in the country. Even the new Goods and Services Tax has left many stakeholders dissatisfied. The issue needs serious consideration by the Government.

Lack of skilled manpower in various positions in all categories of jobs in the travel and tourism sector prevents the Indian tourism industry from ensuring professionalism and value of money to the travellers. While the issue of skills shortages in this sector was flagged for the first time in the Tenth Five Year Plan (2002–07), not enough ground work has been done to address the issue of skill shortages in the sector. Given the importance of skilled manpower in the T&T sector, the issues needs to be discussed in detail.

Skills Requirements and Skill Gaps

Backed by government policy and market forces, the T&T sector is growing in India but there are concerns over whether there will be enough skilled manpower to meet the ever increasing demand in the sector (Kumar, 2015-16). In 2008, the Government approved a "Coordinated Action on Skill Development" to formulate policies to harness the benefits of demographic dividend by skilling 500 million persons in high growth sectors by 2022. The T&T sector was one of the high growth sectors identified and was supposed to have major skill gaps that could not be bridged without pro-active policy action.

Another study was conducted by the Ministry of Tourism to assess manpower requirements in the hospitality and travel trade sector in 2012. The study found that there is a demand and supply gap in manpower especially at the non-managerial level. As per this study, the gap is expected to be 755,000 in non–managerial manpower and 109,000 in management by 2020-21. To bridge the skill gaps, the Government geared up to conduct skill development and capacity building courses across the country including pilgrimage places through the Central Institutes of Hotel Management/State Institutes of Hotel Management/Food Craft Institutes/Indian Institute of Tourism and Travel Management (IITTM)/ India Tourism Development Corporation (ITDC)/ Kerala Institute of Tourism and Travel Studies (KITTS)/Private affiliated Institutes/ Institutes identified by State Governments, Hotels/equivalent establishments under the State Tourism Development Corporations. The Ministry of Tourism has also launched a Pan India-Incredible India Tourist Facilitators Certification Program (IITFC) to enable creation of a pool of well-trained and professional tourism facilitators. It is surprising that while skill gaps in the sector were assessed in 2007 and again in 2012, there have been no assessments in the recent past that could guide the players in the sector – both private and Government - to upscale and accelerate their skill development efforts in the fast changing industry[14].

The Ministry of Tourism launched *Hunar Se Rozgar* in 2009 offering short-term quality courses of 8 weeks and 6 weeks duration under the Capacity Building for Service Providers Scheme in disciplines such as multi-cuisine cooking, room attendants, food and beverage service-steward and front office associate. These courses are fully funded by the Government so that people are encouraged to take up professions in the hospitality industry and to ensure that the industry gets enough trained manpower.

As the industry does not place much value on the prior learning or training received in the colleges and universities, many industry players are active in the supply side, trying to cater to the needs of the sector as a whole. The *Oberoi Group* has a *Systematic Training and Education Program (STEP)* in one of its hotels. STEP is an opportunity for students to participate in a three-year program that offers practical training. The training is provided in the four core operational departments of a hotel: front office, housekeeping, food & beverage service, and kitchen. *Kuoni travels* runs courses that include industry-integrated modules and provide a balanced mix of theory and hands-on training with a leading edge of experiential learning. The *Tata Institute of Social sciences* – School of Vocational Education and *Taj* Group of industries organize a 3-year Bachelor of Vocation degree in Hotel Management, which also combines academic excellence with on-the-job training to equip participants to become leaders in the hospitality sector.

Safety and Security of Tourists

The Ministry of Tourism, the main nodal department for all matters relating to tourism in India, along with all stakeholders including the tourism departments of all states, have adopted the *'Code of Conduct for Safe & Honourable Tourism'* which lays down guidelines to encourage tourism activities to be undertaken with respect for basic rights such as dignity, safety and freedom from exploitation of both tourists and local residents - in particular, women and children. In early 2016, the Ministry of Tourism launched the 24x7 Multi Lingual Tourist Info-Helpline on the toll free number 1800111363 in 12 languages including 10 international languages. This was supposed to provide support services in the form of information relating to travel in India and also offer proactive guidance to tourists in distress. The Ministry also issued the Guidelines on Safety and Security of Tourists for State Governments and tips for travelers in September 2014, stressing the importance of safety and risk management, assisting in identifying best practices and encouraging closer cooperation for ensuring a pleasant and valuable tourist product. The security of tourists is a state government responsibility; however, with efforts of Ministry of Tourism, the state governments / union territory administrations of *Delhi, Goa, Himachal Pradesh, Jammu & Kashmir, Karnataka, Kerala, Maharashtra, Odisha, Punjab, Madhya Pradesh, Uttar Pradesh, Rajasthan* and *Andhra Pradesh* have deployed police in and around places of tourist interest. The Ministry of Tourism conducts a constant dialogue with state governments and various tourism-related institutions for development and promotion of tourism in the country including ensuring safe and honorable tourism. As no information is available on the outcome of such schemes, it is suggested that a third party independent evaluation be undertaken to assess the exact outcome of these measures. The extent to which the various components of the scheme such as tourist helpline numbers were made use by tourists needs to be placed in the public domain.

Apart from issues relating to the safety of tourists in India, the tourism industry is exposed to risks arising out of terrorism, global meltdown and fear of recession, pandemics like H1N1 flu, SARS, Coronovirus etc. While most of these risks are global in nature and beyond the capability of tourism departments to control, timely information dissemination and proper risk management through 360 degrees coordination can go a long way toward mitigating the inherent risks.

Travel & Tourism Traffic from India to Australia

For Indian visitors, Australia possesses many iconic landmarks and attractions including World Heritage sites. These attractions include the Opera House in Sydney, the Great Barrier Reef which itself is home to over 3000 coral reefs, 600 continental islands, 300 coral cays and mangrove islands, *Uluru-kata Tjuta* National park (formerly Ayers rock) and Bondi beach. Indian tourists also visit Australia to meet family and friends many of whom came to Australia earlier on student visas and decided to acquire residency status and stay there.

Sustained economic growth in India in the post-1991 phase of economic liberalisation has increased considerably the disposable incomes of Indians and the emergence of a large middle class which aspires to demonstrate its newly acquired wealth and consolidate its position in the social hierarchy. Undertaking foreign travel is one such *demonstration effect*. During 2000-15, outbound tourism from India showed a four-fold increase to 21. 8 million departures. Out of this four-fold increase in outbound tourism, a disproportionately large number flew to Australia. It is expected that sustained economic growth in India and a growing trade relationship with Australia will increase outbound tourism to Australia. During 2005-16, a significant increase in the number of Indian tourists in Australia was matched by an increase in their per capita spending, causing their total tourism spending to rise by 350 percent, to $1.2 billion in 2016.

As pointed out above, total outbound departures from India to Australia can also be viewed in terms of those who visit Australia for purely tourist purposes and those who visit friends and relatives. Australia has registered a significant jump in tourist numbers due to the growing Indian diaspora in the country. The latest figures released in *Austrade's* International Visitor Survey show that during the year ending March 2019 the number of Indian visitors jumped 15 per cent to 343,000 and their spending rose by 12 per cent to $1.7 billion. The survey also reveals that the per capita spending by Indian tourists was much higher than that by tourists from other countries. The average stay of 61 nights by Indian tourists to Australia against overall average stay of 32 nights is explained by the fact that more than 50 per cent of Indian tourists visit Australia to meet friends and relatives and combine tourism with family visits.

According to projections by "Tourism Australia" - a Government of Australia agency responsible for promoting Australia to the world as a destination for business and leisure travel, the number of Indian tourists in Australia could swell to half a million a year by 2025. Along with various other measures, the agency has appointed the popular Bollywood actress – *Parineeti Chopra* - as the first Indian woman ambassador to be a part of their 'Friend of Australia' (FOA) panel.

Medical and Wellness Tourism

While there may not be a standard textbook definition of medical tourism[15], it may be defined as the process of traveling abroad for the purpose of receiving medical care, procedure and services. The major considerations for seeking medical treatment in another country include: (i) a shortage of supply of medical treatment at home, as reflected in long waiting lists, (ii) the higher cost of medical treatment at home (Bhat, 2015). Based on these primary considerations, the factors such as advances in information technology easing the access to information and knowledge, lower transport costs, reduced language barriers, ability to remain anonymous and maintain privacy overseas (may be required in procedures like cosmetic surgery or treatment of HIV/AIDS), cultural affinity in terms of language, food and religion, geographical proximity and the added benefit of a holiday are behind the global expansion of medical tourism. Specifically, the growth of medical tourism in India is attributed to the following factors:

Low Cost, Low Prices

The major growth driver of medical tourism to India is quality medical treatment at affordable prices. Due to the relatively low cost of operations and salaries of supporting staff, the value-for-money of medical services in India compares favourably with that provided by German, Korean, Turkish and Israeli hospitals. In some fields like organ transplantation, India is among the best in the world[16].

Quality Medical Services

As mandated by the policy regime in India, all the private hospitals have to be certified by the National Accreditation Board for Hospitals & Healthcare Providers (NABH). The certificate confirms compliance of hospitals with world quality standards. For global recognition the hospitals obtain accreditation from Joint Commission International (JCI). As of January, 2019, 41 hospitals/clinics in India have received JCI accreditation which provides assurance on the high level of equipment, doctors' qualification and safety of medical services. List of these 41 hospitals/clinics is provided in Table 16.

Table 16. Oragnizations/ Hospitals Accredited by Joint Commission International (JCI): India

S No	Hospital	City In India	JCI accreditation	Date of Accreditation
1	Grewal Eye Institute Private Limited	Chandigarh	Ambulatory Care program	26 May 2007
2	Indraprastha Apollo Hospitals	New Delhi	Hospital Program	18 June 2005
3	Kokilaben Dhirubhai Ambani Hospital & Medical Research Institute	Mumbai	Hospital Program	13 December 2015
4	Maharaja Agrasen Hospital, Punjabi Bagh	Delhi	Hospital Program	28 January 2017
5	Max Super Speciality Hospital (A Unit of Devki Devi Foundation))	Delhi	Hospital Program	18 February 2017
6	Max Super Speciality Hospital (A Unit of Max Healthcare Institute Limited)	Delhi	Hospital Program	15 February 2017
7	Medanta - The Medicity	Gurugram	Hospital Program	31 August 2013
8	Moolchand Hospital	Delhi	Hospital Program	5 December 2009
9	Narayana Institute of Cardiac Sciences	Bangalore	Hospital Program	21 January 2011
10	National Institute of Ophthalmology	Pune	Ambulatory Care Program	27 June 2015
11	Rajagiri Hospital	Ernakulum, Kerala	Hospital Program	26 November 2016
12	Shroff Eye Hospital/Shroff Eye Clinic	Mumbai	Ambulatory Care Program	13 February 2009
13	Wockhardt Hospitals Ltd Unit: Adams Wylie Memorial	Mumbai	Hospital Program	29 April 2017
14	Ahalia Foundation Eye Hospital	Palakkad, kerala	Hospital Program	1 January 2010
15	Apex Heart Institute (A Unit of TCVS Pvt. Ltd.)	Ahmedabad	Hospital Program	27 January 2018
16	Apollo Gleneagles Hospitals	Kolkatta	Hospital Program	24 January 2009
17	Apollo Hospital	Chennai	Hospital Program	29 January 2006
18	Apollo Hospital	Hyderabad	Hospital Program	28 April 2006
19	Apollo Hospitals Enterprise Limited	Mumbai	Hospital Program	3 June 2017
20	Apollo Hospitals International Limited	GandhiNagar/ Ahmedabad	Hospital Program	25 June 2016
21	Apollo Hospitals	Bengaluru	Hospital Program	18 July 2008
22	Artemis Hospital (a unit of Artemis Medicare Services Ltd.)	Gurugram	Hospital Program	12 January 2013
23	Asian Heart Institute and Research Center Pvt Ltd	Mumbai	Hospital Program	20 October 2006
24	Aster Medcity	Kochi	Hospital Program	20 June 2015
25	Care Institute of Medical Sciences	Ahmedabad	Hospital Program	24 September 2016
26	Columbia Asia Referral Hospital, Yeshwanthupur	Bengaluru	Hospital Program	27 august 2016
27	Continental Hospitals Limited, Hyderabad	Hyderabad	Hospital Program	24 January 2015
28	Dhirubhai Ambani Occupational Health And Family Welfare Centre	Jamnagar, Gujarat	Ambulatory Care Program	23 August 2014
29	Dr. B. L. Kapur Memorial Hospital	New Delhi	Hospital Program	21 April 2018
30	Eternal Heart Care Center & Research Institute	Jaipur	Hospital Program	25 January 2019
31	Fortis Escorts Heart Institute	New Delhi	Ambulatory Care Ashtama	20 August 2011 31 October 2012
32	Fortis Hospital Limited	Mumbai	Hospital Care	26 August 2005
33	Fortis Hospital	Bengaluru	Hospital Care	9 February 2008
34	Fortis Hospital	Mohali/Chandigarh	Hospital Care	15 June 2007
35	Grewal Eye Institute Private Limited	Chandigarh	Ambulatory Care Program	26 May 2007
36	Indraprastha Apollo Hospitals	New Delhi	Hospital Program	18 June 2005
37	Kokilaben Dhirubhai Ambani Hospital & Medical Research Institute	Mumbai	Hospital Program	13 December 2015
38	Maharaja Agrasen Hospital	New Delhi	Hospital Program	28 January 2017
39	Max Super Speciality Hospital (A Unit of Devki Devi Foundation)	New Delhi	Hospital Program	18 February 2017
40	Max Super Speciality Hospital (A Unit of Max Healthcare Institute Limited)	New Delhi	Hospital Program	15 February 2017
41	National Institute of Ophthalmology	Pune	Ambulatory Care	27 June 2015

Effective Drugs

Most Indian hospitals use the licensed analogs (generics) of American drugs. The Indian pharmaceutical companies produce medicines with cost of production which in many cases is 10-18 times lower than drugs imported from the USA .

Qualified and World-recognized Doctors

A big proportion of doctors working in hospitals/hospital chains mentioned earlier are internationally recognized. Most of these doctors are trained in North America, the United Kingdom and Western Europe in state of the art surgeries and procedures involving liver, pancreas, heart and lungs transplants. Most of them also acquire great hands on experience while working in the public health system in India.

Language Skills

Most of the medical tourists coming to India feel advantaged as English is almost the *lingua franca* in the country. Many South Asian medical patients and their families are able to communicate even with their respective mother tongues. This is one of the important drivers of growth of medical tourism in India.

Organ Transplantation

India is one of the few countries where organ transplantation is feasible in a cost effective manner. The National Organ & Tissue Transplant Organization (NOTTO) develops Organ Transplantation in India. Indian transplantologists perform the advanced transplant surgeries of the pancreas, liver, and heart-lung complex.

Globally, the medical value travel (MVT) market is expected to cross US$ 100 billion in 2019, growing at a CAGR of 19.4 percent and India's share could rise significantly from 3.8 per cent of the global medical tourists and 5.5 per cent of the global revenue from medical tourism achieved in 2014 (Medhekar, 2019). The sustained growth of Indian medical tourism industry can also be traced primarily to public policy driven cultivation of medical tourism eco- system in the country.

Box 2. Government Policy Initiatives: Medical Tourism

Government has taken various Policy initiatives and measures to promote Health and Medical Tourism in India. The Ministry of Tourism as well as National Health Policy have recognized Medical and Wellness Tourism including *Ayurveda* as a Niche product to promote India as a 365 days' destination and attract tourists with specific interests.
The market size of medical tourism in India is estimated at US$ 3 billion in 2017. The value of medical tourism is forecasted to reach US$ 9 billion by 2020[17]. Share of Medical Tourists to India is 4.9 per cent out of total FTAs in 2017. The arrival in India on Medical visa increased from 1,39,447 in 2014 to 2,33,918 in 2015 showing a growth of 67.7 per cent. A total of 4,27,014 arrivals were there in 2016 which further increased to 4,95,056 in 2017 showing a growth of 15.93 per cent.
Government offers financial support as Marketing Development Assistance, for Publicity and for organizing Wellness and Medical Tourism Promotion shows. Medical Tourism is regularly highlighted for promotion as part of the *Incredible India* Campaign in the print, electronic, online and outdoor media in India and abroad as well as at the various travel trade exhibitions overseas. Ambit of 'Medical Visa' is being expanded in terms of scope as well as number of countries covered. Currently, 'E- Medical Visa' facility is introduced for citizens of 166 countries.

Source: Economic Survey 218-19, Ministry of Finance, Government of India July 2018

While a reference has already been made to the National Health Policy, it is important to mention that government policy visualized importance of medical tourism way back in 2002. The policy clearly mentions that *"to capitalize on the comparative cost advantage enjoyed by domestic health facilities in the secondary and tertiary sector, the policy will encourage the supply of services to patients of foreign origin on payment. The rendering of such services on payment in foreign exchange will be treated as 'deemed exports' and will be made eligible for all fiscal incentives extended to export earnings"*[18].

Since 2015, a large number of initiatives have been taken by the Government of India to make India a Medical Value Travel as well as wellness destination (Box 2). To realize these objectives, the Ministry of Tourism has formulated guidelines for the promotion of Medical Tourism. As per these guidelines following assistance is provided to eligible stakeholders:

Financial Assistance for participating in fairs/events/road shows approved by the Government in the overseas markets under the Marketing Development Assistance (MDA) Scheme.

- Financial Assistance in the ratio 50:50 for making publicity and promotional material subject to a maximum ceiling of INR 1.0 million.
- Financial Assistance up to a maximum of INR 2.5 million on 50:50 sharing basis for organizing Wellness & Medical Tourism promotion shows.
- Permission for the use of *Incredible India logo* for the Wellness & Medical tourism promotion events, films, literature
- Financial support for training courses focused on skill provision, skill up-gradation and skill certification for the persons engaged in Wellness &

Table 15. Tourist arrivals in terms of Purpose of Visa - 2017

Country Grouping/ Country	Arrivals	Business &Professional (percent share)	Leisure, Holiday, Recreation (percentShare)	Medical (percentShare)	Indian Diaspora (percentShare)	Others (percentShare)
North America	1712358	9.31	43.42	0.06	44.15	3.07
Central & S America	92067	17.83	73.17	0.12	6.60	2.29
Western Europe	2133673	17.99	49.43	0.07	30.04	2.48
Eastern Europe	472872	12.89	81.15	2.37	2.16	1.44
Africa	318023	17.46	40.43	15.70	17.80	8.60
West Asia	457760	9.94	62.66	21.93	3.34	2.13
South Asia	2951665	6.07	78.42	10.79	2.39	2.33
South East Asia	824575	11.42	66.89	0.43	17.21	4.05
East Asia	663295	50.43	44.27	0.06	3.91	1.33
Australasia	386059	8.36	38.05	0.33	51.03	2.22

Source: India Tourism Statistics, Government of India, 2018

Medical Tourism sector as per the Capacity Building for Service Providers (CBSP) Scheme guidelines formulated by the Ministry of Tourism.

- Provision of space to Wellness and/or Medical Tourism Associations at major international fairs for promoting Wellness & Medical Tourism.

In addition to MDA scheme mentioned above, the Ministry of Tourism has taken various steps to boost medical tourism which inter-alia include:

- Medical tourism is being promoted on social media across various platforms.
- Department of Commerce and Services Export Promotion Council have launched a Healthcare Portal www.indiahealthcaretourism.com, as a single source platform providing comprehensive information to medical travelers on the top healthcare institutions in the country in various languages.

In order to provide dedicated institutional framework to take forward medical tourism, a 'National Medical and Wellness Tourism Board' has been constituted which works as an umbrella organization that promotes this segment of tourism in an organized manner.

The major initiatives of National Medical and Wellness Tourism Promotion Board include: (i) Facilitating procedural simplification of formalities for applicants of medical visas such as doing away with the procedure for reporting of those coming on medical visas to Foreigner Regional Registration Offices (FRRO) and following on hospital's reports. (ii) Emphasizing accreditation of institutions and organizations dealing with Medical and Wellness Tourism at all levels for ensuring minimum standards of quality of medical care to the patients. In this context, it may, however be noted that whereas at the level of the Central Government some action in this regard is visible, similar efforts at the level of various State Governments are not visible and needs to be initiated for sustaining medical tourism industry. (iii) Encouraging the Medical and Wellness Tourism stakeholders to work in a transparent and fair manner by listing out indicative cost of procedures and ensuring fair pricing in the market.

These initiatives by the National Medical and wellness Tourism Board to promote medical Tourism are likely to sustain the existing trade and also attract more tourists to the country.

An analysis of the purpose wise tourist arrivals in India in 2017 reveals that around 22 per cent arrivals from West Asia was for medical purpose followed by Africa with 15.70 per cent and South Asia with 10.79 per cent. Majority of visitors from three African countries namely, Nigeria, Sudan, Tanzania visited India primarily for medical purposes in 2017. Majority of visitors from three West Asian countries namely, Iraq, Yemen and Oman also visited India primarily for medical purposes in 2017. Similarly, visitors from three South Asian countries namely, Maldives, Afghanistan and Bangladesh were top recipients of medical visas issued in India in 2017. Majority of the patients from these countries come for treatment for specialized services in wide ranging areas such as neurology, cardiology, endocrinology, nephrology, and urology . Citizens of North America, Western Europe and Australasia primarily visited India for leisure and tourism related activities and their share in medical visa is miniscule. Australian interest in availing cost advantages of Medical facilities in India is very less as less than 1 per cent of medical visas were availed by Australians. Citizens from developed countries may be interested to explore the opportunities of life style improvements based on alternative systems of medicines such as *Aurveda, Yoga, Unani, Siddha and Homeopathy* (AYUSH). In this context, the need to formulate a proper country specific marketing strategy in consultation with various stakeholders and industry bodies (Table 15) may be explored.

Alternative Systems of Wellness and Medicines

Ayurveda is an ancient Hindu system of medicine based on the notion of balance within the body. It uses herbal treatment and yogic breathing for overall wellness of the mind and the body. *Ayurveda* and Spa tourism is one of the fastest growing segments today in India.

Siddha and Unani are similar in their holistic approach to finding harmony between the mind and body, with the origins of *Siddha* lying in the Southern state of *Tamil Nadu*, while *Unani* can trace its roots in history to the time of ancient Greece.

Wellness tourism is different from medical tourism, and usually describes people travelling for the purposes of maintaining or promoting their health and wellbeing. Wellbeing services may include: (i) beauty, such as body and facial treatments, (ii) lifestyle, such as detoxification and rejuvenation, and (iii) spiritual, such as meditation and *yoga* retreats.

There is also a growing demand for Indian medical talent and know-how in geographies that are lacking in advanced medical infrastructure, and several players in African countries are approaching Indian players to help them set up and run hospitals, both as advisors as well as O&M partners.

Corporate Hospitals

Some of the prominent hospitals/hospital chains offering health care to medical tourists are Fortis Escorts Heart institute, Fortis Health care, Max Health Care,, Apollo Hospitals Group, Tata Memorial Centre, Global health care, Medanta, SP Hinduja Hospital, Naryana Hospital, Hiranandani Hospital, Artemis Health Institute, Christian Medical Centre, Vellore, BM Birla Heart Research Centre, Wockhardt Hospitals, Manipal Hospitals and Indian Spinal Injuries Centre.

In order to ensure World class quality treatment and value of money to international medical tourists, these corporate hospitals have geared themselves to get certified by international accreditation systems. Corporate chains such as Apollo Hospitals and Wockhardt Hospitals Group are working through agencies like InduShealth, PlanetHospital and the Medical Tourist Company in Britain to build business across the West. The industry is also promoting the National Accreditation Board for Hospitals and has started the process of granting accreditation to about 70 hospitals across the country.

SUMMARY AND CONCLUSIONS

As the economies grow the relative proportion of services sector in a country's GDP increases. Whereas the services sector constitute a large number of diverse services, the focus on service sectors with high spillover effects such as tourism should become a central focus of the policy action. In India, it is already established that tourism sector is a major engine of economic growth which contributes significantly in terms of GDP, foreign exchange earnings and employment.

India's tourism sector derives its growth from its exotic image with its rich cultural heritage, flora & fauna, cuisine, languages, festivals and diverse geographical landscape offered by it — from the mountains, rivers and deserts, to backwaters and wildlife reserves spread across the country. Lately, medical facilities backed by experienced and skilled medical professionals duly certified by eminent authorities in India and abroad is also driving the growth of medical tourism.

An analysis of the trends in foreign tourist arrivals from 2014 onwards indicate that three major geographical regions namely South Asia, North America and Western Europe contribute close to sixty per cent of total tourists in India. Within these regions too, tourists come from small number of countries and, therefore, efforts of the Government and the industry needs to be focused on inter as well as intra- regional diversification of tourist growth. This can be done through understanding the requirements of the individual regions/countries and providing them tailored solutions marketed through vigorous outreach campaigns. Australasia of which Australia is the major country has never accounted for more than 4 per cent of total tourists inflow to India. Improvements in tourism infrastructure and aggressive marketing of brand India specially in the niche areas of wellness tourism are urgently needed.

While India has a very comprehensive National Tourism Policy for promoting tourism through an array of schemes and projects, it is difficult to come across third party independent evaluations of these schemes for measuring the exact outcomes. Institutional mechanisms need to be devised for determining the outcome of the plethora of schemes and if possible, they should also suggest mid-course corrections for achieving the targets.

While the revival of economic growth at the international level and movement of exchange rates will largely determine the tourist inflows to India, a lot depends upon the availability of quality infrastructure (well maintained and clean hotels, airports, lounges, waiting areas, safe modes of transport) hotel tariffs, air fares, security/safety of the tourists specially women and children, political stability, extremist threats and the overall tourism offerings. Any lapses in terms of these parameters could shift the tourists to alternative cheap destinations within South Asia or towards South East Asia.

According to industry observers, Indian tourism industry in the organized sector such as star hotels are subject to high tax rates and this factor alone puts them at disadvantage vis-a-vis their counterparts in the unorganized sector. According to one estimate, in India, the travel industry may create 46 million job opportunities by 2025. To realize this much needed objective, the industry should be taxed at lower and competitive rates across various States. This factor will also encourage more investment in the sector. The cost of compliance to tax regime also needs to be reduced for providing industry a competitive and transparent environment.

Travel and tourism sector may be given infrastructure status as it will allow large capital-intensive hotel projects to avail loans with longer repayment tenures at lower rates of interest and higher debt-to-equity ratios. Other measures aimed at facilitating capital inflows to the sector at lower costs should also be considered.

Skills gaps act as a big constraint to the growth of tourism in the country. The various vocational training programs offered under a variety of schemes needs to have strong practical orientation so that they meet the requirements of the industry on completion of the courses. Strong linkages of the training providers with the industry must be ensured. National and International giants like ITC, Indian Hotels, Hotel Leelaventure, Fairmont, MarriotBonvoy, Intercontinental and Carlson who intend to build more hotels in India and expand the existing properties must not be discouraged because of lack of skilled manpower at various levels of tourism supply chain.

Currently, India has US$ 3 billion medical tourism industry. Majority of the tourists come from South Asia, West Asia and Africa. India's main advantage in this mode lies in the availability of highly qualified doctors, skilled nurses, paramedics, and hospital staff and its ability to provide high quality yet cost effective treatment relative to that available in their home countries and other countries offering medical visas. India also excels in providing follow up treatments to African patients in their home countries through the Pan-African e-Network which promotes *tele*-education and *tele*-medicine to ensure continuity and follow up of care for African patients treated in India. Tele-education allows already treated patients to electronically receive further guidance and advice while *tele*-medicine ensures medical advice & health care from remote locations. Such an arrangement allows African patients to access care through local hospitals in Africa that have partnerships and alliances with hospitals in India. While India needs to continue to leverage such technologies for retaining the current market shares, it must be aware that countries like South Africa are moving ahead in providing facilities to African patients and they need to be countered through suitable cost effective service oriented strategies. To ensure that medical service providers retain their comparative advantage, the Policy regime must fulfill their requirement of import of technology, equipment and related products at prudent custom duty rates.

REFERENCES

Bhat, T. P. (2015). *India: Trade in Healthcare Services*. Working Paper 180, Institute for Studies in Industrial Development. Retrieved from https://ideas.repec.org/p/sid/wpaper/180.html

Brewster, D. (2010). Australia and India: The Indian Ocean and the limits of strategic convergence. *Australian Journal of International Affairs*, *64*(5), 549–565. doi:10.1080/10357718.2010.513369

Bureau of Immigration. (2017). *Tourism Growth in India: 1981 to 2016*. Government of India. Retrieved from https://www.indiastat.com/tourism-data/29/foreign-tourists/280/stats.aspx

Kumar, S. (2016). Skill Development in India for tourism and hospitality sector. *Journal of Information, Knowledge and Research in Humanities and Social Sciences, 4*(1).

Medhekar, A. (2019). Emerging Trends of Wellness and Medical Tourism in India. in S. Paul & S. K. Kulshreshtha (Eds.), Global Developments in Healthcare and Medical Tourism. Academic Press.

Prasad, H. A. C., & Singh, S. S. (2016). *India's Services sector: Performance,some issues and suggestions*. Department of Economic Affairs, Ministry of Finance, Government of India.

Sengupta, A., & Nundy, S. (2005). The private health sector in India [editorial]. *BMJ (Clinical Research Ed.), 331*(7526), 1157–1158. doi:10.1136/bmj.331.7526.1157 PMID:16293815

ADDITIONAL READING

Bureau of Immigration. (2018). Ministry of External Affairs, Government of India.

Chanda, R. (2017). ADBI Working Paper series 668: Trade in Health Services and Sustainable Development. Retrieved from https://www.adb.org/sites/default/files/publication/229661/adbi-wp668.pdf

Deliotte Access Economics. (2011). *Medical Tourism in Australia – a Scoping study*. Department of Resources, Energy and Tourism.

Economic Survey. (2018). Department of Economic Affairs, Ministry of Finance, Government of India, pages, 231, 237, 249

Economic Survey.(2019). Department of Economic Affairs, Ministry of Finance, Government of India.

Gupta, Amit S. (2008). Medical tourism in India: winners and losers. Retrieved from doi:10.20529/IJME.2008.002

Gurry, M. (2012). India, the new centre of gravity: Australia-India relations under the Howards Government. *Journal of South Asian Studies*

Human Resource and Skill Requirement in the travel, tourism and the hospitality sector. (2013-17, 2017-22), National Skill Development Corporation, Ministry of Skill Development and Entrepreneurship, Government of India

IBEF. (2019). Indian Tourism and Hospitality Industry Analysis. Retrieved from https://www.ibef.org/industry/indian-tourism-and-hospitality-industry-analysis-presentation

Investment, T. (2018).Global Greenfield Investment trends in tourism, A publication from the Financial Times Tourism Research Australia.(April 2019). State of the Industry, 2017-18, Austrade, Australian Government

National Tourism Policy. (2002). *Department of Tourism, Ministry of Tourism and Culture*. Government of India.

Prasad, H. A. C., & Singh, S. S. (2017). *Services sector: Challenges, issues and policy suggestions with special focus on IT-BPM, Tourism, Shipping, Real Estate services and Project exports*. Department of Economic Affairs, Ministry of Finance, Government of India.

Reserve Bank of Australia (RBA). (2019). Monetary Policy. Retrieved from https://www.rba.gov.au/

Reserve Bank of India. (2018). Annual Reports of various Years

Tourism, H. India. (2007). Growth of the medical tourism industry. Retrieved from http://www.health-tourism-india.com/growth-of-the-medical-tourism-industry.html

Tourism Research Australia (TRA). (2019). International Tourism Results. Retrieved from https://www.tra.gov.au/International/international-tourism-results

Travel and Tourism Competitiveness Report. 2019. World Economic Forum

UNCTAD. Trade and Development Report 2016.The catch-up challenge: Industrialization and structural change, chapter III World Bank. (2001). Health, Nutrition, Population Sector Unit India South Asia Region. Raising the sights: better health systems for India's poor. Washington

United Nations. (2019). Sustainable Development Goals. Retrieved from https://www.un.org/sustainabledevelopment/sustainable-development-goals/

World Travel and Tourism Council (WTTC). (2018). Travel and Tourism Power and Performance Report

WTTC. (2019). Contribution of Travel and Tourism to GDP of Australia and India. Retrieved from https://www.wttc.org/economic-impact/country-analysis/country-data

ENDNOTES

1 Economic Survey, Ministry of Finance, Government of India, 2018-19 page 249

2 Economic Survey, Ministry of Finance, Government of India, 2018-19 page 237

3 Economic Survey, Ministry of Finance, Government of India, 2018-19 page 231

4 www.wttc.org, 2018

5 The foreign exchange earnings data provided by the RBI-Central Bank of India and Ministry of Finance has shown differences due to differing contexts in which two agencies release data. Whereas, RBI data is closer to accounting numbers, Ministry of Finance data may be adjusted for GDP deflators to capture the real movement in the economy.

6 Wide volatility in tourism receipts in Rupee and Dollar terms cannot be fully explained by mere variations in the exchange rates

7 According to another data set released by Ministry of Finance, Government of India in Economic Survey, 2018-19 (July 2019), figures for 2016-17 for India was US $ 23.8 billion, For meaningful comparison of earnings share, single source data is used in this table

8 Tourism offerings mentioned here are generic and applicable for domestic tourists as well as international visitors of all countries

9 In Jainism, a tirthankara (Sanskrit: tīrthaṅkara; English: literally a 'ford-maker') is a saviour and spiritual teacher of the dharma (righteous path). The word tirthankara signifies the founder of a tirtha, which is a fordable passage across the sea of interminable births and deaths, the saṃsāra.

10 Sufism, known as tasawwuf in the Arabic-speaking world, is a form of Islamic mysticism that emphasizes introspection and spiritual closeness with God. While it is sometimes misunderstood as a sect of Islam, it is actually a broader style of worship that transcends sects, directing followers' attention inward.

11 In the table on e visas, figures for January to June 2017 have been used as the country wise break up of e-visas for January –September 2017 was not available at the time of preparing this write up.

[12] Atithi Devo Bhava - The Guest is God. A 'tourist' is one who travels to or visits another place for their own pleasure or interest. ... In one of the ancient Hindu Scriptures called Taittiriya Upanishads, the Sanskrit phrase Atithi Devo Bhava holds sacred meaning and translates to 'The Guest is God'.

[13] One of the prominent freedom fighter and first Home Minister of Independent India who is remembered for his resolve to make India a unified country after Independence in 1947.

[14] Parliament (Lok Sabha) Question No.2282 answered by Minister of Tourism, Government of India on 08.07.2019 regarding SHORTAGE OF PROFESSIONALS IN TOURISM SECTOR www.tourism.gov.in 2019.

[15] There is sometimes a distinction between 'medical tourists' and 'medical travellers', where medical tourists are those who travel overseas in addition to a holiday, while medical travellers generally travel overseas for the sole purpose of medical treatment. For the purposes of this study, 'medical tourists' and 'medical travellers' are used interchangeably.

[16] Currently, India is the world center for organ transplantation as donation of organs from the living donors is legally allowed, provided it is done without exchange of any pecuniary benefits. Despite this, organ trafficking does happen and there is an **ethical dimension** of allowing Organ transplantation in India which is not covered here and is beyond the scope of this chapter.

[17] Source: Services Export Promotion Council, Ministry of Commerce, Government of India.

[18] National Tourism Policy 2002, Ministry of Tourism, Government of India.

APPENDIX

Acronyms

ATOI: Adventure of Tour Operators of India
AYUSH: Ayurvedic, Yoga and Naturopathy, Unani, Siddha and Homeopathy
CBSP: Capacity Building for Service Providers
CSR: Corporate Social Responsibility
FOA: friend of Australia
GDP: Gross Domestic Product
IITM: Indian Institute of Tourism & Travel Management
ITDC: India Tourism Development Corporation
JCI: Joint Commission International
KITTS: Kerala Institute of Tourism and Travel Studies
MDA: Marketing Development Assistance
MOU: Memorandum of Understanding
MVT: Medical Value Travel
NABH: National Accreditation Board for Hospitals & Healthcare Providers
PRASAD: Pilgrimage Rejuvenation and Spiritual Augmentation Drive for development of tourism infrastructure
STEP: Systematic Training and Education Programme
TFC: Tourist Facilitators Certification Programme
UNCTAD: United Nations Conference on Trade and Development
WTTC: World Travel and tourism Council

Chapter 8
Medical Tourism:
Trade and Business Opportunities Between Oceania and India

Jeayaram Subramanian
International School of Business and Media (ISB&M), Pune, India

Hardik Vachharajani
https://orcid.org/0000-0002-7342-730X
Crown Institute of Higher Education, Australia

ABSTRACT

Medical tourism, perhaps a late 20th century phenomenon, is said to be making a huge impact across the world in many countries, especially in developing world. According to the Medical Tourism Association in the United States, the term "medical tourism" is where people who live in one country travel to another country to receive medical, dental, and surgical care while at the same time receiving equal to or greater care that they could have received at their own country. Many people across the globe are taking to the wheels to various destinations for their medical needs owing to critical reasons like affordability, better access to care at a higher level of quality, etc. Medical tourism is a fast-growing Indo-Pacific region too. The chapter starts with a literature review of the industry followed by identifying the global hubs of medical tourism especially in the Indo-pacific region. It concludes with looking at potentials and challenges of medical tourism industry between India and Australia.

DOI: 10.4018/978-1-7998-4126-5.ch008

INTRODUCTION:

An Overview of Medical Tourism

Medical tourism, perhaps a late twentieth century phenomenon is said to be making a huge impact across the world in many countries, especially in developing world. According to the Medical Tourism Association in the United States, the term "Medical Tourism" is where people who live in one country travel to another country to receive medical, dental and surgical care while at the same time, receiving equal to or greater care that they could have received at their own country. Many people across the globe are taking to the wheels to various destinations for their medical needs owing to critical reasons like affordability, better access to care at a higher level of quality, etc. "Medical Tourism" can broadly be classified into "International Medical Tourism" and "Domestic Medical Tourism". While the primary focus across the world is on the former, the latter is gaining significance in many countries as well. Again, the Medical Tourism Association defines "Domestic Medical Tourism" as the phenomenon where people travel within their country to different cities, regions or states to receive medical, dental and surgical care. Predominantly, the reasons why people undertake "Domestic Medical Tourism" are the same as those for the "International Medical Tourism", perhaps the "affordability" factor might be a bit more enhanced as domestic travel is always considered to be lesser expensive than making an international travel.

Moghavvemi et.al., (2017) reiterate and drive home the important point that this "Medical tourism" has attracted significant attention in the recent years. Thanks to the ever-growing population of the upper-income countries people undertake travel to the lower and the middle-income countries in search of better healthcare and state-of-the-art robust infrastructure (Behrmann & Smith, 2010; Keckley, 2008). Of course it should be remembered that the present day is a day wherein the internet and the social media is on an all-time boom. Moghavvemi et.al., (2017) also recognize this fact by undermining the significance of internet as an increasingly important source of health and healthcare information. They further iterate the point that this has contributed a significant level in the development and shaping up of this "Medical Tourism" Industry. Interestingly many researchers (For e.g. Hohm & Snyder, 2015; Huang & Chang, 2012; Lunt, Hardey & Mannion, 2010, etc.) have also echoed on the same point in their own respective ways. Von Knoop et al., 2010 also adds an important insight to this discussion that patients especially in the United States, use the internet as a source not only to gather and obtain information on general health but also to obtain information on the specific types of medical services that are available in select hospitals both at home as well as overseas. This important point is again echoed by innumerable researchers in this domain in the likes of Grigoroudis et al., 2008, Taylor et al., 2005, etc. To add more to this, even the renowned Medical Tourism Association in 2009 gives more clarity with some worthwhile statistics. It reported that around 49% of the American medical tourists that were surveyed, learned about medical tourism via the internet and more than 73% of them sought specific information online with regards to various aspects and dimensions of care abroad. Thus from all the above discussed points, it becomes seemingly evident that medical tourism as an industry is fast catching up, thanks to a variety of factors, especially the internet.

Travelling to different domestic destinations and overseas for obtaining quality medical treatment has long been existing now for several decades and Connell (2013) reiterates this same viewpoint too. In fact, Connell (2013) talks extensively about Harley Street in London (UK) and how was it popular amongst tourists from all over the world. However the recent trend has been a bit different. Many contemporary researchers in this domain are of the opinion that a form of "reverse globalization" is currently taking place, wherein patients from the more developed countries flock towards the seemingly lesser developed countries in search of quality medical treatment. Reasons are aplenty such as cost, access, service among the prominent ones. Moreover, Connell (2013) also emphasizes heavily that Medical Tourism has started to grow explosively especially after the late 1990s with thousands of patients making their way into countries such as India, Thailand and Mexico in search of quality medical care, which might be too expensive, inadequate and/or unavailable in their home countries. In fact, many researchers (Eg. Bookman & Bookman, 2007; Connell, 2006, 2008; Reisman, 2010) have subsequently documented the emergence of Asian, few European and Latin American countries as potential medical tourism destinations for the world, as their economies have been shaped up and diversified on existing tourism industries and healthcare systems. Connell (2011.a) also makes a point here that an increasing number of countries from these regions are better marketing themselves to the world as excellent Medical Tourist destinations. Taking advantage of this, hundreds of medical tourism companies have become travel agents, where they try to broker between tourists and hospitals, thereby facilitating their travel and stay.

1. Medical Tourism – Worldwide Industry Profile:

While exploring the size of the Medical Tourism Industry worldwide, there seems to be no common consensus amongst researchers or industry practitioners as of now. However there have been few reports from various corners trying to find an estimate of this industry globally. One such report by the Global Healthcare Resources (2017) feels that Visa estimates that over 11 million tourists travel to different destinations across the world for medical purposes. This might be roughly around 3 to 4% of the total global population. Some other reports (For e.g. "Patients beyond Borders") come up with an estimate that the Medical Tourism industry's worth globally is around USD 45.5-72 Billion with around 14 million travellers spending approximately USD 3600-7600 per medical visit. The Medical Tourism Association pegs the industry's estimate to be a mammoth USD 100 billion owing to various factors considered. However having estimated a few statistics, the report from Global Healthcare Resources (2017) also feels that it might be a complicated task to estimate the sheer size of this mammoth industry owing to various parameters like diaspora patients in each country, expatriates who live within a country for a longer duration of time, short-term drop-ins, spa visitors, purchasers and suppliers of pharmaceutical products, friends and family accompanying patients from various countries. The renowned researcher J. Connell also echoes the similar view that it is complicated to estimate the size of this industry owing to all the above mentioned factors. Another challenge faced by industry estimators according to the Global Healthcare Resources (2017) is that, governments of many countries do not record official data on visitors arriving and departing their countries specifically on account of Medical Tourism. Moreover from the hospitals' front too, there seems to be no specific and verified data on the number of medical tourists, thus becoming difficult to discern the true size of the industry.

However all said and done, it can be inferred that the Medical Tourism industry is a promising one for the future and there are again different estimates of substantial growth to back up the point. Visa estimates that this industry would witness a robust growth of around 25% annually and Deloitte putting its weight behind the industry much more with around 35% year-on-year growth. It is estimated that Americans make up the largest pie of the travelling population on account of Medical Tourism. However, China, with the sheer size of its population is all set to surpass America by 2025. Of course, lot of work needs to go in to set up measurable metrics to estimate the size of the industry. Once metrics are formulated, we might hope to get more authenticated figures.

Interestingly the report of the Global Healthcare Resources (2017) also goes on to say that every region of the world has its own success stories of medical tourism. For instance, India has been one of the most prolific countries in the world in documenting and publishing these success stories in the form of case studies and best practices. These measures are essential to paint a positive picture in the minds of global patients who are on the constant look out for quality medical care and services. Also, it is a known fact that apart from India, many Southeast Asian countries have shown more aggression and thus have become successful in their endeavour to attract medical tourists from across the world. In fact it might be very interesting for us to know that six out of the top ten medical tourism destinations are from this region. This shows the intensity with which these countries compete with each other to offer the best facilities and in attracting global medical tourists. Apart from this, there are other clusters that are at the beginning stage of development as medical tourism destinations. To name couple of them, Sri Lanka and Puerto Rico are examples of this.

Thus, it is imperative that the Medical Tourism industry is a burgeoning one, with a mammoth industry size, which is only going to show robust growth numbers in the near future. Of course there are established medical tourism destinations across the world that offer excellent facilities, there are few other destinations that are in the queue to make it into this list.

In the next section, we shall witness some key medical tourism destinations across the world and how do they contribute in terms of various factors, both internally and externally as well.

2. Global Hubs of Medical Tourism:

"Deloitte Access Economics" had come up with an exhaustive report in August 2011 and this report brings to the table, an extremely interesting snapshot of the Medical Tourism Industry across the globe. This report gives a detailed accord on how Asia, as a continent is driving and propelling this industry forward. Notable Asian countries that lead the charge are Thailand, Singapore, India, Malaysia, Hong Kong, Mainland China, Japan and Korea. Many of these countries gain a competitive advantage mainly owing to their cost-structure and availability of excellent infrastructure and world-class medical facilities. Now we shall witness a brief discussion on how each of these Asian countries position themselves as global hubs for medical tourism.

2.1. Thailand:

As per various reports and studies, (E.g. ESCAP, 2009; France, 2009; Thailand Investment Review, 2010; Deloitte Access Economics, 2011), Thailand is considered to be the global hub of medical tourism. According to a report from ESCAP 2009, Thailand has witnessed phenomenal growth in terms of number of foreign patients visiting various Thai hospitals. Numbers suggest that the figure was around 500,000 in the year 2001, and has considerably grown to around 1.4 million in 2006. Tourism Authority of Thailand News Room reported that in the year 2008, over 1.5million of medical tourists flocked the country's hospitals, thus generating a staggering US$ 6 billion towards the country's economy. Banking upon this huge success, the government is also trying to play its part in encouraging the industry to flourish further by creating active promotions regarding various healthcare options that the country offers. In addition, the government has also come up with various types of incentives for foreign investment including tax holidays, land ownership rights, key permissions that are required to bring in foreign experts in various fields of medicine, etc. (Thailand Investment Review, 2010; Deloitte Access Economics, 2011).

According to the Joint Commission International (JCI), in early 2011, around 14 hospitals in Thailand were accredited according to their prescribed set of international standards. Thailand Investment Review (2010) further goes on to list various reasons why foreign medical tourists are attracted to visit Thailand. They are as follows:

1. Assurance of quality services
2. Competitive pricing wherein some complex medical procedures might just cost 10% of what would be the cost in North America, Europe, etc.
3. Offering a wide variety of medical services such as cosmetic surgeries, organ transplants, joint replacements, dental treatment, CT scans for early detection of cancer, heart problems, brain disorders, etc.

Thus, it is evident from the above projections that Thailand enjoys a paramount place in the medical tourism industry. Various statistics in this regard project a constant upward tick in terms of this industry's growth in the future, thus plotting the country clearly in the global map of medical tourism.

2.2. Singapore:

According to Singh (2009), Singapore is one of the primed destinations for medical tourism in the world. Given its strategic location advantage, in 2006, it was estimated that around 410,000 foreign medical tourists travelled to Singapore for healthcare purposes alone. This huge influx generated approximately US$ 560 million for the economy. Some of the most preferred medical procedures by foreign tourists arriving at Singapore include liver and heart transplantation, neurological procedures, cardiac surgeries and joint replacements. The Deloitte Access Economics report (2011) points out an important point made by Singh (2009) that being an island nation, Singapore has a very negligible domestic local population, its delivery of sophisticated and specialized medical care and retention of the best medical practitioners is highly contingent on it, thus maintaining a critical mass of foreign tourists.

Of course, like any other medical tourism hub, the government has its role to play. Governmental support is rendered through the dedicated Ministry of Health and is supported by three other governmental agencies – The Economic Development Board, promoting new investments in the healthcare sector, Singapore Tourism Board that actively takes initiatives in marketing and promotion activities and the International Enterprise Singapore that promotes growth and expansion of the medical tourism industry in Singapore.

The exhaustive report of Deloitte Access Economics (2011) captures a very important challenge that Singapore confronts in this regard. Chee (2010) points out the critical aspect that there is a severe "drain of expertise" from the public to private healthcare setup, wherein more remuneration and other HR benefits were available. This situation, as Chee (2010) puts it, is not much pronounced in other medical tourist hubs such as Thailand, Malaysia, etc. Normally, Singapore's public healthcare setup offers very competitive salaries to its employees, and as a result, the proportion of people working in the public healthcare setup (as per Deloitte Access Economics, 2011) stood at 65%, which is considered to be one of the highest in the world. This is much higher than world leaders, Thailand and Malaysia (pegged at 25 – 30%) (Pocock & Phua, 2011). Because of this, the gap between public and private healthcare services is much lesser compared with many other countries. But what concerns more is that, the average healthcare costs have been escalating and this is increasingly being paid from the pockets of the end-users of the service. Statistics show that the medical costs have gone up by almost 30% from the year 2005 to 2008.

Despite this, and of course with the positive steps taken by the government of Singapore, Deloitte Access Economics report (2011) clearly shows that still, Singapore's patients come mostly come from its neighbouring countries such as Indonesia, Malaysia, etc. Interestingly, the report points out that Singapore is also attracting a considerable chunk of medical tourists from mainland China, the Middle East and even from the US, owing to the affordability and mainly its clean image. As of 2011, Singapore had around 16 medical facilities that were JCI accredited, including 12 hospital program accreditation.

2.3. Malaysia:

Similar to Thailand and Singapore, Malaysia has also emerged a key player in the medical tourism industry over two decades or so. Various studies and reports (E.g. Tourism Malaysia, 2008; ESCAP, 2009; Pocock & Phua, 2011) peg the numbers as 341,288 foreign patients being treated at Malaysian hospitals, thus contributing a whopping US$ 78 million to the country's economy. Major medical procedures that are preferred by foreign patients in Malaysia include cardiothoracic procedures, cosmetic surgeries, radiotherapy and radiology. These reports also bring to light that a major chunk of foreign medical tourists arrive in Malaysia from neighbouring Indonesia (Figure pegged at almost 72%), Singapore (10%), Japan (5%) and West Asia (2%).

ESCAP (2009) highlights the salient features of Malaysia being an important player in the global medical tourism sector. Malaysia is one of those few countries in the world that offers state-of-the-art medical facilities with a presence of highly trained medical specialists from all over the globe holding post-graduations from countries such as the United States, United Kingdom, Australia, and the likes. There are numerous private medical centres across the country that offer high quality medical treatment at competitive prices. Moreover, there are options for luxury accommodation for foreign patients, which might be helpful for their rehabilitation and recuperation.

On the governmental front, the Malaysian government is supporting the medical tourism industry by relaxing the regulations for advertising and media services. Moreover, the government has established an accreditation system for all hospitals through the Malaysian Society in Quality Health (MSQH) that was founded in the year 1997. This is also significantly lesser expensive for hospitals to go for it, as compared to that of the JCI (Chee, 2010). To go along with this trend, the government has also come up in the recent years with a slew of tax incentives. Notably in 2009, revenues arising out of foreign patients were exempted from the Income tax bracket by almost 50% on the value of increased exports and by the subsequent year (2010), this was doubled to 100%. To go with it, the government announced tax deductions for setting up international patient units and for expenses in obtaining international accreditations. Private hospitals can also claim double deduction on expenses that they might incur from advertising their medical offerings in other countries (Chee, 2010; Deloitte Access Economics report, 2011).

2.4. India:

Medical Tourism in India is considered to be a key growth driver for its economy and there has been consensus amongst many researchers in this domain for this. For instance, Binoy, (2017) indicates that India has emerged successfully as one of the most significant Medical and Welfare tourism destinations in the world. Pollard (2017) establishes the fact that the Indian medical tourism market is expected to clock in USD 7-8 billion in size by the year 2020, as for the current size of around USD 3 billion. The Medical Tourism Report (2015) reveals that India is "one of the lowest cost and highest quality of all medical tourist destinations and it offers a wide variety of procedures at about one-tenth of the cost of similar procedures in the United States. Thus unsurprisingly India is one amongst the most preferred medical tourism destinations in the world".

Binoy (2017) continues to emphasize that the annual growth rate of medical tourists flocking into India is consistently in double digits. Most of the medical tourists arriving from countries like the United States, England and other European countries such as France, Germany, Italy and the likes. Having said this, a report drafted by the Confederation of Indian Industries (CII) in 2015 points out that Afghanistan and Bangladesh accounted to almost 34% of all the medical tourists who arrived in India. It can be inferred that the influx of medical tourists from both these countries are high because of their close proximity to India (In fact, both countries share territorial borders with India). Also it might be due to the fact that healthcare facilities in these countries are often found wanting and are of sub-standard levels and it is perhaps this reason which forces people to travel into India for their medical needs. Apart from Bangladesh and Afghanistan, Russia and few other Commonwealth nations occupied a pie of around 30% of the influx of medical tourists into India, followed by few countries from Africa and the Middle-East.

If we have a look at the major hubs of Medical Tourism within India, the cities of Chennai, Bangalore, Hyderabad, Delhi and Mumbai stand out as prime locations for tourists from across the world. The Indian state of Kerala is well known for a niche type of medical therapy called "Ayurveda". The city of Chennai is considered to be the hub of all activity in the area of Medical Tourism in India and is rightly termed as "India's Health Capital".

"The Presence of World Class hospitals and skilled medical practitioners has strengthened India's position as preferred medical tourism destination. The treatment for major surgeries in India costs only a fraction - in some cases as low as 10% of that in developed countries". "Majority of the patients coming to India for treatment are from the Middle East, Africa, Bangladesh, Afghanistan, Maldives, Pakistan, Bhutan and Sri Lanka. India's cost advantage will significantly open doors to the US and Europe over future, due to lower cost than the US and almost half that of Europe." Dental tourism accounts for 10% of the medical tourism and the government is keen to promote it. "India provides competitive cost advantage at one tenth of the cost of the US and Europe. By 2020, medical tourism industry of India is expected to touch $8 billion," - Confederation of Indian Industries (CII) Report 2017.

There are a few major hospitals in India that serve as the nerve-centre for Medical Tourism and these include Apollo Hospitals, Fortis, Narayana Healthcare, Manipal Hospitals, Max Healthcare and the likes. Binoy (2017) goes on to explain that there are close to 600,000 hospital beds available in India in a year that includes both public and private hospitals.

Thus from all these details it can seemingly be inferred that India has grown into one of the world's most preferred destination for medical tourism. In the coming future, this is only going to get more prominent with the burgeoning infrastructure, coordinated efforts from both the government of India coupled with that of the private sector.

2.5. A special focus on India - A visible boom in the Medical Tourism Industry:

Taking cues from the previous section, we shall witness here as to why India is now being considered as one of the major hubs of Medical Tourism in the world. One of the most prominent and reputed India's print media house "The Hindu" clearly points out India's upper hand in this booming sector amidst a host of positives – A rare combination of advanced facilities, skilled doctors and lower costs of treatment have made India a popular hub for Medical Tourism. The media house adds on to some important statistical data that is worth considering at this point. The Government of India (in 2017) puts the total number of medical tourists who travelled into India as 495,000, as compared to 427,000 in 2016 and 234,000 in 2015. These numbers clearly indicate a paradigm shift of India's position in the global Medical Tourism map. Of the total number of people in the year 2017, the Ministry of Tourism, Government of India pegs the highest influx of medical tourists from Bangladesh as 221,000 and from Afghanistan as 55,681. Other countries from where there is a significant influx of medical tourists coming into India are Iraq, Oman, Maldives, Yemen, Uzbekistan and Sudan. The government of India values the country's share of Medical tourism as 18% of the global market, with a Compounded Annual Growth Rate (CAGR) of around 15% year-on-year. It is also estimated that the market size of India's medical tourism industry would touch USD 9 Billion by the year 2020, if the current growth rate sustains. It is also clearly pointed out that India was the most preferred destination for cardiology, orthopaedics, transplants and ophthalmology. Apart from these, India also enjoys a high credibility amongst global medical tourists in the areas of wellness, preventive and alternative medicine.

2.5.1. Reasons for this boom:

According to a detailed blog titled "Unbeatable stories of India's Medical Tourism Industry" published by "Tour My India" – An organization that serves as a guide for inbound medical tourists in India, the major credit for such a boom in the Medical tourism industry in India goes to the Indian government. The blog explains that there is a dedicated National Medical and Wellness Tourism Board formed by the Government of India that provides a well-formed framework for the promotion of medical tourism in India, encompassing modern medical sciences coupled with those ancient traditional Indian forms of medicine such as Siddha, Ayurveda, Unani, etc. Understanding the global demands of medical tourists across the world, the Indian government has partnered with many leading private and corporate hospitals across the country to extend joint support to patients globally. This is of course one of the reasons for the enormous success and boom of this industry in India. "Tour My India" lists down many more reasons as discussed below:

2.5.1.1. Availability of high-quality treatment:

In the present day scenario wherein many countries around the world could not afford to offer quality medical treatment to its citizens owing to various factors, India has the upper hand where a patient can undergo any type of medical treatment at an extremely affordable cost with the best quality guaranteed! Here the term "Quality" not only refers to the standard of medical and/or surgical services but also includes the availability of the latest cutting-edge technology used to conduct various medical procedures with complete precision and accuracy.

2.5.1.2. Cost Effectiveness:

This is seen as one of the greatest advantage that India offers to the world, as compared to many of its counterparts. It is estimated that a medical tourist travelling to India from any country would be able to save almost 50-70% of the money, which would also include the cost of travel and accommodation in any metro city in India. Such is the scale of saving India offers to its medical tourists. Hence "Cost effectiveness" becomes one of the most important talking points for researchers in this domain to ascertain the significance of India in the global arena.

2.5.1.3. Travelling & Leisure Options:

Although it is a known fact that Medical tourism is a specific travel segment that comes only for medical treatments, if given an opportunity to combine it with some leisure travel and visits to some popular destinations, many of them would be more than happy to undertake. This is especially a big possibility for those people who travel for dental and cosmetic treatments. India offers a host of tourist destinations across the length and breadth of its huge geography and these places add to the required spice that global trotters are exactly looking for!

The blog from "Tour My India" also offers some deeper insights as to why should global medical tourists choose India for their treatment needs, rather than any other country. This clearly explains the list of competitive advantages India has over many other medical tourism destinations in the world.

- Of course, the low-cost advantage that India offers can be one of the biggest growth-drivers for this industry.
- The best hospitals that India has, have the capability to perform complex surgeries and other medical procedures at a low cost with state-of-the-art technology.
- Indian medical visa process is a hassle-free experience for inbound global medical tourists.
- Several corporate hospitals offer several "Treatment Packages" to its international patients and these can be customized to suit individual needs
- Round the clock availability of the country's best doctors and surgeons at the best hospitals.

- Complete hand-holding given to international patients' right from their point of entry till the point of exit. Robust care post-discharge and recovery procedures too aid the cause.
- Extremely negligible waiting time for patients
- Excellent hospitality and cultural acceptance draws more and more medical tourists into India.
- A strong network of air connectivity into India also eases the travel-related stress for inbound patients. Strong domestic connectivity through roads, rail and air aid as catalysts for growth.

3. Australia vs. Rest of the World – Growth Drivers of the Medical Tourism Industry:

As we've witnessed so far in the previous sections, medical tourism is a booming industry in many parts of the world. Apart from the above-mentioned countries of Thailand, Singapore, Malaysia and India, there are other countries as well, that are significant contributors and players in this industry, viz. Hong Kong, Mainland China, Korea, United Arab Emirates and the likes. Of course, each country has its own competitive advantages in terms of various parameters, which enable them to project themselves to the world as a global player in this industry.

As we discuss the various trade and business opportunities for various countries, we now turn our focus to witness where does Australia stand amidst this big clout. As it might be known, if an industry should prosper, there should be few prominent growth drivers that would propel the country forward. The Deloitte Access Economics report (2011) identifies some of the key growth drivers for the medical tourism in Australia as follows:

1. Relative cost of healthcare services in Australia
2. Quality and Availability of those key medical services that might potentially be unavailable in other parts of the world
3. Australia's reputation as a "safe medical destination"
4. Income levels of medical professionals and the country's exchange rates, that would be a key factor in determining the cost
5. Other miscellaneous factors involving migration rules, medical visas, leisure tourism opportunities, Australia's proximity to Asia's fastest growing economies and cultural affinity.

Now let us witness each of these points in a bit more detail, thus outlining various opportunities between Australia and Asia, particularly India.

3.1. Relative Cost of Healthcare services:

As we've discussed in the previous sections, cost of medical offerings play a vital role in the growth of the medical tourism industry in any country. Lesser the price of medical procedures, greater is the probability of attracting more foreign medical tourists. This is where, Asian countries like Thailand, India, etc. have been able to capture a huge chunk of the medical tourist influx, as compared to many other countries. Given this significance, where does Australia stand in this?

Deloitte Access Economics (2011) shares an important dataset that talks about costs of few selected medical procedures across various countries such as the United States, Korea, India, Thailand, Costa Rica, Singapore, France and the United Kingdom, in comparison with that of Australia. As per the figures projected in this dataset (Sourced also from Voigt, et.al., 2010; Deloitte, 2010; Tattara, 2010; Treatment Abroad, 2008), a bypass heart surgery is slated to cost around US$ 11,000 in Thailand, US$9,300 in India, US$ 16,500 in Singapore, US$ 24, 000 in Costa Rica and US$ 34,150 in South Korea. The same procedure costs around US$ 23,070 in Australia. In similar lines, if we consider the cost data of hip replacement surgery across various countries, it comes up to around US$ 7,100 in India, US$ 9,200 in Singapore, US$ 12,000 in Thailand and Costa Rica and US$ 14,000 in Australia. For the procedure of knee replacement, it comes to around US$ 8,500 in India, US$11,000 in Singapore and Costa Rica and US$ 13,192 in Australia.

Now if we compare the costs between the various countries, it is anybody's guess that the competitive advantage with respect to cost of medical procedures are not in Australia's favour. In other words, Australia is unable to compete with many other medical tourism hubs around the world with respect to cost.

However, there is an interesting indication in the dataset accessed by Deloitte Access Economics (2011) (and sourced also from Voigt, et.al. 2010; Deloitte, 2010; Tattara, 2010; Treatment Abroad, 2008) that when compared to few other countries like the United States, United Kingdom, etc. Australia has a huge cost advantage. For instance, the same bypass heart surgery when performed in the United States, comes around to US$ 130,000, whereas in Australia, it is just US$ 23, 070. Similarly for a hip replacement procedure, the cost in the United States comes to around US$ 43, 000, whereas in Australia it comes to just around US$ 16,470. For knee replacement procedure, the cost comes to around US$ 40, 000 in the United States, whereas the cost in Australia hovers around US$ 13,902. This signifies that Australia has a huge cost advantage over the United States, which can be a great opportunity for Australia to capture. As United States is a huge market with high healthcare costs, and with the fact that the healthcare prices in the United States are on the rise (Gan and Frederik, 2011), many stakeholders across the world are realizing that Australia might be able to target patients from here for medical treatment. Also, given the tag that Australia is a developed and an English-speaking country, this adds to the competitive advantage of the country.

3.2. Quality of key healthcare services:

While a lot has been spoken about cost of healthcare services across various global medical tourism hubs across the world, in comparison with that of Australia, we had an overall view that Australia still has a long way to go in terms of containing costs and bringing it on par with several other countries. However having said that, when it comes to quality of medical services and availability of key medical procedures, Australia has a definitive competitive advantage. To substantiate this point further, Deloitte Access Economics report (2011) comes up with a detailed analysis by explaining that each state and territory in Australia provides specific legislations and policies that are very specific to safety and quality standards for both public and private hospitals that fall within their jurisdiction. Although unlike countries like Thailand, India, Malaysia, etc. Australian hospitals are not mandated to go in for international accreditations such as JCI, almost 85% of all public hospitals and 56% of all private hospitals were accredited for quality and safety standards in June 2010, according to a report published by the Australian Institute of Health and Welfare (2011), with few hospitals in Australia also have the International Organization for Standardization (ISO) 9000 accreditation. This proves the point that Australia's hospitals are indeed providing a high quality service that definitely meets internationally recognised standards.

3.3. Exchange Rates and Income level:

The Australian Dollar has fairly been stable over the past 4-5 years since 2015, against major currencies of the world, after rising by over 50% in the decade prior to 2015. The appreciation of the Australian dollar was more pronounced with respect to the US Dollar, Euro and the Pound. However, the Australian Dollar has depreciated over time against other currencies of the world such as the Indian rupee. If however we look into the currency exchange rates between the Australian Dollar and the India from 2015 to 2019, it has been hovering around the rate of INR 46 to INR 52 per Australian Dollar. This 5-year data indicates that the currency rate is fairly stable and this is a good sign.

As per Tourism Australia's 2011 study on the impact of exchange rates on the travel patterns of people across the globe, exchange rates are considered to be of paramount importance, both by domestic and global travellers, but other factors like that of income also has a significant influence on people's expenditure patterns. When it comes to leisure travellers, these factors of exchange rate differences seem to assume lot of significance and can affect travel patterns across the world. However, when it comes to those travelling for medical purposes, there are different views from different stakeholders. Some are of the view that medical tourists do not really respond to the fluctuation in the currency exchange rates, as they're in a way compelled to travel, owing to emergency-like conditions in their personal lives. For instance, if a high-intensity cardiac surgery needs to be done, the medical tourist in this case might go for the best quality treatment that might be available at any part of the world, irrespective of whatever the currency rates are. Some other stakeholders also feel that those people who travel as medical tourists are relatively richer as compared to others, and even if there are small fluctuations in the exchange rates of currencies, it would not figure out as big factors affecting their travel. However, having said that, many stakeholders do agree that this exchange rate might not figure in much in the short-term, but will definitely have an impact on tourism (both leisure and medical) on the long-term (Deloitte Access Economics report, 2011).

3.4. Miscellaneous factors:

Apart from the above-mentioned factors, there might be other factors that might have an impact on the Australian medical tourism opportunities. The Deloitte Access Economics report (2011) discusses the following in brief:

3.4.1. Cultural Affinity:

As it is known to the world, Australia is an attractive tourist destination for people from many countries across the world, and when it comes to medical tourism, people from primarily English-speaking countries such as the United States, United Kingdom, etc. find it more advantageous to travel to Australia for their critical medical requirements. Language is a very important factor that is considered by people while travelling from one country to the other for such purposes, because medical sciences involve "technical terminologies" that might have to be explained by doctors to patients. If patients do not understand the language in which the doctor is trying to communicate, it can be a concern. Since Australia is an English-speaking country, medical tourists who arrive from other English-speaking countries such as the United States, United Kingdom and the likes. Moreover, cultural sensitivity is also an important parameter to be considered for people who travel for medical purposes. Some people might be very sensitive to food habits (vegetarian vs. non-vegetarian, halal foods, etc.) which, hospitals should take care of. (Deloitte Access Economics report, 2011)

3.4.2. Migration rules and visa regulations for medical tourists:

Australia maintains a comprehensive variety of visa options to foreign tourists, thus enabling them to travel in and out of the country for a range of reasons (including medical tourism). According to the Deloitte Access Economics report (2011), visa rules and regulations need to be stricter and implemented properly for medical tourists owing to the risk factors that are involved when a patient arrives with some severe bacterial infection like that of tuberculosis, and this might cause a threat to the local public health within the country. Hence, all requisite pre-medical examination techniques are to be put in place at all arriving points of tourists, predominantly at all international airports. This is to contain the threat of communicable diseases that might spread into the local population rapidly.

Also having said thus, there might be another form of risk wherein if the condition of the patient becomes extremely critical during the medical procedure, he / she might not be able to leave Australia easily. Hospitals and government agencies should look into this factor and address it in such a way that the patient doesn't face diplomatic hassles.

CONCLUSION

Having iterated and re-iterated various aspects of the Medical Tourism Industry in a global perspective and with special reference to the Indian and Australian contexts, it can be viewed that this industry has enormous potential for growth in the future and a co-ordinated effort from governments and the private sectors of countries projecting themselves as hubs, would certainly help the cause. With special reference to Australia, as mentioned above, the industry with its sustained growth numbers annually, should be possible to put the country on the global map of medical tourism at a prominent position by ensuring that, costs are kept under control and at competitive levels (in comparison with potential competitor countries), tapping of the huge English-speaking population of other developed countries around the world, easing visa regulations and by maintaining a healthy currency exchange rate. These key parameters, if achieved, would signify an extremely prominent emergence of a global medical tourist hub in Australia in the near future.

REFERENCES

Admin. (2017, September 18). Tour My India. *Unbeatable Success Story Of Medical Tourism Industry In India.* Retrieved March 01, 2019, from https://www.tourmyindia.com/medical-tourism/blog/success-story-medical-tourism-india/

Australian Institute of Health and Welfare (AIHW). (2011). *Australian hospital statistics 2009- 10, Health services series no. 40, Cat. no. HSE 107.* Canberra: AIHW.

Behrmann, J., & Smith, E. (2010). Top 7 issues in medical tourism: Challenges, knowledge gaps, and future directions for research and policy development. *Global Journal of Health Science*, *2*(2), 80. doi:10.5539/gjhs.v2n2p80

Bhargava, Y. (2018, July 23). Medical tourists flocking to India. *The Hindu.* Retrieved from https://www.thehindu.com/news/national/medical-tourists-flocking-to-india/article24497896.ece

Binoy, T.A. (2017). Dynamics of medical tourism in India-A microscopic analysis. *Asia Pacific Journal of Research, 1*(58).

Bookman, M., & Bookman, K. (2007). *Medical tourism in developing countries.* Palgrave Macmillan. doi:10.1057/9780230605657

Chee, H. (2010). Medical tourism and the state in Malaysia and Singapore. *Global Social Policy*, *10*(3), 336–357. doi:10.1177/1468018110379978

Confederation of Indian Industry (CII) report titled "India Services Sector—A Multi -trillion Dollar Opportunity for Global Symbiotic Growth 2017.

Connell, J. (2006). Medical tourism: sea, sun, sand and surgery. *Tourism Management, 27*, 1093-1100.

Connell, J. (2008). Tummy tucks and the Taj Mahal? Medical tourism and the globalization of health care. In A. Woodside & D. Martin (Eds.), *Tourism management (pp. 232-244).* CABI. doi:10.1079/9781845933234.0232

Connell, J. (2011a). *Medical tourism.* CABI. doi:10.1079/9781845936600.0000

Connell, J. (2013). Contemporary medical tourism: Conceptualisation, culture and commodification. *Tourism Management*, *34*, 1–13. doi:10.1016/j.tourman.2012.05.009

Deloitte. (2010). *Medical Tourism in New Zealand.* Author.

Department of Resources, Energy & Tourism. (2011). *Medical tourism in Australia A scoping study*. Deloitte Access Economics.

Economic and Social Commission for Asia and the Pacific (ESCAP). (2009). *Medical travel in Asia and the Pacific Challenges and opportunities*. United Nations.

France, T. (2009). Holidays for health: some medical options for two weeks or less. *e-Magazine News Room Tourism Authority of Thailand*. http://www.tatnews.org/emagazine/4524.asp

Gan, L., & Frederick, J. (2011). *Consumers' attitudes towards medical tourism*. http://papers.ssrn.com/sol3/papers.cfm?abstract_id=1837062

Grigoroudis, E., Litos, C., Moustakis, V. A., Politis, Y., & Tsironis, L. (2008). The assessment of user-perceived web quality: Application of a satisfaction benchmarking approach. *European Journal of Operational Research, 187*(3), 1346-1357.

Hohm, C., & Snyder, J. (2015). It was the best decision of my life: A thematic content analysis of former medical tourists' patient testimonials. *BMC Medical Ethics*, *16*(1), 8. doi:10.1186/1472-6939-16-8 PMID:25614083

Huang, E., & Chang, C.-C. A. (2012). Patient-oriented interactive e-health tools on US hospital web sites. *Health Marketing Quarterly, 29*(4), 329e345

Joint Commission International (JCI). (2011). http://www.jointcommissioninternational.org/

Keckley, P. H. (2008). *Medical tourism: Update and implications*. Deloitte Center for Health Solutions. Available at: http://www.deloitte.com/assets/ DcomUnitedStates/Local%20assets/documents/us_chs_medicaltourism_ 111209_web.pdf

Lunt, N., Hardey, M., & Mannion, R. (2010). Nip, tuck and click: Medical tourism and the emergence of web-based health information. *The Open Medical Informatics Journal, 3*, 77-87.

Medical Tourism Association. (2017). *2016-2017 global buyers survey brief.* Retrieved February 28, 2019, from https://medicaltourismassociation.com/userfiles/files/GLOBAL_BUYERS_REPORT_BRIEF.pdf

Medical Tourism Association - Medical travel & health tourism: Medical Tourism Association. (2019). *Medical Tourism Association | Medical Tourism FAQ's: Medical Tourism Association.* Retrieved February 16, 2019, from http://www.medicaltourismassociation.com/en/medical-tourism-faq-s.html

Medical tourism Market Report: 2015. (n.d.). *Worldwide Market size, Share, Trends, Analysis, Growth and research Report*. Academic Press.

Moghavvemi, S., Ormond, M., Musa, G., Isa, C. R. M., Thirumoorthi, T., Mustapha, M. Z. B., Kanapathy, K. A., & Chandy, J. J. C. (2017). Connecting with prospective medical tourists online: A cross-sectional analysis of private hospital websites promoting medical tourism in India, Malaysia and Thailand. *Tourism Management*, *58*, 154–163. doi:10.1016/j.tourman.2016.10.010

Pocock, N., & Phua, K. (2011). Medical tourism and policy implications for health systems: A conceptual framework from a comparative study of Thailand Singapore and Malaysia. *Globalization and Health*, *7*(12). Retrieved June 30, 2011, from http://www.globalizationandhealth.com/content/7/1/12 PMID:21539751

Pollard, K. (2017, Nov.). Measuring the ROI from medical tourism promotion. *International Medical Travel Journal*.

Reisman, D. (2010). *Health tourism. Social welfare through international trade*. Edward Elgar.

Singh, V. (2009). *Public policies for facilitating medical tourism industry in Asia*. IV Annual International Conference on Public Policy and Management, IIM, Bangalore.

Tattara, G. (2010). Medical tourism and domestic population health. Department of Economics, Ca' Foscari University of Venice. doi:10.2139srn.1544224

Taylor, J., Gombeski, W. R., Jr., & Dillon, B. W. (2005). Web wellness. *Marketing Health Services, 25*(2), 32-37.

Thailand Investment Review. (2010). *Thailand Service Industry Pleases, Profits Amid Invigorating Growth*. http://www.boi.go.th/english/download/publication_investment/108/January_10.pdf

Tourism Malaysia. (2008). *Media Release: Health Tourism in Malaysia*. http://corporate.tourism.gov.my/mediacentre.asp?page=feature_malaysia&pagemode=search&news_id=16&subpage=archive

Treatment Abroad. (2008). *Treatment Abroad Price Watch Survey 2008*. http://www.treatmentabroad.com/cost/cosmetic-surgery-abroad-cost/

Voigt, C., Laing, J., Wray, M., Brown, G., Howat, G., Weiler, B., & Trembath, R. (2010). *Health tourism in Australia: Supply, Demand and Opportunities*. CRC for Sustainable Tourism Pty Ltd.

Von Knoop, C., Lovich, D., Silverstein, M. B., & Tutty, M. (2003). *Vital signs: E-health in the United States*. Boston Consulting Group.

Section 3

Chapter 9
The Coaching Dance:
Beyond Nonaka – Knowledge Management in Post-Tayloristic Confucian China

Will Percy
Zeng Associates, LLC, China

Kevin Dow
University of Auckland, New Zealand

ABSTRACT

Given the continued popularity of coaching in the West and its increasing use in China, this chapter examines how the predominantly Western-driven coaching methodology can be modified for more effective use in a Confucian culture and its potential positive impact on knowledge exchange and innovation. Through this exploration, the authors examine how a mixed methodology of coaching, wherein team coaching is deployed with internal coaches, can improve coachee's Positive Career Behaviors and as a result the socialisation of knowledge within the organisation. In exploring this dynamic the authors seek to raise awareness of the potential for coaching to address a number of issues within Nonaka's SECI model and to particularly focus on how team coaching may both increase organisational learning and opportunities for knowledge creation.

DOI: 10.4018/978-1-7998-4126-5.ch009

INTRODUCTION

The surpassing of Foreign Direct Investment by Outward Foreign Direct Investment in China, coupled with an increasing shift from China as the 'factory of the world' to Hi-Tech manufacturing and tertiary sector development is likely to see the development of a continued rising number of Sino-foreign partnerships and joint ventures, both inside and outside of China. The focus of such partnerships is likely to be on the sharing and exploitation of knowledge to meet the needs of service development and Hi-Tech industry.

Such partnerships have the potential to be highly profitable. However, the Volatile, Uncertain, Complex and Ambiguous (VUCA) environment, alongside major cultural differences, can create pressure that both highlights and magnifies the weaknesses of senior executives and organisations alike -- resulting in the significantly shorter life span of CEOs' tenure in China and the failure of many global giants to successfully enter the marketplace. Such a dynamic gives rise to the need for both executive development and knowledge exchange models to meet the needs of this demanding and unique environment.

Given the steady rise of executive coaching in the West over the last decade, it would not be unusual to consider executive coaching as a viable option for executive development. However, the issue of the often non-directive, highly individualistic and dyadic nature of Western coaching models must be considered as to their appropriateness for deployment in an often highly autocratic and collectivist Confucian culture. The social nature of coaching, when exploited at both team and individual levels, can provide an insight into the capacity for coaching to be utilised to leverage socialisation in the knowledge exchange process.

If such a process of knowledge exchange is to be realised, it is essential to move beyond the ideal of 'knowledge as data' shared in an IT retrieval system to one of knowledge as the 'property of the individual' only created through applying their understanding to data and information. In this paradigm, the question becomes not how we capture and share knowledge, but how we create an environment in which individual knowledge can be unlocked and shared within the organisation.

This chapter can help those engaged in executive development, business professionals and academics alike, as we explore how coaching models can be modified for use in China, or within Sino-foreign partnerships, and how this may create a sound foundation for the socialisation of knowledge and the considered development of organisational knowledge management (KM) strategies.

BACKGROUND

This chapter investigates the opportunities for knowledge exchange and innovation through the introduction of a culturally-sensitive coaching model to Sino-foreign joint venture partnerships. China is often seen as an easy target for expansion, yet well-established MNCs (such as Tesla) often overestimate the potential of the market and fail to deliver on promises made to shareholders (Perkowski, 2015) and robust business models, proven globally, fail to produce. For instance, Amazon has seen its market share fall from 16% to less than 1% over two years as it battles against domestic firms (Dunn, 2017). To those who have operated in the market for some time, such stories are of no surprise, where business is often seen as 'war' – and foreigners as incapable of engaging meaningfully with its cultural and political intricacies. Yet, the government increasingly continues to push for increased innovation and creativity, whilst legislating to use Sino-foreign partnerships as a driver for this change. Although the need for organisational change and knowledge management is increasingly highlighted, in a China context, it should be noted that this takes place amidst rapid organisational change (on a global scale) as technological and social economic changes see organisations struggling to meet the demands of an increasingly complex global market.

This observation may seem counterintuitive in a global environment of increased communication, increased trade and ever shortening travel times, as it could be expected that the gap between cultures would be narrowed; yet, this may not be the case. The increased placement of expatriate managers around the world has had little impact, as they are often deployed with inadequate preparation to promote cross-cultural understanding. Indeed, in some countries and organisations, expatriate management teams note increased incidence of xenophobia (Littrel, 2002). It is therefore no wonder that the role of the effective cross-cultural manager is critical.

It is in this context, and with the ever-increasing presence of Chinese business on the global stage, that the critical importance of Western business managers understanding Chinese culture and business practices is noted. Yet, few Western business schools reference Chinese business practices and leadership in their curriculum. Management theories often over-simplify the complexity of leadership development in an international context (McCall, 2010) and fail to recognise how philosophical and ideological differences drive a distinctly different approach to leadership and management in Asia (Alves, Manz & Butterfield, 2005).

Although seen as a source of potential strategic advantage, it should be noted that current KM efforts may be seen as significantly under-delivering. Given this major failure of current KM practice, it is of no surprise that there has been a demand for a shift in thinking, toward strategies focused on innovation and knowledge creation toward a strategy that focuses on innovation, creativity and collaboration.

Although the call for a shift in thinking and strategy has received increasing interest over the last decade, return on investment in training remains low. In seeking to move to a post-industrialist approach to KM, there is increasing interest in developing environments where knowledge is able to evolve and lead to innovation. However, to do so, there is a need to move beyond a simple Tayloristic approach to understanding the working environment of knowledge workers and to apply Tayloristic thinking not to how knowledge workers undertake their tasks, but to focus on knowledge work and KM itself (Schütt, 2003).

A shift to post-industrialist KM entails a move away from individual skills and capability as a core focus (as organisations no longer focus on repetitive manual labour); there is a need to identify, hire and develop individuals with the 'right knowledge' and mind set, understanding that knowledge is the domain of the individual and that most organisational knowledge may be held by individuals (Rasmus, 2002). Therefore, focus must be placed on how to utilise effective KM strategies to create environments in which knowledge can be shared, evolve and become part of the organisational DNA (Schütt, 2003). The biggest challenge to organisations may not be in implementing IT systems and strategies to formalise KM strategies, but in changing employees' behaviour with regard to knowledge sharing, not only focusing on individual performance, but on effective teamwork and development of collaborative teams.

In the West, organisations have increasingly adopted coaching as they seek to build internal capability to support effective collaborative practices and the development of individuals (Ellinger, Ellinger, Bachrach, Wang, & Elmadagbas, 2011), whilst seeking to ensure that individual or team performance and productivity are well-aligned to organisational goals. Unsurprisingly, therefore, effective coaching is seen as an increasingly critical part of a manager's role and as a precursor to success (Boyatzis, Jack, Cesaro, Khawaja, & Passarelli, 2010).

From a KM perspective, an adoption of coaching may have potential benefits as there is increasing anecdotal evidence that coaching may increase socialisation and collaboration. However, for these benefits to be realised, coaching needs to be seen as more than an individual endeavour, but as part of a wider organisational strategy and, as such, potentially impacted by social processes and power structures (Cushion, 2018). Whilst coaching has strong potential to be leveraged for KM, the use of managers as internal coaches may present challenges, as we recognise that managers' behaviour and leadership style or capability impact employee and team commitment to the organisation (Chen, Sharma, Edinger & Shapiro, 2011), and therefore potentially on the effectiveness of both the coaching process and wider KM strategies. One of the largest risks in using managers as internal coaches may arise from their coaching style and choice of coaching tools, as a facilitative approach aligned with a developmental mind set, goal-driven performance and support to achieve goals (Hui, Sue-Chan, & Wood, 2013) is likely to be congruous with effective KM strategies.

It is increasingly important to acknowledge that much of current coaching research is based on Western business practices and conducted in Western organisations (Beattie, Kim, Hagen, Egan, Ellinger & Hamlin, 2014) and despite the increased use of coaching in China, there is very little research into the effectiveness of coaching intervention in a Chinese context (Chau, 2016) although, there is significant demand for the development of a culturally-specific coaching model, the absence of which is a significant barrier to the development of Chinese executives, both junior and senior (Chau, 2016).

As the government seeks to rapidly move away from an economy built on 'Made in China' to one built on 'Designed in China', emphasising the need for management innovation with rising foreign acquisitions (to stimulate Chinese innovation and creativity) and senior Western executives more likely to work for Chinese companies both in China or at home, meaning that it is not just Chinese executives that suffer from a lack of a coherent model, but all executives in a Sino-foreign partnership.

In this context, it is critical that the effective international manager understands Chinese business practices and its leadership needs, being able to innovate and survive in what can be a very volatile business environment, where the turnover of expatriate CEOs is approximately four times higher than the global average (Paine, 2010).

A COACHING APPROACH TO KNOWLEDGE MANAGEMENT

Unlocking the Power of Individual Knowledge Through Socialisation

Although there is little literature regarding the effectiveness of coaching in Mainland China or of coaching models amended for this environment, there is a significant amount of literature surrounding knowledge exchange, Chinese culture, along with its potential impact on HR practice, and the nature of coaching. Through literature review of these areas, elements of a culturally sensitive coaching strategy and potential barriers to implementation will be identified.

Knowledge Exchange and Innovation

Viewing organisational learning from a systemic perspective and placing systemic awareness at the centre of their organisational learning model may be a critical piece of innovative strategy (Senge, 2006) as Sino-foreign partnerships seek to make the best possible corporate decisions through effective management and efficient use of corporate knowledge. Recognising the importance of systems, they must also acknowledge that knowledge is more than just data or information. It must also be recognised that in an increasingly technology-driven society data and information become easily searchable and, as such, are external to the individual becoming 'objective properties of the world'. Therefore, knowledge is the 'property' of the individual, only created through applying their understandings to data and information (Swan, 2011).

Acknowledging the 'duality' between individual and organisational knowledge, Bhatt (2002) argues that that knowledge-creating activities are both difficult to monitor and control, demanding unique management strategies. Figures 1 and 2 explore the relationship between individual and organisational knowledge (Fig.1) and strategies for knowledge management (Fig.2).

Figure 1. The Relationship Between Individual and Organisational Knowledge
Source: (Bhatt, 2002)

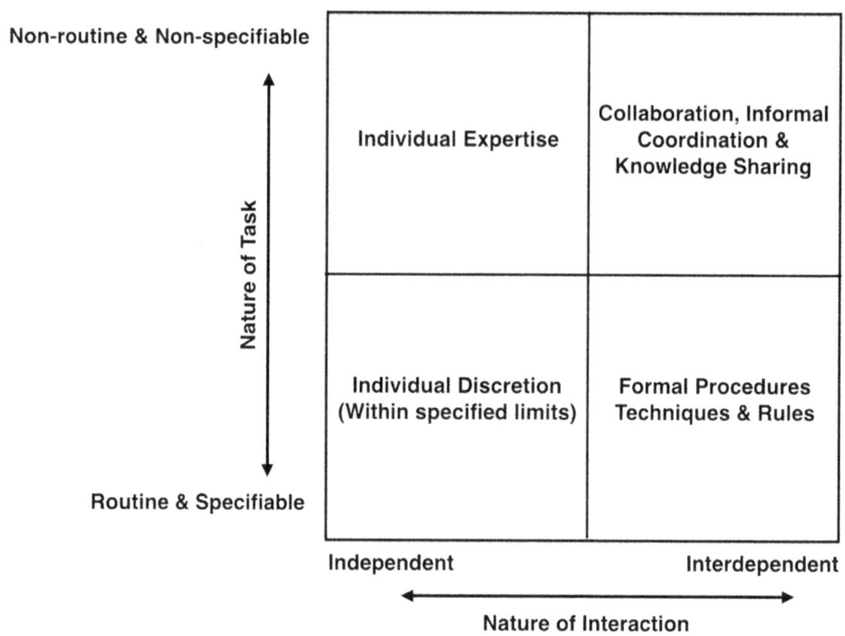

Figure 2. Knowledge Management Strategies
Source: (Bhatt, 2002)

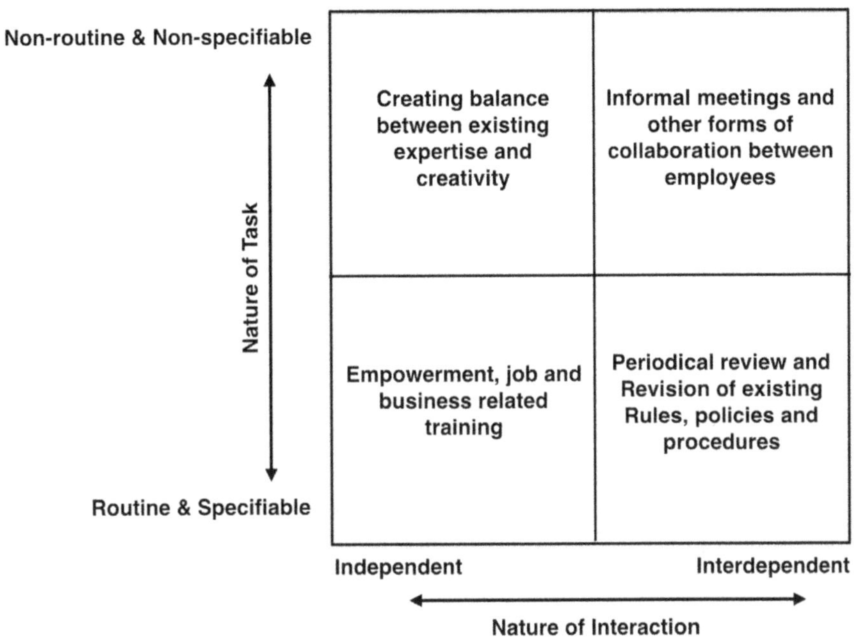

It becomes clear that the key organisational challenge is how individual knowledge can be 'unlocked' and shared within the organisation. Rather than how do we deploy technological systems and databases to capture knowledge? Given this observation and the need for heightened collaboration and knowledge sharing, socialisation may have some bearing on the potential use of coaching; therefore, Nonaka's SECI model (Nonaka, 2000) becomes a critical component of KM.

The model suggests that knowledge is transferred or created through four sequential process, namely socialisation, externalisation, combination and internalisation, after which the model returns to socialisation and suggests that through a virtuous cycle, in which phases are continuously revisited, each circuit of the model provides increasing returns in the exchange and development of knowledge.

The application of the process requires that managers do not slavishly follow it, but create a culture of knowledge sharing, striking a balance between all factors (Brown, 2000). Critical to this is 'ba', the cultural environment in which knowledge resources are exchanged. However, shaping the culture can be the most significant barrier to overcome, particularly when national culture can exert a stronger pull than corporate culture. Indeed, it can result in expatriates more forcefully exerting their own culture as they struggle to align their own ideals with their environment (Adler, 2002).

Recognising the importance of 'ba' is critical to aligning learning strategy with corporate strategy (Shlomo, 2013) and to ensuring that leadership is rewarded for inter-departmental interaction and bringing together those who need information with those who have it (Hansen & Oetinger, 2001). Creating new organisational knowledge is dependent on recognising the role of the manager as 'sense maker' in the work place and the role that the group plays in the development of new meaning and organisational narrative, disrupting 'taken-for-granted meanings' and engaging in 'sense breaking'.

Figure 3. The SECI Model of Knowledge Exchange
Source: (Nonaka, 2000)

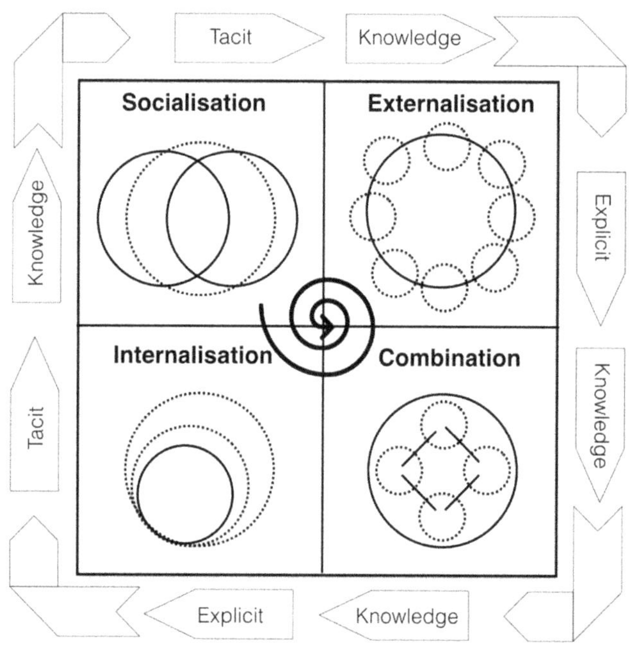

In the context of KM, there are several key criticisms in that the model fails to take account of learning theory, the model neither address how new ideas are produced nor how the collaborative process works (Bereiter, 2002). Additionally, the model does not address the effect of inevitable managerial conflict, the desire of individuals to hold onto their ideas or the power dynamics at play within the organisation (Essers and Schreinemakers, 1997).

Coaching may provide a process through which these key criticisms are addressed when considering knowledge socialisation; we are able to see coaching through a social constructivist lens (Cunliffe, 2008) as a driver of transformational learning. Through the coaching dialogue, individuals and groups become sense makers and breakers, forming a new reality applying their previous experience to information in order to plan for a new future (Reissner, 2008). Through this dialogue, the coach helps frame experiences in order to both sense make and break as the individual or group create new realities and possible futures (Fairhurst and Sarr, 1996).

Defining a Coaching Philosophy

Defining a clear coaching philosophy and underlying coaching rational may be key to ensuring that the positive benefits of coaching can be leveraged for socialisation and improved KM practice. However, this is not often a straightforward process as there is little agreement on a definition of coaching (CIPD, 2009) and much of the coaching literature is focused on executive coaching, wherein external coaches focus on helping individuals achieve short-term goals in order to achieve executive development and career goals (Gessnitzer & Kauffeld, 2015). In contrast to this approach, focus will be placed on employee coaching, using managers as internal coaches and developing this relationship over time to foster continued incremental improvement at both a team and individual level (e.g. Joo, Suchko, & McLean, 2012). In adopting this approach, organisations may seek to leverage the potential socialisation and collaboration that a coaching process may provide to achieve the benefits of a virtuous SECI cycle and to develop more effective KM practices.

A successful coaching philosophy will need to have the following attributes if it is to support socialisation and be dynamic enough to address emerging issues in the organisation, whilst fostering development of a positive environment for knowledge creation and exchange or 'ba':

- A philosophy that supports training, transfer of knowledge and incremental improvement.
- A philosophy that can be deployed at individual, team and organisational levels.
- A philosophy that is facilitative, supporting collaboration and socialisation.

At the heart of such a KM strategy, supported by the socialisation and collaboration processes or development of 'ba', is a social exchange between managers and subordinates as future, often unspecified obligations to managers, are reciprocated by subordinates who feel that they have been treated fairly and therefore reciprocate in a beneficial manner, sharing knowledge and collaborating with others. Viewing

KM and coaching through the lens of social exchange, it becomes clearer still that the role of the manager is critical in the coaching process (Huang and Hsie, 2015).

This section will seek to provide a definition and underlying rational to modify a coaching model that supports socialisation whilst taking into account Chinese culture to align with the Chinese government's call for the modernisation of Chinese business. In doing so, we recognise the development of coaching theory has mainly been driven by Western business practice and has not had a strong presence in Asia (Abbott, 2010), hence the strong need for the development of well-qualified coaches and a strong coaching culture.

Sino-foreign partnerships may seek to maximise the potential of coaching to help with the socialisation of institutional learning, thereby driving and accelerating change. Coaching may also support the development and promotion of junior executives whilst growing a team's emotional intelligence, resulting in a happier workplace with lower staff turnover.

The Chartered Institute of Professional Development (CIPD) also notes that, although there is lack of agreement on a precise definition of coaching, there are a number of generally agreed characteristics of organisational or executive coaching. The following traits may have bearing in this context.

- A non-directive approach.
- A facilitative or developmental approach is adopted.
- Feedback is provided on both strengths and weaknesses.
- The coaching process addresses both organisational and individual goals (although the emphasis is likely to be on work performance).
- There is an implicit belief that the coachee is self-aware or can achieve self-awareness.

In addition to the observations of the CIPD, key elements of coaching can be considered through several continuum as noted in Figure 4 below.

Figure 4. Coaching Continuum
Source: Adapted from Britnor-Guest and Willis, 2004 and Horner, 2002.

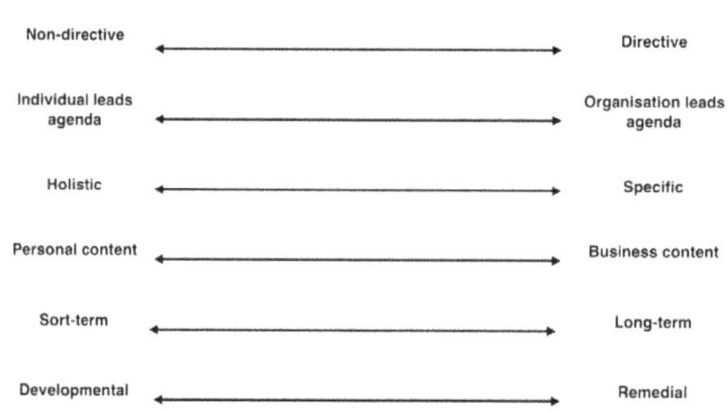

Given the absence of a universally accepted definition of coaching, we advocate the use of a definition developed by Bob Thomson and used within the executive coaching programme at Warwick University:

Coaching is a relationship of rapport and trust in which the coach uses their ability to listen, to ask questions and to play back what the client has communicated in order to help the client to clarify what matters to them and to work out what to do to achieve their aspirations (Thomson, 2014).

Thomson's definition is well-aligned to the elements that have been identified as supporting both the deployment of coaching to support the SECI process and effective KM. There are also several elements within the definition that can be used when considering the cultural implications of developing a coaching model that will be revisited in the next section.

- Coaching as a relationship of rapport and trust.
- Listening.
- Questioning.
- Playback.
- Raising the coachee's awareness (as they clarify what matters to them most).
- The coachee must take action (to achieve their aspirations).

The elements of raising awareness and the need for the coachee to take responsibility for action are also captured in the following equation provided by Whitmore (2002):

Awareness + Responsibility = Performance

Rather than merely being a list of things that the coach does, listening, playback and questioning are skills essential to effective non-directive coaching, and perhaps to fostering innovation and creativity.

The quality of the coach's attention determines the quality of the coachee's thinking, questions will open their mind and heart and that in playback we should use the coachee's own words as 'they came from somewhere rich with the thinker's history, culture, experience' (Kline, 2016). In an organisational context, Thomson highlights a cycle of development (as depicted in Figure 5) that may be deployed, highlighting the need for ongoing feedback as the coachee takes increasing responsibility for meeting increasingly challenging objectives.

Thomson clearly distinguishes mentoring from coaching thus:

Mentoring is a relationship of rapport and trust in which one person draws on their experience, expertise and knowledge to advise and guide a less experienced person in order to enhance their performance or support their development (Thomson, 2009).

Figure 5. Thomson's Cycle of Development
Source: Thomson, 2014

This clearly places mentoring at the directive end of the spectrum, highlighting the need for a mentor with domain-specific experience, expertise and knowledge.

Figure 6. The Coaching Dance
Source: Thomson, 2009.

MANAGER CENTERED (Pushing) (Telling)		Performer Centered (Pulling) (Asking)
• Set by manager.	GOALS & TARGETS	• Discuss and agree with performer.
• Reward and punish; • Encourage.	MOTIVATION	• Ask what interests the performer; • Performer challenges self.
• Pass judgments; • Praise and criticise; • Give feedback to performer.	FEEDBACK	• Draw out performer's experience; • Help performer to generate feedback.
• Tell what went well and what didn't; • Show how it could have been done better.	LEARNING	• From self-awareness; • By reflection and discovery.

Thomson's definition of coaching, along with an understanding of the Coaching Dance (Figure 6), provides a clear philosophical approach to coaching that resonates well with the needs of a KM environment as it potentially supports the effective deployment of SECI and its socialisation process, whilst providing a structure that clearly highlights the elements of effective facilitative coaching for managers. The addition of Thomson's development cycle also provides a deeper underlying rational that potentially helps to bridge the gap between SECI and the application of effective learning theory.

Chinese Culture in a Coaching Context

Much has been said and written about the role of Confucianism as a guiding force in Chinese life andbusiness. This is not surprising given that after 2,500 years, it is still recognised as the strongest guiding force in Chinese society (Cheung and King, 2004). Yet, the role of Taoism, Buddhism and 'Bing Fa' (texts on the art of war) should not be forgotten (Hennig, 2013). More recently, Communist ideology and Western values have also had significant impact.

East Asia's recent success may be caused by Confucian influence (Han, 1992), therefore, it is considered critical for those who wish to work with Chinese or trade with China to have an understanding of Confucianism. It is also critical to understand in order to apply the cultural lessons from Hofstede and Meyer with greater finesse. Confucianism is based on the basic doctrine of 'Li' (礼) – rites, which seek to maintain social harmony through the establishment of a society in which everybody should behave according to their rank, having a fixed place in it. Given these hierarchical states, five key aspects of Confucian values can be identified (Wang, Wang & Rouna, 2005):

- Hierarchy and harmony.
- Collectivism.
- 'Guanxi' (系) – networks – and reciprocity in relations.
- 'Mianzi' (面子) – face – showing respect for social status.
- A long-term time orientation towards past – present – future.

In many studies, collectivist and hierarchical values are noted as being barriers to implementing Western HR practices (Chen, Bishop & Scott, 2000). Over time, many Confucian scholars have argued that the concept of Li should lead to "rule by man" rather than "rule by law". Resultantly, senior decision makers not only have the final say, but also, should not be questioned. In theory, a Confucian business leader should seek to be an 'honest gentleman' (Ip, 2009). Yet, the absence of checks and balances for this power paternalistic management may be a significant barrier for modernisation in China.

Closely related to the concept of "rule by man" is a 'junzi' (君子) – or the virtuous man/leader. Although derived from Confucian philosophy, 'junzi' is still present in the business world as subordinates seek to emulate senior leaders (Romar, 2002), even taking blame for their superiors in order to help them save face, although, unfortunately this is often abused (Cardon, 2009). Confucianism has experienced resurgence since the establishment of the market economy (Wall, Lin, Zhang & Lei, 2009), whilst Communism has strengthened its hierarchical ideals.

Face is often linked with the idea of having dignity and being held in high esteem by your peers. Such measures of status are very important in Chinese society. In order to preserve a harmonious society, Confucianism has clear patterns for interpersonal relationships and failure to work within these or meet expectations of the 'collective' can cause great loss of face and lead to serious social consequences. A key element of interpersonal relationships is 'guanxi' or relationships (often friendships) with an expectation of reciprocity. These debts are referred to as 'renqing'(人情) and must be repaid if one is to maintain their status.

For many centuries, 'Bing Fa' have been a core element of Chinese culture and form a part of upbringing for many Chinese. The resurgence of Bing Fa, in the business world, over recent years should be of some note to foreigners in their business dealings and the application of 'Bing Fa' can lead to brutal business decision-making.

The high power distance in Chinese culture may be a barrier to implementation. The hierarchical environment may cause the coachee to desire a more directive approach and a relationship that is not on an equal footing. Nangalia & Nangalia (2010) note that the coach in Asia is expected to be someone who is more senior, more qualified and a source of wisdom. These hierarchical barriers may be further augmented by the complexity of 'junzi' and power structure within the organisation posing a significant threat to knowledge exchange and creativity. Promotion may often be a matter of 'time-served' rather than through merit, with the socialisation of ideas being inhibited, as junior members are afraid or reluctant to share ideas that may go against current practice.

The coach must be sensitive to the social context, and given the collective nature of Chinese society, individuals are likely to carefully consider the implications of their actions on their wider community before committing to a course of action. Whilst this may have some positive implications, the wider implications may create barriers to implementation of a programme as individuals seek to avoid high performance, not wanting to stand out from the crowd, as they fear being viewed as a 'traitor to the team' (Vorhauser-Smith, 2012). Resultantly, many prefer rewards to be distributed across the team in order to maintain harmony within the organisation (Stone, Stone-Romero & Lukaszewski, 2007).

These issues are likely to hamper knowledge exchange and socialisation of ideas, as individuals do not wish to risk standing out from the crowd by taking action and taking responsibility for their ideas. Indeed, in Chinese organisations, subordinates often take the smallest issue to their manager for direction as they fear to take responsibility for an individual decision.

As Aycan (2005) notes, the worst-case scenario can be seen when elements of collectivist and high power distance combine as negative feedback on performance, creating resentment and mistrust and leading to employee resignations. This may be due to the unpleasant feeling of losing face as for the Chinese, losing face is as bad as losing your mouth or nose (Zinzius, 2004). Such issues may be connected to the reluctance of managers to give subordinates poor ratings (Lu and Bjorkman, 1997) and with the observation that feedback is often not given to subordinates and not seen as being necessary (Shen, 2008).

Losing face can also result from expectation not being met or from indelicate feedback (Qian, Abdur Razzaque & Ah, 2007); such complexities of face, when coupled with the rigid hierarchy, may make honest communication difficult and projected external appearances may be very different to the internal realities. To some degree, these issues may also contribute to Chinese subordinates blaming problems and poor performance on external factors that are beyond their control (Stipek, Weiner & Li, 1989).

The combination of these factors re-emphasises the need for skilful listening, questioning and playback. Yet, it also highlights the potential barriers to implementation from difficulty in providing feedback, raising awareness and encouraging individuals to take responsibility for their actions. In recognising this complexity and the need to deal with it at an individual level, a number of 'coachable issues' for Chinese workers and managers have been highlighted, ranging from helping them to find a voice, putting authority into perspective and transitioning to leadership (Wearley, 2006).

Having thus far reviewed the impact of power difference and collectivism, we are mindful that workplace innovation is often implemented at the team level (Drach-Zahavy and Somech, 2001), yet, as Fang (1995) notes there is significant conflict between Chinese cultural values and a number of entrepreneurial attributes:

- A desire for and positive response to change.
- Desire to take initiative.
- A high internal locus of control.

However, perhaps more difficult to contend with are the oft-cited absent cultural values of flexibility, creativity and innovation.

Having noted the more negative areas, it is important to acknowledge and consider the areas of Confucian value that are positive and have congruence with the coaching model (Yeh and Xu, 2010). Particularly given that Confucianism provides a strong work ethic, coupled with perseverance, diligence and a strong desire for learning (Hofstede and Bond, 1988; Oh, 1992) – elements that all have strong congruence with effective coaching environments.

Tulpa and Bresser (2013) note that coaching requires a medium- to long-term orientation, medium masculinity and low uncertainty avoidance. China has reasonable congruence with these areas, yet mention should be made of both uncertainty avoidance and long-term orientation. Low uncertainty avoidance may be surprising, given the discussion about power-distance and collectivism; however, strong Confucian values and remnants of the Cultural Revolution have made the Chinese very pragmatic (Chong & Liu, 2002). With regard to time orientation, it should be noted that this references both the strong desire of the Chinese to maintain their cultural identity and to their ability to focus on the medium- to long-term. Coupled with low indulgence, the Chinese are able to set medium- to long-term goals and defer reward as they pursue them.

Whilst Hofstede's cultural dimensions and an understanding of the driving Confucian philosophy provide an insight to Chinese culture from a group perspective, they somewhat lack the finesse required to examine coaching interaction from the individual level. Meyer (2015) provides a series of continuum that can be used to consider a more individualistic approach to managing across cultures.

Meyer's Culture Map is based on interviews with executives and uses standard deviation to define normative patterns, from which the culture is placed on the continuum. It is important to recognise that 'cultural relativity' is critically important in interpreting the results; it is not the positioning on the map that makes the difference, but the 'gap' between cultures being compared. Meyer would suggest that this is significant for the UK and China.

The more relationship based nature of trust in China may mean that it takes longer for the coach to develop a relationship with the client, whilst high context communication may mean that the coach needs to listen with greater intent, listening 'between the lines' for inferred meaning. In providing feedback and using the feedback of others to examine workplace reality it may be important to remember that in China negative feedback is given indirectly and that confrontation is often avoided. This may have implication for both playback and feedback, perhaps necessitating a need to peel back layers over time and in turn using a more high context communication method to provide this negative feedback and to explore its implications (Meyer, 2015). When providing information or seeking to persuade within the coaching relationship it may be beneficial to present facts first and underlying logic to follow, remembering the more mathematical approach to logic of the Chinese.

SOLUTIONS AND RECOMMENDATIONS

Examination of Nonaka's SECI model places the focus on the human side of KM practices and highlights that the potentially most difficult challenge facing organisations (as they seek to implement KM strategies) is how to unlock individual knowledge, rather than how they capture data in IT systems. Nonaka suggests that socialisation is the key to unlocking this knowledge and provides a cycle by which knowledge, innovation and new ideas can be created. However, the SECI model is not without its critics – as the model fails to take account of learning theory, politics or power and neither addresses how socialisation and combination take place nor how new knowledge is created.

Given that emergent research in the field of coaching suggests that coaching may support the socialisation of ideas and knowledge exchange, it is proposed that coaching may bridge the gaps between the SECI model and learning theory, as well as providing strategies for enhancing socialisation and combination. Effective application of social exchange theory and developing IRB and PCB, through the use of individual and team coaching, may further support socialisation and, this may provide strategies for addressing the gaps around politics and power created by reluctance to share knowledge in the SECI model.

In seeking to provide solutions and recommendations for organisations to adopt effective KM strategies and to move beyond Nonka's SECI model in post-Tayloristic China, we outline a culturally sensitive coaching mix that supports effective KM. By asking not 'if coaching works' but 'how does it work' (Fillery–Travis 2006), we can develop a strategy that unlocks individual and group knowledge to transform the organisational KM environment.

In recommending the following coaching mix, we seek to provide a solution that recognises that KM is a social exchange and that team members will often share knowledge due to the intrinsic reward of positive feeling generated by social exchange. As coaching promotes positive In Role Behaviour (IRB) and Proactive Career Behaviour (PCB), highly committed team members are more likely to engage in positive social behaviours aimed at achieving shared goals. However, the role of the manager cannot be ignored, as a facilitative coaching approach is likely to foster an environment of collaboration (Neubert, Kaemar, Carlson, Chonko & Roberts 2008) that is likely to foster knowledge exchange. Conversely, a pressure-based coaching style is likely to inhibit knowledge exchange as it inhibits socialisation (Huang & Hsieh, 2015). Finally, the coaching mix must address the need for transfer of knowledge from on-the-job training as suggested in coaching literature.

In order to provide a coherent structure to the coaching mix, the following issues are addressed (CIPD, 2009):

- Who will be coached.
- Who will do the coaching.
- What type of coaching model will be deployed and what issues will it address.
- How will institutional fit be ensured?

In advocating who to coach, we are mindful that much of coaching literature places a strong emphasis on developmental learning and knowledge sharing (Caplan, 2003) and that many organisations would best benefit from coaching as they are often fast growing businesses, facing a talent shortage with a need to rapidly develop employee potential and KM strategies (CIPD, 2009). Therefore, we recognise that good leaders are hard to find and that the time has come to grow and develop them in China. Consequently, we advocate coaching (Donde and Rock 2008) for:

- Future leaders or senior executives.
- Expatriates as they transition to their new environment.
- For those changing job or role.
- For those involved in organisational change.

Given the focus on KM and developing an approach of socialization, we further suggest that teams of knowledge workers may benefit from engaging in a cyclical approach to coaching to build cycles of continuous improvement. The cultural pressure for senior and experienced coaches, a need for cultural understanding and the tension between using internal or external coaches must also be considered.

In selecting a model for the coaching process, it is important that it fits both the cultural environment and supports the underlying coaching philosophy that has been adopted from Thomson. Therefore, the GROW model (Goal, Reality, Options, Way Forward) (Whitmore, 2002) cognitive behavioural model is advocated as this model can be easily deployed, given the above considerations.

This model is recommended as it is able to be deployed in both individual, group and team settings. Although most organisational coaching takes the form of one-to-one (dyadic) coaching, it may be advisable to deploy group coaching alongside individual coaching to better suit the collectivist culture of China. This will simultaneously provide an opportunity for coachees to become more comfortable in a shared environment, building a stronger relationship of trust, before tackling more difficult issues of feedback and development in individual coaching sessions. This approach may create an environment conducive to stronger KM.

Although the evidence for positive outcomes of group coaching are mainly anecdotal, Brown (2010) notes that there are many potential benefits noted within literature on the subject. Given the potential cultural barriers to implementation previously discussed, the following benefits may help to achieve the development of a stronger knowledge exchange and coaching culture:

- More likely and more durable changes to behaviour.
- Stronger trust and support within the group.
- Improved skills of communication and listening within the group.
- More constructive conflict resolution.
- Stronger appreciation and alignment of individual goals, strengths and values.
- Greater commitment and accountability within the group.
- Greater knowledge exchange achieved through improved systemic awareness.

Having noted the potential benefits of team or group coaching it should also be recognised that choosing when to intervene and the nature of coaching intervention must be a considered choice. Hackman and Wageman (2005) suggest that there are three key points at which coaching intervention can have significant impact. The beginning of a project or as a team forms motivational interventions may help establish norms and get the team off to a positive start. At midpoints, the team have a significant understanding of the project and know what is working and are primed for consultative coaching as they feel the pressure of the project drawing to a close. At the end of the project, coaching may be used for educational purposes and for explicit knowledge transfer. Hackman and Wageman also note that teams working together for longer periods of time will often discover a rhythm that supports a cyclical approach suited to their own environment

To achieve knowledge exchange the coaches will, at times, need to deploy a systemic approach to their coaching interactions at both an individual and group level. Given the ability of a sponsor to facilitate wider institutional learning we suggest that sponsors are identified and allocated. This may also provide an opportunity to, positively, engage 'junzi' in the change process and to align senior leaders outside of the coaching process with knowledge exchange initiatives.

In line with this systemic element of this approach, we advocate the use of a data-driven approach to help inform a systemic understanding of the 'Reality' in the GROW model, and advocate the use of 360-degree review for the individual coaching and data-driven professional learning communities within the group environment. In doing so, we hope to achieve an increase in goal achievement and resilience for coachees (Grant et al. 2009).

This systemic approach may help to drive organisational change and help individuals to know what needs to be changed; yet it is only part of the complex puzzle to achieving improved organisational effectiveness. A behavioural approach can be used to augment this approach, particularly in individual sessions, as coachees consider their behaviour, how to achieve their aspirations and, as appropriate, modify behaviour to meet organisational expectations (Skiffington and Zeus, 2003). Given Kegan's observations about the complexity of adopting apposing ideas from other cultures and belief systems (Appendix 1) skilful use of the individual sessions and a behavioural approach is likely to be key to realising the desired outcomes of knowledge exchange.

Given the role of socialisation and social constructivism in knowledge exchange, we also recognise the need to embrace a social constructivist approach to support the behavioural and systemic elements of both individual and group coaching. It should be noted that the language used does not just describe the reality, but shapes and frames it (Ford, 1999), acting as a driving force for constructive change (Cooperrider, 1990).

In order to achieve strong organisational fit, we recognise the need to provide clear parameters for operation to the coaching team, therefore, revisit the coaching continuum previously outlined and reapply them to define parameters and to provide a summary of key dynamics of the proposed coaching strategy.

In a KM environment, a predominantly non-directive, facilitative approach to the coaching relationship is advocated as this is well aligned to knowledge transfer and building positive IRB and PCB. However, we echo Thomson regarding the importance of engaging in the coaching dance to better meet the needs of the organisation, team or individual and making considered use of a more directive approach if appropriate.

The individual or team in the coaching process must be empowered to drive the agenda; however, this should take place within the boundaries of the organisational and team goals. Coaching at all levels may need to move between being holistic or specific and we advocate the use of a data-driven cyclical approaches to team and individual coaching in order that both more holistic and specific coaching interventions can be made as appropriate. This approach supports the use of more business driven sessions and a focus on KM within a knowledge working environment as appropriate.

FUTURE RESEARCH DIRECTIONS

Given the mixed approach to coaching advocated in this chapter, it must be acknowledged that although the advantages for individuals from coaching are increasingly well-documented, there is still little research on the impact of group team coaching. Therefore, greater research is needed in this area and into the 'black box' of socialisation as presented in the SECI model, and the potential benefits of a blended coaching mix in achieving socialisation as well as examining the potential impact on knowledge transfer in work based learning.

Whilst there is increasing evidence of the cumulative positive effect of one-on-one or dyadic coaching (Weer, DiRenzo & Shipper, 2016), there is little research either about the negative impact of coaching or the mechanisms through which coaching can lead to improved individual or organizational performance (Liu & Batt, 2010). Therefore, additional research is needed into both group and team coaching, as well as the potential negative impacts of coaching and techniques used by coaches in achieving coaching outcomes.

Given the Chinese context for the development of the coaching mix advocated, it must be noted that additional research is required to more fully develop an appropriate coaching philosophy, rational and interventions for a non-Western environment. However, it should also be noted that that the blended coaching mix presented in this chapter is a marked departure from the often dyadic approach to coaching used in the West and, given the potential impact of group or team coaching on socialisation and KM, further research into its potential deployment in non-Chinese environments may be beneficial to organisations with a desire to enrich their KM practices.

CONCLUSION

In a context of rapid development and transition from a predominantly manufacturing to knowledge based economy in China, this chapter has viewed knowledge management and transfer through the lens of Nonaka's SECI model. Despite the emphasis on socialisation in the SECI model, there is little to link it to learning theory and Nonaka neither addresses how knowledge is created nor how the socialisation approach may work.

Thomson's definition of coaching and its underlying rational have been explored and are advocated for use within a Chinese KM environment. The cycle of learning is highly likely to support a developmental, facilitative approach to coaching at team or individual level and an awareness of the coaching dance may allow Chinese managers to embrace a more non-directive approach as needed to support KM strategies, whilst, continuing to deploy directive strategies as the environment may demand.

ACKNOWLEDGMENT

The authors wish to acknowledge the significant support of Professor Bob Thomson for his helpful comments on early versions of this chapter.

This research received no specific grant from any funding agency in the public, commercial, or not-for-profit sectors.

REFERENCES

Abbott, G. (2010). Cross Cultural Coaching: A Paradoxical Perspective. In *The Complete Handbook of Coaching*. Sage.

Adler, N. J. (2002). *International dimensions of organizational behavior*. South-Western.

Alves, J., Manz, C., & Butterfield, D. (2005). Developing leadership theory in Asia: The role of Chinese philosophy. *International Journal of Leadership Studies*, *1*(1), 3–27.

Aycan, Z. (2005). The Interplay Between Cultural and Institutional / Structural Contingencies In Human Resource Management Practices. *International Journal of Human Resource Management*, *16*(7), 1083–1119. doi:10.1080/09585190500143956

Beattie, R. S., Kim, S., Hagen, M. S., Egan, T. M., Ellinger, A. D., & Hamlin, R. G. (2014). Managerial Coaching: A Review of the Empirical Literature and Development of a Model to Guide Future Practice. *Advances in Developing Human Resources*, *16*(2), 184–201. doi:10.1177/1523422313520476

Bereiter, C. (2002). *Education and mind in the knowledge age*. Lawrence Erlbaum Associates.

Bhatt, G. D. (2002). Knowledge management in organizations: Examining the interaction between technologies, techniques, and people. *Journal of Knowledge Management*, *5*(1), 68–75. doi:10.1108/13673270110384419

Boyatzis, R., Jack, A., Cesaro, R., Khawaja, M., & Passarelli, A. (2010). *Coaching with compassion: An fMRI study of coaching to the positive and negative emotional attractor*. Academy.

Brown, J. S., & Duguid, P. (2000). Balancing act: How to capture knowledge without killing it. *Harvard Business Review*, *78*(3), 73–80. PMID:11183980

Brown, S. W., & Grant, A. M. (2010). From GROW to GROUP: Theoretical issues and a practical model for group coaching in organisations. Coaching. *An International Journal of Theory. Research and Practice*, *3*(1), 30–45.

Caplan, J. (2003). *Coaching for the future: How smart companies use coaching and mentoring*. CIPD.

Cardon, P. (2009). A model of face practices in Chinese business culture: Implications for western businesspersons. *Thunderbird International Business Review*, *51*(1), 19–36. doi:10.1002/tie.20242

Chau, R. C. P. (2016). *Culturally sensitive coaching for Chinese business leaders* (Unpublished doctoral dissertation). Widener University, Chester, PA.

Chen, G., Sharma, P., Edinger, S., Shapiro, D., & Farh, J. (2011). Motivating and demotivating forces in teams: Cross-level influences of empowering leadership and relationship conflict. The Journal of Applied Psychology, 96, 441–557.

Chen, X., Bishop, J. W., & Scott, K. D. (2000). Teamwork in China: Where Reality Challenges Theory and Practice. In J. T. Li, A. S. Tsui, & E. Weldon (Eds.), *Management and Organizations in the Chinese Context* (pp. 269–282). Macmillan. doi:10.1057/9780230511590_11

Cheung, T. S., & King, A. Y. (2004). Righteousness and Profitableness: The Moral. *Journal of Business Ethics*, *54*, 245–260.

Chong, F., & Liu, H. (2002). Indigenous counselling in the Chinese cultural context: Experience transformed model. *Asian Journal of Counselling*, *9*(1), 49–68.

CIPD. (2009). *Taking The Temperature of coaching*. Retrieved from http://www2.cipd.co.uk/NR/rdonlyres/E27F313C-FFBC-466F-84D8-A240893A2A22/0/Taking_temperature_coaching.pdf

CIPD. (2009). *Taking The Temperature of coaching*. Retrieved from http://www2.cipd.co.uk/NR/rdonlyres/E27F313C-FFBC-466F-84D8- A240893A2A22/0/Taking_temperature_coaching.pdf

Cooperrider, D. L. (1990). Positive image, positive action: the affirmative basis for organizing. In S. Srivastva & D. L. Cooperrider (Eds.), *Appreciative Management and Leadership*. Jossey-Bass.

Cunliffe, A. L. (2008). Orientations to social constructionism: Relationally responsive social constructionism and its implications for knowledge and learning. *Management Learning*, *39*(2), 123–139. doi:10.1177/1350507607087578

Cushion, C. J. (2018). Reflection and reflective practice discourses in coaching: A critical analysis. *Sport Education and Society*, *23*(1), 82–94. doi:10.1080/13573322.2016.1142961

Drach-Zahavy, A., & Somech, A. (2001). Understanding Team Innovation: The Role of Team Processes and Structures. *Group Dynamics*, *5*(2), 111–123. doi:10.1037/1089-2699.5.2.111

Dunn, J. (2017). *Amazon is still getting dominated in China.* Retrieved from http://www.businessinsider.com/amazon-market-share-china-alibaba-jd-chart-2017-2

Ellinger, A. D., Ellinger, A. E., Bachrach, D. G., Wang, Y.-L., & Elmadagbas, A. B. (2011). Organizational investments in social capital, managerial coaching, and employee work-related performance. *Management Learning*, *42*(1), 67–85. doi:10.1177/1350507610384329

Essers, J., & Schreinemakers, J. (1997). Nonaka's subjectivist conception of knowledge in corporate knowledge management. *Knowledge Organization*, *24*(1), 24–32.

Fairhurst, G. T., & Sarr, R. A. (1996). *The Art of Framing: Managing the Language of Leadership*. Jossey-Bass.

Fang, Y. (1995). Chinese Value Survey by the Chinese Culture Connection. *Journal of Cross-Cultural Psychology*, *18*(2), 147–148.

Fillery-Travis, A., & Passmore, J. (2011). A critical review of executive coaching research: A decade of progress and what's to come. *Coaching: An International Journal of Theory, Practice & Research*, *4*, 70–88.

Ford, J. D. (1999). Organizational change and shifting conversations. *Journal of Organizational Change Management*, *12*(6), 480–500. doi:10.1108/09534819910300855

Galliers, R. D., & Currie, W. (Eds.). (2011). The Oxford handbook of management information systems: Critical perspectives and new directions. Oxford University Press.

Gessnitzer, S., & Kauffeld, S. (2015). The working alliance in coaching: Why behavior is the key to success. *The Journal of Applied Behavioral Science*, *51*(2), 177–197. doi:10.1177/0021886315576407

Grant, A. M., Curtayne, L., & Burton, G. (2009). Executive coaching enhances goal attainment, resilience and workplace well-being: A randomized controlled study. *The Journal of Positive* Psychology, 4(1), 396–407.

Hackman, J. R., & Wageman, R. (2005). A theory of team coaching. *Academy of Management Review*, *30*(2), 269–287. doi:10.5465/amr.2005.16387885

Han, C. K. (1992). The positive contribution of Confucianism to the modernization of East Asian business enterprises. *Journal of Chinese Philosophy*, *19*(2), 171–181. doi:10.1111/j.1540-6253.1992.tb00117.x

Hansen, M. T., & Von Oetinger, B. (2001). Introducing T-shaped managers. Knowledge management's next generation. *Harvard Business Review*, *79*(3), 106–116. PMID:11246918

Hennig, A. (2013). *The Ethical Background of Business in China – An Outline. academia.edu*. Retrieved from: https://www.researchgate.net/publication/269403615_The_Ethical_Background_of_Business_in_China_-_An_Outline

Hofstede, G., & Bond, M. H. (1988). The Confucius Connection: From Culture Roots to Economic Growth. *Organizational Dynamics, 16*(4), 4–21. doi:10.1016/0090-2616(88)90009-5

Horner, C. (2002) *Executive coaching: the leadership development tool of the future?* (Unpublished MBA dissertation), Imperial College of Science, Technology and Medicine.

Huang, J., & Hsieh, H. (2015). Huang, Supervisors as good coaches: Influences of coaching on employees' in-role behaviors and proactive career behaviors. *International Journal of Human Resource Management, 26*(1), 42–58. doi:10.1080/09585192.2014.940993

Hui, R. T., Sue-Chan, C., & Wood, R. E. (2013). The contrasting effects of coaching style on task performance: The mediating roles of subjective task complexity and self-set goal. *Human Resource Development Quarterly, 24*(4), 429–458. doi:10.1002/hrdq.21170

Ip, P. (2009). The Challenge of Developing a Business Ethics in China. *Journal of Business Ethics, 88*(1), 211–224. doi:10.100710551-008-9820-2

Johnson, R., Chang, C., & Yang, L. (2010). Commitment and motivation at work: The relevance of employee identity and regulatory focus. *Academy of Management Review, 35*, 226–245.

Joo, B., Suchko, J. S., & McLean, G. N. (2012). Multiple faces of coaching: Manager-as-coach, executive coaching, and formal mentoring. *Organization Development Journal, 30*, 19–38.

Kegan, R. (1994). *In over our heads: The mental demands of modern life*. Harvard University Press.

Kline, N. (2016). *Time to think: listening to ignite the human mind*. Cassell Illustrated.

Littrell, R. F. (2002). Desirable leadership behaviours of multi-cultural managers in China. *Journal of Management Development, 21*(1), 5–74. doi:10.1108/02621710210413190

Lu, Y., & Bjorkman, I. (1997). HRM practices in China-Western joint ventures: MNC standardization versus localization. *International Journal of Human Resource Management, 8*(5), 614–628. doi:10.1080/095851997341414

McCall, M. Jr. (2010). Recasting leadership development. *Industrial and Organizational Psychology: Perspectives on Science and Practice, 3*(1), 3–19. doi:10.1111/j.1754-9434.2009.01189.x

Meyer, E. (2015). *The culture map: decoding how people think, lead, and get things done across cultures.*

Nangalia, L., & Nangalia, A. (2010). The Coach in Asian Society: Impact of social hierarchy on the coaching relationship. *International Journal of Evidence Based Coaching and Mentoring, 8*(1), 51.

Neubert, M. J., Kacmar, K. M., Carlson, D. S., Chonko, L. B., & Roberts, J. A. (2008). Regulatory focus as a mediator of the influence of initiating structure and servant leader- ship on employee behavior. *The Journal of Applied Psychology, 93*(6), 1220–1233. doi:10.1037/a0012695 PMID:19025244

Nonaka, I. (1994). A Dynamic Theory of Organizational Knowledge Creation. *Organization Science, 5*(1), 14–37. doi:10.1287/orsc.5.1.14

Nonaka, I., Toyama, R., & Konno, N. (2000). SECI, Ba and Leadership: A Unified Model of Dynamic Knowledge Creation. *Long Range Planning, 33*(1), 5–34. doi:10.1016/S0024-6301(99)00115-6

Oh, T. K. (1992). Inherent Limitations of The Confucian Tradition in Contemporary East Asian Business Enterprises. *Journal of Chinese Philosophy, 19*(2), 155–169. doi:10.1111/j.1540-6253.1992.tb00116.x

Paine, L. S. (2010). *The China Rules: A Practical Guide for CEOs Managing Multinational Corporations in the People's Republic.* Retrieved from: https://hbr.org/2010/06/the-globe-the-china-rules

Perkowski, J. (2015). *Tesla Overestimates the Chinese Market.* Retrieved from: https://www.forbes.com/sites/jackperkowski/2015/02/17/tesla- overestimates-the-china-market/#5b3fd2a44346

Qian, W., Abdur Razzaque, M., & Ah Keng, K. (2007). Chinese Cultural Values and Gift-giving Behavior. *Journal of Consumer Marketing, 24*(4), 214–228. doi:10.1108/07363760710756002

Rasmus, D. W. (2002). *Collaboration, Content and Communities.* GigaTel.

Reissner, S. C. (2008). Narrative and story: New perspectives on coaching. *International Journal of Mentoring and Coaching, 6*(3), 1–5.

Rock, D., & Donde, R. (2008). Driving organizational change with internal coaching programs: Part one. *Industrial and Commercial Training*, *40*(1), 10–18. doi:10.1108/00197850810841594

Romar, E. J. (2002). Virtue Is Good Business: Confucianism as a Practical Business Ethics. *Journal of Business Ethics*, *38*(1/2), 119–131. doi:10.1023/A:1015760710802

Schütt, P. (2003). The post-Nonaka Knowledge Management. *Journal of Universal Computer Science*, *9*(6), 451–462.

Senge, P. M. (2006). *The fifth discipline: The art & practice of the learning organisation*. Random House.

Shen, J. (2008). HRM in Chinese privately owned enterprises. *Thunderbird International Business Review*, *50*(2), 91–104. doi:10.1002/tie.20181

Shlomo, B. (2013). *The business of corporate learning: insights from practice*. Cambridge University Press.

Skiffington, S., & Zeus, P. (2003). *Behavioral Coaching: How to Build Sustainable Personal and Organizational Change*. McGraw-Hill Education.

Stipek, D., Weiner, B., & Li, K. (1989). Testing some attribution-motion relations in the People's Republic of China. *Journal of Personality and Social Psychology*, *56*(1), 109–116. doi:10.1037/0022-3514.56.1.109 PMID:2926613

Stone, D., Stone-Romero, E., & Lukaszewski, K. (2007). The impact of cultural values on the acceptance and effectiveness of human resource management policies and practices. *Human Resource Management Review*, *17*(2), 152–165. doi:10.1016/j.hrmr.2007.04.003

Thomson, B. (2009). *Don't just do something, sit there: an introduction to non-directive coaching*. Chandos. doi:10.1533/9781780632063

Thomson, B. (2014). *First steps in coaching*. SAGE. doi:10.4135/9781526401649

Thornhill, A., & Saunders, M. N. K. (1998). What if line managers don't realize they're responsible for HR? Lessons from an organization experiencing rapid change. *Personnel Review*, *27*(6), 460–476. doi:10.1108/00483489810238903

Tulpa, K., & Bresser, F. (2013). Coaching in Europe. In J. Passmore (Ed.), *Diversity in coaching: Working with gender, culture, race and age* (2nd ed.). Kogan Page.

Vorhauser-Smith, S. (2012). *Performance Management in China - Three Factors to Watch*. Retrieved from: http://www.forbes.com/sites/sylviavorhausersmith/2012/08/22/performance- management-in-china-three-factors-to-watch/2/#2a590c07481a

Wall, K., Lin, H., Zhang, R., & Lei, X. (2009). A Study on the Chinese Ethical Evolution and Its Effects on SMB in China Today. *International Journal of Business and Management*, *4*(3), 15–25. doi:10.5539/ijbm.v4n3p15

Wang, J., Wang, G. G., Rouna, W. E. A., & Rojewski, J. W. (2005). Confucian Values and the Implications for International HRD. *Human Resource Development International*, *8*(3), 311–326. doi:10.1080/13678860500143285

Weer, C., DiRenzo, M., & Shipper, F. (2016). A Holistic View of Employee Coaching: Longitudinal Investigation of the Impact of Facilitative and Pressure-Based Coaching on Team Effectiveness. *The Journal of Applied Behavioral Science*, *52*(2), 187–21. doi:10.1177/0021886315594007

Yeh, Q. J., & Xu, X. (2010). The Effect of Confucian Work Ethics on Learning about Science and Technology Knowledge and Mobility. *Journal of Business Ethics*, *95*(1), 111–128. doi:10.100710551-009-0352-1

Zinzius, B. (2004). *Doing Business in the New China: A Handbook and Guide*. Conneticut.

ADDITIONAL READING

Abravane, M., & James, G. (2017). Exploring the evolution of coaching through the lens of innovation. *Coaching: An International Journal of Theory. Research and Practice*, *15*(1), 24–51.

Boyatzis, R., Smith, M., & Blaize, N. (2006). Developing Sustainable Leaders through Coaching and Compassion. *Academy of Management Learning & Education*, *5*(1), 8–24. doi:10.5465/amle.2006.20388381

Hackman, J., & Wageman, R. (2005). A Theory of Team Coaching. *Academy of Management Review*, *30*(2), 269–287. doi:10.5465/amr.2005.16387885

Meyer, E. (2015). *The culture map: decoding how people think, lead, and get things done across cultures*. Public Affairs.

Parish, P. (2016). A coaching framework for developing the psychological capital of a global mindset. *Coaching: An International Journal of Theory, Research and Practice*, Special Issue No 10, 172-184.

Peters, J., & Carr, C. (2013). Team effectiveness and team coaching literature review. *Coaching: An International Journal of Theory. Research and Practice*, *6*(2), 116–136.

Rock, D., & Donde, R. (2008). Driving organisational change with internal coaching programmes: Part two. *Industrial and Commercial Training*, *40*(2), 75–80. doi:10.1108/00197850810858901

Thomson, B. (2014). *First steps in coaching*. Sage. doi:10.4135/9781526401649

KEY TERMS AND DEFINITIONS

Coaching Mix: The combination of coaching continuum elements to define and structure an organisation's approach to coaching.

Internal Coaching: The use of employees within the organisation, often line managers, to provide work-based coaching to other employees.

Knowledge Combination: The process through which groups and individuals combine knowledge, potentially creating new knowledge.

Knowledge Externalisation: Individuals form groups and share tacit knowledge, therefore making it explicit and shared within the organisation.

Knowledge Internalisation: This is the process through which new explicit knowledge is codified and captured, becoming tacit again as it now becomes embedded in organisational culture and processes.

Knowledge Management: The systematic and systemic management of the organisation's knowledge assets with an emphasis on organisational learning and innovation.

Knowledge Socialisation: The process through which tacit knowledge is transferred through interaction with others. Although this may be through discussion, it may also be through observation and demonstration.

Sense Breaking: The process through which the coach supports the coachee to break away from old systems and thought processes as they engage with organisational change.

Sense Making: The process through which the coach supports the coachee to envision a brighter future and to create a new 'reality' as they engage with organisational change.

Appendix 1

Kegan's Development Phases (Kegan, 1994).

Phase	Adults generally in This phase	Core Characteristics	Major Limitations
Phase 3: The Socialised Mind	43-46% of all adults between 19-55 usually entered in adolescence.	Able to internalize the ideas or emotions of others who represent their meaning system Guided by the ideologies, institutions, or people that are most important to them. They are able to think abstractly, be self-reflective about their actions and the actions of others, and be devoted to something that's greater than their own needs.	When there is a conflict between important ideologies, institutions, or people, those at the Third order feel torn in two and cannot find a way to make a decision Their esteem is entirely reliant on others because they are, in many ways, made up of those around them.
Phase 4: The Self Authored Mind	18 – 34% of all adults between 19-55.	Have created a self that is the author of its connections to the ideologies, Able to examine those various rule-systems, opinions, and expectations and are able to mediate among them using an internal set of rules and regulations – a self-governing system.	May feel torn apart by disagreeing pieces of themselves which are both working in service of a larger, self-authored (but relatively unquestioned) goal. May become embedded in (and is Subject to) their self-authored system.
Phase 5: The Self Transforming Mind	3-6% of all adults between 19-55. Not entered before midlife.	Learned the limits of their own inner system – and the limits of full identification with any one inner system in general. Less likely to see the world in terms of dichotomies. They are more likely to understand and deal well with paradox and with managing the tension of opposites.	

Chapter 10
The Coaching Dance Applied:
A Culturally Sensitive Approach to Knowledge Management and Nondirective Coaching in Confucian China

William Percy
Zeng Associates, LLC, China

Kevin Dow
University of Auckland, New Zealand

ABSTRACT

Through the application of a culturally sensitive coaching model, in a Sino-foreign education partnership, this chapter explores a non-directive coaching model and its positive impact on knowledge exchange and innovation. Whilst acknowledging the call from some quarters for the use of a directive approach to coaching, in mainland China, this chapter explores the positive relationship between the non-directive approach and socialisation of knowledge amongst teachers. The chapter also sheds light on the potential positive impact of the GROW model to support the 'Coaching Dance' and facilitate movement towards a more non-directive approach to enhance knowledge exchange. It is also important of further research into both the GROW model and the development of a coaching approach built upon the foundation of Confucian culture.

DOI: 10.4018/978-1-7998-4126-5.ch010

INTRODUCTION

This chapter applies a culturally sensitive coaching model to investigate the opportunities provided for knowledge exchange and innovation in a Sino-foreign partnership. Particularly, the model is deployed and analysed in the context of a bilingual school based in mainland China.

The current education environment in mainland China provides a rich context for an investigation as it has many parallels with the wider business environment. There is significant political pressure on the education sector to 'internationalise' by adopting best global practices (with a significant shift in the legal and political environment aimed at rewarding those who innovate and comply with Central Government's reforms, whilst embracing Chinese culture) and moving beyond rote learning to a more innovative and collaborative approach to education. This *step change* and the many fast paced legal reforms have led to an increasingly Volatile, Uncertain, Complex and Ambiguous (VUCA) environment.

It is in this context, and with the ever-increasing presence of Chinese business on the global stage, that we note the critical importance of Western business managers' understanding of Chinese culture and business practices (Paine, 2010). Yet, few Western business schools reference Chinese business practice and leadership. Management theories often over-simplify the complexity of leadership development in an international context and fail to recognise how philosophical and ideological differences drive a distinctly different approach to leadership and management in Asia (Alves, Manz and Butterfield, 2005).

The field of coaching also suffers from this deficit. Despite the increased use of coaching in China, there is very little research into the effectiveness of coaching intervention in a Chinese context, although, there is significant demand for the development of a culturally specific coaching model (Gallo, 2012; Kim, Egan and Kim, 2013). According to Chau (2016), this is a significant barrier to the development of Chinese executives.

Chinese junior executives often fail to develop career plans and do not take the initiative to set targets with their bosses. Whilst Chinese senior executives, buffeted by the Volatile Uncertain Complex and Ambiguous business environment in China and how they perceive, react to and understand its rapid modernisation are suffering 'mid-life crisis' at a far younger age than their Western counterparts (Woo 2011).

As the Chinese government seeks to rapidly move away from an economy built on 'Made in China' to one 'Designed in China' it emphasises the need for management innovation with rising foreign acquisitions (to stimulate Chinese innovation and creativity), and senior Western executives more likely to work for Chinese companies both in China or in their home country (Regina, Abrami, Kirby and McFarlan, 2014). As such, it is not just Chinese executives that suffer from a lack of a coherent model, but all executives in Sino-foreign partnerships. Such partnerships are likely to continue through the One Belt & One Road initiative, with Foreign Minister Wang Yi calling for continued business collaboration and a greater 'Think Tank'.

In this context it is critical that an effective international manager understands Chinese business practices and the corresponding leadership needs, being able to innovate and survive in what can be a very volatile business environment, where the turnover of expat CEOs is approximately four times higher than the global average (Paine, 2010).

The cultural context of Sino-foreign partnerships certainly adds a great deal of complexity to the knowledge exchange and innovation processes and whilst Knowledge Management models, such as Nonaka's SECI model, may provide critical insights for executives engaged in change management and innovation (Percy and Dow, 2020) there are significant gaps in these models as they neither address how new ideas are produced nor how the collaborative process works (Bereiter, 2002).

Coaching may provide a process through which these key criticisms are addressed as in considering knowledge socialisation, we are able to see coaching through a social constructivist lens as a driver of transformational learning. Through the coaching dialogue, individuals and groups become sense makers and breakers, forming a new reality applying their previous experience to information in order to plan for a new future. Through this dialogue, the coach helps frame experiences in order to both sense make and sense break as the individual or group create new realities and possible futures (Fairhurst and Sarr, 1996).

Given such an emphasis on the social context, culture and its impact on the coaching process must be addressed. Much has been said and written about the role of Confucianism as a guiding force in Chinese life and business. This is not surprising given that after 2,500 years it is still recognised as the strongest guiding force in Chinese society (Cheung and King, 2004). Yet, the role of Taoism, Buddhism and 'Bing Fa' (texts on the art of war), should not be forgotten. More recently, Communist ideology and Western values have also had significant impact on Chinese socialisation.

Within this context, the following elements must be addressed in deploying a culturally sensitive coaching model (Percy and Dow 2020):

- Building a coaching approach on a foundation of Confucian culture.
- Acknowledging and working with the need for social harmony.
- Acknowledging and working within the constraints of high power distance and a high collectivism by deploying both individual and group coaching.
- The need to focus and further develop coaching skills as we:
    - Engage in the coaching dance, although predominantly deploying a non-directive approach.

- ◦ Take longer to form a relationship of trust.
- ◦ Learn to listen, question and playback within this cultural context.

Research Questions

The abovementioned needs will be addressed through examination of a three-tiered coaching programme that focuses on group, individual and peer coaching, the themes of knowledge exchange, innovation and culturally-sensitive coaching in a Chinese context by focusing on the following questions:

- How can the implementation of a coaching programme lead to closer collaboration and innovation amongst its teaching professionals?
- What are the barriers to the implementation of a culturally-sensitive coaching approach and how can these be overcome?
- What are the benefits to the implementation of a culturally-sensitive coaching approach and how can these be maximised?

In posing these questions, it is essential to move beyond adjustment of coaching models to developing a model that is built on a foundation of Chinese culture – which will require deeper immersion, collaboration and reflection on the application of coaching models that is beyond the scope of this paper. Therefore, this paper deploy a culturally sensitive coaching model (Percy and Dow, 2020). Examining the perceived need for changes to the 'Western' model and potentially highlighting areas for future research and modification in future iterations of the coaching programme.

Methodology

Given the social constructivist approach to both knowledge exchange and coaching alongside cultural considerations, an ontological approach was adopted. In doing so, we recognised the continuous change in the environment and that players may construct multiple complex realities (Whitehead, 2005).

In adopting a constructivist stance, we assert that our 'knowledge' arises not only from our experiences, but also from our 'understandings' in many ways driven by reflection on experience and the language that we use to define them (Bryman, 2008). In recognising this, we acknowledge that methodologies used in the 'natural sciences' may not fit an environment where social reality is defined by multiple perspectives and understandings (Cohen, Manion and Morrison, 2007).

In embracing the phenomenologically oriented paradigm that is inherent in ethnographic research, we must accept that, although few explicit assumptions should be made, inductive analysis will allow themes to emerge from the data.

Figure 1. Timeline and Key Events of the Research

Timeline	Key Events
First Half of Semester One	• Negotiation of pilot project terms; • Weekly sessions focus on introducing coaching; • Weekend coaching workshop; • Individual and peer coaching sessions begin in earnest using Thomson's appraisal questions (Thomson, 2009); • Lesson walk throughs begin.
Second Half of Semester One	• Group coaching begins; • Individual and peer coaching are driven by the coachee's agenda; • PLCs are introduced; • 360 degree review performance criteria are collaboratively developed; • Lesson walk throughs progress to lesson observations; • 1st 360 degree review.
First Half of Semester Two	• Learning Facilitators undertake a major project; • Lesson observations continue; • 360 degree reviews 3 & 4 take place; • Group, per and individual coaching are at their height and are data driven.

The authors adopted an Ethnographic Action Research strategy to explore cultural issues to develop a coaching strategy and then to take 'action'. The methodology is particularly useful as a strategy in this setting as it uses immersive ethnography to guide research, whilst the action research component links back to considered and purposeful actions.

In recognising that time is required for observation to develop credible description, the project was conducted across a full academic year, allowing for a series of cycles of emic (culturally immersive) observation to be followed by etic (reflection from a researcher's perspective) allowing research to be progressively shaped and focused by the ethnographic investigation.

During the course of the investigation a three-tiered coaching programme that focused on the use of the GROW model (Whitmore, 2009) in group, individual and peer coaching was deployed. After negotiation, two expatriate coaches delivered a pilot project working with eight Learning Facilitators who were seeking to make the transition to full teaching posts.

Following a period of training and familiarisation with the coaching process, weekly group coaching sessions were held alongside peer and individual coaching, which took place on alternate weeks.

Throughout the project, the coaching team immersed themselves through emic observation in the cultural environment, engaging with the Cultural Systems Paradigm and periodically pausing and undertaking etic evaluation to continue to amend and develop the coaching strategy for continued delivery. In undertaking emic observations, we acknowledged the significantly different nature of Chinese culture and resultantly adopted Whitehead's (2005) Natural Cultural Learning process recognising the 'Child' as an ethnographic model. Ethnographers observe, interview, participate and make interpretations. Throughout the project, the following data gathering tools were used:

- Emic and etic participatory observation.
- Individual coaching session notes (also used to inform group coaching).
- Group coaching session notes.
- Semi-structured individual and group interviews.
- Maintenance of personal 'field' notes.
- 360 Degree data analysis from online systems.
- Modified Fitzpatrick coaching survey.

The gathering and representation of data is closely linked to the inclusion of peer coaching and coaching training within the study, as we recognise the ethical and social responsibility not to treat participants as objects and that participants should grow and learn from the ethnographic interaction, becoming 'informant and fellow analyst'.

As the authors form these relationships, and organise the data into a meaning narrative and decide what to tell others, it is essential to highlight the weaknesses in the methodology – as there are significant questions regarding validity and reliability (Bath, 2009) given that neutrality is impossible and the narrative subjective, this methodology lacks the validity of a quantitative methodology – as there is no control for validity threats or testing of hypothesis, therefore, such subjectivity may lead to a loss of objectivity (Cohen, Manion and Morrison, 2007).

Scientists have long accepted the inadequacy for more qualitative methods to engage with the 'complexities of the human condition' and that as the researcher becomes more focused on the contradictions, they are able to gain an increased consciousness. Therefore, in monitoring the quality of their reflection and data gathering, the researcher ensures the rigour of the process (Ball, 1990).

Results and Findings

Recognising that labels may follow a coachee throughout their career, colouring the way the coachee is perceived by managers and other important community members, results are presented using aggregated data to maintain anonymity of the participants.

Negotiation of Project Terms

Given that initial stages of a project should be included in reflection of the action research cycle and that the initial collaboration with the researcher is often ignored, this section will focus on the initial negotiation to begin the coaching project.

The coaching project was discussed as a potential staff development programme and presented to a mixed panel of both Chinese and Western Headmasters. Junior teachers had highlighted the fact that they were unhappy with development opportunities and that they felt unsupported in their role. Many of their concerns and confusions seemed to stem from the fact that they were unclear or unsure of how to bring together 'the best from East and West'. The initial concept to be presented was that Junior Teachers and Learning Facilitators would be given the opportunity to be coached, and that Heads of Department would be trained in Personal Learning Community strategies and offered training to develop coaching skills.

During the course of the meeting, it became clear that there were very different models of professional development held in the minds of the Western and Chinese leaders present. Generally, the Western team was clear that Professional Development is a process (or journey), rather than a one-off event, and that through empowering teams and individuals to drive their own professional development that the organisation and its professionalism would grow. The Chinese leaders present expressed the view that training should take the form of presentation or prescribed reading/study material and that participants should be expected to present back what they had learned. In essence, expressing the view that professional development is an event at a given time and place, and that participants cannot be trusted to engage with training or to apply it. It was also clear that the preference was for a senior teacher to be assigned to mentor them showing them the 'right' way to teach.

Just when it appeared that there might be an impasse, one of the senior Chinese leaders spoke out and shared his experience with a trusted American colleague who had explained the effectiveness of coaching in driving change in his school. From this point, the tone of the meeting changed to discussing how the programme could be implemented. Several critical issues were discussed:

- A feeling that Western coaches should not be training Chinese teachers.
- That assessment criterion should not be used as part of 360 degree review.

- That coaching is not suitable for senior colleagues such as master teachers or headmasters.
- That all Learning Facilitators should take part in the coaching programme.

The coaching team agreed that they would coach all learning facilitators and that, with regard to Chinese being coached by Westerners, they had agreed that they would be providing training to the coachees to raise awareness of the nature of coaching, and being passionate about developing capacity in Chinese colleagues they agreed to train Chinese coaches over time. A compromise was reached with regard to the 360-degree criteria and coaches could run the Professional Learning Communities (PLCs), rather than training the Heads of Department.

This was the first interaction that the coaching team had with the leadership team and it highlighted several important issues that would re-emerge. Not least of these was the need to engage all stakeholders and particularly 'system change levers' if the coaching programme were to have systemic impact, and that by aligning with the desire for change and building capacity within local resources, the programme was more likely to be accepted. The idea that all learning facilitators must be coached because some people may be unhappy was the first exposure the team had to the idea of harmonious society within the workplace, and that such training decisions would also be made from a collective perspective.

Cultural Systems Paradigm Applied

From a Chinese perspective, there are significant differences in social systems, behavioural patterns and idea systems that need to be better understood if coaching is to be a driver of knowledge exchange.

Not least of these differences is a Confucian approach to HR. The team found that individually a Confucian belief system was prevalent and concurred with Kim, Atkinson and Yang (1999), in that although Western ideals may be affecting the outward presentation of behaviour, the cultural core remains stable. Yet, we also acknowledge we found the younger generation, who had spent time overseas, retained some Western values. However, the collision and resultant synergy of these ideals could be seen from an organisational perspective with a desire to develop a HR practices that are both modern and embrace Confucian ideals.

This is not unusual as many overseas returning Chinese apply HR lessons learned in the West (Ding, Goodall, & Warner, 2000). Yet, many note these strategies do not meet the needs of China. This is perhaps due to a Western tension between the 'bottom line' and the individual (Beer, Broselie and Brewster, 2015) not being appropriate for a Chinese environment and business practices.

In China, amongst forwarding thinking organisations, a Confucian belief drives an HR system that values delayering and a 'family' style approach. This belief drives engagement with the employee's home life and sometimes to company time and resources being used to help solve personal issues. This can be can be very confusing for Western executives, who failing to understand the Confucian implications belief that this is a relic of the command economy 'iron rice bowl'.

In seeking to further understand this important dynamic, the coaching team adopted a Confucian Model of HR developed by Lamond and Zheng (2010) (as depicted in Figure 2) as it more fully captures the desire for a 'harmonious' workplace (through equality and fairness), the 'guanxi' networks that bind us together from individual to the group and the wider business context, driven by the Confucian ideal of a more holistic view of HR.

Figure 2. A Confucian Approach to HR Systems (adapted from Lamond and Zheng, 2010)

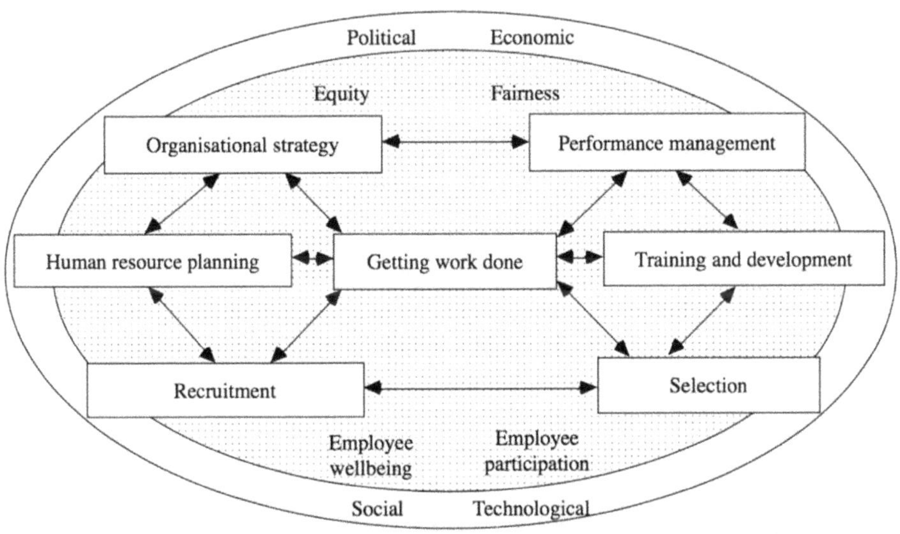

Many Chinese organisations are now seeking more entrepreneurial employees that can cope with a tough and uncertain business environment, this matches the coaches' observation of the environment in which the coachees must operate (as depicted in Figure 3). The political environment continues to become increasingly complex and volatile, as the government enforces legislation to stop, what has been described as, the 'imperialistic' behaviour of some Western education providers in

China. Alongside this has come an increased mistrust and questioning of Western education practices on a local level.

The Learning Facilitators found themselves caught up in this tension as they received advice from both Western and Chinese colleagues on how to develop their classroom practice. Beyond the implications of the political environment, the wider social context is also less than conducive to the idea of trialling and experimenting with new practice. Parents are very judgmental and will complain quickly and, surprisingly individualistically, are likely to be critical of the teacher seeking change to benefit their child. This perhaps reflects the Confucian morality of relationships with strangers and those not close to you, certainly creating a somewhat hostile environment for a young teacher as they develop and deliver lessons in the classroom.

Figure 3. A Hostile Environment

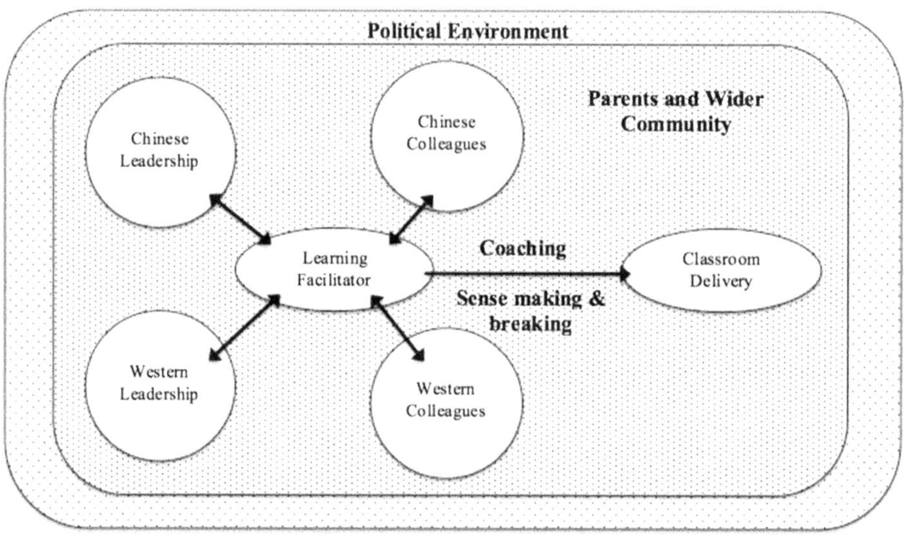

Training and Introducing Coaching

The coaching team approached the training and introduction of coaching as a critical element of the programme, realising that if they were unable to create a convincing narrative for the programme that it would be highly unlikely to succeed. Given their experience with the Chinese members of the leadership team and the somewhat tense legislative environment, they approached the session with a feeling of trepidation.

However, their fear was generally well-received. Rather than assert their own opinion that there was a need for change in Chinese education, the team used several quotes from the national government that called for change, and then explained how the coaching programme would empower the young professionals to develop their own approach to teaching, taking the 'best from East and West'. Thomson's silent coaching questions (Thomson, 2009) were then used to introduce the GROW model and a non-directive approach to coaching. This was then expanded on in a series of one-hour sessions over the following three weeks.

During these sessions, several observations were made by the coaching team, which led to a discussion with regard to the effectiveness of only using Hofstede's cultural dimensions and a strong understanding of Confucianism to inform their coaching work. This was driven by the observation that many of the teachers had initially engaged with the need for education reform through what appeared to be feelings of patriotism, yet over the next two weeks there were several conversations that focused on the fact that China was achieving better examination results, globally, and that China had a longer history and more respect for teachers than the West.

As a result of these discussions, the team initially looked at the Chinese Value Survey, and was intrigued to note that under the category of National Traits, patriotism, cultural superiority and respect for tradition. Some of the finer detail in this survey helped with deeper insight and also to the realisation that rather than just being barriers or supports for the coaching environment, cultural traits could cause conflict and confusion. For instance, the drive for reform by a patriotic desire was certainly conflicting with respect for tradition.

The training phase ended with a one-day coaching workshop, aimed at developing coaching skills, which was attended by all of the Learning Facilitators. Upon being asked what was driving their enthusiasm they spoke about the need to succeed at work and to achieve by adopting new ways of doing things. This demonstrated that Chinese decision-making is becoming more rational and that Confucianism alongside modern Chinese values places emphasis on pragmatism. We also noted the presence of virtues such as persistence, industry and adaptability in the Chinese Value Survey as these cultural values were significant in creating a positive coaching environment.

One unexpected outcome from the training phase was the unexpected enduring success of the silent coaching questions. Many of the Learning Facilitators related how they had continued to use these silent coaching questions well beyond the training and that they had used them with their students. Further questioning about 'why' revealed that they liked the 'logic' of the questions, perhaps appealing to the mathematical logic of the Chinese (Meyer, 2016) and the support they gave in problem solving, with one Learning Facilitator noting:

Silent coaching helped me to work out how to solve my own problems and to decide what I needed to take to coaching.

Coaching Effectiveness

Using the Fitzpatrick Scale (Renton, 2009) the average rating for all elements of the coaching programme was 4.1 or 'Very Strong' with most of the respondents saying that they would recommend the programme to others and that it was effective (see Figure 4). However, two of the respondents rated the effectiveness as 2 or 'below expectation'. This is somewhat incongruous with the development of executive skills (as can be seen in Figure 5), having a section average of 4.4 or 'very strong' towards 'outstanding'. With a mind to improving future cycles of the programme, follow-up conversations were held with both respondents, who when asked why they rated effectiveness as 2, answered truthfully and directly:

I wanted the coach to tell me what to do.

Figure 4. Effectiveness of Coaching (The Coach)

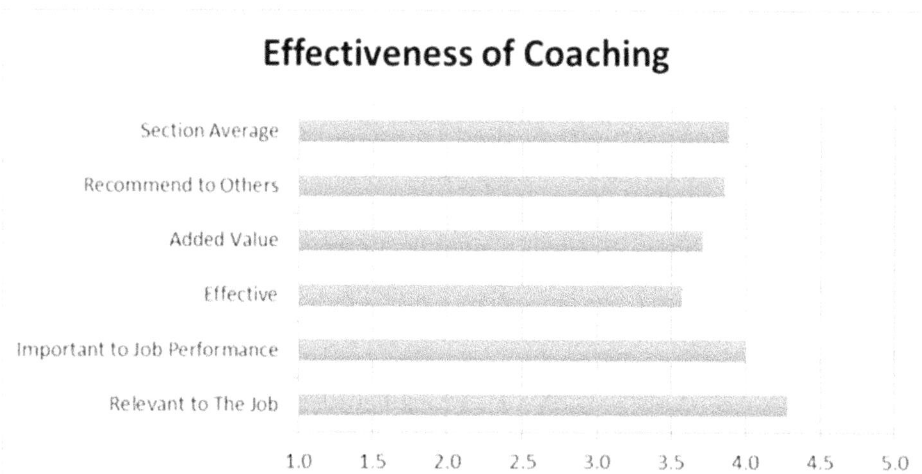

Figure 5. Effectiveness of Coaching (Developing Executive Behaviour)

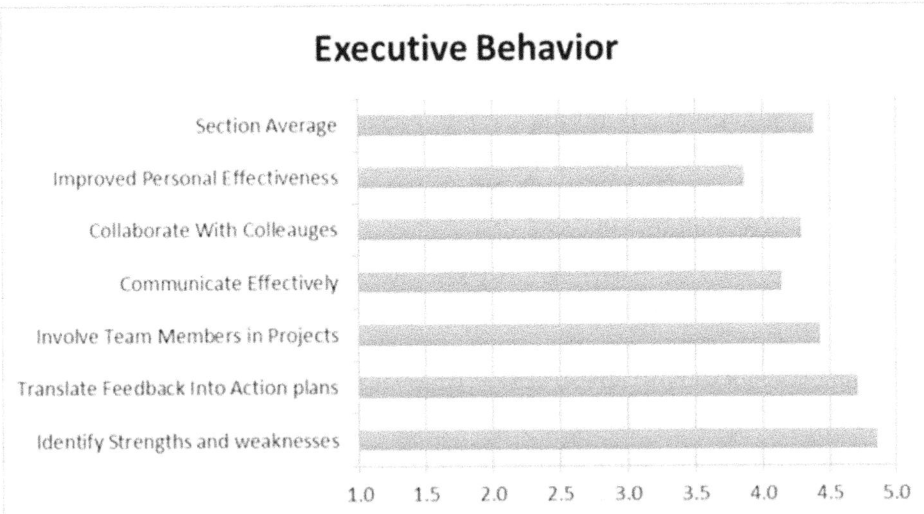

Therefore, a coach can be judged to be impersonal and ineffective (in China) if they do not take responsibility for the both session structure and driving outcomes (Chang, Tong and Zeng, 2005) or that the coach should be a highly qualified 'source of knowledge' (Nangalia and Nangalia, 2010). As this would be reflected in a directive style of coaching, we must ask whether mentoring or a directive style of coaching would have worked better than non-directive coaching.

Noting the strong scores for areas that would improve socialisation, and resultant knowledge exchange, such as collaborating with colleagues and involving team members in projects (as noted in Figure 5), we cannot concur that a directive approach would have been better, and that it would have led to less socialisation. In addressing the need to be highly qualified and drive outcomes, both coaches were able to leverage their many years' coaching and involvement in executive and teacher development to demonstrate their qualification for the role. Rather than viewing the need to drive success as telling coachees what to do, both coaches were proactive in supporting coachees and changing systems, thereby 'removing obstacles' to success in the work environment. We assert that this helped with developing a deeper relationship of rapport and trust, whilst demonstrating a strong desire to support coachees beyond the sessions. Coaches must note that in the early stages of developing coaching relationships, it was difficult to encourage individuals to take personal responsibility as they lacked initiative.

Group and Peer Coaching

Although collectivism has been noted as a barrier to implementing Western HR systems, it has proved to be a significant positive factor in the roll-out of the coaching programme and particularly during the group coaching. We noted that coaching drives discussion, whilst creating a more positive environment and by doing so, increases socialisation (leading to knowledge exchange) and facilitates the alignment of individual to organisational goals.

This is particularly significant, in a Chinese context, as collectivist and hierarchical pressure often mean junior employees are reluctant to share ideas. In this context, meetings are often seen as one-way communication, where information is delivered and comment is not sought. As can be seen from the following quote from a coachee, group coaching helped to overcome this:

[Chinese] meetings are about spreading news, I get information.... In [group] coaching, we discuss problems and find solutions... I don't regard coaching as a meeting, it's more like talking and learning together.

In this context, we can see that group and peer coaching allows for informal sharing and collaboration across department and by doing so increases socialisation. This was also noted by a coachee:

[Coachees] Shared experience across departmental groups... sometimes more like a 'sharing of ideas' than 'coaching.'

This, along with the ability of a systems approach to group coaching to facilitate concurrent change and alignment of organisational systems has been particularly beneficial, as it demonstrated to coachees that the organisation is serious about facilitating change. Therefore, every action in the coaching interaction truly impacts the coaching relationship. Particularly in this case, positive actions, in group coaching, provided a solid foundation for individual coaching relationships to develop. However, we also note that both coaches found these sessions particularly demanding, given that group coaching in this context requires a strong cultural understanding, alongside the ability to develop rapport with the group and understand group dynamics (Brown and Grant, 2010).

Figure 6. Sustained Improvement resulting from coaching

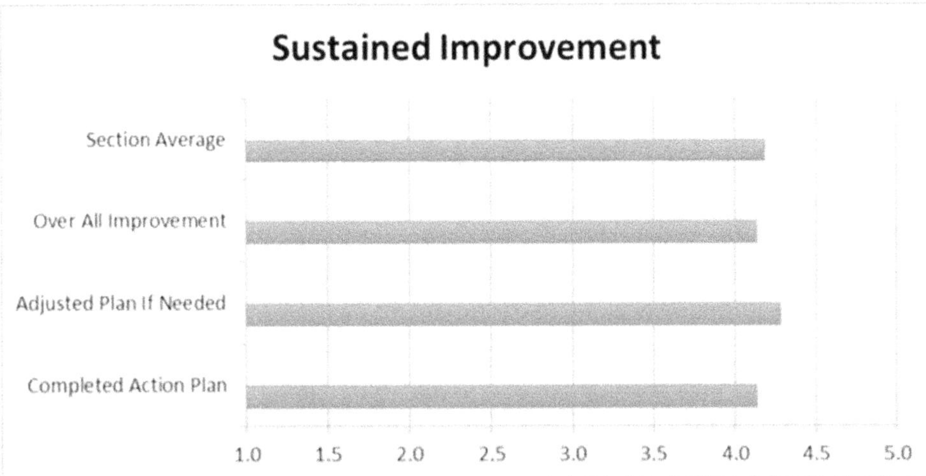

Figure 7. Key Performance Indicators resulting from coaching

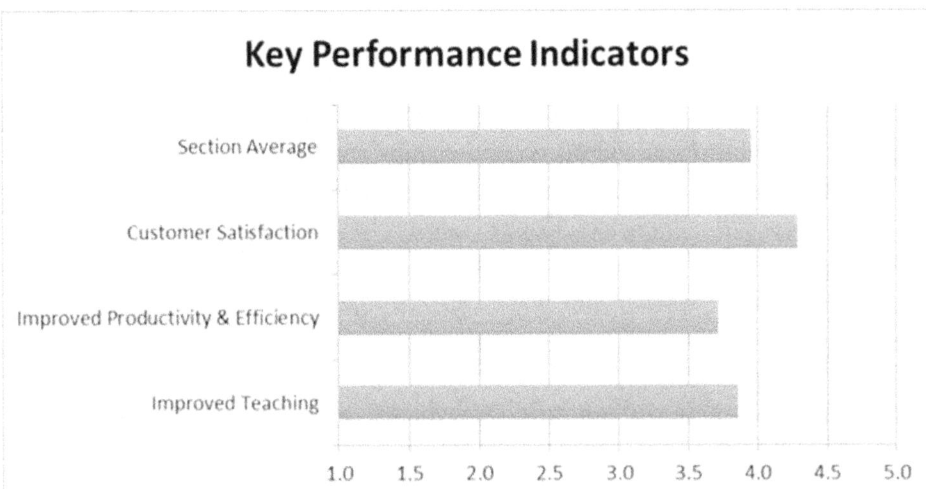

Individual Coaching

Having begun with group coaching, the aim was to transfer to individual coaching running alongside peer coaching. Both coaches made a short presentation to the group to outline their coaching qualifications and coaching style. Coachees were then invited to choose the coach that they would like to work with and let them know during the week. The aim was to hold a first coaching session the week after and to use the FUEL (Zenger, 2010) model to contract with the coaches.

Towards the end of the coaching sessions, no coachees had approached the coaches and both began to be concerned that there may be difficulty in transitioning to individual coaching. However, a representative came to find the coaches and let them know that the coachees would prefer to discuss the ground rules for individual sessions, and who would coach in a group session.

Interestingly, the coachees used the group coaching session to contract as a group, agreeing how sessions would be conducted and how information would be shared back to a group coaching sessions (themes to be identified and shared by the coaches), and how to split the coaching to get the best balance and benefit for the group. Neither coach had previously contracted in this manner; however, both were impressed by the desire to seek 'social harmony' alongside the best project outcomes. By the end of the project, the coachees were generally very enthusiastic about the experience, stating that their self-belief and confidence had improved alongside better communication and knowledge exchange, leading to improvement (Figures 6-7).

As Flaherty (2005) notes, relationship is the first principal of coaching. Unfortunately, both coaches noted that significant gaps between their cultural make-up and that of China meant that they had to be particularly vigilant in building relationships. Although those that had some education oversees tended to form relationships quicker and benefited from coaching faster, relationships still took longer than usual to form and once relationships were deeper, it was not unusual for some time to be spent discussing personal issues. During one session, one of the coaches was left helping a colleague consider how best to reduce pressure from their parents to marry; however, given the need for a more paternalistic approach and that in China personal and work can become blurred (Hout and Michael 2014), the coach spent the time on the subject and was later rewarded with a much strengthened relationship.

Coaches also reported listening to be both intensive and energy draining, given the need to listen for what was not being said. This manifested mainly through follow-up on activities that had not been completed, followed by circular conversations in the coaching session, and then the coach later discovering that a superior or colleague had not played their part or blocked an initiative, and the coachee did not wish to speak badly of them or to admit they had not completed the task. With regard to playback and feedback, coaches found that as the relationships began, they needed to be careful and were very concerned about issues of face; however, as relationships progressed and trust deepened, they found this to be much less of a concern.

Both coaches noted that their biggest difficulty, by far, was not snapping back to their own cultural perspective, particularly when they were struggling to align with and make sense of the rapidly changing political environment, and when decisions being made were in conflict with their core ideals (Adler, 2000).

For the coachees, it was clear that the starting situation was not going to be an easy one (Fig. 3) with advice and sometimes contradicting demands, from superiors, coming from all directions in a constantly changing political environment where the wider community are extremely critical, it would not be surprising if a junior employee could not find the momentum to take action and make change.

Recognising the leader as an intrinsic part of the organisation, we must also recognize that there was great pressure on some of the coachees to emulate leaders or 'junzi' who had little faith or trust in the foreigners and the coaching programme.

In the formative stages of the individual coaching, many of the coaching sessions focused on the coachable issues of helping the coachee put authority into perspective and to find their voice, alongside the need to help coachees to deal with the internal conflict of bringing together strategies from apposing value systems and cultures (Kegan, 1994).

The individual coaching began with the use of Thomson's Cycle of Development and its associated questions (Thomson, 2009). Many of the coachees had not engaged in such performance management previously, not an unusual situation given that a 'no feedback' condition is not unusual in collectivist culture where managers may find it difficult to tackle poor performance or the need for change (Aycan, 2005). It was therefore not surprising when several sought to avoid taking responsibility and blamed factors beyond their control for poor performance (Stipek et al. 1989). However, with patience and time, many of the coachees came to enjoy both the coaching and use of the structure with one commenting:

Individual coaching provided structure [rather than informal discussion] and opportunity for 'deep' discussion.

For those coachees that found it difficult to embrace change using a solely non-directive approach, the coaches entered into the coaching dance (Thomson, 2009) and become more directive. In keeping with the desire to exchange knowledge through socialisation, the first directive task was often to have a discussion with a colleague about a named area with which the coachee was struggling. In a desire to return quickly to a non-directive approach and empower the coachee, they were then asked how they could be supported in this. Often the coaching session was then spent helping the coachee to rehearse and prepare for the upcoming interaction, as for many this was a daunting prospect. However, this was a successful strategy, with one coachee noting:

Coaching motivated me... pushed me to speak to more experienced teachers... because I heard from coaches what they were doing.

...he [the coach] believed in me so it made me feel more confident.

Undertaking the coaching dance and moving along the spectrum of directive and non-directive coaching allowed the coach to help the coachee break the inertia, caused by an overly critical environment, to move beyond their fear and remain solution focused.

One of the clear benefits of managers doing the coaching was that it helped to move beyond hierarchical relationships and gave the coachee opportunity to speak out whilst still maintaining a harmonious workplace, with one coachee noting:

Informal discussion about real problems helped reduce stress and pressure [compared to a formal meeting] it removed the feeling of "reporting on others" and gave permission to speak out about important issues.

The coaches were strongly impressed with the coachees' perseverance, diligence and strong desire for learning as they used the individual and group coaching sessions to work with each other and prepare their 'project' to demonstrate their readiness to become teachers and to show how they had engaged with knowledge exchange and professional development. Given time and support, the coachees willingly shared trialled and improved ideas as they sought to sense make and break, constructing a new reality for their learning and teaching environments.

Throughout the process, they showed again and again that socialisation and collaboration could lead to knowledge exchange, one coachee noted that:

Coaching taught me I can pause, talk to myself and find solutions, slow down the process... analyse and if necessary work with others to find solutions.

Yet, one problem that arose was the difficulty for coachees in arriving at their very next action point or the tactics that they would deploy to achieve their goals. Ironically, as they sought to transform the education system, they were products and prisoners of it, being so used to rote learning and direction they found it hard to take responsibility for or to define the next step. One coachee talking of this feeling noted:

After coaching sessions, sometimes I was confused, sometimes it gave everything and sometimes nothing.

As the coaches grappled with this problem, they were fortunate to have a conversation with Dr. Christian van Nieuwerburgh who introduced them to the GROWTH model of coaching, adding the idea of generating clear Tactics and Habits to the GROW model. This was a significant development, with the same coachee noting

[The] GROWTH model links the dots so they become a line... tactics come from joining ideas together from the session so I know what to do next.

The coaches became aware of the GROWTH model at a time when it made perfect sense to deploy it; however, one of the coaches notes that he believes that this transition was so smooth as through a process of 'gradual release' that the GROW model had helped the coachees develop responsibility for their actions and that, through this raised awareness, they were now ready to take responsibility for tactics and habits, using the GROWTH model. Therefore, he advocates gradual release from GROW to GROWTH.

The Role of Data

There can be no doubt that including the requirement for the Learning Facilitators to produce a project that showed their engagement with developing new ideas and exchanging knowledge is in many ways responsible for the very strong results achieved for sustained improvement. Yet the role of data and formalised process cannot be ignored, as although culture may appear to be an 'initial barrier' to appraisal, its organisational systems that make or break the process.

Although many of the managers involved in the 360-degree feedback process did not see feedback as necessary (Shen, 2008) and were reluctant to give poor feedback (Lu and Bjorkman, 1997), opting to give average marks rather than poor or outstanding (Chen and Eldridge 2010), the 360-degree feedback system was invaluable to the coachees, who, by the end of the programme, craved specific and actionable feedback.

Without the feedback, coachees were coming to sessions with an agenda, that, albeit subconsciously, was driven by a narrative that was an edited view of the world as we all selectively highlight and ignore portions of our story. The data from the 360-degree review helped the coaches to support the coachees in framing their current experiences and creating an aspirational narrative (Fairhurst and Sarr, 1996). The power of such a narrative cannot be ignored as the language that the coachees use in describing their preferred future and aspirations is a driver of constructive change.

As the coachees began to work with the data and develop their own goals for development they began to realise that to develop ability, they would need training and began to seek opportunities for training and to demand that the organisation presented more such opportunities. Given this observation and the earlier observation that developing confidence was necessary to beat the inertia caused by the fear to take action, we amend the equation previously provided by Whitemore (1992),

Awareness + Responsibility = Performance

and concur with Thomson (2009) as he notes that:

Awareness + Responsibility + Confidence + Ability = Performance.

SOLUTIONS AND RECOMMENDATIONS

Although the use of standard Mandarin (普通话) /Putonghua or the people's language) has begun to unify the Chinese mainland (Irwin, 2015), its vast geography and many ethnic cultures make it hard to speak of one China. Therefore, recommendations and conclusions from this study should be applied with caution, particularly given the small sample size of the study and its application to one location.

However, a coaching model is key to organising the conceptual framework, highlighting key elements of the coaching approach and through its application, guiding decisions made during the coaching intervention. As such, it serves as a robust tool for reflection and continued learning of the coach. Therefore, conclusions and recommendations are presented in a spirit of continued reflection with a desire for continued learning towards the development of a coaching model with cultural foundations.

We recognise the role of the individual as 'knowledge owner' sense maker and sense breaker, creating new realities as the coach and coaching process help to reframe experiences and develop new possibilities. Throughout the study, coachees have acknowledged that the systems, and collaboration that these promoted, have increased knowledge exchange and the development of new strategies for deployment in the classroom. This observation is supported through the overall rating of the coaching programme.

Therefore, in seeking to answer the question "How can the implementation of a coaching programme lead to closer collaboration and innovation amongst teaching professionals?" we assert that the use of PLCs and 360-degree review, accompanied by a systemic approach to coaching, provided formal systems for knowledge exchange, whilst the coaching sessions also created informal communication and collaboration opportunities (Bhatt, 2002). The coaching process led to greater socialisation of ideas and that this in turn supported the SECI process (Nonaka, 2000) and led to greater knowledge exchange.

In order to develop a sustainable and replicable coaching model, it is critical to highlight 'the key elements of a successful culturally sensitive coaching approach".

Given the current political environment and the strong desire of the Chinese people to both maintain and modernise their cultural heritage it is key that a 'non-imperialist approach' be taken and that those engaged in Sino-foreign partnership recognise the expectation that they will align with the ideal of creating a 'harmonious society' and, as such, should seek to adopt an approach that also leads to the creation of public value.

In seeking to create a socially-sensitive coaching model, we recognise that Confucianism continues to be the key-driving factor of Chinese culture and that whilst Hofstede's cultural dimensions, coupled with a strong understanding of Confucian values, give a good understanding of national culture, a richer tapestry provided by elements such as Meyer's Culture Map and the Chinese Cultural Values Survey is required to gain a deeper understanding at an organisational, group and individual level (Percy and Dow, 2020).

Experience during the study suggests that there is still a wide and broad spectrum of belief about HR practice ranging from the highly authoritarian and hierarchical to those driven by Confucian value and best modern practice. Therefore, we recognise the aspirational nature of the Confucian HR model presented by Lammond and Zheng (2010) and concur that equity, fairness, connectivity and the ideals of the harmonious work place are significant factors at an organisational level. Therefore, we assert that there is a need to keep an open mind during the contracting process and that this may benefit from being a group activity.

When considering the impact of culture on the group, we recognise the impact of collectivism and hierarchy and that their influence is further augmented by the highly competitive, volatile, uncertain complex and ambiguous nature of the modern Chinese business environment. These elements combine to create change inertia caused by a fear to speak out and to make change to the accepted norm through sense breaking and making. Therefore, we assert that group coaching is a critical part of the coaching model and intervention in a Chinese context, and that when combined with a systemic approach, it develops confidence within the group to both speak out and to challenge the status quo. The group becomes a support mechanism and encourages the exchange of knowledge alongside the development of more effective systems.

From an individual perspective, we recognise that Power Difference is a significant cultural factor leading to preference for directive coaching interaction, we do not concur with calls for a directive approach to coaching. Asserting that the coach should skilfully engage in the 'coaching dance' and support the coachee in their individual development. We note that the evidence presented within the study also suggests that a non-directive approach may lead to higher socialisation and knowledge exchange, therefore, it is a critical element in fostering creativity and innovation.

Cultural elements of hierarchy, collectivism, power difference and the desire for a harmonious workplace do cause a high likelihood of common themes developing in individual coaching sessions (Wearley 2010); particularly, the need to help the coachee find their voice and to adjust their perception of power. However, given the high emphasis of rote learning and knowledge recall in the Chinese education system, we note the difficulty that coachees had in visualising and implementing next steps. Therefore, we recommend that the GROWTH model be further investigated, given the addition of Tactics and Habits and the observation that is supported by the coachees in taking action beyond the session.

The idea of pre-identified coachable issues may encourage coaches to oversimplify the cultural impact on the coaching environment. Therefore, we note the significant issues that arose during individual coaching sessions as coachees sought to strike balance between issues arising from their cultural tension, such as the conflict between the patriotic drive to reform and the desire to preserve national culture. Further complexity was added by the internal conflict generated by the need to adopt practices from an ideal system that is incongruous with the coachees' core values (Kegan, 1994).

Whilst interacting in both group and individual coaching environments, the coach must be mindful of the impact of culture on the coaching relationship. We note the insights provided by Meyer (2016) that the coach should expect to take longer to develop rapport and trust alongside being mindful of the need to 'listen between the lines' and using questioning, playback and feedback in ways that do not cause a loss of face, particularly, in the formative stages of the relationship.

There are barriers to the successful implementation of a coaching programme, given the significant need to ensure that the overriding corporate strategy and environment are aligned to the knowledge strategy. However, there is significant tension between the more hierarchical, traditional Chinese HR strategy and the coaching approach. Confucian values surrounding trust and relationships mean that expatriates and Western business theories may be treated with distrust, and some may deploy hostile strategies to derail these projects.

The benefits reported by the coachees suggest that there were significant benefits to addressing the need for cultural adjustment to the coaching model and overcoming implementation barriers. Particularly, the use of individual and group coaching in parallel with the GROW and GROWTH models in a non-directive coaching environment supported socialisation of ideas and knowledge exchange, whilst, raising the confidence of coachees and through a raised awareness empowering them to take responsibility for their actions.

A significant element to the coaching environment was the use of the PLC and 360-degree review strategies to facilitate a systemic approach to coaching and by reframing the coachees' narrative to empower them to be co-author of new and improved realities. Given the reported desire from coachees to have more feedback and the impact this had on their performance, we recommend that there is further exploration of the role of coaching in the appraisal process and its potential to facilitate both feedback and development, thereby overcoming the reticence of Chinese managers to provide feedback and engage in meaningful appraisal.

CONCLUSION

In conclusion, we assert that the with a culturally-sensitive approach that coaching and Thomson's underlying ethos have significant potential to positively impact knowledge exchange and innovation in Sino-foreign partnerships and to improve performance. Therefore, we concur with Thomson (2009) and his observation that:

Awareness + Responsibility + Confidence + Ability = Performance.

Key to this approach is the use of a non-directive approach to coaching and, despite the call for a directive approach in a Chinese context, the case study provides some insight into the positive impact of a non-directive approach in fostering innovation and knowledge exchange. Further research into this area and in particular the application of the GROWTH model is highly recommended.

ACKNOWLEDGMENT

The authors wish to acknowledge the significant support Professor Bob Thomson for his helpful comments on early versions of this chapter.

The authors also wish to acknowledge the support of the team at Mr. Elmer, LLC for their support in data capture through the deployment of Intervention Compass.

This research received no specific grant from any funding agency in the public, commercial, or not-for-profit sectors.

REFERENCES

Adler, N. J. (2002). *International dimensions of organizational behavior*. South-Western.

Alves, J., Manz, C., & Butterfield, D. (2005). Developing leadership theory in Asia: The role of Chinese philosophy. *International Journal of Leadership Studies*, *1*(1), 3–27.

Aycan, Z. (2005). The Interplay Between Cultural and Institutional / Structural Contingencies In Human Resource Management Practices. *International Journal of Human Resource Management, 16*(7), 1083–1119. doi:10.1080/09585190500143956

Ball, S. J. (1990). Self-doubt and Soft Data: social and technical trajectories in ethnographic fieldwork. In M. Hammersley (Ed.), *Educational Research: current issues*. Paul Chapman.

Beer, M., Boselie, P., & Brewster, C. (2015, May). Boselie. P and Brewster. C. Implications For The Field Of HRM Of The Multistakeholder Perspective Proposed 30 Years Ago. *Human Resource Management, 54*(3), 427–438. doi:10.1002/hrm.21726

Bereiter, C. (2002). *Education and mind in the knowledge age*. Lawrence Erlbaum Associates.

Bhatt, G. D. (2002). Knowledge management in organizations: Examining the interaction between technologies, techniques, and people. *Journal of Knowledge Management, 5*(1), 68–75. doi:10.1108/13673270110384419

Brown, S. W., & Grant, A. M. (2010). From GROW to GROUP: Theoretical issues and a practical model for group coaching in organisations. Coaching. An International Journal of Theory. *Research and Practice, 3*(1), 30–45.

Bryman, A. (2008). *Social research methods*. Oxford University Press.

Chang, D. F., Tong, H., Shi, Q., & Zeng, Q. (2005). Letting a Hundred Flowers Bloom: Counseling and Psychotherapy in the People's Republic of China. *Journal of Mental Health Counseling, 27*(2), 104–116. doi:10.17744/mehc.27.2.hxfupdhht26b30a6

Chen, J., & Eldridge, D. (2010). Are "standardized performance appraisal practices" really preferred? A case study in China. *Chinese Management Studies, 4*(3), 244–257. doi:10.1108/17506141011074138

Cheung, T. S., & King, A. Y. (2004). Righteousness and Profitableness: The Moral Choice of Contemporary Confucian Entrepreneurs. *Journal of Business Ethics, 54*(3), 245–260. doi:10.100710551-004-6405-6

Cohen, L., Manion, L., & Morrison, K. (2007). *Research Methods in Education*. Routledge. doi:10.4324/9780203029053

Ding, D. Z., Goodall, K., & Warner, M. (2000). The end of the "iron rice bowl"? Whither Chinese human resource management. *International Journal of Human Resource Management, 11*(2), 217–236. doi:10.1080/095851900339837

Fairhurst, G. T., & Sarr, R. A. (1996). *The Art of Framing: Managing the Language of Leadership*. Jossey-Bass.

Flaherty, J. (2005). *Coaching: Evoking Excellence in Others* (2nd ed.). Elsevier.

Gallo, F. (2012). How Chinese managers can become effective global leaders. *People & Strategy*, *35*(2), 24–30.

Hout, T., & Michael, D. (2014). *A Chinese Approach To Management*. https://hbr.org/2014/09/a-chinese-approach-to-management

Irwin, J. (2012). *Doing Business in China: An overview of ethical aspects*. Institute of Business Ethics.

Kegan, R. (1994). *In over our heads: The mental demands of modern life*. Harvard University Press.

Kim, B. S. K., Atkinson, D. R., & Yang, P. H. (1999). The Asian values scale: Development, factor analysis, validation, and reliability. *Journal of Counseling Psychology*, *46*(3), 342–352. doi:10.1037/0022-0167.46.3.342

Kim, S., Egan, T. M., Kim, W., & Kim, J. (2013). The impact of managerial coaching behavior on employee work-related reactions. *Journal of Business and Psychology*, *28*(3), 315–330. doi:10.100710869-013-9286-9

Lamond, D., & Zheng, C. (2010). HRM research in China: Looking back and looking forward. *Journal of Chinese Human Resource Management*, *1*(1), 6–16. doi:10.1108/20408001011051179

Meyer, E. (2015). The culture map: decoding how people think, lead, and get things done across cultures. Academic Press.

Nangalia, L., & Nangalia, A. (2010). The Coach in Asian Society: Impact of social hierarchy on the coaching relationship. *International Journal of Evidence Based Coaching and Mentoring*, *8*(1), 51.

Nonaka, I., Toyama, R., & Konno, N. (2000). SECI, Ba and Leadership: A Unified Model of Dynamic Knowledge Creation. *Long Range Planning*, *33*(1), 5–34. doi:10.1016/S0024-6301(99)00115-6

Paine, L. S. (2010). *The China Rules: A Practical Guide for CEOs Managing Multinational Corporations in the People's Republic*. Retrieved from: https://hbr.org/2010/06/the-globe-the-china-rules

Percy, W., & Dow, K. (2020). The Coaching Dance: Beyond Nonaka, Knowledge Management in Post Tayloristic Confucian China. In G. Hooke (Ed.), *Emerging Trade and Investment Opportunities Between Oceania and Asia*. IGI Global.

Regina, M., Abrami, C., Kirby, F., & McFarlan, W. (2014). Why China Can't Innovate. *Harvard Business Review*. Available at: https://hbr.org/2014/03/why-china-cant-innovate

Renton, J. (2009). *Coaching and mentoring: What they are and how to make the most of them*. Economist.

Thomson, B. (2009). *Don't just do something, sit there: an introduction to non-directive coaching*. Chandos. doi:10.1533/9781780632063

Wearley, L. (2006). *Coaching with Confucian Values: Reflections on Coaching Asian-Americans*. Grovewell's Knowledge Center.

Whitehead, T. L. (2005). Basic classical ethnographic research methods. *Community and Cultural Assessment Research*, 1-28.

Whitmore, J. (2009). *Coaching For Performance* (4th ed.). Nicholas Brealey.

Woo, M. J. (2011). Human developmental and cultural perspectives on coaching mid-career executives in China. *Advances in Global Leadership*, *6*, 315–331. doi:10.1108/S1535-1203(2011)0000006016

Zenger, J., & Stinnett, K. (2010). *The Extraordinary Coach: How the Best Leaders Help Others Grow*. McGraw-Hill.

ADDITIONAL READING

Abravane, M., & James, G. (2017). Exploring the evolution of coaching through the lens of innovation. *Coaching: An International Journal of Theory. Research and Practice*, *15*(1), 24–51.

Boyatzis, R., Smith, M., & Blaize, N. (2006). Developing Sustainable Leaders through Coaching and Compassion. *Academy of Management Learning & Education*, *5*(1), 8–24. doi:10.5465/amle.2006.20388381

Fang, Y. (1987). Chinese values and the search for culture- free dimensions of culture. *Journal of Cross-Cultural Psychology*, *18*(2), 143–164. doi:10.1177/0022002187018002002

Hackman, J., & Wageman, R. (2005). A Theory of Team Coaching. *Academy of Management Review, 30*(2), 269–287. doi:10.5465/amr.2005.16387885

Parish, P. (2016). A coaching framework for developing the psychological capital of a global mindset. *Coaching: An International Journal of Theory, Research and Practice*, Special Issue No 10, 172-184.

Peters, J., & Carr, C. (2013). Team effectiveness and team coaching literature review. *Coaching: An International Journal of Theory. Research and Practice, 6*(2), 116–136.

Rock, D., & Donde, R. (2008). Driving organisational change with internal coaching programmes: Part two. *Industrial and Commercial Training, 40*(2), 75–80. doi:10.1108/00197850810858901

Thomson, B. (2014). *First steps in coaching*. Sage. doi:10.4135/9781526401649

KEY TERMS AND DEFINITIONS

Coaching Mix: The combination of coaching continuum elements to define and structure an organisation's approach to coaching.

Group Coaching: Coaching of a group of employees who come together to be coached. They may have common purpose or shared experience but are not in a team relationship and may not be seeking to achieve the same business objectives.

Internal Coaching: The use of employees within the organisation, often line managers, to provide work-based coaching to other employees.

Knowledge Management: The systematic and systemic management of the organisation's knowledge assets with an emphasis on organisational learning and innovation.

Sense Breaking: The process through which the coach supports the coachee to break away from old systems and thought processes as they engage with organisational change.

Sense Making: The process through which the coach supports the coachee to envision a brighter future and to create a new 'reality' as they engage with organisational change.

Team Coaching: Coaching of a team (often from a work unit) that come together to achieve a common business purpose or objective.

Chapter 11
Enterprise Resource Planning Development in China in the Age of Intelligent Manufacturing:
Exploring Barriers, Strategies, and Education

David Edwards
University of Nottingham, China

ABSTRACT

Enterprise resource planning (ERP) systems, an important software enabler of intelligent manufacturing, are the core of the "Made in China 2025" initiative to comprehensively upgrade the Chinese industry. However, ERP is notoriously difficult to adopt. In this chapter, the author discusses the Chinese ERP adoption landscape and explores important issues facing organizations adopting ERP. The chapter presents the findings of a large-scale survey of Chinese management by identifying and overcoming major barriers to further success in ERP development. The chapter highlights the influence of organizational culture, education, and training on future success. The challenge will be to provide education and training that addresses both culturally specific organizational issues and technical challenges. Providers with specific cultural understanding, including vendors and universities in Oceania and Asia, will benefit from this study.

DOI: 10.4018/978-1-7998-4126-5.ch011

INTRODUCTION

The "Made in China 2025" initiative aims to comprehensively upgrade the Chinese industry. Its core focus, intelligent manufacturing, applies the tools of information technology (IT) to production, making it more efficient and integrated to occupy the highest parts of global production chains. As the Chinese government pushes to implement the initiative, a new round of scientific and technological industrial upgrading and transformations may be needed.

Intelligent manufacturing applies new IT to all aspects of industrial production, including design, manufacturing, management, and service. As the informational backbone of intelligent manufacturing, enterprise resource planning (ERP) is the essential core information software in the manufacturing industry. ERP systems are essential for real-time data shared across an organization, as well as for the integration and automation of business processes. This is particularly important in a new business environment where automation, effectiveness and efficiency in operations and real-time data are valuable contributors to business success.

Successful ERP implementation is essential in developing technological innovations like blockchain and Internet of things (IoT) applications. For example, the ERP system is home to critical data like purchase orders, invoices and business partner payment information. The ability to transmit this type of data via blockchain improves business-to-business (B2B) processes like invoice processing and payments. The success of these types of initiative is dependent on a well-functioning ERP system. ERP development in China as the information backbone of an organization is crucial for efficient, data-driven business practice.

ERP, a highly innovative and sophisticated technology, provides an advanced information system to support daily management planning and coordinate the cooperative relationship among departments in an enterprise. This technology supports multiple functions, including product planning, manufacturing, inventory management, and finance. ERP adoption across a business requires large investments in time and efforts. The complexity of ERP implementation has led many firms to give up adoption projects. This is evident in China, where ERP adoption is particularly complex due to culturally specific aspects of Chinese business organizations (Chofreh et al., 2014; Sheu, Chae, & Yang, 2004; Sheu, Yen, & Krumwiede, 2003).

Education is key to the success of ERP. Globalized systems are not always applicable in different contexts, especially Asia. Therefore, education about globalized system development is essential to create Asian technology leaders of the future. ERP education plays an important role in ERP projects.

The ERP skills shortage has reached an all-time high, especially in the Asian region. Major global ERP vendors and a limited number of universities offer training. However, a drawback to vendor training is that the system is culturally specific. The challenge will be to design training that addresses the culturally specific organizational issues discussed in this chapter. Providers with specific cultural understanding, including vendors and universities in Oceania and Asia, will be better placed to undertake this effort.

In this chapter, the author discusses the main features of ERP adoption in China. The chapter also reviews how the ERP landscape has changed in recent years. ERP implementation is a complex and difficult task. Therefore, the author explores significant issues for organizations adopting ERP, discussing the findings of a large-scale survey of Chinese management. The study asks the following questions: (1) What are the major barriers to further success in ERP development? and (2) How can these barriers be overcome?

The survey presented covers the following issues related to ERP adoption research and Chinese managers' attitudes toward ERP: (1) motivation systems; (2) knowledge accommodation; (3) level of authorization; and (4) implementation cycling period. The chapter highlights how issues of adoption are intertwined with the cultural dynamics of Chinese organizations. This may explain the recent turn against standard systems offered by major global suppliers to domestically produced systems.

Chinese enterprises no longer import ERP systems. Instead, they are using local high-quality ERP systems made by Chinese companies. Even with major localized systems development, there is a need for a renewed focus on organizational dynamics for ERP success. The author points to the need for education and development of employee motivation for supporting ERP systems.

ERP Systems

In 1990, Gartner Group Inc. introduced the concept of ERP to the field of supply chain management. It was regarded as the next generation of material requirements planning (MRP) and manufacturing resources planning (MRP2). Its suite of integrated applications focuses on a set of business processes to deal with daily work in different stages. Database and information repository technology is applied to support the integration of data across departments. In doing so, the information and data flow between business functions is facilitated without time and geographical limitations.

ERP supports capabilities in the process of supply chain management, including recapitulative concepts like supply resources integration, lean production and agile manufacturing, error-free transactions, finance, and tax collaborative management. ERP systems are widely used in different industries. For instance, the Navision system, part of the Dynamics series by Microsoft in 2002, is widely applied in manufacturing and the food industry. In addition, myERP is a high efficiency, practical ERP system used in the transportation industry. It provides strategic planning about business development, data sharing, and process monitoring.

Most ERP systems need to be customized to meet industry requirements. This period of secondary development requires significant investments and data integration. Thus, it is large enterprises or multinational corporations that commonly implement ERP. Cloud-based ERP offers small- to medium-sized businesses a scalable, less resource-intensive option. However, similar issues of adoption come into play at a smaller scale.

Decisions regarding which packages to buy and how they fit an organization are greatly influenced by nontechnical factors from outside the organization including vendor influence, marketing promises of major vendors, and isomorphic influence (Howcroft & Light, 2010). Regardless of such persuasive rhetoric, decision makers need to be able to make reasonable assessments of how their company will adopt ERP. IT vendors and consulting firms rely heavily on the power of advertising to persuade potential adopters that their products provide the solutions to their organizational problems. They also downplay the limited generalizability, complexity and risk (Swanson & Ramiller, 2004).

In China, organizations face cultural challenges in addition to ERP implementation. It is often assumed that ERP packages can transfer across contexts or organizations and countries with little modification (Howcroft & Light, 2010). However, the problems of transferability of standardized products across organizations are often cited as a primary reason for failure (Willis & Chiasson, 2007).

In practice, ERP system implementation in China is associated with several well-documented problems. A major issue is the customization of standard software to Chinese contexts. For example, some customized ERP systems for the Chinese market mistakenly analyzed the functions and requirements of local enterprises. Also, the costs of ERP implementation in China can be substantial and unpredictable. Firms are forced to re-engineer business processes to fit the ERP system, which may damage competitiveness or distract from other critical activities. Accordingly, business plans may need to be re-engineered. However, Martin and Cheung (2005) drew a different conclusion with a case study of Mobil Oil Australia Limited, describing how business process re-engineering can achieve dramatic improvements in cost, quality, service and speed even after an ERP solution was implemented.

A study by Plaza and Rohlf (2008) used a learning curve model to analyze consulting costs from implementation, particularly the potential cost of "lock-in" with one supplier. They found that the high switching cost between existing and new ERP systems can increase the vendor's negotiating power. This can lead to high cost of support and upgrades.

Training is another significant cost, with significant training requirements of ERP adoption taking resources from daily operations (Rajan & Baral, 2015; Ranjan, Jha, & Pal, 2016; Saide & Mahendrawathi, 2015). However, some scholars explained that:

companies should not complain the about costs of their investment, as the skills and capabilities they acquired during the implementation process will permit them to improve their enterprise resources planning applications incrementally, adding considerable value. (James & Wolf, 2000, p. 100)

ERP implementation is both a social/cultural and technical project. For example, in their research of ERP implementation in large Iranian organizations, Babaei, Gholami, and Altafi (2015) concluded that organizational barriers are the most important challenges facing ERP implementation. They found that technological factors and individual aspects are less important. For example, complex management levels and cultures of information sharing in a large enterprise weaken the quality and speed of information transmission. This can lead to unnecessary misunderstandings between departments, reducing the motivation to share important data when workers use an ERP system.

A study by Pan and Jang (2008) found that ERP adaptation is strongly influenced by top management commitment. In the Chinese context, the concept of top management commitment means "one hand." The leader makes the final decisions and holds every section's permission. If the leader understands and supports the use of ERP, it will be easier to acquire their commitment. This will encourage ERP usage and improve the perception of usefulness by employers.

ERP is an organizational project. Therefore, communication and training are key influences on beliefs in the benefits of an ERP system. Appropriate communication can lead to better understanding among organizational participants, promoting necessary information flow between sections. Training is an effective way to explore the system from technical and functional perspectives and helps employers test and experience the system with first-hand information.

ERP education increases communication and discussion regarding difficulties faced during the use of ERP. This enhances shared beliefs and congruence between users and the organization. It assumes that the main problem in ERP implementation is knowledge management and transformation. ERP scholars argue that operational knowledge needs to be made explicit in new systems, requiring the active participation of users (Costa, Ferreira, Bento, & Aparicio, 2016; Saide & Mahendrawathi, 2015). This can be achieved during the training process.

It has been nearly 30 years since ERP systems first entered China. Early ERP products in the Chinese domestic market were custom software. Initial efforts were plagued by high prices, unfamiliar business environments and cultural incompatibilities. Many Chinese users think that ERP is merely a supplementary tool to increase work efficiency. They do not realize the core value of the ERP system (Li, 2011).

In China, most ERP software vendors are asked to redesign management software to correspond to enterprise properties. Firms are generally not willing to re-engineer their business process to align with advanced ERP systems design. This can lead to situations where firms do not significantly improve their efficiency and competitiveness (Zhou, 2005).

ERP implementation has changed along with an understanding of its technology. Local software companies began to develop contextually aligned ERP systems, focusing on creating ERP systems more suitable for firms in China, multinational corporations and small developing companies.

Chinese IT vendors, in understanding the challenge of global ERP suppliers, have invested substantial resources to develop systems. However, the implementation of ERP systems in China is still restricted by social-cultural aspects. Although many enterprise vendors (predominantly Western) participate in the Chinese marketplace, local Chinese vendors have dominated the market since 2005. This highlights the advantage of local suppliers given that Western ERP vendor product maturity far exceeds that of the local vendors (Zhou, 2005).

Much of the literature focuses on identifying factors that influence Chinese users' acceptance and use of ERP systems. According to Xue, Liang, Boulton and Snyder (2005), cultural impacts on ERP implementation are related to the relationship between individuals or cooperation partners. The authors argue that Chinese culture is based on relationship networks and business culture is shaped by private or stealthy communication. The norm is that individuals or departments in an organization are not willing to exchange or share useful information with workers or project teams. Instead, they prefer to use this kind of resource as a bargaining power or competitive advantage. Even in the same company, business information is used to gain management confidence. Therefore, it is not casually transferred between teams or departments.

An information sharing culture is an embodiment of organizational culture, playing an important role in the process of ERP implementation. In China, organizational culture is dominated by Guanxi. This type of interrelationship replaces a set of shared assumptions or understanding about organizational basic functions. In fact, Guanxi is a more complex system than shared values and express beliefs. Guanxi can influence communication aspects of organizational life, including interpersonal trust, frequency of communication, favorable evaluation by members who share connections and preferential actions like offering information or resources. It has been argued that structures embedded in a Western-developed ERP system do not support important Guanxi-based business practices (Malaurent & Avison, 2015). These are considered very important for transactions and marketing. Without a match between organizational culture and cultural assumptions embedded within an information system, ERP implementation may fail (and often does in China).

Xue et al. (2005) noted that language is an important factor restricting the development of ERP in China. Their research used a case study to illustrate how the ERP system deletes shortcuts or program commands during the process of Chinese version translation. In turn, it reduces its efficiency. Some ERP systems still use the English operation language to keep the original design. This is difficult for Chinese users to learn and use. Therefore, local workers' enthusiasm for ERP systems usage decreases, leading to the failure of ERP implementation (Candra, 2012; James & Wolf, 2000; Sheu et al., 2004; Xue et al., 2005). A summary of ERP implementation issues is presented in Table 1.

Table 1. Summary of ERP adoption issues in China

Functionality	Cost	Management Systems	Knowledge Management
Customization of standard software to Chinese contexts	Re-engineering business processes	Complex management levels	Willingness to make implicit business processes explicit
System language	Training	Cultures of information sharing	
	Vendor costs	Top management commitment	

CONCLUSION

Most Chinese enterprises want a customised ERP system with redesign according to the requests of firms. They are not willing to re-engineer business processes to adapt to ERP system implementation. Also, Chinese organizational culture means that local enterprises are more reluctant to execute organizational transformations. Not surprisingly, scholars point out that Chinese firms do not wish to undertake the risk of business process re-engineering. Instead, they ask ERP vendors to change the system to satisfy a firm's running restructure, even if leads to the failure of the ERP system (Xue et al., 2005).

Support from top management is essential for intricate changes (Saide and Mahendrawathi, 2015). This support, however, has been notably absent in some Chinese firms. Frequently, senior leaders have neglected to grasp the strategic implication of ERP. Instead, they have sat back while the project has been intermittently stripped of resources and important workers.

BACKGROUND RESEARCH

Survey

This research surveyed Chinese managers about their attitudes and perceptions toward ERP success. The questionnaire was delivered through e-mail and WeChat. The group included 50 participants from Chinese businesses. The research focused on the following factors:

1. **Motivation:** This was linked to the organization's effort to motivate users to use the system through psychological satisfaction or practical reward.
2. **Knowledge Accommodation:** This was not simply defined as familiarity, awareness, or understanding. It was regarded as an opinion toward ERP and acceptance in a specific period. Here, the research incorporated age structure in consideration of employees' receptivity. Moreover, even the concept of ERP system training had been noted by previous literature as a determinant of ERP acceptance. Also noted was the effect of educational level on user experience and attitude.
3. **Level of Authorization:** This was ERP users' access levels in enterprise data. In China, it is to what extent employees have control of data independent of top management. A higher level of authorization brings a stronger motivation to use an ERP system.
4. **Implementation Cycling:** A project, from start to finish, is a process of growth and change. For example, knowledge increases, ERP systems adapt, users accept ERP systems, and intention of use changes. This process was divided into the forming period, storming period, norming period, performing period and slacking period.

All participants originated from China. None had been abroad for more than four years. Their average age was 30 years. The 50 participants studied in universities (26 with bachelor's degrees; 21 master's degrees; 3 educational certificates). Most participants worked in large firms with ERP systems. Some were from multinational corporations with rich experience of ERP systems. Others began their careers in smaller firms with recent adoption of systems. The research included users in management positions and ERP project managers. Accordingly, the study interviewed five ERP users from different firms' top management. They had used ERP systems for extended periods and were familiar with issues related to ERP implementation.

Findings

ERP development remains a complex technology in which social and human factors play significant roles in adoption and implementation. ERP systems, which can be difficult to grasp, are affected by internal factors. Before using ERP systems, employees must understand the ERP concept and benefits. Users must establish a knowledge reserve to realize the necessity of ERP system implementation. This research data illustrates that knowledge accommodation influences user-acceptance of the ERP system.

Figure 1. Age structure

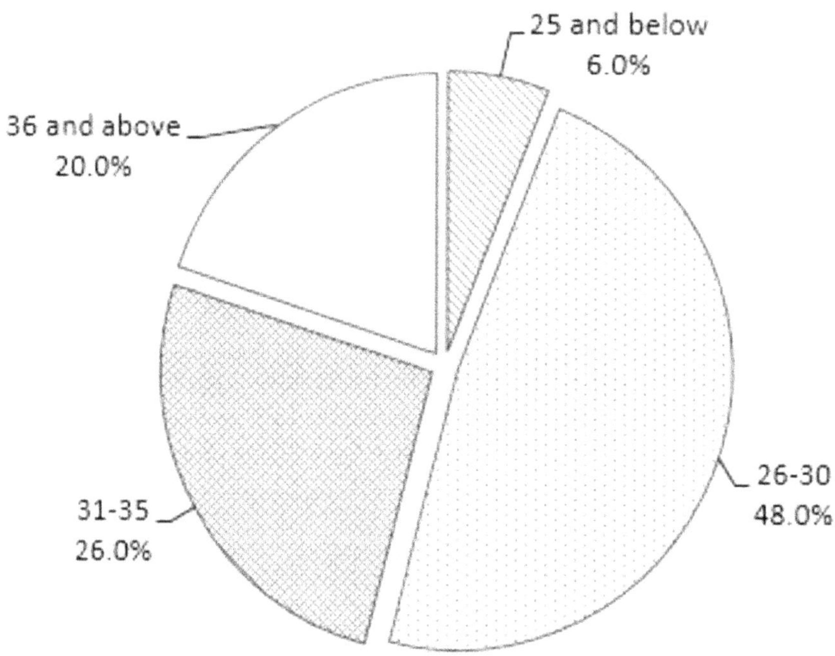

According to Figure 1, respondents' ages and scores had significant differences within the four factors.

Table 2. Respondents' factor scores related to issues and age

	25 and below	26-30	31-35	36 and above	F	Sig.
Motivation system	1.762±0.923	1.512±0.856	1.199±0.335	0.772±1.143	2.879	0.015
Knowledge accommodation	2.670±0.905	2.216±0.701	1.148±1.018	1.295±0.032	7.794	0.000
Level of authorization	1.390±0.727	1.123±0.924	0.508±0.807	-0.520±0.424	7.605	0.000
Implementation cycling period	2.577±1.445	2.151±0.737	1.709±0.771	1.609±0.420	2.538	0.028
Note: the significant level of the test is 0.05.						

Figure 2. Educational levels

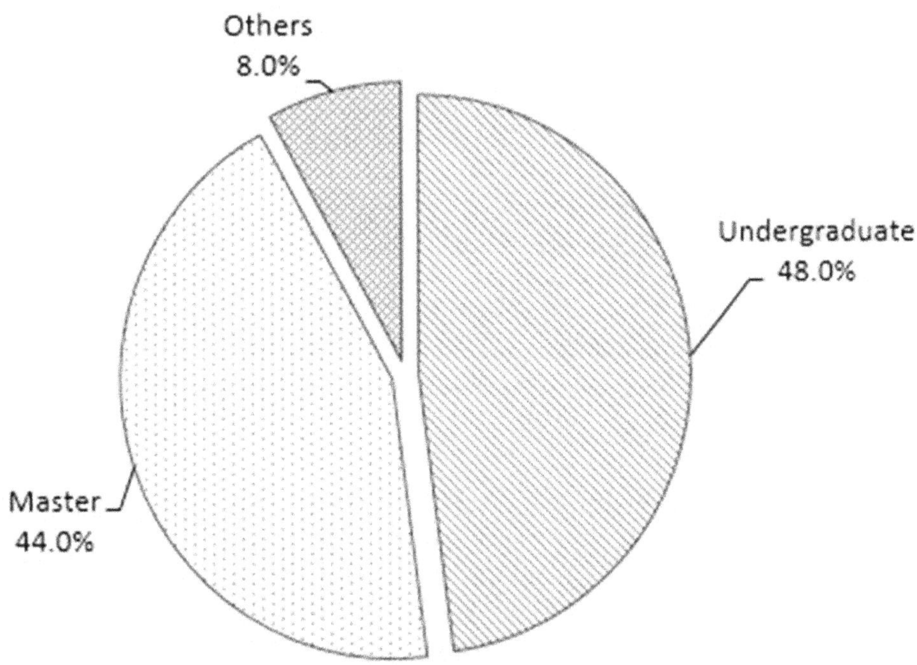

Based on Table 2, the questionnaire data illustrates that different educational levels show significant differences in "motivation system" and "knowledge accommodation."

Regarding the mean score, respondents with a higher level of education have a higher score when compared to respondents with a lower level of education. This is especially true for respondents with a master's degree and high acceptance of ERP.

Table 3. Respondents' factor scores of major issues in different educational levels

	Undergraduate	Master	Others	F	Sig.
Motivation system	1.359±0.606	2.046±0.667	0.902±1.284	2.869	0.017
Knowledge accommodation	1.560±0.927	2.572±0.708	1.802±1.199	8.348	0.001
Level of authorization	0.875±0.853	1.139±1.028	0.898±0.837	0.480	0.622
Implementation cycling period	1.848±0.577	2.300±1.115	2.093±1.253	0.586	0.561
Note: Significant level of test is 0.05					

Figure 3. Increasing user support for ERP development

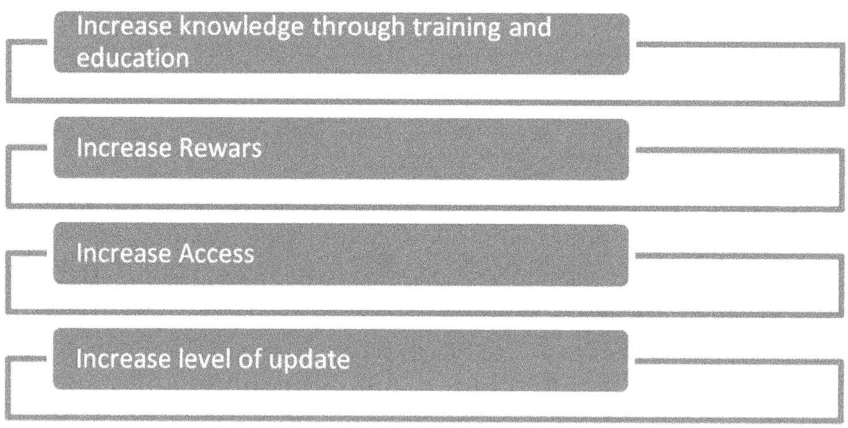

CONCLUSIONS

First, age affects users' enthusiasm for ERP. However, it is not a determinant of user support for ERP development. Younger, more educated employees tend to accept and learn to use ERP. Yet older workers who are willing to use the system are likely to continue its use of them as their expert knowledge increases. Skilled operation and experience bring a sense of achievement, leading to the perceived usefulness of the ERP system.

Academic education has a profound impact on individual enterprise workers' acceptance of ERP. According to Zhou (2005), a strong link exists between employees' educational level, knowledge structure and attitude toward a firm's business re-engineering. If a team or firm has more educated members, it will increase the use of management and technology innovation. This is more conducive to the implementation of the ERP system.

The data analysis found that age structure also offers interesting findings. Younger employees may be more willing to accept or try new things and take risks. Older workers find it more difficult to adapt to changes brought by enterprise reform.

Second, a functioning motivation system is a necessary mechanism to increase the Chinese users' acceptance of an ERP system. In some Chinese enterprises, employees claim that they do not experience the benefits of an ERP system although it may improve management. This results in the reduction of enthusiasm for the system. However, this attitude will change if support for the system is embedded in a reward system.

Some employees argue that they rarely meet with senior leaders and are, therefore, unable to express their ideas about company development. If ERP implementation provides opportunities for feedback to top management, it will incentivize the system's use.

During the research process, some employees noted that they are limited in ERP system use or have no access to check and utilize data and information. In a Chinese firm, senior managers tend to have authorization to use a large part of the ERP system's functionality. Employees are asked to finish basic operations. Research suggests that this is not conducive to achieving the most benefit from the system. Additional authorizations should be given to employees to maximize the use and efficiency of the ERP system.

Finally, the research finds that the ERP implementation cycling period influences employees' use and acceptance of the system. Results show that employees are most likely to use a system in the performing period due to higher skill levels and knowledge accommodation. However, with increasing time, its utility can decrease due to changes in the business environment. Therefore, ERP systems must be regularly updated to adapt to changing conditions.

According to the author, specific factors (software supplier, investments, and top management support) promote ERP implementation and user support in Chinese organizations. This may involve changing or adjusting aspects of the organizational culture to encourage interorganizational coordination both horizontally and vertically.

There is a clear relationship between national objectives for SMART production and education. Higher education will be a significant enabler for rapid progress toward intelligent manufacturing visions. In China, the development of ERP has lagged, calling for a renewed educational focus (Fan et al., 2011). The broad array of ERP competencies could be better embedded in curricula, particularly business schools. Oceanic universities have led industry partnerships (for example, SAP educational alliance in 2007). The research highlights the need for general ERP education for a range of organizational users. Although computer science students may graduate with specific SAP skills, they lack the understanding of how these skills are used in a business environment and business processes. Business students should, therefore, be encouraged in this direction as the study of ERP exemplifies principles of sociotechnical development that can inform techno-savvy managers of the future.

REFERENCES

Babaei, M., Gholami, Z., & Altafi, S. (2015). Challenges of enterprise resource planning implementation in Iran large organizations. *Information Systems*, *54*, 15–27. doi:10.1016/j.is.2015.05.003

Candra, S. (2012). ERP implementation success and knowledge capability. *Procedia: Social and Behavioral Sciences*, *65*, 141–149. doi:10.1016/j.sbspro.2012.11.103

Chofreh, A., Goni, F., Shaharoun, A., Ismail, S., & Klemeš, J. (2014). Sustainable enterprise resource planning: Imperatives and research directions. *Journal of Cleaner Production*, *71*, 139–147. doi:10.1016/j.jclepro.2014.01.010

Costa, C., Ferreira, E., Bento, F., & Aparicio, M. (2016). Enterprise resource planning adoption and satisfaction determinants. *Computers in Human Behavior*, *63*, 659–671. doi:10.1016/j.chb.2016.05.090

Fan, C. J., Zhang, P., Liu, Q., Yang, J. Z., & Xi, W. Y. (2011). Research on ERP teaching model reform for application-oriented talents education. *International Education Studies*, *4*(2), 25–30. doi:10.5539/ies.v4n2p25

Howcroft, D., & Light, B. (2010). The social shaping of packaged software selection. *Journal of the Association for Information Systems*, *11*(3), 2. doi:10.17705/1jais.00224

James, D., & Wolf, M. L. (2000, Spring). A second wind for ERP. *The McKinsey Quarterly*, 100.

Li, Y. L. (2011). ERP adoption in Chinese small enterprise: An exploratory case study. *Journal of Manufacturing Technology Management*, *22*(4), 489–505. doi:10.1108/17410381111143130

Malaurent, J., & Avison, D. (2015). From an apparent failure to a success story: ERP in China—Post implementation. *International Journal of Information Management*, *35*(5), 643–646. doi:10.1016/j.ijinfomgt.2015.06.004

Martin, I., & Cheung, Y. (2005). Business process re-engineering pays after enterprise resource planning. *Business Process Management Journal, 11*(2), 185–197. doi:10.1108/14637150510591174

Pan, M. J., & Jang, W. Y. (2008). Determinants of the adoption of enterprise resource planning within the technology-organization-environment framework: Taiwan's communications industry. *JCIS, 48*, 94–102.

Plaza, M., & Rohlf, K. (2008). Learning and performance in ERP implementation projects: A learning-curve model for analyzing and managing consulting costs. *International Journal of Production Economics, 115*(1), 72–85. doi:10.1016/j.ijpe.2008.05.005

Rajan, C., & Baral, R. (2015). Adoption of ERP system: An empirical study of factors influencing the usage of ERP and its impact on end user. *IIMB Management Review, 27*(2), 77. doi:10.1016/j.iimb.2015.04.004

Ranjan, S., Jha, V., & Pal, P. (2016). Literature review on ERP implementation challenges. *IJBIS, 21*(3), 388. doi:10.1504/IJBIS.2016.074766

Saide, E. R., & Mahendrawathi, E. (2015). Knowledge management support for enterprise resource planning implementation. *Procedia Computer Science, 72*, 613–621. doi:10.1016/j.procs.2015.12.170

Sheu, C., Chae, B., & Yang, C. (2004). National differences and ERP implementation: Issues and challenges. *Omega, 32*(5), 361–371. doi:10.1016/j.omega.2004.02.001

Sheu, C., Yen, H., & Krumwiede, D. (2003). The effect of national differences on multinational ERP implementation: An exploratory study. *Total Quality Management & Business Excellence, 14*(6), 641–657. doi:10.1080/1478336032000053807

Swanson, E. B., & Ramiller, N. C. (2004). Innovating mindfully with information technology. *Management Information Systems Quarterly, 28*(4), 553. doi:10.2307/25148655

Willis, R., & Chiasson, M. (2007). Do the ends justify the means? A Gramscian critique of the processes of consent during an ERP implementation. *Information Technology & People, 20*(3), 212–234. doi:10.1108/09593840710822840

Xue, Y., Liang, H., Boulton, W., & Snyder, C. (2005). ERP implementation failures in China: Case studies with implications for ERP vendors. *International Journal of Production Economics, 97*(3), 279–295. doi:10.1016/j.ijpe.2004.07.008

Zhou, P. (2005). *Organizational culture impact on ERP implementation in China*. Swedish School of Economics and Business Administration.

Chapter 12
Funding Disruptive Innovation Startups in Asia-Oceania

Brian Jack Mcnaughton
https://orcid.org/0000-0003-4541-1412
Participant Capital Partners LLP, Australia

ABSTRACT

The opening up of new markets, foreign or domestic, and the organizational development from the craft shop to such concerns as U.S. Steel illustrate the same process of industrial mutation—if the author may use that biological term—that incessantly revolutionizes the economic structure from within, incessantly destroying the old one, incessantly creating a new one. This process of Creative Destruction is the essential fact about capitalism. This chapter addresses disruptive innovation in the 21st century and how new ventures that might produce such innovation in Oceania and Asia can obtain the funds they need to survive and prosper.

OVERVIEW

Most people with a novel business idea want to raise capital to allow their vision to become a reality. These are our Entrepreneurs, and their venture is called a "startup". The venture is most likely a new business created by a Founder and possibly a few friends and colleagues. Small businesses are significant employers in an economy. Those small businesses are not necessarily startups. Many are long-standing family businesses having commenced generations before. The ventures that we most commonly like to think about as startups are those disruptive innovators that could grow to become major corporations.

DOI: 10.4018/978-1-7998-4126-5.ch012

The reality is that most startups are poorly financed businesses that are struggling to survive. Those employed in the business are often lowly paid, and many are unskilled. Isenberg noted in his HBR article that *"the Danish Business Authority shows that among beneficiaries of its programs, 72% of jobs are created by existing firms, 10% by startups, and, incidentally, public investment per startup job created through business support programs costs three times more for startups than for existing firms."*

The Global Entrepreneurship Monitor (GEM) has previously noted that two-thirds of startups create no jobs at all or at most 1 to 5 jobs inside five years. Fewer than 3% of all startups can be called "High Potential" - that is, they have a product that buyers want, they have few competitors, they involve a disruptive innovation and they use state of the art technology.

Within Asia -Oceania regions, India is estimated to need 10 million new jobs yearly to take advantage of its favourable demographic characteristics – the median age is only 28 years and 45% of the population are less than 25 years old, implying very strong work force growth in the coming decades. The Indian NASSCOM in 2016 estimated that there would be 10,000 startups by 2020. However, the assumption that startups will address the employment situation is not readily supported.

Delving deeper into the issue of job creation, numerous reports find that innovative startups are usually "growth-drivers" and that *"survival and a more (than) above average post-entry performance in terms of profitability, export performance and job creation....(Pg7)... that only innovative startups (rather than startups in general) should be considered the core of that kind of entrepreneurship which can be conducive of genuine Schumpeterian destruction leading to competitive pressure, productivity growth and ultimately economic development and employment creation ....(Pg. 17)"* (Colombelli *et al.* 2016).

The preferred focus on innovative startups as the driver of future productivity, growth, and employment recognizes their importance and suggests an increase in emphasis on maximizing the strength and number of those startups so they can improve the chances of enough succeeding to have a significant impact on economic growth, living standards and employment. Strengthening startups usually involves ensuring that the funding base is adequate and the management team is supported. This approach can also be supported by the statistical approach of increasing the number of innovative startups so that the number of successful ventures increases.

The GEM 2018/2019 report identified the sectors where entrepreneurs are most active relative to the income levels of their country: *"Few early-stage entrepreneurs in low-income economies start finance/real estate/business services or ICT businesses. In contrast, in over half of high-income economies, 20% or more of startup activity is in finance/real estate/business services. While ICT is less prevalent, in over half of high-income economies, more than 5% of early-stage entrepreneurs are starting these types of businesses" (GEM 2018/2019 Report page 29).*

Various entities are used by Governments and private enterprises to access and support startups such as incubators, accelerators, angel investors, venture capital and private equity. Governments across Asia and Oceania all make use of such entities to help different classes of innovative startups to succeed by helping them access development money. The Gust 2016 accelerator reports that in the accelerator sector 63.5% of funding comes solely from th developers, with the remainder being a mix of government and private funding.

Many startup programs exist across Asia and Oceania. The test of success now rests within the hands of the entrepreneur to develop an idea and then execute that idea. Part of the execution involves the ability to go from the idea and conceptual phase towards the fully-funded, operational delivery of the innovation. The focus also now shifts entirely to disruptive and innovative startups as these most likely to bring about growth and high-productivity employment in the Asia-Oceania region.

ACCESSING STARTUP FUNDS

Traditional funding solutions for early-stage companies revolve around "bootstrapping" and tapping into the savings and assets of the entrepreneur and their friends and families before progressing onto debt, incubators, accelerators, and angel financiers. Tools have been devised to aid in the fund-raising process for new and developing ventures such as business plans, elevator pitches and pitch decks. These tools serve as the presentation material designed to sell a business as a viable entity to investors. They focus on how to showcase the business so as to raise capital successfully. Unfortunately, they fail many times to recognize the investor's interests in the process.

The fund-raising market is a very crowded. Moreover, it is impacted by economic and political cycles and by geographic and sovereign risks. To improve their chances of successfully raising funds for a venture, the entrepreneur needs an arrow-like focus, pointing at the potential investors' concerns, issues and drivers and delivered with the right tools to close a funding round. Any improvement in a startup's ability to access financing already on offer will improve the outcome for the startup and so contribute to the disruptive innovation needed for an economy to grow its GDP and increase overall employment.

It is a pre-condition of being a successful startup to know how to develop an idea, commence implementation of the idea and raise the funds required to complete the implementation. The interplay between conceptualizing and implementing an idea, represented by the 1949 Earl Prevette "laws" of Faith, Imagination, Repetition and Persistence (FIRP), and expanded upon by Mcnaughton in *Monetizing Ideas* (2019), points to the need for the entrepreneur to develop the required skills. Without those skills, the toolbox of techniques that follows is unlikely to be enough to transform the ideas into a thriving, disruptive and innovative business and to support the work of governments in creating an eco-system of disruptive innovation.

GETTING STARTED

Most first-time entrepreneurs commence their project with the goal of being disruptive and bringing about change. Like a young person going out into the world, these new entrepreneurs are often unaware of the dangers that exist to both themselves and their new enterprise. There are several primary considerations that should be taken into account before launching into a new venture. The marketplace is not a jungle, albeit at the time it appears to be like one. The nature, extent, and features of the market are often considered too late by the entrepreneur. It is imperative that proper analysis of the market occurs before launching into detailed product design, improvements, and development.

Another common mistake is to use a desk-bound approach to marketplace analysis and research to the exclusion of faster, cheaper and generally more effective approaches. Walking around, asking friends, family and even those in the street will help provide a check on the ideas and solutions under consideration. This "walk-about approach" needs to form an integral part of the entrepreneur's "feedback-loop". It works to streamline the development process. All too often, we continue down the wrong development path in the belief that we fully understood the opportunity, only to find that the marketplace has a different view.

A word of caution to budding entrepreneurs: in receiving comments and inputs from the marketplace do not assume that those interviewed are experts and fully understand trends and opportunities relevant to your innovation. It is the "wisdom of the crowd" - the views and insights of the collective marketplace - that is being accumulated, not just the thoughts of a few. At times there will also be inputs that appear very negative, but the collective opinion around the centre of the feedback is the desired insight, not the outlier responses. Assessing the person delivering those comments, their experience and their abilities can help determine if there is merit in their comments. Feedback such as the view of the crowd can allow that information to be assimilated into the development of the innovation and can lead to variations in the development plans before large amounts of time and money are invested.

The ever-increasing speed at which new and innovative goods and services are reaching the market can engender a view that "speed-to-market is of the essence". There are many instances where that is true. However, many more exist where the first product to market only served to make the way cheaper and more accessible for those following. The market for ride-sharing cars has already seen the trailblazer, Uber, under threat from competitors like Ola and Didi. Conservation of the venture's most precious resources, namely its business capital and the founder/entrepreneur, should be the mantra.

Allowing the entrepreneur to be consumed by the project is as bad as having the business capital consumed before demonstratable progress is achieved. The selection of the team collaborating with the entrepreneur is a large part of the supporting structure that needs to be put in place for the venture to succeed. Putting the wrong people in the wrong position can do more damage than having a scarcity of funds. The startup project's real and immediate needs should be the first consideration in team selection. For example, bringing on board an experienced sales manager before there is a product to sell may prove an unnecessary and expensive early investment. Likewise, spending early funding on the wrong priority, either for other team members that are not needed yet, or wasteful extras such as extravagant offices, consume precious resources on the wrong priorities. Understanding and maintaining the focus on the venture's main goals are important parts of the discipline needed by the entrepreneur and the team to achieve business success.

Many entrepreneurs who have prepared a sound business plan and implemented it correctly have discovered that the initial \$50,000 to \$200,000 "seed-round" capital needed to commence their business was not as hard to access as they had originally thought. However, the difficulties escalate when the capital needs to be topped up. Usually, the next significant capital raising, referred to as the "SERIES A round", involves going to venture capitalists (VCs) and private equity firms. The amounts needed to bring the product or service to the market are often in the \$ millions. The degree of difficulty in accessing these funds comes as a shock to the entrepreneur. The time, the number of interviews and the amount of work needed to access this level of funding are orders of magnitude higher than for the "seed-round". Questions asked and materials wanted by the potential investors include in-depth information on plans, costs, revenues, competitors, the product road-map, and the implementation team. Even when these points are covered, the bridge over this so-called funding "valley-of-death" is long and difficult to traverse, and many fail to cross it. The entrepreneur's capacity to "make it across" is even more important to now consider.

It is understandable given the issues raised that the entrepreneur can feel overwhelmed. Mental fatigue and depression can and do occur. The entrepreneur is the greatest asset of the business and as such, must be protected. Maintaining a balanced lifestyle while trying to raise money, develop an acceptable market product and manage and motivate a team is daunting. More damage than running out of money is caused when there is no plan in place to achieve that balance. That the entrepreneur has already decided there is an innovative solution waiting to be developed demonstrates that he may have the ideas. The drive to take on the task of finding that solution does require that he looks at himself and answers the question: "Do I have the will needed to succeed?"

Knowing the desire and passion are there to undertake the task is only a part of the equation. Expertise, capital requirements, lifestyle issues and the recognition that the odds are against succeeding must all be taken into account.

FUNDING METHODS

The methods for funding new and growing ventures have been continuously evolving. Typically, methods are grouped into steps that match the development of a startup from the initial idea and conceptualization stage through the planning, establishment and growth stages. There is no defined ladder to successful fundraising. However, it is likely that the starting point is with the entrepreneur commencing with his own money.

Bootstrapping:

The founder/entrepreneur starts by exploring and then choosing ways to obtain resources to finance the operation. Bootstrapping is the most common source of startup funding, with entrepreneurs reportedly using their personal resources to provide 77% of the funds needed. It is also common for the entrepreneur to undertake a range of jobs over and above the roles of chief technical director and managing director/CEO. The entrepreneur does whatever work is needed regardless of how it relates to their skills. They take on all roles, from "the CEO to the janitor". The task of developing new businesses, however, may require other sacrifices. It often happens that existing work and employment have to be closed-out to allow the time and commitment needed to get "the entrepreneurial job done". It is dangerous to believe that any significant undertaking can have two masters.

It has been reported by the USA Small Business Administration (SBA) that 44% of new businesses fail. Other sources report that the main reason for these failures is a lack of money, being as high as 82%, and that 27% of businesses surveyed state that they were not able to receive the funding they needed. It can be expected that the situation would be similar for start-ups across the Asia-Oceania region.

There are reasons other than financial to bootstrap. Some entrepreneurs decide early on that they either do not want to share their vision and venture with others, or expose them to the risk associated with committing to a new and disruptive startup. Others take the view that their disruptive concepts are never going to be understood by the marketplace until they are launched, so they prefer to "black-out" information about their startup until this stage is reached.

Friends and Family Investments:

Those closest to the founder often find themselves providing financial support to support the launch, growth and maintenance of the operation. Family and friends have been reported to supply 16% of the funding and to provide 9% as a "donation". Obtaining capital from close associates and family carries many non-business risks, but has the advantages of:

1) reducing the risk that knowledge about the innovation will "leak" out,
2) avoiding time-consuming due diligence, and
3) speeding up the fund-raising process.

The non-business risks associated with any financing from family and friends can be, and usually is, significant. Pressure on relationships caused by money issues can create new and unwelcome distractions as well as changes to the implementation plan as the entrepreneur "rushes" to positive cash-flows and the repayment of money.

Accelerators and Incubators:

Specific business ventures are at different stages of the business lifecycle. Organisations designed to support them offer a range of cash, mentoring and other products, including business training, tailored to these different stages. They expect to be rewarded for providing these support products by being granted an appropriate share of the business venture.

Accelerators help entrepreneurs by grouping in one location those in the same stage of the development cycle. This facilitates the creation of networks that can support the entrepreneur. Other services, in addition to providing access to money and a working environment conducive to the development of the startup, can include connections with corporations and other suitable links that will foster the startup's development and implementation of the product or service.

The literature on accelerators covers incubators and early-stage funders through to more advanced-funding-stage entities. Gust's *"Asia and Oceania Accelerator Report of 2016"* states that 1,368 start-ups raised over USD$17 billion in 76 accelerator programs across Asia and Oceania. By country, the top five in funds raisings for accelerators were:

- Australia USD 4.3 billion 251 companies
- India USD 3.9 billion 267 companies
- Malaysia USD 2.9 billion 175 companies
- China USD 2.75 billion 142 companies

- South Korea USD 2.15 billion 130 companies

The accelerators in the Asia-Oceania area are primarily focused upon investments in fintech, health, big data analytics and the "Internet of Things". These are the sectors most likely to be the focus of growth in the region during the coming decades and are likely to include many of the disruptive and innovative startups that are most likely to contribute to GDP and employment growth across the region.

Government Funding:

Government support is replete with complex application forms, time-consuming meetings and many competitors vying for limited funds. The availability of grants and other types of government-supported investments has created an industry of consultants who understand and assist in the process in return for fees. Direct government supports differ markedly across countries.

China has adopted a very supportive approach that includes the creation of Government Guidance Bonds. About 780 different funds have raised 1.5 trillion yuan (equal to 10% of China's GDP). The country has 1600 high-tech incubators designed to attract and support development of the innovative startups the government believes are needed to maintain China's impressive record of economic and employment growth. This approach will likely produce positive results if only due to its sheer size.

The likelihood that the funds will be used most efficiently is more uncertain. However, the China approach is an example of the massed-support method where many "winners" in the disruptive innovation success game will likely surface because of the sheer number of ventures supported.

The percentage of ventures that make it to the top will depend upon more than the entrepreneurs and will require support from the incubators/accelerators to maximize the opportunities this level of funding creates.

Incubator programs are being established throughout China and appear to be focused on the same sectors as elsewhere in Asia-Oceania. The China Banking News reported in December 2018 on one such incubator in Guangdong Financial Hi-Tech Zone " *Yihive chair Zhang Jinxi said that the company had established a 200 million yuan private equity fund to focus on "Blockchain+" fintech investments and that it would use the incubation centre to deploy the company's four-facet model of "education – innovation – incubation – investment.*" This holistic support concept, when carried out effectively, can improve the odds of an entrepreneur successfully launchng their product in the market place.

Australia has a multi-level system of startup support ranging from early-stage venture capital LLPs that make use of government tax incentives to direct funding via refundable tax offsets through the Research and Development tax incentive. These programs do not require the supporting infrastructure of an accelerator. They can, however, help ventures to succeed. In Monetizing Ideas (Mcnaughton, 2019), the importance of mentoring and other supports in a venture's early stages was noted and supported with quotes from the founders of Google and Facebook.

A wider industry and university public-private approach exists through the Cooperative Research Centres (CRC) program. The CRC's are not focused upon startups, but their influence, educational impact and technology-driven approach create many opportunities for startups. They have proven time and again to facilitate a successful harnessing of private-government-university strengths to support and develop innovative products and services.

India also makes use of the taxation system to support new ventures by allowing up to three years of tax exemption for eligible and registered startups. Other benefits include more relaxed compliance requirements, less stringent labour laws, and self-assessment in respect of environmental and other laws. Further benefits are available from the State Bank of India which, amongst others, provides strong support for startups.

Malaysia operates a variety of government-supported programs aimed at bridging the gap between initial seed-funding and later VC investments. The programs range from flexible loans without collateral and grants for incubation-style startups to hybrid grant-equity style arrangements. Programs are also in place to help startups acquire global technologies that will support Malaysia's manufacturing industry. The consistent theme among these arrangements is the focus on startups that are innovatve. Support for a cross-border IP style transfer is a significant game-changing approach in Asia-Oceania. Fostering the development of transnational startups in the region can significantly enhance the adoption of disruptive innovations that bring economic and employment growth to the entire region.

Indonesia encourages the development of incubators and offers educational programs, However, it provides very little financial support Funding from private VCs grew from a little more than $2 million in 2014 to $136 million by 2017. The government has announced that it is targeting the commencement of 1,000 startups with value of $10 billion by 2020. The focus is on startups using innovative technologies. This is another example of the massed-startup strategy that aims to encourage disruptive innovation. The wider is the range of of funding options and other supports, the more likely is it that successful outcomes will ensue.

South Korea's Ministry of Small and Medium Enterprises (SMEs) and Startups has the status of a full government department. This indicates the importance that the South Korean Government places on startups. With a massive budget, exceeding $7.5 billion, the Ministry is able to allocate over $400 million to support startups. The rationale behind so much support is the belief that it "*is nurturing talents in young people. We need to create new jobs. This is a necessary and urgent mission,*" (Park

Tae-Hyun, president of the Korea Foundation for the Advancement of Science and Creativity (KOFAC)). Eric Kim, co-founder and managing partner at Goodwater Capital, explains the advantages of these efforts as follows: *"The Korean government realized that the economy has been dependent on Korean conglomerates. They see startups as a great way to diversify the economy and help job creation. For instance, Kakao started from 10 people, and now they have thousands of employees."*

The South Korea Government's also supports cross-border startups, which may lead to opportuntieis for innovative enterpreneurs in neighbouring countries such as Japan, China and Taiwan. In July 2016, the South Korean Ministry of SMEs and Startups established an investment fund, the "Foreign VC Investment Fund "(FVICF) with the Korea Venture Investment Corp. Having a unique mandate of helping Korean companies grow and expand their businesses abroad, CBA Ventures, a South Korean licensed VC is one of a few select co-General Partners (GP) tasked with helping exceptional, committed and accredited offshore GPs and fund managers to invest alongside the South Korean Government's FVICF. With an expected lifespan of 19 years and a partnership period of 10 years, the budget is approximately $USD 90 million with up to 40% of the total fund provided by the FVICF and the remainder coming from an offshore co-GP. While funds are invested by the FVICF and offshore GPs that will promote the overseas expansion of Korean companies, the sector and stage of investment are not fixed, leaving GPs free to make investment proposals based on the wishes of their limited partners. The development of this style of internationalized startup funding augers well for the region's attempt to foster disruptive innovative ventures with access to significant, patient capital

Debt

Debt such as secured and unsecured loans, working capital overdrafts, inventory financing, invoice factoring, purchase-order factoring (Del Credere), and car, office and equipment leasing are typically secured against the personal assets and guarantees of directors and other associates, friends and family. Various governments do have programs that encourage debt financing, but it is a problematic area for financiers given the very high failure rate of startups. Accordingly, debt funding of an early-stage venture usually involves collateral and personal guarantees. Such financing arrangements, which normally carry the requirement of regular interest payments and principal repayments, add to the pressure on the entrepreneur and create a further impediment to the successful implementation of their development plan.

Venture Capital and Private Equity:

The distinction between angel investors, venture capitalists and private equity providers is blurred, but all these organisations are in the business of providing capital in return for an agreed interest and profit "mark-up" over their costs of capital. The risk premium is usually very high. About 6% of funding for startups in the Asia-Oceania region is from this funding source, comprising 3% from angels and 3% from venture capitalists. Getting access to these investors is usually tricky. A referral is the best approach, and the venture's law firm may be a first channel to accessing them. The challenge is to find someone in the startup's network who can make that introduction.

The entrepreneur needs to exhibit many charismatic skills and demonstrate great persistence to "get in the door". Often, it comes down to good fortune or luck. Salespeople confront this same issue in attempting to make sales by cold-calling potential clients. They know that by continuing to "knock on doors," they will eventually get a meeting that they may convert to a sale. Investors can also be approached using a "cold-call" technique once the entrepreneur has clarified where interest in the startup's innovation may exist.

As the entrepreneur becomes more polished in making presentations of their venture, the chances of closing an investment with the venture capitalists, angels, and others will increase. Remember that these investors are not looking primarily at the team or product and services for the perceived benefits. Their principal interest is finding out whether the venture could make them a return that is 10 to 25 times their investment.

Consider the experience of those raising funds for a company called Burbn. The service Burbn offered enabled people using an iPhone to share photos. In 2010, the developers had to sell their vision that smartphones would become the main computer used by people and this would lead to a people-sharing photos app becoming a "killer app". The team sole their vision, and within two years the renamed company, Instagram, was sold to Facebook for $1 billion.

How is the investor's interest recorded? The Investor interest can be represented, initially, via several typical agreements such as:

a) a SAFE (Simple Agreement for Future Equity),
b) a convertible note (debt to equity at a defined event and based upon an agreed algorithm),
c) convertible preference shares (this method is defined both in terms of timing and quantum of any conversion from a preference share to ordinary shares), and finally
d) ordinary shares.

The approach adopter is often dependent upon the venture's characteristics and the preferences of the venture capitalist or private equity company.

More substantial corporations also offer venture funding, especially where the new investment provides a benefit for the corporation's existing business, products or processes. Such corporate venture funding may be direct or via the corporation's own venture fund structure. There are numerous examples of corporate venture capitlists, including most of the Big Pharma groups, Apple, Facebook, and the oil majors. Universities are also now developing their own venture capitalist style of approach that makes use of their R&D capacity to assist startups while enabling the university to share in the knowledge acquired and any subsequent growth in the startup's value. Google was developed out of Stanford University's Digital Libraries Project, with the entrepreneurs being able to use the Standford computers to crawl the web and, eventually, create the Google search product.

Alternatives Such as Crowdfunding, Equity Crowdfunding, and Cryptocurrency ICOs and STOs:

These are the modern variations of existing approaches. They add features that may be more attractive to an investor. Total resources from Crowdfunding is still minor, at about 2% of the total. Nevertheless, legal changes that permit smaller investors to participate in the funding of startups have facilitated a new, if still mostly immature, method of supporting startups. In Australia, startups with less than AUD 25 million (USD 17.5 million) can access up to AUD 5 million (USD3.5m) per year from retail investors providing a maximum of AUD10,000 to the company. Such arrangements are strictly controlled and require licensed intermediaries to facilitate and complete the offer and investment. They have, however, expanded the potential pool of investors. The Australian model is still significantly less in terms of amounts and more demanding in terms of intermediaries than the USA Jump Start Our Small Business Startups Act (JOBS Act) of 2012. Amongst other rules, retail or "unaccredited" small investors could make an equity investment in the startup of USD2,000 (or 5% of their salary under $100,000 pa) up to $10,000 (or 10% of their salary if over $100,000 pa).

The rural areas of Australia have been in steady decline for decades. CRC Partners LLP, an Australian promoter of crowd-sourced funding for regional Australia, notes that disruptive innovation can play a useful role in returning prosperity, growth and employment to country areas. Improved productivity has seen the slow but sustained decline in the population in agricultural areas, particularly in developed economies. The Worldwatch Institute study of June 29, 2019, noted "Population trends…for *China, India, and the United States: Between 1980 and 2011, the economically active agricultural populations of China and India grew by 33 and*

50 per cent, respectively, due to overall population growth. The economically active agricultural population of the United States, on the other hand, declined by 37 per cent as a result of large-scale mechanization, improved crop varieties, fertilizers, pesticides, and federal subsidies—all of which contributed to economies of scale and consolidation in U.S. agriculture". There is every reason to expect improved productivity in India, China, Indonesia, and others in Asia-Oceania will follow a similar trend of declining employment in regional areas and a general population migration to ever-growing cities.

CRC Partner's initiative is attempting to promote disruptive innovation that could change the dynamics in predominately agricultural areas by creating **a regional resilience startup fund** to help the areas become locations for innovation surges. CRC's methodology is to use a master fund that offers investors a rate of return based upon both interest and capital growth. A master fund structure allows risk to be spread over several ventures and technologies and in that regard is not dissimilar to a typical private equity fund approach. It differs, however, in that it attempts to retain an incubator/accelerator, rather than a private equity fund approach, with the startup. Additionally, such a fund structure is permitted to receive investments from Australia's massive pension pool which, according to AFSA, exceeds AUD2.2 trillion or around 130% of Australia's GDP, and is one of the world's largest pension savings pool.

Establishing a link between startups and significant funding pools opens the door for a significant injection of money into areas with declining growth and employment prospects. The careful allocation of this resource to under-serviced areas could create an opportunity to renew and revitalize depressed communities. The relocation of young and energetic innovators and entrepreneurs to regional areas reduces the pressure of migration, particularly of youth, on those ever-growing cities and is a model that can be replicated in agricultural communities across Asia-Oceania.

Stock Exchange IPOs

The original purpose of the Stock Exchange was to facilitate a marketplace where businesses could access capital. Also, they provided a mechanism for investors to exit their business interests if buyers exist prepared to take the quantity and price offered for the share. The development of listed venture funds, private equity firms, hedge funds and the like have produced an eco-system based around a more structured approach to funding new ventures including startups. Quarterly profit disclosures as well as dividend, and capital growth targets are, however, challenging short-term goals for startup investments and as a result, very few stock exchange IPOs could be constructed to suit the sector.

There are stock exchange listings for exploration "startups", but they have a unique characteristic. Even Facebook and Google waited many years before listing. Attempts have been made to address this shortcoming, with the European Union, in particular, creating "Multi-Lateral Trading Facilities (MTFs)". These quickly became second-tier stock exchanges and were are a popular early-stage listing option for startups. They have not proved very successful. However, the EURONEXT exchange product called Euronext Access has maintained a solid track record and is pitched at the startup and SME categories. It raised EUR 8.7 billion between 2013-2017. Exchanges such as the UK's London Stock Exchange second market called the Alternative Investment Market (AIM) comes in and out of favour for startups depending on economic (boom) conditions prevalent at the time. They are appealing mainly to sophisticated investors. Once again, the opportunity to access capital funding is the primary goal of these exchanges. So the measure of success has to be the sums raised, with AIM raising some USD 140 billion for 3,500 companies globally over the period 1995 -2015. The global nature of these exchanges allows the benefits to be accessible to the startups of the Asia-Oceania region.

NEXT STEPS

What has become apparent from the funding and structures discussed here is the need to be able to access the funds on offer in a constructive manner. Startups will continuously require money to further the implementation of their plan, so fundraising is a commonly recurring feature of a startup. Chasing money requires the entrepreneur to understand the fundraising process and to be able to deliver their ideas and implement them. The tools needed are limited initially to a business plan, elevator pitch, pitch deck, and later, a due diligence pack. The ability to understand how these tools work and how they are presented to investors is vital to a startup's success.

Knowledge is power? No. Knowledge on its own is nothing, but the application of useful knowledge, now that is powerful. – **Rob Liano**

Business Plan

A new venture should develop a business plan that seeks to quantify the parameters and assumptions underpinning the Founder's belief in the viability of the business and its likely future performance. Creating a business plan, however, needs more than a spreadsheet of numbers. A deep understanding of the WHY of the business also needs to be clearly demonstrated. Selecting a likely cash-flow generative business makes any fund-raising easier for an investor to grasp. Moreover, there are other features, such as the potential for capital growth or market disruption and dominance that can be among the features of a startup's business model. Such a selection of a concept or business can be improved by making a careful and well thought systematic analysis of the venture's features for success. One method to use is the concept of the **VRIN** score. By understanding how to use this score, it is possible to demonstrate to an investor the reasons why there is a belief that the startup is viable.

The VRIN score assumes that by understanding and applying a score against several different factors, a more rational appraisal can be made of the likely success of the business. It provides a way that this rationale can be conveyed to investors. Each letter in "VRIN" presents one such factor and is scored between 1 to 10, with a higher score denoting a more positive appraisal.

a) The "**V**" denotes the"Value" for the business or more correctly the need for the product or service. The "Value" can be subjective and should not be a simple guess by the entrepreneur; instead, it should be based upon feedback from your marketplace testing of the business idea.
b) The "**R**" is the "Rarity" of the product or service being put forward. Again, this score is based upon a valid appraisal of the perceived "Rarity" or lack of competition in the marketplace. The lack of a competing product should not be construed as demand. It may be that there is simply no need for the idea.
c) The "**I**" denotes the "Inimitability" (or imitation) of the product or service. A high score for "I" implies the target market cannot do the idea on their own.
d) The "**N**" is a score based on the ability to substitute the new idea for another product or service, generally from another category.

Another approach that is not mutually exclusive to the VRIN approach is to review and research existing successful businesses. The wealth of information and market reaction enables consideration of a better way to supply the market. The concept called the "Blue Ocean Strategy" was initially put forward by W. Chan Kim and Renee Mauborgne in the book of the same name as the concept. Their 4-point approach looked at

a) **"Raise"** being those factors that could be elevated above the industry norms;
b) **"Reduce"** refers to the factors affecting the ability to compete against others;
c) **"Eliminate"** concerns those factors that can be eliminated; and
d) **"Create"** refers to offerings not currently available.

Examples are Uber, Ola, Airbnb and Amazon, which all eliminated the expensive property, plant, and equipment from their products.

This technique can be used both to create potential disruptive ideas and to rank new ideas against the existing marketplace. Potential investors and others are allowed to see how the disruptive venture fits into its environment. The resulting business plan forms the basis for both the value justification surrounding the investment decision and proof of the venture's viability.

The assumptions around both revenue and costs in any business plan are mostly very subjective, raising the question as to the value in preparing such a plan as a tool for getting investment in addition to demonstrating the viability of a venture. A study by Babson College found that a business plan made no difference to a venture's outcome (Lange et al., 2007). That is, the business plan is not a predictor of business success. This raises doubts about the value of the business plan as a tool to be used in a funding round to close an investment.

While creating a business plan does not ensure funding or business success, it is a useful tool to aid in the understanding of a business. It provides a mechanism to help focus on those many factors that make up the operation and how their interplay affects the ultimate performance of the business. This approach is constructive in highlighting the really critical factors where 80% of the team's time must be focused if the business is to succeed. Knowing what is essential and what is of secondary importance provides a tool that enables the entrepreneur and the team to monitor and control the parts of the operation of the venture that matter and avoid spending time in areas that do not contribute to the success or failure of the venture.

A business plan has may aspects, and while there is no set list of things to incorporate, it should include:

- A Heading page containing a clear name, website, and date;
- An Executive Summary, which is only written after completion of the plan, to ensure that it adequately summarises the key points that arise. It must be those key points that are brought to the reader's attention, and it is those points that are appealing to the targeted audience.
- The plan needs a description of the market environment within which the venture operates, and covers points like:
    a) The future direction of that environment also needs to be expressed to show the relevance of the venture into the future;
    b) The nature, description, and uniqueness of the Product going into a market, and why it is vital and how it fits into that market.
    c) It positioning, pricing, competition, and
    d) The total value of the likely market,
- An understanding of why someone would buy the venture's good or service.

- The competitive landscape, especially if the product is going "head-to-head" against existing products. Being able to identify how to enter and beat competitors is an essential validation of the likelihood of the chances of success.
- A range of operational matters, such as the product design and development work and timetable, how the operations will be managed and the Team that will do this work.
- A forecast of financial needs and projected results, summarized into the main categories. No benefit is derived from detailing the expenditures on paper or coffee. Instead, the main variable factors and the underlying assumptions will help a reader to understand the way the key factors affect the profit outcomes.

Due Diligence

An understanding and acknowledgement that the plan has been built up from underlying supporting documents is vital. These supporting documents become very important when the investors are at the due diligence stage. At that time, the intimate and detailed checking of what is in the business plan is undertaken, and the work to create the plan is reviewed in-depth. It is often at this point that any "pie in the sky" calculations will come to light and materially impact the regard any investor has of the team's skills and capacity to deliver on the ideas and concepts promoted.

Due Diligence, as the name implies, is a detailed check to ensure that what has been claimed in the Business Plan is fully supported with sound documents, that the Venture owns the patent, trademark, copyright or other IP, that employees are correctly contracted under appropriate agreements and books, records, share registers, and corporate documentation are complete and up-to-date.

The due diligence program dpends on access to very detailed record keeping, and its preparation is a must-have skill.

Before the due diligence stage of any investment and even before a review of the business plan, it is necessary to engage with a potential investor. Investors are inundated with plans asking for financial aupport, so be mindful that there is competition from others for this scarce resource. It has been estimated that there are globally about 100 million startup businesses formed each year. Not all are searching for money, but even, as noted, 3% of companies are funded from VC's - potentially 3 million per year across all categories of funding. To ensure the venture, at the very least, gets noticed, requires an understanding of and training in the art of presentation and selling.

PRESENTATION TOOLS

The presentation tools that are used such as the "elevator" pitch and the venture presentation "pitch deck" serve the purpose of telling a story about a venture in a way that will cause potential funders to consider an investment in the venture. The investor is taken on a journey via these tools into aspects of the business that usually focus on the technical and descriptive aspects, sometimes in exquisite detail. The focus is, unfortunately, often directed towards in-depth details about the venture about which the Founder is most proud. However, it is a story that needs to engage, entertain and above all, keep the potential investor interested rather than provide the entrepreneur with the opportunity to speak about and show off their concept.

Elevator Pitch

To reach this point, the entrepreneur must be prepared for the investment journey. Every interaction could lead to the contact needed to bring an investment closer. The entrepreneur needs to have a story that is sharp, quick and exciting, ready to go. Any such encounter is usually a chance event, so it is doubtful that a conversation can be structured beforehand. Rather, such a chance event will be a free-flowing and straightforward chat, and that means the conversation will need to be guided into the "story" about the venture, idea, and opportunity in a way that is both logical and compelling.

The single most crucial approach to adopt is to know the audience. Start any approach with a key quote that best creates an image for the remainder of the short story. An elevator pitch, as the name implies, is only a 30-second grab. There is no time for lengthy introductions. The audience is being hit with a quick message that makes them agree to receive the next more extensive presentation. The simple question to be answered is: Is what is being said likely to create a memorable meeting? There is considerable pressure when delivering this quick encapsulation of the venture, yet the delivery has to appear calm and the storyteller charismatic.

However, it is one of only several hurdles to master. Increasing the pool of contacts that can hear the venture's story is vital, and many have recognised that it is easier to delve deeply into personal networks to locate "warm contacts" with possible investors. It is well known that the "warm" network will help you get past the elevator pitch and onto the presentation with a little more time to show your message to a potential investor and with less pressure.

Pitch Deck

Investors are a limited and scarce resource, and entrepreneurs seem to be an endless line of people searching for this scarce resource. Seen in terms of a scarce resource, the rules needed to obtain scarce investment are the same as searching for that elusive gold mine. Firstly, locate the most likely area to conduct the exploration, which constitutes the target audience. Secondly, engage with that audience by preparing the right material to demonstrate the value of the business.

The task of a pitch deck is to convey this story entertainingly and quickly. Investors have a fundamental need to understand the business and environment within which the business will operate. Helping an investor understand the size of the market being entered into may require a change to their paradigm. When Uber looked at the taxi industry, it was not focusing on the actual amount of taxi usage. They knew that consumers had issues with taxi usage, such as price, convenience, taxi license costs and availability. The Uber product, in addressing the restrictions on taxi usage, substantially increased the potential market.

Being able to define the market adequately is imperative to the message being conveyed to an investor. Kim Cutler and Professor Tom Eisenmann conducted a study in 2015 and discovered that VCs spent as little as 3 minutes and 44 seconds reviewing a pitch deck. They also noted that most companies *need an average 40 investor meetings and took a little over 12 weeks to close a Round". The forecast financials, team and the competition were the most studied parts of the pitch decks.*

An entrepreneur's ability to sell the unique skill-sets of the chosen team helps investors understand why it can be successful. Many potentially great businesses fail to achieve "lift-off" because their team did not perform as expected. Investors realize that a successful venture will need a team that can execute the business plan, be flexible in the face of obstacles and remain persistently committed to getting the business functioning. The planned success may be the result of the team having a range of skills that could be unusual. Investors are aware that possessing a qualification in any field is by no means a guarantee of success. What they are looking for is to be convinced that the team has what it takes to make this business work. It may be an instinctive understanding on the investors part, and it could be the power of the explanation of the team's aptitude given to the investor by the entrepreneur. Whichever method works to convince an investor of the team's skill and substance is the crucial element and not the approach used.

Presentations made to an investor consist of more than what is in the written presentation. The thinking behind the business and how the entrepreneur arrived at the solutions put forward tells the investor more about the entrepreneur's capacity to deliver the right result. Understanding the product or service developed is a part of the investors understanding but the beliefs, feelings of the strength of the development and implementation skills and resilience to stand up and argue vehemently about the business case all contribute to an investors "feelings" about the team and its abilities to deliver on the business plan.

Investors are also aware that during any development of the business, a point may be reached where the way forward is determined to be a likely "failure". Action to stop or pivot to another area is a strength. The ability to be realistic and practical is an advantage and recognizing the limitations of the business plan avoids wasting an investment entirely. The hugely successful product *Slack* was not the result of the original investment. Instead, during the development of a multi-user game, the developers realized that their business plan would not succeed. However, they had developed a convenient communication tool that they realized was an excellent product. By pivoting away from the game to the communication product, they introduced *Slack* to the world and developed a product now valued at many $ billions.

Milestones

Any investor is unlikely to provide all the funding needed to carry out the business plan. It is vital to understand that the business can be funded in smaller steps, or tranches. These tranches need to be planned and are best linked to defined goals and targets. Investors like "milestones". They provide a measurable target against which the venture and more importantly, others, can identify that progress is being made. In planning for investments, be prepared to break down the investments proposed into tranches. Tranches help demonstrate that the importance of the venture performance is understood and the scarcity of funds and the need to show success through continuous meaningful progress is a central tenet of the venture.

CROWDFUNDING AND CRYPTOCURRENCY APPROACH

Crowdfunding has introduced large numbers of small investors to ventures that had traditionally approached only more significant venture funders. The additional potential funders coming online has created new opportunities to mobilize many smaller investors to add to the pool of the limited number of larger investors. The most popular and successful crowdfund method is built around "pre-orders" for products that are yet to be made. (Mollick, 2014). "*No longer are we looking to the venture's capital growth and future profitability but rather the output product from the venture*". Mollick goes on to use the Mathew Effect (Merton, 1957) - that the venture's product nature and quality are the critical parameters in achieving a successful decision *"to make this "pre-order" decision. The pre-order buy is not a traditional investment decision and relies on the product attractiveness to the consumers prepared to buy it in advance at some beneficial discount or purchase terms".*

Pre-order crowdfunding is different from the equity crowd-sourced funding discussed earlier. The significant advantage of the pre-order type of funding is that the business is selling a product or service. There is no dilution of equity or investment in the venture itself. Such is the nature of this approach that it can be seen as a way of test-marketing the business plan while gaining sales. Naturally, care is needed as the "pre-orders" need to be filled and should be included in calculations of the costs. If this is not done, financial losses arise or worse, charges of fraudulent behaviour may be levelled for non-performance.

The more recent advent of the blockchain and the rise of "utility" coins and "asset-backed tokens" has created a new opportunity for ventures to access capital. While having many different features, the purpose of these tokens is not dissimilar to crowdfunding (which is like using token ICOs) and share issue (which is like token STOs). The delivery of a token has a perceived inherent value to the buyer. It is not an investment in the venture, albeit it is conceivable that the promotion of the token sells the venture's future success to create the tokens perceived underlying value. In many respects, the nature of the blockchain coins is not dissimilar to a "collective investment scheme" but without the protections afforded by those heavily regulated schemes.

THE INVESTOR'S WANTS

Leaving aside pre-order and token buying "investments" and discussions on behavioral investing psychology and neuroscience in financial decision making, an investor is, or should be, primarily analyzing risk in any investment decision. This analysis follows a few simple steps: firstly, the likely loss of the investor's capital; secondly, the actual and opportunity costs of the investor's returns; and finally, an exit strategy for capital and the receipt of profits. It is an investor's calculation of risk that is relevant and not the view of the founder or others as to the value on offer. The investor's focus on the actual product or service and other intangible benefits will figure in any decision making only after these more basic risks are addressed.

Understanding and focusing upon the investor's main risk parameters should be the first goal in seeking out a successful investment decision.

A CHANGE IN FOCUS

An investment process is like the sale of a product. The product is not a venture. The product is an investment offering and has the same features as any product for sale. When the focus is placed upon the investment as the thing being sold, then the focus is switched from discussions around the intricate detail of the venture and over to what makes the investment work. Once the focus is realigned to this "investment product", then all documents and discussions can be altered to align to the Investor's priority decision making interests using the essential investment presentation tools.

Those presentation tools serve a purpose in providing a structure to present the venture. The entrepreneur, however, must act as the salesman and use that presentation material in a sale-like situation with an investor. By using sale techniques, an entrepreneur can increase his ability to achieve the desired result. Basic selling techniques make clear that mimicry and mirroring between the "salesman" and the customer lead to higher sales closing success (Jacob et al., 2011). Increases in positive evaluation, greater liking, rapport and affiliation were leading to greater persuasion and rate of buying. Transferring this approach to the investment area requires not only the education of the founder in the selling techniques associated with mimicry but just as importantly needs the investment product to mimic the investor's risk profile.

The result is that the significant features of an investor's risk assessment must be analyzed and understood to gain any advantage in using mimicry. Such an approach aids capital raising by making the focus clear and unambiguous, removing the distractions of emphasis on other details about the venture and can lead to the successful conversion of the investment decision. The other details of the venture are both relevant and vital but are usually handled in-depth during the due diligence phase and not at the investment sale phase. The due diligence phase occurs after the investor is locked in via agreements such as Heads of Agreement, Non-Disclosure agreements (NDS) and Non-circumvention agreements (NCA).

The development of a compelling investment decision is venture-dependent. However, any "investor pitch" and other tools used must ensure that the risk that the specifically targeted investor takes is addressed as part of the investment product development. Moreover, the "sale" to the investor should proceed by enquiring about the investor's financial requirements, expectations on returns, timing and exit, thereby creating the elements needed to mimic the investor's wants.

COMMUNICATION SKILLS

Being able to sell the venture effectively requires mastery of the art of effective communication and speaking. It is often the difference between success and failure. The art of speaking, however, is only one part of the process. It is noticeable that certain people always have new and exciting contacts. They seem to be able to produce names quickly whenever asked: "Do you know anyone who does this?". The skill to access a network like these people is not some undiscoverable ancient art. It is the continuous attendance at gatherings such as social events, seminars, meetings, conferences, gatherings of those influencers in areas of interest and an ongoing awareness that meeting an ever-growing circle of different people is the key.

To convert any attendance at these various networking events does require development of the skills that will make the individual "worth" knowing. To achieve that level means there is a need to read widely so a conversation can be held on numerous subjects. Knowledge of events globally, history, advances and current affairs ensures active participation with an opinion, rather than passive listening. and improves the chances of becoming memorable. Knowing about business and business sectors generally and some areas individually will add to the current affairs knowledgebase. It takes practice to adopt a smooth and engaging conversational approach that provides an exciting experience for those involved. Avoid boorish behaviours such as dominating *ad nauseam* a conversation by exhibiting in-depth knowledge. The purpose of networking is to connect with people not to show off.

When engaging with people and finding that there is the opportunity to present material, then that presentation must be delivered without reading it. The presentation is the chance to demonstrate that the entrepreneur has a plan and can talk about the subject, entertainingly, without reading out what the investor can also read. Reading a presentation achieves nothing. The opportunity to expand on a presentation allows for depth and "flavour" to be given to what is written. The passion for the subject can then resonate in the spoken words appealing to the other senses of the listener. Learning the skill of effective communication provides an advantage over others. Do not be afraid to consider voice training and communication and speaking courses to give that edge. Remember, in any interaction with an investor; there is a need to identify with the audience and know the message to convey.

Finally, there needs to be clarity as to what exactly is expected to be achieved: a sale, a network contact, an introduction or an investment. Knowing the goal will help the entrepreneur stay on track and avoid the flow of the "sale" and investors attention being diverted away from the objective.

INVESTMENT CLOSING

Any investment decision requires documentation and a clear understanding of the steps to the receipt of the funding. Once an investor has expressed interest, documentation is needed to ensure clarity of what the parties are aiming to achieve. A non-binding Heads of Agreement allows each party to detail what their goals are, as well as the conditions and steps needed. After a Heads of Agreement comes the completion of various documents (NDA, NCA) designed to protect the IP of the targeted investment venture.

The nature of the investment, such as debt, convertible debt, convertible preference shares, ordinary shares, investment in kind, crypto tokens or product pre-purchase and other solutions, all have a variety of applicable agreements. Each agreement has its use and is dependent on the type of deal, size of the investment, exit considerations and investor preference.

THE IMPORTANCE OF SUCCESSFUL FUNDING

A business venture that can raise enough funding has the potential to move beyond being a small business. Within the general economy, small businesses mostly fail within five years. Those that can disrupt and innovate develop from this pool provided the funding exists for their growth.

Waterhouse (2017) points out that real employment growth arises mostly from fast-growing companies and "*small firms' worth came not from promoting competition or preserving local values, but rather from their potential to cease to be small businesses.*" Getting the investment pitch correct and the sales techniques properly developed is vital to the growth of an economy and increased employment by using the capital available allowing a startup, with disruptive innovation, to move to an economic powerhouse. The resulting reallocation of resources within the total economy, guided by Adam Smith's *Invisible Hand*, is stimulated by Schumpeter's understanding that innovation is the driver to growth and employment.

REFERENCES

Bosma, N. (2018/2019). *Kelley D Global Entrepreneurship Monitor (GEM)*. Global Report Babson University.

Clare, R., & Craston, A. (2017). *The Australia superannuation industry*. AFSA Research and Resource Centre.

Colombelli, A., Krafft, J., & Vivarelli, M. (2016). *To Be Born is Not Enough: The Key Role of Innovative Startups*. Discussion Paper No.9733. IZA Research.

Isenberg, D. (2016, June 6). Do Startups really Create Lots of Good Jobs? *Harvard Business Review*.

Jacob, C., Gueguen, N., Martin, A., & Boulbry, G. (2011). Retail salespeople's mimicry of customers: Effects on consumer behaviour. *Journal of Retailing and Consumer Services*, *18*(5), 381–388. doi:10.1016/j.jretconser.2010.11.006

Lange. J.E., Mollov A., Pearlmutter M., Singh S. & Bygrave W.D. (2007). Pre-start-up formal business plans and post-start-up performance: A study of 116 new ventures. *Venture Capital: An International Journal of Entrepreneurial Finance*, *9*(4).

Maslow, A. (1943). The Theory of Human Motivation. *Psychological Review*, *50*(4), 370–396. doi:10.1037/h0054346

Mcnaughton, J. (2019). *Monetizing Ideas from Startup to Success*. Lakeland House Publishing LLP.

Merton, R.K. (1957). Priorities in scientific discovery: a chapter in the sociology of science. *Am. Social. Rev.*, *22*(7), 635-659.

Mollick, E. (2014). The dynamics of crowdfunding: an exploratory study. *J. Bus. Ventur.*, *29*(1), 1-16.

Schumpeter, J. A. (1942). *Capitalism, Socialism, and Democracy*. New Yory Harper & Brothers.

Waterhouse Benjamin. C. (2017). *The Small Business Myth*. Aeon Co.

Compilation of References

ABARES. (2019). *Australian Agriculture Import--export*. Retrieved from http://www.agriculture.gov.au/abares

Abbott, G. (2010). Cross Cultural Coaching: A Paradoxical Perspective. In *The Complete Handbook of Coaching*. Sage.

ABC News. (2019). *Adani protesters pick peak hour in Brisbane to 'stop the city'*. Retrieved from https://www.abc.net.au/news/2019-07-05/adani-protest-brisbane-cbd-promp-train-delay-warnings/11282030

ABS. (2019). *Statistics*. Retrieved from https://www.abs.gov.au/

Adler, N. J. (2002). *International dimensions of organizational behavior*. South-Western.

Admin. (2017, September 18). Tour My India. *Unbeatable Success Story Of Medical Tourism Industry In India*. Retrieved March 01, 2019, from https://www.tourmyindia.com/medical-tourism/blog/success-story-medical-tourism-india/

Ahluwalia, M. S., & Little, I. M. D. (1998). *India's Economic Reforms and Development: Essays for Manmohan Singh*. Oxford University Press.

Ahn Kwan-ok, G. (2016). *Elderly community centers a unique feature of aged life in South Korea*. Retrieved from http://english.hani.co.kr/arti/english_edition/e_national/776262.html

Alves, J., Manz, C., & Butterfield, D. (2005). Developing leadership theory in Asia: The role of Chinese philosophy. *International Journal of Leadership Studies*, *1*(1), 3–27.

Ashiana Housing Ltd. (2019). *Senior Living VS Old Age Homes VS Retirement Homes in India*. Retrieved from https://www.ashianahousing.com/real-estate-blog/old-age-homes-vs-retirement-village-vs-retirement-homes-in-india-and-senior-living

Asialink. (2019). *Where we Live. Address to Asialink PM Scott Morrison*. Retrieved from https://asialink.unimelb.edu.au/stories/australia-and-the-indo-pacific-an-address-by-prime-minister-scott-morrison

Australia-India Council (AIC). (2019). *Australia-India Council*. Available from dfat.gov.au/people-to-people/foundations-councils-institutes/australia-india-council/governance/Pages/australia-india-council-strategic-plan-2017-2020.aspx

Australian Bureau of Statistics. (2019). *Population clock*. Retrieved from https://www.abs.gov.au/AUSSTATS/abs@.nsf/Web+Pages/Population+Clock?opendocument&ref=HPKI

Australian Institute of Health and Welfare (AIHW). (2011). *Australian hospital statistics 2009-10, Health services series no. 40, Cat. no. HSE 107*. Canberra: AIHW.

Australian Institute of Health and Welfare. (2018). *Older Australia at a glance*. Canberra: AIHW. Retrieved from https://www.aihw.gov.au/reports/older-people/older-australia-at-a-glance

Australian Institute of Health and Welfare. (2019). *Australia's welfare 2019 data insights*. Canberra: AIHW.

Aycan, Z. (2005). The Interplay Between Cultural and Institutional / Structural Contingencies In Human Resource Management Practices. *International Journal of Human Resource Management*, *16*(7), 1083–1119. doi:10.1080/09585190500143956

Babaei, M., Gholami, Z., & Altafi, S. (2015). Challenges of enterprise resource planning implementation in Iran large organizations. *Information Systems*, *54*, 15–27. doi:10.1016/j.is.2015.05.003

Ball, S. J. (1990). Self-doubt and Soft Data: social and technical trajectories in ethnographic fieldwork. In M. Hammersley (Ed.), *Educational Research: current issues*. Paul Chapman.

Banister, J., Bloom, D. E., & Rosenberg, L. (2012). Population aging and economic growth in China. In M. Aoki & J. Wu (Eds.), *The Chinese economy, International economic association series* (pp. 114–149). Palgrave Macmillan. doi:10.1057/9781137034298_7

Bayly, S. (1999). *Caste, Society and Politics in India from the Eighteenth Century to the Modern Age*. Cambridge University Press. doi:10.1017/CHOL9780521264341

Beattie, R. S., Kim, S., Hagen, M. S., Egan, T. M., Ellinger, A. D., & Hamlin, R. G. (2014). Managerial Coaching: A Review of the Empirical Literature and Development of a Model to Guide Future Practice. *Advances in Developing Human Resources*, *16*(2), 184–201. doi:10.1177/1523422313520476

Beer, M., Boselie, P., & Brewster, C. (2015, May). Boselie. P and Brewster. C. Implications For The Field Of HRM Of The Multistakeholder Perspective Proposed 30 Years Ago. *Human Resource Management*, *54*(3), 427–438. doi:10.1002/hrm.21726

Behrmann, J., & Smith, E. (2010). Top 7 issues in medical tourism: Challenges, knowledge gaps, and future directions for research and policy development. *Global Journal of Health Science*, *2*(2), 80. doi:10.5539/gjhs.v2n2p80

Bereiter, C. (2002). *Education and mind in the knowledge age*. Lawrence Erlbaum Associates.

Bergenwall, S. (2016). Assessing India's Rise and the Road Ahead. *Strategic Analysis*, *40*(5), 386–404. doi:10.1080/09700161.2016.1209905

Bhagwati, J. (1993). *India in Transition: Freeing the Economy*. Clarendon Press. doi:10.1093/acprof:oso/9780198288473.001.0001

Bhargava, A. (2015). Elderly care: Why India is one of the worst countries to grow old? *Daily News Analysis India*. Retrieved from https://www.dnaindia.com/analysis/standpoint-elderly-care-why-india-is-one-of-the-worst-countries-to-grow-old-in-2138686

Bhargava, Y. (2018, July 23). Medical tourists flocking to India. *The Hindu*. Retrieved from https://www.thehindu.com/news/national/medical-tourists-flocking-to-india/article24497896.ece

Bhat, T. P. (2015). *India: Trade in Healthcare Services*. Working Paper 180, Institute for Studies in Industrial Development. Retrieved from https://ideas.repec.org/p/sid/wpaper/180.html

Bhattacharya, S. C., & Jana, C. (2009). Renewable Energy in India: Historical Developments and Prospects. *Energy*, *38*(8), 981–991. doi:10.1016/j.energy.2008.10.017

Bhatt, G. D. (2002). Knowledge management in organizations: Examining the interaction between technologies, techniques, and people. *Journal of Knowledge Management*, *5*(1), 68–75. doi:10.1108/13673270110384419

Bhosale, S. (2018). Why India is Emerging as Australia's Natural Ally. *The Sydney Moring Herald*. Retrieved from https://www.smh.com.au/world/asia/why-india-is-emerging-as-australia-s-natural-ally-20180905-p501yp.html

Binoy, T.A. (2017). Dynamics of medical tourism in India-A microscopic analysis. *Asia Pacific Journal of Research*, *1*(58).

Blake, D., Cairns, A., & Dowd, K. (2011). The new life market: from survivor bonds to life settlements securitization. In Q.-P. Ma (Ed.), *Private capital and road to developed economy* (pp. 111–151). Economic Science Press.

Blanchet, G. (1991). *A Survey of the Economy of French Polynesia, 1960 to 1990*. The Australian National University.

Bookman, M., & Bookman, K. (2007). *Medical tourism in developing countries*. Palgrave Macmillan. doi:10.1057/9780230605657

Bose, A. (2016). Vegetarian India A Myth? Survey Shows Over 70% Indians Eat Non-Veg, Telangana Tops List. *Huffpost*. Retrieved from https://www.huffingtonpost.in/2016/06/14/how-india-eats_n_10434374.html

Bosma, N. (2018/2019). *Kelley D Global Entrepreneurship Monitor (GEM)*. Global Report Babson University.

Boyatzis, R., Jack, A., Cesaro, R., Khawaja, M., & Passarelli, A. (2010). *Coaching with compassion: An fMRI study of coaching to the positive and negative emotional attractor*. Academy.

Brewster, D. (2010). Australia and India: The Indian Ocean and the limits of strategic convergence. *Australian Journal of International Affairs*, *64*(5), 549–565. doi:10.1080/10357718.2010.513369

Brijnath, B. (2012). Why does institutionalised care not appeal to Indian families? Legislative and social answers from urban India. *Ageing and Society*, *32*(4), 697–717. doi:10.1017/S0144686X11000584

Brown, J. S., & Duguid, P. (2000). Balancing act: How to capture knowledge without killing it. *Harvard Business Review*, *78*(3), 73–80. PMID:11183980

Brown, S. W., & Grant, A. M. (2010). From GROW to GROUP: Theoretical issues and a practical model for group coaching in organisations. Coaching. *An International Journal of Theory. Research and Practice*, *3*(1), 30–45.

Bryman, A. (2008). *Social research methods*. Oxford University Press.

Bureau of immigration. (2017). *Tourism Growth in India: 1981 to 2016*. Government of India. Retrieved from https://www.indiastat.com/tourism-data/29/foreign-tourists/280/stats.aspx

Campos, M. L., Morini, C., De Moraes, G. H., & Inacio, E. (2018). A Performance Model for Public–Private Partnerships: The authorized economic operator as an example. *RAUSP Management Journal*, *53*(2), 288–279. doi:10.1016/j.rausp.2017.07.002

Candra, S. (2012). ERP implementation success and knowledge capability. *Procedia: Social and Behavioral Sciences*, *65*, 141–149. doi:10.1016/j.sbspro.2012.11.103

Canlas, D., & Fujisaki, S. (2001). *The Philippine Economy: Alternatives for the 21st Century*. University of Philippines Press.

Caplan, J. (2003). *Coaching for the future: How smart companies use coaching and mentoring*. CIPD.

Cardon, P. (2009). A model of face practices in Chinese business culture: Implications for western businesspersons. *Thunderbird International Business Review*, *51*(1), 19–36. doi:10.1002/tie.20242

Carnes, B. A., Olshansky, S. J., & Grahn, D. (2003). Biological evidence for limits to the duration of life. *Biogerontology*, *4*(1), 31–45. doi:10.1023/A:1022425317536 PMID:12652187

CECA. (2019). *Comprehensive Economic Cooperation Agreement*. Retrieved from https://dfat.gov.au/trade/agreements/negotiations/aifta/Pages/australia-india-comprehensive-economic-cooperation-agreement.aspx

Chacko, P., & Davis, A. E. (2017). The natural/neglected relationship: Liberalism, identity and India-Australia relations. *The Pacific Review*, *30*(1), 26–50. doi:10.1080/09512748.2015.1100665

Chandel, S. S., Shrivastava, R., Sharma, V., & Ramasamy, P. (2016). Overview of the initiatives in renewable energy sector under the national action plan on climate change in India. *Renewable & Sustainable Energy Reviews*, *54*, 686–873. doi:10.1016/j.rser.2015.10.057

Chang, D. F., Tong, H., Shi, Q., & Zeng, Q. (2005). Letting a Hundred Flowers Bloom: Counseling and Psychotherapy in the People's Republic of China. *Journal of Mental Health Counseling*, *27*(2), 104–116. doi:10.17744/mehc.27.2.hxfupdhht26b30a6

Chatterjee, S., Rae, A., & Ray, R. (2006). *Food Consumption, Trade Reforms and Trade Patterns in Contemporary India: How Do Australia and NZ Fit in?* Centre for Applied Economics and Policy Studies, Working Paper 2/06. Massey University, Palmerston North, New Zealand.

Chau, R. C. P. (2016). *Culturally sensitive coaching for Chinese business leaders* (Unpublished doctoral dissertation). Widener University, Chester, PA.

Chee, H. (2010). Medical tourism and the state in Malaysia and Singapore. *Global Social Policy*, *10*(3), 336–357. doi:10.1177/1468018110379978

Chen, G., Sharma, P., Edinger, S., Shapiro, D., & Farh, J. (2011). Motivating and demotivating forces in teams: Cross-level influences of empowering leadership and relationship conflict. The Journal of Applied Psychology, 96, 441–557.

Chen, J., & Eldridge, D. (2010). Are "standardized performance appraisal practices" really preferred? A case study in China. *Chinese Management Studies*, *4*(3), 244–257. doi:10.1108/17506141011074138

Chen, X., Bishop, J. W., & Scott, K. D. (2000). Teamwork in China: Where Reality Challenges Theory and Practice. In J. T. Li, A. S. Tsui, & E. Weldon (Eds.), *Management and Organizations in the Chinese Context* (pp. 269–282). Macmillan. doi:10.1057/9780230511590_11

Cheung, T. S., & King, A. Y. (2004). Righteousness and Profitableness: The Moral Choice of Contemporary Confucian Entrepreneurs. *Journal of Business Ethics*, *54*(3), 245–260. doi:10.100710551-004-6405-6

Cheung, T. S., & King, A. Y. (2004). Righteousness and Profitableness: The Moral. *Journal of Business Ethics*, *54*, 245–260.

China Radio Network. (2014). *A relatively complete government procurement service system will be established in 2020*. Retrieved from http://www.chinanews.com/gn/2014/10-06/6651510.shtml

Chofreh, A., Goni, F., Shaharoun, A., Ismail, S., & Klemeš, J. (2014). Sustainable enterprise resource planning: Imperatives and research directions. *Journal of Cleaner Production*, *71*, 139–147. doi:10.1016/j.jclepro.2014.01.010

Chong, F., & Liu, H. (2002). Indigenous counselling in the Chinese cultural context: Experience transformed model. *Asian Journal of Counselling*, *9*(1), 49–68.

CIA. (2020). *The World Factbook*. https://www.cia.gov/library/publications/the-world-factbook/

CIPD. (2009). *Taking The Temperature of coaching*. Retrieved from http://www2.cipd.co.uk/NR/rdonlyres/E27F313C-FFBC-466F-84D8- A240893A2A22/0/Taking_temperature_coaching.pdf

CIPD. (2009). *Taking The Temperature of coaching*. Retrieved from http://www2.cipd.co.uk/NR/rdonlyres/E27F313C-FFBC-466F-84D8-A240893A2A22/0/Taking_temperature_coaching.pdf

Clare, R., & Craston, A. (2017). *The Australia superannuation industry*. AFSA Research and Resource Centre.

Cohen, L., Manion, L., & Morrison, K. (2007). *Research Methods in Education*. Routledge. doi:10.4324/9780203029053

Colombelli, A., Krafft, J., & Vivarelli, M. (2016). *To Be Born is Not Enough: The Key Role of Innovative Startups*. Discussion Paper No.9733. IZA Research.

Commonwealth of Australia. (2010). *Australia-India: Joint Free Trade Agreement Feasibility Study*. Australian-Indian Government, DFAT.

Confederation of Indian Industry (CII) report titled "India Services Sector —A Multi -trillion Dollar Opportunity for Global Symbiotic Growth 2017.

Confederation of Indian Industry. (2018). *CII - Senior Care Industry Report India 2018: Igniting potential in senior care services*. Retrieved from https://www.slideshare.net/saileshmishra1/cii-senior-care-industry-report-india-2018?from_action=save

Connell, J. (2006). Medical tourism: sea, sun, sand and surgery. *Tourism Management, 27*, 1093-1100.

Connell, J. (2008). Tummy tucks and the Taj Mahal? Medical tourism and the globalization of health care. In A. Woodside & D. Martin (Eds.), *Tourism management (pp. 232-244)*. CABI. doi:10.1079/9781845933234.0232

Connell, J. (2011a). *Medical tourism*. CABI. doi:10.1079/9781845936600.0000

Connell, J. (2013). Contemporary medical tourism: Conceptualisation, culture and commodification. *Tourism Management, 34*, 1–13. doi:10.1016/j.tourman.2012.05.009

Cooperrider, D. L. (1990). Positive image, positive action: the affirmative basis for organizing. In S. Srivastva & D. L. Cooperrider (Eds.), *Appreciative Management and Leadership*. Jossey-Bass.

Coronado, D. (2015). Singapore: Focus on eldercare. *Health Management, 15*(2).

Costa, C., Ferreira, E., Bento, F., & Aparicio, M. (2016). Enterprise resource planning adoption and satisfaction determinants. *Computers in Human Behavior, 63*, 659–671. doi:10.1016/j.chb.2016.05.090

Cunliffe, A. L. (2008). Orientations to social constructionism: Relationally responsive social constructionism and its implications for knowledge and learning. *Management Learning, 39*(2), 123–139. doi:10.1177/1350507607087578

Cushion, C. J. (2018). Reflection and reflective practice discourses in coaching: A critical analysis. *Sport Education and Society, 23*(1), 82–94. doi:10.1080/13573322.2016.1142961

Dalal, S., & Basu, D. (2019). *Retirement Homes in India*. Retrieved from Mumbai, Mharashtra, India: https://foundation.moneylife.in/memorandum/report-on-retirement-homes-in-india-by-moneylife-foundation-for-hdfc-ltd/48.html

Damodaran, H., & Nilekani, N. (2011). *India's New Capitalists: Castes, Business, and Industry in a Modern Nation*. AIAA.

Dang, J. (2016). *Aging industry is the largest new economy in the future*. Retrieved from http://www.cncaprc.gov.cn/contents/20/177814.html

Davis, M. J. (2020). Australia and China: Framing an Ambivalent Relationship. *Asian Studies Review*, *44*(2), 278–296. Advance online publication. doi:10.1080/10357823.2019.1698006

Dawson, P., Blake, D., Cairns, A., & Dowd, K. (2010). Survor derivatives: A consistent pricing framework. *The Journal of Risk and Insurance*, *77*(3), 579–596. doi:10.1111/j.1539-6975.2010.01356.x

Deloitte. (2010). *Medical Tourism in New Zealand*. Author.

Deloitte. (2014). *Ensuring care for the golden years - Way forward for India*. Paper presented at the FICCI 7th Annual Health Conference, New Delhi. https://www2.deloitte.com/content/dam/Deloitte/in/Documents/life-sciences-health-care/in-lshc-ficci-elderly-care-noexp.pdf

Department of Foreign Affairs and Trade. (2018). *Government response to An India Economic Strategy to 2035*. Retrieved from https://dfat.gov.au/about-us/publications/Pages/government-response-india-economic-strategy.aspx

Department of Foreign Affairs and Trade. (2019). *India Country Brief*. Canberra, Australia: Australian Government Retrieved from https://www.dfat.gov.au/geo/india/Pages/india-country-brief

Department of Innovation Industry & Science (DIIS). (2019). *Collaborating with India on Science and Research*. Retrieved from www.industry.gov.au/funding-and-incentives/science-and-research/collaborating-with-india-on-science-and-research

Department of Resources, Energy & Tourism. (2011). *Medical tourism in Australia A scoping study*. Deloitte Access Economics.

Dey, S., Nambiar, D., Lakshmi, J., Sheikh, K., & Reddy, K. S. (2012). Health of the elderly in India: challenges of access and affordability. In *Aging in Asia: findings from new and emerging data initiatives*. National Academies Press.

DFAT. (2017). https://dfat.gov.au/about-us/publications/Documents/cot-cy-2017.pdf

DFAT. (2018a). https://dfat.gov.au/about-us/publications/Documents/cot-2017-18.pdf

DFAT. (2018b). *Indian Economic Strategy 2035*. Department of Foreign Affairs and Trade. Retrieved from https://dfat.gov.au/geo/india/ies/index.html

Ding, D. Z., Goodall, K., & Warner, M. (2000). The end of the "iron rice bowl"? Whither Chinese human resource management. *International Journal of Human Resource Management, 11*(2), 217–236. doi:10.1080/095851900339837

Drach-Zahavy, A., & Somech, A. (2001). Understanding Team Innovation: The Role of Team Processes and Structures. *Group Dynamics, 5*(2), 111–123. doi:10.1037/1089-2699.5.2.111

Dunn, J. (2017). *Amazon is still getting dominated in China.* Retrieved from http://www.businessinsider.com/amazon-market-share-china-alibaba-jd-chart-2017-2

Dyer, S. M., Valeri, M., Arora, N., Ross, T., Winsall, M., Tilden, D., & Crotty, M. (2019). *Review of International Systems for Long-Term Care of Older People.* Retrieved from Adelaide, Australia: https://agedcare.royalcommission.gov.au/publications/Documents/research-paper-2-review-international-systems-long-term-care.pdf

Economic and Social Commission for Asia and the Pacific (ESCAP). (2009). *Medical travel in Asia and the Pacific Challenges and opportunities.* United Nations.

Elley, D. (2003, Nov. 24). Baghban. *Variety.*

Ellinger, A. D., Ellinger, A. E., Bachrach, D. G., Wang, Y.-L., & Elmadagbas, A. B. (2011). Organizational investments in social capital, managerial coaching, and employee work-related performance. *Management Learning, 42*(1), 67–85. doi:10.1177/1350507610384329

Enomoto, N. (2008). *Changing Consumer Values and Behavior in Japan: Adaptation of Keio Department Store Shinjuku. In The Silver Market Phenomenon.* Springer.

Essers, J., & Schreinemakers, J. (1997). Nonaka's subjectivist conception of knowledge in corporate knowledge management. *Knowledge Organization, 24*(1), 24–32.

Fairhurst, G. T., & Sarr, R. A. (1996). *The Art of Framing: Managing the Language of Leadership.* Jossey-Bass.

Fan, C. J., Zhang, P., Liu, Q., Yang, J. Z., & Xi, W. Y. (2011). Research on ERP teaching model reform for application-oriented talents education. *International Education Studies, 4*(2), 25–30. doi:10.5539/ies.v4n2p25

Fang, Y. (1995). Chinese Value Survey by the Chinese Culture Connection. *Journal of Cross-Cultural Psychology, 18*(2), 147–148.

Feng, Z., Zhan, H. J., Feng, X., Liu, C., Sun, M., & Mor, V. (2011). An industry in the making: The emergence of institutional elder care in urban China. *Journal of the American Geriatrics Society, 59*(4), 738–744. doi:10.1111/j.1532-5415.2011.03330.x PMID:21410445

Ferry, T. (2017). *Long-Term care for Taiwan's elderly.* Retrieved from https://topics.amcham.com.tw/2017/03/caring-taiwans-elderly/

Fillery-Travis, A., & Passmore, J. (2011). A critical review of executive coaching research: A decade of progress and what's to come. *Coaching: An International Journal of Theory, Practice & Research*, *4*, 70–88.

Flaherty, J. (2005). *Coaching: Evoking Excellence in Others* (2nd ed.). Elsevier.

Flath, D. (2014). *The Japanese Economy*. Oxford University Press.

Ford, J. D. (1999). Organizational change and shifting conversations. *Journal of Organizational Change Management*, *12*(6), 480–500. doi:10.1108/09534819910300855

Foreign Direct Investment. (2019). Retrieved from https://dipp.gov.in/foreign-direct-investment/foreign-direct-investment-policy

France, T. (2009). Holidays for health: some medical options for two weeks or less. *e-Magazine News Room Tourism Authority of Thailand*. http://www.tatnews.org/emagazine/4524.asp

Fries, J. F. (1980). Aging, natural death and the compression of morbidity. *The New England Journal of Medicine*, *303*(3), 130–135. doi:10.1056/NEJM198007173030304 PMID:7383070

Galliers, R. D., & Currie, W. (Eds.). (2011). The Oxford handbook of management information systems: Critical perspectives and new directions. Oxford University Press.

Gallo, F. (2012). How Chinese managers can become effective global leaders. *People & Strategy*, *35*(2), 24–30.

Gan, L., & Frederick, J. (2011). *Consumers' attitudes towards medical tourism*. http://papers.ssrn.com/sol3/papers.cfm?abstract_id=1837062

Ganguly, S. (2017). Had Modi truly changed India's foreign Policy? *The Washington Quarterly*, *40*(2), 131–143. doi:10.1080/0163660X.2017.1328929

Gessnitzer, S., & Kauffeld, S. (2015). The working alliance in coaching: Why behavior is the key to success. *The Journal of Applied Behavioral Science*, *51*(2), 177–197. doi:10.1177/0021886315576407

Golechha, M. (2015). Healthcare agenda for the Indian government. *The Indian Journal of Medical Research*, *141*(2), 151–153. doi:10.4103/0971-5916.155541 PMID:25900948

Goodman, D. S. (2017). Australia and the China threat: Managing ambiguity. *The Pacific Review*, *30*(5), 769–782. doi:10.1080/09512748.2017.1339118

Goodman, R., & Lepani, C. (1997). *The Economy of Papua New Guinea*. The Australian National University.

Grant, A. M., Curtayne, L., & Burton, G. (2009). Executive coaching enhances goal attainment, resilience and workplace well-being: A randomized controlled study. *The Journal of Positive* Psychology, 4(1), 396–407.

Grigoroudis, E., Litos, C., Moustakis, V. A., Politis, Y., & Tsironis, L. (2008). The assessment of user-perceived web quality: Application of a satisfaction benchmarking approach. *European Journal of Operational Research, 187*(3), 1346-1357.

Grove, A. (2016). *Aged care: a quick guide*. Research paper series, 2016-17. Parliament of Australia, Department of Parliament Services, Social Policy Section.

Guo, L., & Zhang, Y. (2014). The changes and evaluation of China's private capital participating in the construction of elderly care service system. *Academic Forum,* (4), 90-94.

Gurry, M. (1993). Leadership and Bilateral Relations: Menzies and Nehru, Australia and India, 1949-1964. *Pacific Affairs*, *65*(4), 510–526. doi:10.2307/2760317

Gurry, M. (2012). India, the new centre of gravity: Australia-India relations under the Howards Government. *Journal of Southeast Asian Studies*, *35*(2), 282–305.

Gurry, M. (2013). A delicate balance: Australia's tilt to Pakistan and its impact on Australia-India relations. *Australian Journal of International Affairs*, *67*(2), 141–156. doi:10.1080/10357718.2012.750641

Hackman, J. R., & Wageman, R. (2005). A theory of team coaching. *Academy of Management Review*, *30*(2), 269–287. doi:10.5465/amr.2005.16387885

Hall, I. (2015). Is a 'Modi doctrine' emerging in India's foreign policy? *Australian Journal of International Affairs*, *69*(3), 247–252. doi:10.1080/10357718.2014.1000263

Han, C. K. (1992). The positive contribution of Confucianism to the modernization of East Asian business enterprises. *Journal of Chinese Philosophy*, *19*(2), 171–181. doi:10.1111/j.1540-6253.1992.tb00117.x

Hansen, M. T., & Von Oetinger, B. (2001). Introducing T-shaped managers. Knowledge management's next generation. *Harvard Business Review*, *79*(3), 106–116. PMID:11246918

Hawke, G. R. (1985). *The Making of New Zealand: An Economic History*. Cambridge University Press.

HelpAge India. (2015). *State of Elderly in India 2014*. Retrieved from New Delhi, India: https://www.helpageindia.org/wp-content/themes/helpageindia/pdf/state-elderly-india-2014.pdf

HelpAge India. (2017). *Old Age Homes*. Retrieved from https://www.helpageindia.org/our-work/welfare-development/old-age-homes/

Hennig, A. (2013). *The Ethical Background of Business in China – An Outline. academia.edu.* Retrieved from: https://www.researchgate.net/publication/269403615_The_Ethical_Background_of_Business_in_China_-_An_Outline

Hiles, G., & Webb, R. (1995). *The Economic Impact of Tourism in Guam*. Bureau of Labor Statistics, Guam Finance Commission.

HKMC. (2019). *Reverse Mortgage Programme*. Retrieved from http://www.hkmc.com.hk/eng/our_business/reverse_mortgage_programme.html

Hofstede, G., & Bond, M. H. (1988). The Confucius Connection: From Culture Roots to Economic Growth. *Organizational Dynamics*, *16*(4), 4–21. doi:10.1016/0090-2616(88)90009-5

Hohm, C., & Snyder, J. (2015). It was the best decision of my life: A thematic content analysis of former medical tourists' patient testimonials. *BMC Medical Ethics*, *16*(1), 8. doi:10.1186/1472-6939-16-8 PMID:25614083

Hooke, A. (2019). *Global Economic Development: Past, Present and Future*. Lakeland House.

Horner, C. (2002) *Executive coaching: the leadership development tool of the future?* (Unpublished MBA dissertation), Imperial College of Science, Technology and Medicine.

Hout, T., & Michael, D. (2014). *A Chinese Approach To Management*. https://hbr.org/2014/09/a-chinese-approach-to-management

Howcroft, D., & Light, B. (2010). The social shaping of packaged software selection. *Journal of the Association for Information Systems*, *11*(3), 2. doi:10.17705/1jais.00224

Hu, Y. (2018). *Measures to boost care for the elderly*. Retrieved from http://www.chinadaily.com.cn/a/201812/04/WS5c05d3a6a310eff30328ed7f.html

Huang, E., & Chang, C.-C. A. (2012). Patient-oriented interactive e-health tools on US hospital web sites. *Health Marketing Quarterly*, *29*(4), 329e345

Huang, J., & Hsieh, H. (2015). Huang, Supervisors as good coaches: Influences of coaching on employees' in-role behaviors and proactive career behaviors. *International Journal of Human Resource Management*, *26*(1), 42–58. doi:10.1080/09585192.2014.940993

Hubbard, R. G., Garrett, A., Lewis, P., & O'Brian, A. (2019). Essentials of Economics, 4th (edn), Sydney: Pearson.

Hui, R. T., Sue-Chan, C., & Wood, R. E. (2013). The contrasting effects of coaching style on task performance: The mediating roles of subjective task complexity and self-set goal. *Human Resource Development Quarterly*, *24*(4), 429–458. doi:10.1002/hrdq.21170

Hu, X., Xia, B., Skitmore, M., Buys, L., & Zuo, J. (2017). Retirement villages in Australia: A literature review. *Pacific Rim Property Research Journal*, *23*(1), 101–122. doi:10.1080/14445921.2017.1298949

Hwang, Y. R., & Park, H. J. (2018). *Comprehensive community care system to allow elderly Koreans to live in their homes by 2025*. Retrieved from http://english.hani.co.kr/arti/english_edition/e_national/871188.html

Indian Budget. (2019). *Indian Budget 2019*. Retrieved from https://www.indiabudget.gov.in/

Institute for Management Development. (2010). *World Competitiveness Yearbook*. Author.

International Institute for Population Sciences. (2017). *National Family Health Survey (NFHS-4), 2015-16: India*. Mumbai: IIPS Retrieved from http://rchiips.org/nfhs/NFHS-4Reports/India.pdf

Ip, P. (2009). The Challenge of Developing a Business Ethics in China. *Journal of Business Ethics*, *88*(1), 211–224. doi:10.100710551-008-9820-2

Irwin, J. (2012). *Doing Business in China: An overview of ethical aspects*. Institute of Business Ethics.

Isenberg, D. (2016, June 6). Do Startups really Create Lots of Good Jobs? *Harvard Business Review*.

Jacob, C., Gueguen, N., Martin, A., & Boulbry, G. (2011). Retail salespeople's mimicry of customers: Effects on consumer behaviour. *Journal of Retailing and Consumer Services*, *18*(5), 381–388. doi:10.1016/j.jretconser.2010.11.006

James, D., & Wolf, M. L. (2000, Spring). A second wind for ERP. *The McKinsey Quarterly*, 100.

Jindal, B. (2012). *Maintenance and welfare of Parents and Senior Citizens*. Academic Press.

Jinks, B., Biskup, P., & Nelson, H. (1973). *Readings in New Guinea History*. Angus & Robertson.

Johnson, R., Chang, C., & Yang, L. (2010). Commitment and motivation at work: The relevance of employee identity and regulatory focus. *Academy of Management Review*, *35*, 226–245.

Johnston, L. A. (2019). The Economic Demography Transition: Is China's 'Not Rich, First Old'Circumstance a Barrier to Growth? *The Australian Economic Review*, *52*(4), 406–426. doi:10.1111/1467-8462.12325

Joint Commission International (JCI). (2011). http://www.jointcommissioninternational.org/

Joo, B., Suchko, J. S., & McLean, G. N. (2012). Multiple faces of coaching: Manager-as-coach, executive coaching, and formal mentoring. *Organization Development Journal*, *30*, 19–38.

Kadoya, Y., & Khan, M. S. R. (2017). Can concern for the long-term care of older parents explain son preference at birth in India? *Journal of Women & Aging*, *29*(3), 254–266. doi:10.1080/08952841.2015.1138048 PMID:27029287

Keckley, P. H. (2008). *Medical tourism: Update and implications*. Deloitte Center for Health Solutions. Available at: http://www.deloitte.com/assets/ DcomUnitedStates/Local%20assets/documents/us_chs_medicaltourism_ 111209_web.pdf

Kegan, R. (1994). *In over our heads: The mental demands of modern life*. Harvard University Press.

Khan, A. R. (2016). *The Economy of Bangladesh: A Quarter Century of Development*. Palgrave Macmillan.

Khare, V., Nema, S., & Baredar, P. (2013). Status of solar wind renewable energy in India. *Renewable & Sustainable Energy Reviews*, *27*, 1–10. doi:10.1016/j.rser.2013.06.018

Khosla, D., Patel, F. D., & Sharma, S. C. (2012). Palliative care in India: Current progress and future needs. *Indian Journal of Palliative Care, 18*(3), 149. doi:10.4103/0973-1075.105683 PMID:23439559

Kim, B. S. K., Atkinson, D. R., & Yang, P. H. (1999). The Asian values scale: Development, factor analysis, validation, and reliability. *Journal of Counseling Psychology, 46*(3), 342–352. doi:10.1037/0022-0167.46.3.342

Kim, M.-Y., Subramaniam, P., & Flicker, L. (2018). The Australian Aged Care and its Implications for the Korean Aging Crisis. *Annals of Geriatric Medicine and Research, 22*(1), 9–19. doi:10.4235/agmr.2018.22.1.9

Kim, S., Egan, T. M., Kim, W., & Kim, J. (2013). The impact of managerial coaching behavior on employee work-related reactions. *Journal of Business and Psychology, 28*(3), 315–330. doi:10.100710869-013-9286-9

Kit, T. S. (2019). *New assisted living model for seniors in the works, public consultations to start soon.* Retrieved from https://www.channelnewsasia.com/news/singapore/new-assisted-living-model-for-seniors-in-the-works-public-11317046

Kline, N. (2016). *Time to think: listening to ignite the human mind.* Cassell Illustrated.

Knowledge Partnership on Migration and Development. (2018). *Migration and Remittances: Recent Developments and Outlook.* Retrieved from https://www.knomad.org/sites/default/files/2018-04/Migration%20and%20Development%20Brief%2029.pdf

Kumar, S. (2016). Skill Development in India for tourism and hospitality sector. *Journal of Information, Knowledge and Research in Humanities and Social Sciences, 4*(1).

Kumar, C. T. S., & Roy, K. J. (2016). Bianca Brijnath, Unforgotten: Love and the Culture of Dementia Care in India, Berghahn Books, Oxford, 2014, 240 pp., hbk£ 60, ISBN 13: 9781782383543. *Ageing and Society, 36*(5), 1111–1113. doi:10.1017/S0144686X1600012X

Kushnir, I. (2019). *Economy of New Caledonia.* Independently published.

Kushnir, I. (2019). *The Economy of Nepal.* Independently published.

Lal, B. V. (1992). *Broken Waves: A History of the Fiji Islands in the Twentieth Century.* University of Hawaii Press.

Lamond, D., & Zheng, C. (2010). HRM research in China: Looking back and looking forward. *Journal of Chinese Human Resource Management, 1*(1), 6–16. doi:10.1108/20408001011051179

Lange. J.E., Mollov A., Pearlmutter M., Singh S. & Bygrave W.D. (2007). Pre-start-up formal business plans and post-start-up performance: A study of 116 new ventures. *Venture Capital: An International Journal of Entrepreneurial Finance, 9*(4).

Lee, J. (1998). *Han Unbound: The Political Economy of South Korea.* Stanford University Press.

Li, B., Tai, S., & Xia, K. (2018). *Coping with aging, see how the capital Beijing "toughs up"*. Retrieved from http://www.xinhuanet.com/2018-06/22/c_1123018685_2.htm

Li, V. J. (2016). *Housing Policies in Hong Kong, China and the People's Republic of China*. ADBI Working Paper. Tokyo: Asian Development Bank Institute (ADBI).

Lin, Y.-Y., & Huang, C.-S. (2016). Aging in Taiwan: Building a society for active aging and aging in place. *The Gerontologist*, *56*(2), 176–183. doi:10.1093/geront/gnv107 PMID:26589450

Littrell, R. F. (2002). Desirable leadership behaviours of multi-cultural managers in China. *Journal of Management Development*, *21*(1), 5–74. doi:10.1108/02621710210413190

Liu, J. (2016). The gap between social health and longevity industry and national health in Japan. *Chinese and Foreign Entrepreneurs,* (13), 114.

Liu, S. (2011). China's aging population status and countermeasures analysis. *Chinese Urban Economy,* (29), 298-298.

Liu, Y. (2018). The marketization development of China's aging industry. Beijing: Social Sciences Academic Press (China).

Li, Y. L. (2011). ERP adoption in Chinese small enterprise: An exploratory case study. *Journal of Manufacturing Technology Management*, *22*(4), 489–505. doi:10.1108/17410381111143130

Lu, L. (2018). *Analysis of smart old-age equipment industry in 2018*. Retrieved from https://www.qianzhan.com/analyst/detail/220/180201-5ff84cbc.html

Lunt, N., Hardey, M., & Mannion, R. (2010). Nip, tuck and click: Medical tourism and the emergence of web-based health information. *The Open Medical Informatics Journal, 3*, 77-87.

Luo, B. (2015). China Will Get Rich Before It Grows Old. *Foreign Affairs*, *94*, 19.

Lu, Y., & Bjorkman, I. (1997). HRM practices in China-Western joint ventures: MNC standardization versus localization. *International Journal of Human Resource Management*, *8*(5), 614–628. doi:10.1080/095851997341414

Majid, A. (2012). Future of untouchables in India: A case study of Dalit. *South Asian Studies*, *27*(1), 263.

Malaurent, J., & Avison, D. (2015). From an apparent failure to a success story: ERP in China—Post implementation. *International Journal of Information Management*, *35*(5), 643–646. doi:10.1016/j.ijinfomgt.2015.06.004

Ma, Q.-P. (2012b). Government and individual strategy for dealing with the increasing post-retirement life expectancy. In A. Tavidze (Ed.), *Progress in Economics Research* (Vol. 26, pp. 1–29). Nova Science Publisher.

Ma, Q.-P. (2014). Financing a fair and efficient pension system: issues and solutions. In T. Reilly (Ed.), *Pensions: policies, new reforms and current challenges* (pp. 1–25). Nova Science Publisher.

Ma, Q.-P. (2017). Pension provision in the robotic age. In A. Webb (Ed.), *Pensions: Global issues, perspectives and challenges* (pp. 1–38). Nova Science Publisher.

Martin, I., & Cheung, Y. (2005). Business process re-engineering pays after enterprise resource planning. *Business Process Management Journal, 11*(2), 185–197. doi:10.1108/14637150510591174

Maslow, A. (1943). The Theory of Human Motivation. *Psychological Review, 50*(4), 370–396. doi:10.1037/h0054346

Matthews, Z., Padmadas, S. S., Hutter, I., McEachran, J., & Brown, J. (2009). Does early childbearing and a sterilization-focused family planning programme in India fuel population growth? *Demographic Research, 20*, 693–720. doi:10.4054/DemRes.2009.20.28

Max India Limited. (2016). *About Max India Limited.* Retrieved from https://www.maxindia.com/wp-content/uploads/2016/01/About-Max-India-Limited1.pdf

Mayer, P., & Jain, P. (2010). Beyond Cricket: Australia–India Evolving Relations. *Australian Journal of Political Science, 45*(1), 133–148. doi:10.1080/10361140903517759

McCall, M. Jr. (2010). Recasting leadership development. *Industrial and Organizational Psychology: Perspectives on Science and Practice, 3*(1), 3–19. doi:10.1111/j.1754-9434.2009.01189.x

Mcnaughton, J. (2019). *Monetizing Ideas from Startup to Success.* Lakeland House Publishing LLP.

Medhekar, A. (2019). Emerging Trends of Wellness and Medical Tourism in India. In S. Paul & S. K. Kulshreshtha (Eds.), Global Developments in Healthcare and Medical Tourism. Academic Press.

Medhekar, A. (2019). Emerging Trends of Wellness and Medical Tourism in India. In S. Paul & S.K. Kulshreshtha, (Eds.), Global Developments in Healthcare and Medical Tourism. IGI Global. doi:091218-104208

Medhekar, A. (2003). Environmental, degradation, population and poverty in India. In R. Ghosh, M. Siddique, & R. Gabbay (Eds.), *Essays on development Issues: India and the Indian Ocean Region* (pp. 67–92). Atlantic Publishers and Distributors.

Medhekar, A. (2012). Managing the Growth of Medical Tourism by Public-Private Partnership in India. In K. Roy & S. Kar (Eds.), *Development Management in the Twenty First Century: Readings in World Development* (pp. 73–90). Nova Science.

Medhekar, A., Wong, H. Y., & Hall, J. E. (2019). Factors influencing inbound medical travel to India. *Journal of Health Organization and Management, 33*(2), 155–172. doi:10.1108/JHOM-08-2018-0234 PMID:30950309

Medical Tourism Association - Medical travel & health tourism: Medical Tourism Association. (2019). *Medical Tourism Association | Medical Tourism FAQ's: Medical Tourism Association.* Retrieved February 16, 2019, from http://www.medicaltourismassociation.com/en/medical-tourism-faq-s.html

Medical Tourism Association. (2017). *2016-2017 global buyers survey brief.* Retrieved February 28, 2019, from https://medicaltourismassociation.com/userfiles/files/GLOBAL_BUYERS_REPORT_BRIEF.pdf

Medical tourism Market Report: 2015. (n.d.). *Worldwide Market size, Share, Trends, Analysis, Growth and research Report*. Academic Press.

Menon, J. (2009). Dealing with the Proliferation of Bilateral Free Trade Agreements. *World Economy*, *32*(10), 1381–1407. doi:10.1111/j.1467-9701.2009.01187.x

Merton, R.K. (1957). Priorities in scientific discovery: a chapter in the sociology of science. *Am. Social. Rev., 22*(7), 635-659.

Meyer, E. (2015). The culture map: decoding how people think, lead, and get things done across cultures. Academic Press.

Meyer, E. (2015). *The culture map: decoding how people think, lead, and get things done across cultures.*

Miltiades, H. B. (2002). The social and psychological effect of an adult child's emigration on non-immigrant Asian Indian elderly parents. *Journal of Cross-Cultural Gerontology*, *17*(1), 33–55. doi:10.1023/A:1014868118739 PMID:14617974

Ministry of Health and Family Welfare. (2017). *National Family Planning Programme*. New Delhi: Government of India Retrieved from https://humdo.nhp.gov.in/about/national-fp-programme/

Ministry of Housing and Urban Affairs. (2019). *Model Guidelines for Development and Regulation of Retirement Homes*. New Delhi, India Retrieved from http://mohua.gov.in/upload/uploadfiles/files/Retirement%20Model%20Guidelines%20Book.pdf

Ministry of Human Resource Development. (2016). *Language Education*. Delhi, India: Government of India Retrieved from https://mhrd.gov.in/sites/upload_files/mhrd/files/upload_document/languagebr.pdf

Ministry of Statistics and Program Implementation. (2016). *Elderly in India - Profiles and Programes*. Retrieved from New Delhi, India: http://mospi.nic.in/sites/default/files/publication_reports/ElderlyinIndia_2016.pdf

Mishra, R. (2012). India-Australia Strategic Relations: Moving to the next level. *Strategic Analysis*, *36*(4), 657–662. doi:10.1080/09700161.2012.689537

Moghavvemi, S., Ormond, M., Musa, G., Isa, C. R. M., Thirumoorthi, T., Mustapha, M. Z. B., Kanapathy, K. A., & Chandy, J. J. C. (2017). Connecting with prospective medical tourists online: A cross-sectional analysis of private hospital websites promoting medical tourism in India, Malaysia and Thailand. *Tourism Management*, *58*, 154–163. doi:10.1016/j.tourman.2016.10.010

Mollick, E. (2014). The dynamics of crowdfunding: an exploratory study. *J. Bus. Ventur., 29*(1), 1-16.

Nangalia, L., & Nangalia, A. (2010). The Coach in Asian Society: Impact of social hierarchy on the coaching relationship. *International Journal of Evidence Based Coaching and Mentoring*, *8*(1), 51.

Narayan, S. M., Varghese, M., Hepburn, K., Lewis, M., Paul, I., & Bhimani, R. (2015). Caregiving experiences of family members of persons with dementia in south India. *American Journal of Alzheimer's Disease and Other Dementias*, *30*(5), 508–516. doi:10.1177/1533317514567125 PMID:25735742

National Insititute of Social Defence. (2016). *Old Age Care*. Delhi, India: Government of India Retrieved from http://www.nisd.gov.in/content/128_1_OldAgeCare.aspx

Naughton, B. (2018). *The Chinese Economy*. MIT Press Ltd.

Neubert, M. J., Kacmar, K. M., Carlson, D. S., Chonko, L. B., & Roberts, J. A. (2008). Regulatory focus as a mediator of the influence of initiating structure and servant leader- ship on employee behavior. *The Journal of Applied Psychology*, *93*(6), 1220–1233. doi:10.1037/a0012695 PMID:19025244

Nguyen, T. H. (2017). Prospects of ASEAN-India Relations: An Analysis. *European Journal of Social and Human Sciences*, *4*(2), 1–8.

Nidhiprabha, B. (2018). *Macroeconomic Policy for Emerging Markets: Lessons from Thailand*. Routledge. doi:10.4324/9781315627472

Nilekani, N. (2010). *Imagining India: The Idea of a Renewed Nation*. Allen Lane.

Nonaka, I. (1994). A Dynamic Theory of Organizational Knowledge Creation. *Organization Science*, *5*(1), 14–37. doi:10.1287/orsc.5.1.14

Nonaka, I., Toyama, R., & Konno, N. (2000). SECI, Ba and Leadership: A Unified Model of Dynamic Knowledge Creation. *Long Range Planning*, *33*(1), 5–34. doi:10.1016/S0024-6301(99)00115-6

NORDEA. (2019). *Australia: Economic and Political Overview*. Retrieved from www.nordeatrade.com/en/explore-new-market/australia/economical-context

Observer Research Foundation (ORF). (2019). *Australia's Opportunity with the return of Narendra Modi*. Retrieved from www.orfonline.org/expert-speak/australias-opportunity-with-the-return-of-narendra-modi-51897/

Office of the Registrar General & Census Commissioner. (2020). *Census and You - Religion*. New Delhi: Government of India. Retrieved from http://censusindia.gov.in/Census_And_You/religion.aspx

Oh, T. K. (1992). Inherent Limitations of The Confucian Tradition in Contemporary East Asian Business Enterprises. *Journal of Chinese Philosophy*, *19*(2), 155–169. doi:10.1111/j.1540-6253.1992.tb00116.x

Olshansky, S. J., Carnes, B. A., & Cassel, C. (1990). In search of Methuselah: Estimating the upper limits to human longevity. *Science*, *250*(4981), 634–640. doi:10.1126cience.2237414 PMID:2237414

Olshansky, S. J., Carnes, B. A., & Désesquelles, A. (2001). Prospects for human longevity. *Science*, *291*(5508), 1491–1492. doi:10.1126cience.291.5508.1491 PMID:11234076

Pachauri, S. (2014). Priority strategies for India's family planning programme. *The Indian Journal of Medical Research*, *140*(Suppl 1), S137. PMID:25673535

Paine, L. S. (2010). *The China Rules: A Practical Guide for CEOs Managing Multinational Corporations in the People's Republic*. Retrieved from: https://hbr.org/2010/06/the-globe-the-china-rules

Palmer, I. (2018). *The Indonesian Economy Since 1965: A Case Study of Political Economy*. Routledge. doi:10.4324/9780429461491

Pan, M. J., & Jang, W. Y. (2008). Determinants of the adoption of enterprise resource planning within the technology-organization-environment framework: Taiwan's communications industry. *JCIS*, *48*, 94–102.

Patra, S. (2016). Role of SAARC in Convergence of South Asian economies. In Handbook of Research on Global Indicators of Economic and Political Convergence (pp. 144-169). IGI Global. doi:10.4018/978-1-5225-0215-9.ch007

Paul, N. S. S., & Asirvatham, M. (2016). Geriatric health policy in India: The need for scaling-up implementation. *Journal of Family Medicine and Primary Care*, *5*(2), 242. doi:10.4103/2249-4863.192333 PMID:27843821

Percy, W., & Dow, K. (2020). The Coaching Dance: Beyond Nonaka, Knowledge Management in Post Tayloristic Confucian China. In G. Hooke (Ed.), *Emerging Trade and Investment Opportunities Between Oceania and Asia*. IGI Global.

Perkowski, J. (2015). *Tesla Overestimates the Chinese Market*. Retrieved from: https://www.forbes.com/sites/jackperkowski/2015/02/17/tesla-overestimates-the-china-market/#5b3fd2a44346

Phan, T., Harvie, C., & Tran, V. (2006). *Vietnam's Economic Transition: Policies, Issues and Prospects*. ICFAI Books.

Phillips, A. (2013). Australia and the challenges of order- building in the Indian Ocean region. *Australian Journal of International Affairs*, *67*(2), 25–140. doi:10.1080/10357718.2012.751965

Piketty, T. (2014) *Harvard University Press.*

Plaza, M., & Rohlf, K. (2008). Learning and performance in ERP implementation projects: A learning-curve model for analyzing and managing consulting costs. *International Journal of Production Economics*, *115*(1), 72–85. doi:10.1016/j.ijpe.2008.05.005

Pocock, N., & Phua, K. (2011). Medical tourism and policy implications for health systems: A conceptual framework from a comparative study of Thailand Singapore and Malaysia. *Globalization and Health, 7*(12). Retrieved June 30, 2011, from http://www.globalizationandhealth.com/content/7/1/12 PMID:21539751

Pollard, K. (2017, Nov.). Measuring the ROI from medical tourism promotion. *International Medical Travel Journal.*

Prasad, H. A. C., & Singh, S. S. (2016). *India's Services sector: Performance,some issues and suggestions*. Department of Economic Affairs, Ministry of Finance, Government of India.

Productivity Commission. (2020). *Report on Government Services*. Retrieved from https://www.gen-agedcaredata.gov.au/Resources/Reports-and-publications/2020/February/Report-on-Government-Services-2020-part-f,-chapter

Qian, W., Abdur Razzaque, M., & Ah Keng, K. (2007). Chinese Cultural Values and Gift-giving Behavior. *Journal of Consumer Marketing, 24*(4), 214–228. doi:10.1108/07363760710756002

Raghuramapatruni, R., & Chary, D. S. (2017). Trends and prospects of bilateral trading relations between India and Australia. *International Journal of Economic Research, 14*(1), 599–616.

Rajan, C., & Baral, R. (2015). Adoption of ERP system: An empirical study of factors influencing the usage of ERP and its impact on end user. *IIMB Management Review, 27*(2), 77. doi:10.1016/j.iimb.2015.04.004

Ranjan, S., Jha, V., & Pal, P. (2016). Literature review on ERP implementation challenges. *IJBIS, 21*(3), 388. doi:10.1504/IJBIS.2016.074766

Ranjan, V. (2016). Australia and India *in Asia:* When 'Look West' Meets Act East. *Strategic Analysis, 40*(5), 425–439. doi:10.1080/09700161.2016.1209906

Rasmus, D. W. (2002). *Collaboration, Content and Communities*. GigaTel.

Regina, M., Abrami, C., Kirby, F., & McFarlan, W. (2014). Why China Can't Innovate. *Harvard Business Review*. Available at: https://hbr.org/2014/03/why-china-cant-innovate

Reisman, D. (2010). *Health tourism. Social welfare through international trade*. Edward Elgar.

Reissner, S. C. (2008). Narrative and story: New perspectives on coaching. *International Journal of Mentoring and Coaching, 6*(3), 1–5.

Renton, J. (2009). *Coaching and mentoring: What they are and how to make the most of them.* Economist.

Reserve Bank of Australia (RBA). (2020). *Monetary Policy*. Retrieved from https://www.rba.gov.au/

Rock, D., & Donde, R. (2008). Driving organizational change with internal coaching programs: Part one. *Industrial and Commercial Training, 40*(1), 10–18. doi:10.1108/00197850810841594

Romar, E. J. (2002). Virtue Is Good Business: Confucianism as a Practical Business Ethics. *Journal of Business Ethics*, *38*(1/2), 119–131. doi:10.1023/A:1015760710802

Roser, M., Ortiz-Ospina, E., & Ritchie, H. (2013). *Life expectancy*. Our World in Data.

Rukmini, S. (2017). India's staggering wealth gap in five charts. *The Hindu*. Retrieved from https://www.thehindu.com/data/indias-staggering-wealth-gap-in-five-charts/article10935670.ece

Ryan, C., Ellem, P., Heaton, L., Mulvogue, J., Cousins, M., & De George–Walker, L. J. N. e. i. p. (2018). *Australian final year nursing students' and registered nurse supervisors' perceptions of a gerontology clinical learning experience: A preliminary appraisal*. Academic Press.

Saeed, K. A. (2010). *The Economy of Pakistan*. Oxford University Press.

Saide, E. R., & Mahendrawathi, E. (2015). Knowledge management support for enterprise resource planning implementation. *Procedia Computer Science*, *72*, 613–621. doi:10.1016/j.procs.2015.12.170

Salaam Balak Trust. (2019). *Industry Partnership Salaam Balak Trust*. Retrieved from www.cqu.edu.au/industry-and-partnerships/partnerships/community/salaam-baalak-trust

Sathyanarayana, K., Kumar, S., & James, K. (2014). Living arrangements of elderly in India: Policy and programmatic implications. *Population Ageing in India, 74*.

Sawe, B. E. (2019). *Countries with the highest rates of vegetarianism*. WorldAtlas.

Schumpeter, J. A. (1942). *Capitalism, Socialism, and Democracy*. New Yory Harper & Brothers.

Schütt, P. (2003). The post-Nonaka Knowledge Management. *Journal of Universal Computer Science*, *9*(6), 451–462.

Senge, P. M. (2006). *The fifth discipline: The art & practice of the learning organisation*. Random House.

Sengupta, A., & Nundy, S. (2005). The private health sector in India [editorial]. *BMJ (Clinical Research Ed.)*, *331*(7526), 1157–1158. doi:10.1136/bmj.331.7526.1157 PMID:16293815

Sharma, K. (2017). *India has 139 million internal migrants. They must not be forgotten*. World Economic Forum. Retrieved from https://www.weforum.org/agenda/2017/10/india-has-139-million-internal-migrants-we-must-not-forget-them/

Sharma, N. K., Tiwari, P. K., & Sood, Y. R. (2013). A comprehensive analysis of strategies, policies and development of hydropower in India: Special emphasis on small hydro power. *Renewable & Sustainable Energy Reviews*, *18*, 460–470. doi:10.1016/j.rser.2012.10.017

Shen, J. (2008). HRM in Chinese privately owned enterprises. *Thunderbird International Business Review*, *50*(2), 91–104. doi:10.1002/tie.20181

Sheu, C., Chae, B., & Yang, C. (2004). National differences and ERP implementation: Issues and challenges. *Omega*, *32*(5), 361–371. doi:10.1016/j.omega.2004.02.001

Sheu, C., Yen, H., & Krumwiede, D. (2003). The effect of national differences on multinational ERP implementation: An exploratory study. *Total Quality Management & Business Excellence, 14*(6), 641–657. doi:10.1080/1478336032000053807

Shlomo, B. (2013). *The business of corporate learning: insights from practice*. Cambridge University Press.

Singh, V. (2009). *Public policies for facilitating medical tourism industry in Asia*. IV Annual International Conference on Public Policy and Management, IIM, Bangalore.

Singh, U. B. (2016). Australia's 2016 Defence White paper: An Indian perspective. *Journal of Defence Studies, 10*(2), 111–120.

Sinha, N. (2018, April 19). Why Elder Care Services is Unexplored in India? *Entrepreneur India*.

Skiffington, S., & Zeus, P. (2003). *Behavioral Coaching: How to Build Sustainable Personal and Organizational Change*. McGraw-Hill Education.

Smith, G. (2010). Australia and the rise of India. *Australian Journal of International Affairs, 64*(5), 566–582. doi:10.1080/10357710903544114

Sonnega, A. (2006). The future of human life expectancy: have we reached the ceiling or is the sky the limit. *Research Highlights in the Demography and Economics of Aging, 8*, 1-4.

Stipek, D., Weiner, B., & Li, K. (1989). Testing some attribution-motion relations in the People's Republic of China. *Journal of Personality and Social Psychology, 56*(1), 109–116. doi:10.1037/0022-3514.56.1.109 PMID:2926613

Stone, D., Stone-Romero, E., & Lukaszewski, K. (2007). The impact of cultural values on the acceptance and effectiveness of human resource management policies and practices. *Human Resource Management Review, 17*(2), 152–165. doi:10.1016/j.hrmr.2007.04.003

Swanson, E. B., & Ramiller, N. C. (2004). Innovating mindfully with information technology. *Management Information Systems Quarterly, 28*(4), 553. doi:10.2307/25148655

Tattara, G. (2010). Medical tourism and domestic population health. Department of Economics, Ca' Foscari University of Venice. doi:10.2139srn.1544224

Taylor, J., Gombeski, W. R., Jr., & Dillon, B. W. (2005). Web wellness. *Marketing Health Services, 25*(2), 32-37.

Thailand Investment Review. (2010). *Thailand Service Industry Pleases, Profits Amid Invigorating Growth*. http://www.boi.go.th/english/download/publication_investment/108/January_10.pdf

Thakur, R., & Sharma, A. (2018). India in Australia's strategic framing in the Indo-Pacific. *Strategic Analysis, 42*(2), 69–83. doi:10.1080/09700161.2018.1439328

The Economic Times. (2018). *India to increase public health spending*. Retrieved from economictimes.indiatimes.com/news/economy/policy/india-to-increase-public-health-spending-to-2-5-of-gdp-pm-modi/articleshow/67055735.cms?from=mdr

The Indian Express. (2018). *Australian agriculture minister to visit India soon to resolve pulse trade issue*. Retrieved from www.newindianexpress.com/business/2018/jan/11/australian-agriculture-minister-to-visit-india-soon-to-resolve-pulses-trade-issue-1750925.html

The Indian Express. (2019). *80 percent framer suicide due to debt, loans from banks, not money lenders*. Retrieved from https://indianexpress.com/article/india/in-80-farmer-suicides-due-to-debt-loans-from-banks-not-moneylenders-4462930/

The World Bank. (2020). Fertility rate, total (births per woman) - India. Author.

Thomson, B. (2009). *Don't just do something, sit there: an introduction to non-directive coaching*. Chandos. doi:10.1533/9781780632063

Thomson, B. (2014). *First steps in coaching*. SAGE. doi:10.4135/9781526401649

Thornhill, A., & Saunders, M. N. K. (1998). What if line managers don't realize they're responsible for HR? Lessons from an organization experiencing rapid change. *Personnel Review*, *27*(6), 460–476. doi:10.1108/00483489810238903

Tourism Malaysia. (2008). *Media Release: Health Tourism in Malaysia*. http://corporate.tourism.gov.my/mediacentre.asp?page=feature_malaysia&pagemo de=search&news_id=16&subpage=archive

Tourism Research Australia (TRA). (2019). *International Tourism Results*. Retrieved from https://www.tra.gov.au/International/international-tourism-results

Treatment Abroad. (2008). *Treatment Abroad PriceWatch Survey 2008*. http://www.treatmentabroad.com/cost/cosmetic-surgery-abroad-cost/

Tulpa, K., & Bresser, F. (2013). Coaching in Europe. In J. Passmore (Ed.), *Diversity in coaching: Working with gender, culture, race and age* (2nd ed.). Kogan Page.

United Nations Development Programme. (2019). *Human Development Reports Data (1990-2018)*. Retrieved from http://hdr.undp.org/en/data#

United Nations Population Division. (2017a). *World Fertility Data 2017*. Retrieved 2020/4/26 https://www.un.org/en/development/desa/population/publications/dataset/fertility/wfd2017.asp

United Nations Population Division. (2017b). *World population prospects 2017*. Retrieved from https://population.un.org/wpp/DataQuery/

United Nations. (2017). *Caring for Our Elders: Early Responses-India Ageing Report*. New Delhi, India: Author.

United Nations. (2019). *Ageing*. Retrieved from https://www.un.org/en/sections/issues-depth/ageing/

United Nations. (2019). *Sustainable Development Goals*. Retrieved from https://www.un.org/sustainabledevelopment/sustainable-development-goals/

United Nations. (2019). *World Population Ageing 2019: Highlights*. New York: United Nations Population Fund.

Varghese, P. N. (2018). *An India Economic Strategy to 2035*. Retrieved from https://www.dfat.gov.au/geo/india/ies/pdf/dfat-an-india-economic-strategy-to-2035.pdf

Vecchio, M. G., Paramesh, E. C., Paramesh, H., Loganes, C., Ballali, S., Gafare, C. E., Verduci, E., & Gulati, A. (2014). Types of Food and Nutrient Intake in India: A Literature Review. *Indian Journal of Pediatrics*, *81*(1), 17–22. doi:10.100712098-014-1465-9 PMID:24928105

VERVE Financial Services Private Limited. (2020). *Guide to Indian Private Limited Company for Foreigners*. Retrieved from https://www.indiafilings.com/learn/guide-to-indian-private-limited-company-for-foreigners/

Voigt, C., Laing, J., Wray, M., Brown, G., Howat, G., Weiler, B., & Trembath, R. (2010). *Health tourism in Australia: Supply, Demand and Opportunities*. CRC for Sustainable Tourism Pty Ltd.

Von Knoop, C., Lovich, D., Silverstein, M. B., & Tutty, M. (2003). *Vital signs: E-health in the United States*. Boston Consulting Group.

Vorhauser-Smith, S. (2012). *Performance Management in China - Three Factors to Watch*. Retrieved from: http://www.forbes.com/sites/sylviavorhausersmith/2012/08/22/performance-management-in-china-three-factors-to-watch/2/#2a590c07481a

Wall, K., Lin, H., Zhang, R., & Lei, X. (2009). A Study on the Chinese Ethical Evolution and Its Effects on SMB in China Today. *International Journal of Business and Management*, *4*(3), 15–25. doi:10.5539/ijbm.v4n3p15

Walton-Robert, M., & Rajan, S. I. (2020). Global demand for medical professionals drives Indians abroad despite acute domestic health-care workers shortages. *Online Journal of the Migration Policy Institute*. Retrieved from https://www.migrationpolicy.org/article/global-demand-medical-professionals-drives-indians-abroad

Wang, F., Zhao, L., & Zhao, Z. (2017). China's family planning policies and their labor market consequences. *Journal of Population Economics*, *30*(1), 31–68. doi:10.100700148-016-0613-0

Wang, J., Wang, G. G., Rouna, W. E. A., & Rojewski, J. W. (2005). Confucian Values and the Implications for International HRD. *Human Resource Development International*, *8*(3), 311–326. doi:10.1080/13678860500143285

Waterhouse Benjamin. C. (2017). *The Small Business Myth*. Aeon Co.

Wearley, L. (2006). *Coaching with Confucian Values: Reflections on Coaching Asian-Americans*. Grovewell's Knowledge Center.

Weer, C., DiRenzo, M., & Shipper, F. (2016). A Holistic View of Employee Coaching: Longitudinal Investigation of the Impact of Facilitative and Pressure-Based Coaching on Team Effectiveness. *The Journal of Applied Behavioral Science*, *52*(2), 187–21. doi:10.1177/0021886315594007

Whitehead, T. L. (2005). Basic classical ethnographic research methods. *Community and Cultural Assessment Research*, 1-28.

Whitmore, J. (2009). *Coaching For Performance* (4th ed.). Nicholas Brealey.

Willis, R., & Chiasson, M. (2007). Do the ends justify the means? A Gramscian critique of the processes of consent during an ERP implementation. *Information Technology & People*, *20*(3), 212–234. doi:10.1108/09593840710822840

Wojczewski, T. (2019). Identity and world order in India's post-Cold War foreign policy discourse. *Third World Quarterly*, *40*(1), 180–198. doi:10.1080/01436597.2018.1552079

Woo, M. J. (2011). Human developmental and cultural perspectives on coaching mid-career executives in China. *Advances in Global Leadership*, *6*, 315–331. doi:10.1108/S1535-1203(2011)0000006016

Xie, Y., & Jin, Y. (2015). Household wealth in China. *Chinese Sociological Review*, *47*(3), 203–229. doi:10.1080/21620555.2015.1032158 PMID:26435882

Xu, J., & Zhang, D. (2016). *Research on investment potential and policy of China's aging industry*. Beijing: Economic Daily Press.

Xue, Y., Liang, H., Boulton, W., & Snyder, C. (2005). ERP implementation failures in China: Case studies with implications for ERP vendors. *International Journal of Production Economics*, *97*(3), 279–295. doi:10.1016/j.ijpe.2004.07.008

Xu, J., & Zhao, T. (2013). The Realistic Dilemma and Path Innovation of Government Purchasing Public Service: Practice in Shanghai. *China Administration*, *8*, 26–30.

Yadav, S. (2013). Why India's Elderly are Moving to Retirement Homes. *BBC News India*. Retrieved from https://www.bbc.com/news/world-asia-india-23176206

Yang, Y. (2014). *Report on the Development of Aging Society and Pension Security in China (2013)*. Tsinghua University Press.

Yeh, Q. J., & Xu, X. (2010). The Effect of Confucian Work Ethics on Learning about Science and Technology Knowledge and Mobility. *Journal of Business Ethics*, *95*(1), 111–128. doi:10.100710551-009-0352-1

Zenger, J., & Stinnett, K. (2010). *The Extraordinary Coach: How the Best Leaders Help Others Grow*. McGraw-Hill.

Zhang, H. (2015). Australia wants to enter the Chinese pension market. *Youth Reference*. Retrieved from http://qnck.cyol.com/html/2015-11/25/nw.D110000qnck_20151125_1-11.htm

Zhou, P. (2005). *Organizational culture impact on ERP implementation in China*. Swedish School of Economics and Business Administration.

Zhu, Y. (2008). Public Policy Analysis of Government's Purchase of Elderly Care Services. *Journal of Tianshui College of Administration, 2008*(4), 72-76.

Zhuang, Z. (2017). *Focus on "Red Sunset", analyze the Australian aged care industry.* Retrieved from https://zhuanlan.zhihu.com/p/30365815

Zinzius, B. (2004). *Doing Business in the New China: A Handbook and Guide.* Conneticut.

About the Contributors

Angus Hooke is a former Professor in Entrepreneurship and Head of the Business School at Nottingham University Business School, China. He has a BEc (First Class Hon, Australian National University), DipEd (University of Sydney), PhD (University of Queensland). Angus has worked in international organisations, governments at all levels, universities and private industries. He was employed for 15 years by the International Monetary Fund (IMF), including two years in Seoul as IMF Advisor to the Minister of Finance and two years in Paris as IMF Representative to the OECD. He has undertaken numerous consultancies for the World Bank, the United Nations Development Programme (UNDP), the Food and Agriculture Organisation (FAO), the Asian Development Bank (ADB) and the Australian Government. Gus has served as Chief Economist and Branch Head of the NSW Treasury Department, and has lectured in universities in Australia, the United States, China and Korea. He was resident in Beijing during 2001-06, as Australian Manager of an AusAID project to help China join the WTO and then as consultant to companies in Australia, the United States, and the United Kingdom seeking to invest in China.

Hardik Vachharajani, is an Associate Professor at the Crown Institute of Higher Education in Sydney, Australia. He has over 15 years of experience in teaching, assessing and supervising undergraduate, postgraduate and PhD students in Australia, Europe and South Asia in face to face, blended and online learning environments. Hardik teaches courses at Crown Institute, Australian Catholic University, University of Canberra (online), Telecom Ecole de Management at Paris and Amrita University in India. His areas of teaching, research and consulting interest are strategy, entrepreneurship and innovation. Hardik is assessor and adviser for Institute of Managers and Leaders Australia and New Zealand.

Harpreet Kaur has a Master of Philosophy and a PhD in Economics. Currently, she teaches Economics, Statistics, Governance and Business Ethics at Charles Sturt University, Central Queensland University, and the Australian Institute of Higher education. Her research interests commenced with development dynamics, socioeconomic conditions and the role of women in India (when very few women were in the labour force and foreign trade was quite limited) and now include upcoming scenarios in the world economy, especially the economic interrelationship between Asia, Oceania and the world economy

Kevin E. Dow is a Professor of Accounting Information Systems at the University of Auckland. He received his Ph.D. from the University of South Carolina, and his MS in Analytics from Columbia University. Dr. Dow's research focuses on the application of predictive analytics and machine learning to help solve business issues. His work has appeared in various journals, including Information Systems Research, Journal of Management Information Systems, European Journal of Information Systems, Database for Advances in Information Systems, International Journal of Accounting Information Systems, Journal of Information Systems, Issues in Accounting Education, Journal of Accounting Education, and the Journal of Forensic and Investigative Accounting and his work has been presented at numerous national and international conferences.

* * *

Lauren Alati is a manager with Argon & Co, world leading operations consultants, headquartered in Paris with global offices including London, Mumbai, and Atlanta. Lauren brings operational and consulting experience in distribution logistics and strategic network design working with leading manufacturers and retailers across Australia, New Zealand, and Oceania. Lauren has global supply chain credentials; certified in Transport Logistics and Distribution by the Association for Supply Chain Management with further tertiary degrees earned in Australia, China, and the USA.

Munish Duggal holds Master's degrees (Economics) from India and the United Kingdom and Doctorate in Economics from India. After teaching assignments for 3 years, he joined the prestigious Indian Economic Service in 1986 and occupied key positions in the various Economic Ministries of the Indian Federal Government including Adviser in the Ministry of Labour and Employment and Economic Adviser in the Ministry of Information and Broadcasting. During his tenure as Director and Additional Adviser in Ministry of Finance he prepared sectoral reports on infrastructure sector, capital market and price and food management. He joined the United Nations in 1999 and worked in various capacities including Dean of the Civil Service Academy in Timor Leste. He was appointed as a member of the Think Tank on Restructuring Higher Education in India by Commonwealth Educational Media Centre for Asia (CEMCA) in 2018. During 34 years of his career, he has travelled extensively to over 25 countries from 6 continents.

David Edwards teaches and researches in business information system. He currently teaches at the University of Nottingham Business School, China and specializes in organizational and technology. His academic background is in the area of Social Informatics. He has published in top international journals, conferences and media on digital journalism, digital transformation, logistics and enterprise systems. He also has professional expertise in e-government and cultural management.

Mei Liu currently works at Nottingham University Business School China. She obtained PhD in Accounting and Finance from University of Strathclyde. Her research interest are international economics, real estate economics, and China's economy.

Qing-Ping Ma currently works at Nottingham University Business School China. He obtained PhD in Physiology/Neuroscience from Peking University and PhD in Economics from University of London. After receiving his PhD in Physiology/Neuroscience, he had worked in Peking University, University College London, and Merck Sharp & Dohme Research Laboratories, with research interests in the mechanisms of pain, analgesia, anxiety and depression. After completing his PhD in Economics part-time, he joined Nottingham University Business School and his research interests in economics are pension economics, China's economic growth, industrial revolutions and technological progress.

Jack Mcnaughton is a qualified accountant and has a master's degree in Change, Management and Leadership from York St. John University in England. He currently provides consulting services to various groups involved with Startups and Companies looking to grow internationally. His expertise in global structuring, business, and project establishment is called upon in such areas as banking, financial services, funds management, affordable housing mining, food trading and supply, cryptocurrencies, and stock exchange listings in different countries. He has been responsible for over 20 stock exchange listings with a total market value in excess of $USD1.5 billion and direct fundraising.

Anita Medhekar is an economist and holds a PhD from Deakin University, Australia. She has taught at undergraduate and post graduate levels in India, Indonesia and Australia. Currently, she is teaching at Central Queensland University, Rockhampton, Australia. Her research interest is in applied micro and macroeconomics, international trade, development economics, public finance, South-Asia, health economics, tourism economics, bilateral trade and development for peace, public policy, and public-private partnerships. She has presented papers at numerous international conferences and has many publications to her credit as refereed conference proceedings, book chapters, and journal articles.

Will Percy has over a decade of experience working and leading in professional learning and development environments in mainland China and supporting organisations that seek to share knowledge across cultures. An accredited Master Executive Coach and Chartered member of the CIPD, will has a passion for people analytics and experiential learning.

Divya Ramachandran was born in and has spent the majority of her life in India. She has experienced first-hand the interplay between India's traditional culture and values, and the sweeping changes in socio-economic patterns over the last few decades, and subsequently their impact on the elderly and ageing in India. Professionally, Divya is an experienced project manager and has worked with large global technology companies including IBM and GE. Divya's became interested in health when she migrated with her family to Australia in 2008. She completed a degree in Public Health and is currently pursuing a PhD in Health and Medicine. Divya is passionate about empowering individuals in taking control of their health and ageing and making fully informed care choices.

Jeayaram Subramanian is Assistant Professor of OB and HR at Department of Management, Amrita Vishwa Vidyapeetham, India. Jeayaram holds his PhD from Institut Mines-Télécom Business School, Paris. He is Chairperson of PhD program at the department.

W. Kathy Tannous is a health economist and a senior lecturer at Western Sydney University who has been researching ageing and aged care for 23 years. She is currently examining the economic impact of lifestyle intervention programs on reduction of obesity in Western Sydney and the economic cost of the diabetic foot. In addition, Dr Tannous has an active research program examining the health and economic cost of residential fires in New South Wales.

Index

www.ingramcontent.com/pod-product-compliance
Lightning Source LLC
LaVergne TN
LVHW081341300926
849161LV00008B/2039